SPENSER'S COURTEOUS PASTORAL

SPENSER'S COURTEOUS PASTORAL

BOOK SIX OF THE
Faerie Queene

HUMPHREY TONKIN

CLARENDON PRESS · OXFORD
1972

Oxford University Press, Ely House, London W.1

GLASGOW NEW YORK TORONTO MELBOURNE WELLINGTON
CAPE TOWN IBADAN NAIROBI DAR ES SALAAM LUSAKA ADDIS ABABA
DELHI BOMBAY CALCUTTA MADRAS KARACHI LAHORE DACCA
KUALA LUMPUR SINGAPORE HONG KONG TOKYO

PRINTED IN GREAT BRITAIN
BY BUTLER & TANNER LTD
FROME AND LONDON

IN MEMORY OF MY MOTHER

PREFACE

My first acquaintance with Spenser goes back to my time as an undergraduate, under the wise tutelage of Mr. George Watson. Later, a seminar with Professor Harry Levin opened my eyes to the range and implications of pastoral literature and drew Spenser and pastoral together. My efforts to understand Book Six of the *Faerie Queene* have been helped in many ways by many scholars. My colleagues Professors Roland Frye and Jason Rosenblatt read parts of my manuscript and put their knowledge and good sense at my disposal, Professors Douglas Bush and Walter Kaiser read an earlier version and gave me much help and notable wisdom, and Professor Craig Thompson read the whole manuscript in final form and offered various helpful suggestions. I presented part of the argument in a paper read to the University of Pennsylvania Seminar on the Renaissance, whose members contributed several instructive observations and criticisms. I am particularly grateful to Professor A. C. Hamilton, whose detailed comments on my argument and manner of presentation were the fruit of a painstaking and generous reading of the complete text shortly before the final revisions. Help also came in the form of a research grant from the University of Pennsylvania and a pleasant summer's hospitality from St. John's College, Cambridge. My main debt, however, is to my wife, who has made much sense of nonsense, turned opaque arguments into lucidity, and sat at typewriter and elbow through many drafts and much discomfort. The book is hers as well as mine. Without her help and that of the others I have mentioned, there could have been no book at all.

The pace of scholarship being what it is, it proved impossible to take into account all of the stimulating studies both of Spenser and of pastoral published while the present work was in its final stages. In addition to a number of works on pastoral in Virgil, Shakespeare and Marvell, Rosemary Freeman, Patrick Cullen, Angus Fletcher, Michael Murrin and Maurice Evans have all added significant new contributions to our understanding of

Spenser. It is both gratifying and humbling to see such attention being paid to so important a poet and so fascinating a literary mode. I hope my own work will throw some small light on Spenser's difficult and significant poem, though I am ever mindful of the chastening words of C. S. Lewis, that best of Spenser's critics: 'If there is any safe generalization in literary history it is this: that the desire for a certain kind of product does not necessarily beget the power to produce it, while it does tend to beget the illusion that it has been produced.'

University of Pennsylvania
May, 1971

CONTENTS

ABBREVIATIONS

BHR	*Bibliothèque d'Humanisme et Renaissance*
BJRL	*Bulletin of the John Rylands Library*
CLS	*Comparative Literature Studies*
DA	*Dissertation Abstracts*
EA	*Études Anglaises*
EETS	Early English Text Society
ELH	*Journal of English Literary History*
ES	*Essays and Studies*
HLQ	*Huntington Library Quarterly*
JEGP	*Journal of English and Germanic Philology*
JHI	*Journal of the History of Ideas*
JWCI	*Journal of the Warburg and Courtauld Institute*
MLN	*Modern Language Notes*
MLQ	*Modern Language Quarterly*
MLR	*Modern Language Review*
MP	*Modern Philology*
N & Q	*Notes and Queries*
PMLA	*Publications of the Modern Language Association of America*
PQ	*Philological Quarterly*
RES	*Review of English Studies*
STC	*Short Title Catalogue of Books Printed . . . 1475–1640*, ed. Pollard and Redgrave (London, 1926)
SEL	*Studies in English Literature*
SP	*Studies in Philology*
SRen	*Studies in the Renaissance*
SVEC	*Studies on Voltaire and the Eighteenth Century*
TSLL	*Texas Studies in Literature and Language*

All quotations from Spenser are drawn from *The Works of Edmund Spenser: a Variorum Edition*, ed. Edwin A. Greenlaw and others, 9 vols. (Baltimore, Md., 1932–49). I have modernized the letters u, v, and j throughout.

I

The Poetry of Reconciliation

1. The Context

THE *Faerie Queene* is a work extraordinarily difficult to come to terms with, as the extent and sophistication of modern scholarship attest. But it is also a work extraordinarily difficult to leave alone, both because of the important literary problems which it poses and because of the fascination which it continues to exercise as a kind of world of its own and an epitome of the Elizabethan age. The present study was written largely for those who know the work well, or for those who wish to know one piece of it better. Yet it is my contention that a knowledge of Spenser's Legend of Courtesy and its ramifications is in large measure the key to the whole work. Book VI sums up and re-examines the issues raised by the work as a whole.[1]

Because this study presupposes some knowledge of Spenser and his age, it seems hardly necessary to rehearse the principal critical approaches to the *Faerie Queene*. But since Book VI comes last, if we except the 'Mutabilitie Cantos', it would perhaps be useful to remind ourselves of the way in which the work begins, and of what we have learned as the work has unfolded itself before us in ever richer variety.

Spenser tells us, in a memorable and famous phrase, that the purpose of his work is 'to fashion a gentleman or noble person in vertuous and gentle discipline'. If we can believe the Letter to Ralegh (and on this point, at least, it has support in the practice of other poets and historians), the aim of the *Faerie Queene* is to improve a man's conduct, to make him a better leader and governor and Christian. To this end, it is set out in a series of books, each

---

[1] The notion that the poem is essentially cumulative has been effectively advanced by Kathleen Williams in her article 'Eterne in Mutabilitie: the Unified World of *The Faerie Queene*', *ELH*, 19 (1952), 115–30, and in her book *Spenser's 'Faerie Queene': the World of Glass* (London, 1966).

dealing with a separate virtue, and the stories it tells are aimed at inculcating these virtues in the reader. Binding this ordered sequence together is the figure of Arthur himself, 'before he was king', the hero and founder of Tudor Englishness, the very measure and example of Elizabethan loyalty.

Not least among the Spenserian's problems, however, is the fact that the neat, watertight system of the Letter to Ralegh hardly accounts for the complex and multiform reality of the work itself. It is all very well to write of separate virtues, but in practice the virtues have a bothersome tendency to run into one another, to coalesce, and to prove mutually dependent. It is all very well to describe the Faerie Queene's annual feast, but the feast scarcely comes into the fictional picture at all when the work gets under way.[2] As for Arthur, his role hardly seems to merit the terms in which it is described in the Letter, and the shadowy figure of the Faerie Queene does not reduce itself to the simple dichotomy set forth in the Letter, where we are told, 'In that Faery Queene I meane glory in my generall intention, but in my particular I conceive the most excellent and glorious person of our soveraine the Queene, and her kingdome in Faery land.'[3]

In fact, the more we look at the Letter, the more we realize that the poem itself defies simple categorization. The division into books does not take into account the close interrelationship of many of the virtues, nor does it explain the recurrent structural devices—the cantos of instruction, the intrusion of the narrator, the unfinished stories—which counterpoint the steady numerical progression stanza by stanza, canto by canto, book by book. The dictum that the poem delights to instruct (the old Horatian formula, so beloved of the Renaissance)[4] is not enough to account

[2] Una mentions her visit to Gloriana's court in passing (1.vii. 46), and Guyon refers to her feast when talking to Amavia (11.ii.42), but these and similar reminiscences hardly play an essential part in the fiction.

[3] On discrepancies between the Letter and the text, see *The Works of Edmund Spenser: a Variorum Edition*, ed. Edwin A. Greenlaw and others (Baltimore, Md., 1932–49), 1: 314–62, *passim*; W. J. B. Owen, 'In These XII Books Severally Handled and Discoursed', *ELH*, 19 (1952), 165–72, and 'Spenser's Letter to Ralegh—a Reply', *MLN*, 75 (1960), 195–7. A. C. Hamilton presents a somewhat different view, arguing for the coherence of the Letter, in *The Structure of Allegory in 'The Faerie Queene'* (Oxford, 1961), pp. 50–8.

[4] On the background to this common view, see Baxter Hathaway, *Marvels and Commonplaces: Renaissance Literary Criticism* (New York, 1968), pp. 52ff.; Geoffrey Shepherd, ed., *An Apology for Poetry*, by Sir Philip Sidney (London, 1965), pp. 66–9; Joel E. Spingarn, *Literary Criticism in the Renaissance* (New York, 1963), pp. 5ff.

for the richness of statement, the complexity of address, with which the virtues are presented to us.

One reason for our difficulty is the fact that the *Faerie Queene* is not quite like any other work we have ever seen. In the Letter its author alludes to the epic tradition—to Homer and Virgil as instructors in virtue. He mentions, too, the Italian romance writers of his own age. But while Ariosto particularly, and Boiardo and Tasso to a lesser extent, may have a great deal to tell us about the nature of the *Faerie Queene*,[5] and while Renaissance theories of the heroic poem afford impressive insight into its purposes, Spenser's work is emphatically not an English imitation of Italian literature, nor is it a neo-classical epic. In a quite peculiar way it is answerable to itself, it is its own universe. Faeryland is not a geographical entity; it *is* the poem. Coleridge, perceptive as always, makes mention of 'the marvellous independence and true imaginative absence of all particular space and time in the *Faerie Queene*'.[6] The poem affords us no sense of geographical distance at all, no sense of time. No boundaries fix the poem spatially or temporally; events do not take place on Thursday or in July or during the summer. We might go so far as to say that Spenser's questing knights, as representatives of the titular virtues, generate the poem's action. They determine the meaning of events, and their own personal qualities actually *create* characters and incidents and encounters.

In this respect Spenser's work is quite unlike Italian models. Nor does it resemble the medieval romances upon which the poet

[5] The topic is most effectively discussed by Graham Hough, *A Preface to 'The Faerie Queene'* (London, 1962), pp. 9–81. See also John Arthos, *On the Poetry of Spenser and the Form of Romances* (London, 1956); C. S. Lewis, *The Allegory of Love* (London, 1936); Paul J. Alpers, *The Poetry of 'The Faerie Queene'* (Princeton, N.J., 1967), pp. 160–99; Robert M. Durling, *The Figure of the Poet in Renaissance Epic* (Cambridge, Mass., 1965).

[6] S. T. Coleridge, *Miscellaneous Criticism*, ed. T. M. Raysor (London, 1936), p. 36. Arnold Williams, *Flower on a Lowly Stalk* (Michigan State University, 1967) suggests that Spenser's method resembles medieval drama: 'Except for the English cycle plays, all medieval drama is built on a station-and-place arrangement of the playing space. A glance at such a play as the *Castle of Perseverance* will make this plain. God, World, Flesh, Devil, and Covetousness have stations or scaffolds assigned to them, as do also the seven virtues. Mankind and six of the deadly sins move from one station to another through the neutral space between and around the stations' (p. 18). The sense of timelessness, of a landscape somehow charged with mystery and significance, is of course fundamental to romance. See John Arthos, *Spenser and Romances*, pp. 79–91; W. P. Ker, *Epic and Romance* (London, 1896), *passim*. But in Spenser this feeling is uniquely strong.

draws freely. The distance between Ariosto's Bradamante and the magic castle where Ruggiero is imprisoned is so many mountains —and we have a fair idea as to how many; Ruggiero's hippogriff takes just so long to reach Alcina's castle; Rinaldo and Sacripante ride off to *Paris*, and Rinaldo goes to *Scotland*; Bradamante goes to the *Pyrenees*. Malory's Lancelot goes to France, Tristram goes to Ireland; if Glastonbury is sometimes disturbingly close to the other end of the country, at least to a degree geography is taken account of, seasons come and go, and fixed periods of time elapse.

If the fabric of the *Faerie Queene* is woven out of many elements —from the classics, from medieval literature, from contemporary poetry and romance and iconography—to form a poetic universe unique to Spenser, this uniqueness raises whole series of questions about the way in which the poem works. We are forced to re-examine Spenser's use of myth, his narrative method, his characterization. Above all, we must ask what actually *happens* when we read the *Faerie Queene*.[7] The fact that the temporal element is missing, or that Faeryland time is quite unlike our own, throws into doubt many of our preconceptions about the nature of the past. There was a time when the critics saw the *Faerie Queene* as a kind of misty nostalgia for values rapidly disappearing, or a conservative attempt to arrest social and literary change. It is not difficult to refute such a view. For one thing, we can point to the fact that the Elizabethans underwent what can only be described as a medieval revival—a bright, almost campy delight in the past, which revealed itself especially strongly in architecture, and in more sober fashion in antiquarianism. It was not an attempt to cling to old values; Elizabethan architects went to great lengths to destroy the old fortifications of earlier years, but they ended by building what frequently looked like imitations of fortifications. In the same way, the *Faerie Queene* imitates the past, it does not seek to re-create it. The architect of St. Pancras railway station, to take an example nearer our own time, never forgot that he was building a railway station, even if the result *looks* more like a Gothic castle: it was an imitation, not a re-creation.[8]

---

[7] The only recent critics to confront this question directly are Alpers, *Poetry*, and Roger Sale, *Reading Spenser* (New York, 1968). Some discussions of allegory touch on this question: see my article 'Some Notes on Myth and Allegory in the *Faerie Queene*', forthcoming in *MP*, and also the introductory chapter in Thomas P. Roche, Jr., *The Kindly Flame* (Princeton, N.J., 1964).

[8] On Elizabethan medievalism, see John Buxton, *Elizabethan Taste* (London,

But this answer to the romantic view of Spenser is itself based on doubtful premises. It takes for granted that Spenser viewed history as a simple continuum, and it ignores the profound crisis in man's view of the past which was a phenomenon of sixteenth-century Europe.[9] In recent years, scholars have traced the growth and decline of the Christian view of history, finding its beginnings in the efforts of the early Christians to establish the historicity of Jesus Christ and hence the eschatalogical significance of historical event, and its ending in the new empiricism of the later Renaissance, which no longer viewed history as a series of events culminating and concluding in the Last Judgement and the New Jerusalem. They have shown, too, how the attraction of the classical view of history, as cyclical, was never wholly absent even in Christian historiography. It exercised particular force in the Renaissance, and it is built into the structure of the *Faerie Queene*.

In fact, Spenser is interested not so much in the past as in history itself. I said that, according to the Christian view, the Last Judgement and the New Jerusalem *conclude* history, but it would be more accurate to suggest that they *contain* history. The purpose, function, and fulfilment of history are contained within the streets and squares of the City of God. Such a view differs wholly from the classical interpretation of history, where the emphasis falls on the recurrence of events, and upon past perfection rather than future apocalypse.[10] Spenser draws on both views, matching primitivism with historical destiny, a perfect past with the promise of a second Golden Age.

Spenser's view of history, while it may acknowledge the concept of anachronism, does no more than pay it lip-service. The *Faerie Queene* is not set in a specific historical period. By choosing as his heroes Arthur and Gloriana, Spenser sums up within his work all of English history and English glory. The fact that he chooses Arthur 'before he was king' suggests an awareness of the fierce

---

1963), *passim*; Mark Girouard, *Robert Smythson and the Architecture of the Elizabethan Era* (London, 1966), pp. 159–74. On medievalism as it manifests itself in language, see especially Rosemond Tuve, 'Ancients, Moderns, and Saxons', *ELH*, 6 (1939), 165–90; Veré L. Rubel, *Poetic Diction in the English Renaissance* (New York, 1941).

[9] See Peter Burke, *The Renaissance Sense of the Past* (London, 1969); F. Smith Fussner, *The Historical Revolution* (London, 1962).

[10] C. A. Patrides, *The Phoenix and the Ladder* (Berkeley and Los Angeles, Calif., 1964); Mircea Eliade, *Cosmos and History: the Myth of the Eternal Return* (New York, 1959).

debate over the historicity of Arthur which preoccupied Elizabethan historians.[11] Spenser sidesteps the issue by concentrating
on a non-historical aspect of this hero of the Tudors. But he tele-
scopes history into the movement of his poem by having the
founder of the Tudor line, the great British hero, set forth on a
quest for Gloriana, the last of her line, childless in her virginity,
and culmination of English history. Contained within the poetic
universe of the *Faerie Queene* is the whole of the English experience.[12] Indeed, the landscape of Faeryland, in this respect like the
Holy City, *is* history.

A world where the past is constantly present and where the
future is contained within this present affords special poetic ad-
vantages but creates major ontological difficulties. Primitivism,
the idea of a perfect past, can be used as an instrument to examine
the present within the simultaneity of all time in the narrative.
The court of Gloriana and the court of Queen Elizabeth, as we
shall see, exist juxtaposed, the one contradicting the other but
both present within the fiction. The garden of Adonis is not
merely a means of coming to terms with our existence through
the use of the paradise myth: it is a present reality to Britomart and
Belphoebe and Amoret and, we are tempted to add, Queen
Elizabeth and her courtiers.

But problems arise when Spenser seeks to set this essentially
cyclical view of time, this neo-classical sense of the constant recurrence of events, into the larger Christian context of creation
and apocalypse, birth and death, quest and fulfilment. There is a
constant pull throughout the *Faerie Queene* between the quest, the
forward movement towards a final goal, and primitivism, the
periodic return toward the beginning. As the stanza and canto
numbers move steadily forward, the action constantly looks back
upon itself; the poet, like Orpheus, looks over his shoulder; quest
and battle are never wholly completed, never wholly won. The
symbols of Quest and Enclosed Garden, the one northern and
Christian and forward-looking, the other Mediterranean and classical and circular, themselves epitomize the intellectual crisis of

[11] See T. D. Kendrick, *British Antiquity* (London, 1950); Edwin Greenlaw,
Studies in Spenser's Historical Allegory (Baltimore, Md., 1932), pp. 1–58; C. B. Millican,
Spenser and the Table Round, rev. edn. (New York, 1967).

[12] On Elizabethan views of history see also F. J. Levy, *Tudor Historical Thought*
(San Marino, Calif., 1967).

Spenser's generation.[13] In a very real sense the *Faerie Queene* is the mirror of Elizabethan England, and Spenser is attempting to solve through poetry the great psychological dilemma of his age. The poetic mechanism mirrors the social dynamics of sixteenth-century England.

According to our temperament, we may feel that in the end the *Faerie Queene* is a glorious failure, that it is based upon a set of irreconcilables, or we may feel that Spenser succeeds in coming to terms with the Janus face of his own intellectual milieu. The 'Mutabilitie Cantos' do surely provide an answer. Nature's famous judgement suggests that Quest and Garden, line and circle, are part of the same pattern:

> I well consider all that ye have sayd,
> And find that all things stedfastnes doe hate
> And changed be: yet being rightly wayd
> They are not changed from their first estate;
> But by their change their being doe dilate:
> And turning to themselves at length againe,
> Doe worke their owne perfection so by fate:
> Then over them Change doth not rule and raigne;
> But they raigne over change, and doe their states maintaine.
>
> (VII. vii. 58)

The verdict reflects back upon Spenser's own poem and upon the nature of England's glory. The quests are not so much battles won, new territory gained, as part of the constant struggle of the human spirit against all manner of enemies without, all manner of disloyalties within. The history of England forms a pattern of quest and achievement and failure, all of them contained *within* the garden of Tudor glory, which is both the result and the cumulation of the story of England. The history of humankind forms a similar pattern and similar cumulation.

Viewed in this light, the evaluation of the precise extent of Spenser's Platonism, or the precise influence of Aristotle, one of those traditional battlegrounds of Spenserian scholars, recedes in

---

[13] On the Quest, see, for example, Charles Moorman, *A Knyght There Was* (Lexington, Ky., 1967); Joseph Campbell, *The Hero with a Thousand Faces* (New York, 1949). On the Enclosed Garden, see A. Bartlett Giamatti, *The Earthly Paradise and the Renaissance Epic* (Princeton, N.J., 1966); Stanley Stewart, *The Enclosed Garden* (Madison, Wis., 1966).

importance.[14] By writing a kind of *summa* of human experience,
Spenser seems almost to repudiate organic change, and yet the
very premiss of the work (the desire to educate), and the basic
structure (the quest), seem to promote it. Of late, Renaissance
scholars have come to understand the full force of the epoch's
faith in paradox.[15] Spenser's method and his philosophy are
grounded in a belief in the simultaneous validity of contradictory
impulses. We find something of the same combination of elements
on a smaller scale in Sidney's *Apology*, which draws heavily upon
the schools of both Plato and Aristotle. In fact it is almost a
hallmark of the age; the Elizabethans practised eclecticism as perhaps no age before or since, and ultimately the *Faerie Queene* is a
very Elizabethan poem.

Its purely poetic qualities are also very much those of its age.
Spenser's use of imagery, his careful rhetorical poise, the fluency
of his verse, are all hallmarks of the 'golden' poetry of the Elizabethans. We should read the *Faerie Queene* also in the context of
the popularity of Ovid. Much of the poem was probably written
at the height of the vogue for erotic epyllia. Some of their lightness and brightness was perhaps borrowed from, and repaid with
interest to, Spenser's poem. This was also the age of the sonnet,
tightest and most precise of the great poetic forms. The capacity
of the sonnet for precision, and of the epyllion for rapid movement, are combined in the *Faerie Queene* in the articulation of the
tightly organized Spenserian stanza in vast sequences of narrative.

At the same time, the poem's sequence of argument, as many
critics have pointed out, is accompanied by a gradual widening of
its frame of reference. Books I, II, and III, with their titular virtues
of Holiness, Temperance, and Chastity, deal with man's proper
governance of himself; Books IV, V, and VI—Friendship, Justice,
Courtesy—are concerned with man's relation with other men.
Alternatively, we can trace a triple sequence, Books I and II concerning virtues strictly personal, Books III and IV our personal

[14] Robert Ellrodt, *Neoplatonism in the Poetry of Spenser* (Geneva, 1960), finally
established that Spenser's alleged Platonism consisted largely of Renaissance
philosophical commonplaces—a view not disturbed by Jon A. Quitslund's excellent
recent article on the *Fowre Hymns*, 'Spenser's Image of Sapience', *SRen*, 16 (1969),
181–213. Rosemond Tuve, *Allegorical Imagery* (Princeton, N.J., 1966), has shown
conclusively that the background of Spenser's virtues and vices is richly medieval
rather than directly Aristotelian.
[15] See Rosalie Colie, *Paradoxia Epidemica* (Princeton, N.J., 1966).

relationships with our fellows, Books v and vi our conduct in society. We move from the individual to his social environment.

The key to each of these categories is the power of love. Holiness is at once the most personal and the most fundamental of all the virtues, since it defines the love of God towards mankind (the pattern of *all* love) and establishes the nature of man's love for God. Through the proper exercise of holiness the Christian is able to regulate his life on earth and move towards his individual salvation. Temperance, a more severe and less conciliatory virtue, is the natural complement of holiness, since it governs our singleness of purpose and our determination to follow virtue here on earth. Seen in the context of Spenser's chivalric metaphor, holiness determines the Christian basis of chivalry, while temperance defines the retributive *virtus* of classical heroism—also the proper attribute of the knight.[16]

The movement from self to society, from treatment of the virtues of the individual to consideration of those of the collective, is effected above all through Books iii and iv, which deal with the nature of love. Most critics are agreed that the two books form a more or less continuous argument (which actually runs over into Book v) concerned with the psychology and, one is tempted to add, sociology of love.[17] Not only is the virtue of chastity redefined in the light of Christian marriage, but the nature of the marriage vow is also examined and, very early on, the link between universal harmony and personal chastity is established unequivocally. The great natural forces of the Garden of Adonis represent the very flux and change of nature itself, but Amoret, as an individual, personalizes these natural forces by contributing the characteristics of marital love to our view of the heroine Britomart.

These central books of the *Faerie Queene* are united by the poet's efforts to bring the cycle of generation into alignment with the historical destiny of England—to bring the natural and the social together. Spenser presents this generative cycle to us through a

---

[16] This broad distinction, supported in A. S. P. Woodhouse's article 'Nature and Grace in *The Faerie Queene*', *ELH*, 16 (1949), 194–228, is useful as far as it goes. Even in Book ii the Christian context is never wholly lost sight of. See Hamilton, *Structure*, pp. 89ff.; A. D. S. Fowler, 'The Image of Mortality: *The Faerie Queene*, 2. 1–2', *HLQ*, 24 (1960–1), 91–110.

[17] See Roche, *Kindly Flame*; Mark Rose, *Heroic Love* (Cambridge, Mass., 1968). My own contribution to our understanding of the central books, 'Spenser's Garden of Adonis and Britomart's Quest', will appear shortly in *PMLA*.

number of myths, or mythic emblems, in Book III and to some
extent in Book II. Book II hints at the preoccupations of the third
book by conveying us from contemplation of the dead body of
Mortdant in Canto i, to the discovery of the bewitched Verdant
in Canto xii: the book's action takes place within the framework
of death and rebirth. Belphoebe's intrusion on Book II, with all
that it implies of Venus and Diana, also serves as a precursor of
the Legend of Chastity.

But the central myth of generation is of course the Garden of
Adonis, with its description of the ongoing processes of creation.
This complex emblem, whose parody we have already met in the
Bower of Bliss, contains within it a separate and parallel myth, that
of Venus and Adonis (already encountered in parodic form in the
tapestry on Malecasta's wall). Both are prefigured in the story of
Chrysogonee, whose spontaneous generation suggests the stirring
of seeds in the spring.

These mythic episodes in Book III are each of them non-
sequential. They are extended, turned into a sequence, principally
through the story of Florimell and Marinell. The union of flower
and sea, of natural world and ocean, suggests the myth of the birth
of Venus, who rose from the seed of Uranus scattered on the
ocean. The neo-Platonists tell us that this miraculous birth symbolizes the creation of the world out of chaos. Such creation, the
search of form for matter, is a central theme in the episode of the
Garden of Adonis.

While Florimell's pursuit of Marinell is like the search of Form
for Matter, in an entirely different way it is also like Arthur's pursuit of Gloriana and Britomart's pursuit of Artegall. Since Britomart's quest is absolutely central to the narrative and thematic
development of these central books, we see that behind and beneath the telling of Britomart's story runs a great mythic under-
song. Myth and heroine finally come together in the episode of the
Temple of Isis, where Britomart's dream is both sexual and political. Her confusion on waking is indicative of a crisis of identity
which is finally resolved with her defeat of Radigund and bestowal
of authority on Artegall.

Books V and VI are a mirror-image of I and II, though their
context is much wider. Artegall's justice (which, admittedly, must
be supplemented by mercy) is severe, uncompromising, single.
The book tells us that the rule of law is fundamental to human

society, but it suggests, through the presence of Britomart and especially through Isis Church and the Court of Mercilla, that there are other, more specifically human, qualities which should form the basis of justice.

If Book v's severity is like the severity of Book ii, the openness of Book vi recalls Book i. Courtesy is one of the manifestations of love. Book i, as the visit to the Mount of Contemplation suggests, is based on man's unselfishness towards his fellow men. (The same subject, in a different context, is taken up in Book iv.) In Book vi, the emphasis falls time after time on man's obligation to help and respect those around him. Aid to the afflicted, honour to superiors, treatment of inferiors humanely, forgiveness, readiness to learn from the best traditions of society—these are the very basis of courtesy, the orderly running of society.

Book vi, then, is concerned essentially with love in relation to the social order. This concern takes us very close to the heart of the work. Its stated purpose was 'to fashion a gentleman or noble person in vertuous and gentle discipline'. The virtuous and gentle discipline of the gentleman was, in Elizabethan eyes, none other than courtesy. Hence Book vi sums up and evaluates the driving purpose of the whole poem; and the fact that it deals with social issues, with the life of the courtier and the standards of the court, makes the sixth book itself a mirror of Elizabethan society: it contains in little the central issues of the whole work.

Most particularly it contains in little those twin symbols of the age, the Quest and the Garden. The pull of pastoral against quest, of movement against stasis, brings the forces to which the goddess Nature alludes into sharp and sudden conflict. The anxieties and doubts of the age are confronted in a new and markedly daring light, and the presence of the poet himself, so close to the poetry, individualizes them and adds to their poignancy.

2. *The Proem*

If Britomart establishes her identity, if Florimell and Marinell are wed, their successes only clear the way for Artegall's efforts to bring about a different type of reconciliation, tied in, to be sure, with Britomart's personality, but having wider public and social implications. In Book iv Artegall appears at Satyrane's tournament 'in quyent disguise';

> For all his armour was like salvage weed,
> With woody mosse bedight, and all his steed
> With oaken leaves attrapt, that seemed fit
> For salvage wight, and thereto well agreed
> His word, which on his ragged shield was writ,
> *Salvagesse sans finesse*, shewing secret wit.   (IV. iv. 39)

Artegall's failing, his unremitting *salvagesse*, has its sexual aspect:
it is like Scudamour's, who did not follow the dictum written up
in Busyrane's castle, 'Be bold, Be bold, Be not too bold', and so
created a wall of fire between himself and his new bride. But it also
has its public aspect. Despite Artegall's growth in knowledge as
Book v progresses, and although he learns the importance of
mercy (though less successfully than Arthur), his *salvagesse* is never
matched with a comparable *finesse*. Mercilla, alone in Book v,
unites the sceptre of clemency and the sword of justice, and the
visit to her court looks forward to the exploration of the nature of
finesse in Book VI.

The problem which Spenser sets himself in Books v and vi is
exploration of the relation between strength and understanding.
In his poetry of reconciliation, the Legend of Courtesy leads on
from the Legend of Justice with a certain thematic inevitability.
Although Artegall himself may seem a limited figure, throughout
Book v we are constantly made aware of a perfect pattern of
justice existing behind Artegall's earthly imitation. There is an
almost painful gap between the perfect virtue bequeathed to the
hero by the departing Astraea and the application of that virtue
in the world of here-and-now. This note of primitivism, while it is
constantly evident in the very structure of Spenser's chivalric
poem, rises to dominance in the two final books of the *Faerie
Queene*, heralded by the unusually elaborate introduction to Book
v, a lament over the decay of the world.

In the proems the poet frequently comments on the progress of
his own work, bypassing the voice of the narrator (who is telling
a story, not reciting a poem). He often sets his poem in perspective
by describing the movement of experience over its surface or by
fixing it metaphorically.[18] His comparison of 'the state of present
time' with 'the image of the antique world' (v. proem. 1) involves
more than a judicious weighing of what the poet sees around him

[18] On the role of the poet in the *Faerie Queene*, see Durling, *Figure of the Poet*,
pp. 211-37. Cf. Arthos, *Spenser and Romances*, pp. 25ff., and *passim*.

against his accumulated knowledge of the Ancients. While that process may indeed be part of both the composition and the experience of the poem, in another sense the 'image of the antique world' is the poem itself. The inhabitants of Faeryland, then, the virtuous heroes whom Spenser has created and set within this 'image', are engaged in a struggle against alien forces massed at the borders of the poem. The delineation of the *Faerie Queene* must take into account both inherent virtue and assailing vice.

Description of the poem as a picture implies a tightness, a clarity of design and style. The metaphor is especially reminiscent of the opening of Book II, whose 'image of mortality' is only one of a number of allusions to artistic form which set the tone for the book and which anticipate a certain constriction in the development of Temperance. Hence the confessional quality of the proem to Book v is offset by a preciseness which can point to waverings in the heavens and cite exact figures (stanzas 7 and 8), and which can speak of a kind of backwards creation, in which men become stones instead of stones becoming men (stanza 2). Book VI, on the other hand, begins with a proem more open and more sympathetic than Book IV's. Here, the metaphor used to describe the poem is not 'image' but 'land', not artistic, but topographical. The poem becomes a country of its own, or a journey through this country, with all the movement and freedom which these metaphors imply. This shift in emphasis bespeaks a total change in mood.

There are those who detect an autobiographical note in the sad beauty of Calidore's adventures—a sense of the failure of the poet's ideals and an intense awareness of the pains of exile. While we may doubt such claims, both because Spenser's biography does not bear them out and because they cannot be proved from the poem, the elegiac tone of much of Book VI, and the poignancy of its story, do carry a strange authenticity.[19] The poet's voice, behind the narrator's, comes through very clearly. Of course, by the time he reaches Book VI, Spenser's reader has learned to expect such changes with each new book. He will readily accept the sharp distinctions Spenser draws between Books v and VI, and he may

[19] See, for example, Kate M. Warren, in *Variorum*, 6: 317ff. Alexander C. Judson has assembled what facts there are in *The Life of Edmund Spenser* (Baltimore, Md., 1945). Note also Rosemond Tuve's remarks in 'Spenserus', in Millar MacLure and F. W. Watt, ed., *Essays in English Literature . . . Presented to A. S. P. Woodhouse* (Toronto, 1964), pp. 3–25, esp. pp. 9–10; and see Raymond Jenkins, 'Spenser with Lord Grey in Ireland', *PMLA*, 52 (1937), 338–53.

feel relief at the distinctly personal tone of the sixth book after the impersonality of Book v. But Book vi is in some respects different in kind from all the previous books. It is the only one in which the validity of the 'quest' framework is seriously questioned; on earlier occasions the issue was somehow avoided. And this questioning of the fundamental element in Spenser's chivalric romance is accompanied by an introspective questioning of the nature of poetry itself: the poet is very close to us, examining, interrogating, reformulating. Just as the *Epithalamion* seems to bring the whole cosmos within the range of a poet's marriage, so the examination of the cohesion of society becomes a highly personal consideration of the role of the poet. It is almost as though Spenser cuts systematically across his reader's expectations: courtesy is no longer in the court, we must look elsewhere; the old order of society can best be understood through the order of poetry.[20]

Since the court stands at the top of the social hierarchy, and since it is to court that gentlemen resort, we expect to find courtesy there. The court of Mercilla, we remember, presented a picture of true justice superior even to Artegall's. Clearly Mercilla was modelled after Elizabeth, and clearly her court was a kind of ideal of justice displaying the proper balance between retribution and forgiveness, *salvagesse* and *finesse*. But if we look for a court of courtesy in Book vi, we shall not find one. The proem alludes to the glories of Elizabeth's court, but only to show that they contrast sharply with the practice of 'present time'. The fact that courtesy is etymologically connected with the court only tells us something about the ideal, nothing about the dislocations of modern times. It is odd indeed that the very book allocated to this courtly virtue has very little to do with the court, particularly since it follows a book much concerned with affairs administrative and political. But whereas Book v brings us very close to the actual court of Elizabeth and the day-to-day affairs of her government, the hero of Book vi reveals his courtly accomplishments not in society but in a rural world. Shepherds tend their flocks in quiet pastures; wild animals roam through the woods; in the wilderness lurk cannibals. Whereas all the previous books have occasional scenes in sumptuous courts—architectural descriptions, lavish

---

[20] The close connection between Book vi and poetic theory has long been recognized. See, for instance, W. W. Greg's passing remark, in *Pastoral Poetry and Pastoral Drama* (London, 1906), pp. 100–1.

works of art, costly raiment—Book VI is without such set pieces. Other heroes have companions on their quests, yet Calidore the exemplar of social virtue is enjoined by Gloriana to travel alone.

Such an unusual narrative strategy requires some explanation. The proem provides it:

> The waies, through which my weary steps I guyde,
> In this delightfull land of Faery,
> Are so exceeding spacious and wyde,
> And sprinckled with such sweet variety,
> Of all that pleasant is to eare or eye,
> That I nigh ravisht with rare thoughts delight,
> My tedious travell doe forget thereby;
> And when I gin to feele decay of might,
> It strength to me supplies, and chears my dulled spright.
>
> (VI. proem. 1)

So Spenser begins his book, anticipating a widening of his subject and justifying it on almost therapeutic grounds. For a poet of epic pretensions, such an apology is very necessary. The Legend of Courtesy will be given a pastoral setting, and pastoral, traditionally the apprentice-work of poets, is strictly speaking unsuited to serious moral statement.[21] But Spenser has a special purpose in thus offending against decorum, since his concentration on his own art in Book VI will bring the very world of the *Faerie Queene*, the premises of the work, under scrutiny.

As with Book V, the proem, especially in this opening stanza, makes no distinction between the narrator telling his story and the poet writing his poem: the poet appropriates to himself the voice of the narrator in order to address us directly. Spenser often begins and ends his books in this way. Book I, for example, concludes with a traditional motif: the poem is like a ship, the poet its steersman:

> Now strike your sailes ye jolly Mariners,
> For we be come unto a quiet rode,
> Where we must land some of our passengers,
> And light this wearie vessell of her lode.
> Here she a while may make her safe abode,
> Till she repaired have her tackles spent,

---

[21] See, for example, *Variorum*, 7: 240.

And wants supplide. And then againe abroad
On the long voyage whereto she is bent:
Well may she speede and fairely finish her intent.

(I. xii. 42)

Many poets have used the ship image before, but Spenser's version
is peculiarly elaborate. Whether we, as readers, stand outside the
fiction, or are passengers, or are mariners, remains delicately un-
clear. But the stanza's third line seems to suggest that we are part
and parcel of the enterprise itself. '*We* must land some of our
passengers.' The ship's voyage, the poem's exposition, becomes a
kind of collective effort involving the co-operation of poet and
reader in active harmony. This feeling of co-operation never quite
leaves us as we read the *Faerie Queene*: proems and apostrophes
help remind us of the presence of the poet, the irregularity of the
structure coupled with the inevitability of the allegory suggests an
inscrutable ordering principle lying above and beyond the poet's
utterances. *We*, as well as the poet, are shaping the poem; and the
poet, as well as ourselves, is participating in a preordained process
of order. The poem in some way is an extension of our own con-
sciousness, expressed to us through the metaphor of the quest. It
is a journey, like the quest of Arthur which parallels it—and like
the quests of the titular heroes, whose search for virtue reflects in
miniature not only Arthur's quest for the final glory of the Faerie
Queene but also the poet's quest for the aesthetic and moral completeness of the poem, his *Faerie Queene*.

But while allusions to the progress of the poem itself frame and
define the quests, the opening of Book VI goes much further in
explaining the relationship of poem and poet. The suggestion that
the poet's movement through the poem parallels the knight's
journey towards his quest is nowhere so explicit as here. The
poet, we are told, 'guydes' his weary steps through 'this delightfull Land of Faery', like the knight travelling on his quest. He
guides his steps, perhaps, because as poet he orders his experience.
But the 'Land of Faery' itself seems to exist independently of the
poet: it is the world of poetry, and the poet's creation of his poem
is a journey through this world of the imagination. Of course, my
use of the term 'world of the imagination' only serves to hint at
the principle fundamental to the technique of all allegorical
poetry. On the one hand, the adventures of the allegorical hero
are extensions of his own psychology. On the other hand, these

adventures answer to an abstract scheme which exists independently of its individual manifestations. So it is with poetry itself; the land of Faery, the idea of poetry, exists beyond the experience of the individual poet, but it is also the source of the individual poet's invention, which he must then order and control. The word 'guyde' seems in fact to make the poet almost two people, both guide and guided; the land of Faery, we are told, is 'sprinckled with such sweet variety' that the poet himself draws strength from his own creation. We, too, seem to participate in the journey, under the poet's guidance, drawing strength as we move, like the 'gentleman or noble person' of the Letter to Ralegh, on the road to 'vertuous and gentle discipline'. Thus the cosmos of the work bears out the Renaissance critical notion, hinted at in the Letter, that poetry delights to instruct. The very topography of Faeryland will be deployed to test this assumption, and by the end of the book, poetry will turn out to be something remarkably like Courtesy, the practice of Courtesy itself becoming a form of artistic creation.

But the stanza hints at a conflict. The fact that the ways are spacious and wide might imply no more than that Book VI will involve a widening of the poem's subject—which is true enough, of course, but tells only part of the story. The five books we have already traversed must surely have taught us to be on our guard against 'pathes and alleies wide'. A 'broad high way' leads to the House of Pride, but the way into the House of Holiness is 'streight and narrow'. In Book II, we remember, Guyon is led astray by the enticements of Phaedria, and only the Palmer prevents him from moral and literal shipwreck through the allurements and entrapments of all manner of creatures as he travels over the sea towards the Bower of Bliss. Guyon's story may be regarded as typical: he is the questing knight *par excellence*. His journey to the Bower repeats and sums up the many perils which he has faced in the earlier eleven cantos of his quest. The sea which he must cross is a kind of literalization of the water imagery which runs right through the book and which is associated with the inactive concupiscence of Cymochles, the Idle Lake of Phaedria, and the 'base murmure of the waters fall' in the Bower itself. What is more, this sea-voyage reminds us of the voyage of the poet and his poem—alluded to again in the final canto of Book II just as it rounded out Book I. But if Guyon keeps to his course in spite of

his surroundings, the poet in Book VI, far from lingering un-
productively before each new beauty, actually draws strength from
what lies around him: 'I nigh ravisht with rare thoughts delight, /
My tedious travell do forget thereby.' Our first reaction to these
lines is likely to be one of dismay: this is precisely what Phaedria
does to questing knights. 'Refuse such fruitlesse toile, and present
pleasures choose', says the song she sings to Cymochles. But,
strangely, the final lines of the stanza in Book VI belie the anxieties
of the opening: 'And when I gin to feele decay of might / It
strength to me supplies, and chears my dulled spright.' The state
bordering on rapture, the 'nigh ravishment', serves to reinforce
the poet's strength rather than debilitate him. In the sixteenth
century the term *ravishment* often implied heavenly rapture. At this
stage, at least, it would be exaggerating to describe the relation
of the poet's poem to the poet himself as that of God's grace to
mankind, but there is a hint of such an idea here. Less exalted but
hardly less arresting is the realization that a knight who draws
strength from the countryside through which he travels is no
knight at all—that harmony between questing knight and the
natural world is the very antithesis of chivalric romance, with its
dragons and bears and wolves, and its sinister enchanted gardens.

The true paradise belongs to pastoral, not chivalry. Ovid and
Hesiod tell us that at first men lived in a Golden Age when the
trees dropped honey and the sun always shone. Far from carving
out a few square yards of civilization from tracts of savagery, like
the knight of romance, the inhabitants of the Golden Age lived
in a world where harmony was the natural state. Arcadia is at one
remove from the Golden Age, and there is still enough in the
world of the shepherds that is reminiscent of the old primeval
order to make the green fields and sunny simplicity of the countryside a happy dream for the discontented city-dweller.[22] Discontent
is the important element. If Phaedria or Acrasia, Armida, Alcina,
even Dido, all with their attractive dwelling-places and still more
attractive persons, can cause the knight to *question* the values of his
society, then he is on the way to his downfall. The chivalric mode
implicitly denies the validity of the pastoral myth. The hero of

[22] On pastoral and the Golden Age, see Arthur O. Lovejoy and George Boas,
Primitivism and Related Ideas in Antiquity: Contributions to the History of Primitivism,
vol. I (Baltimore, Md., 1935); Harry Levin, *The Myth of the Golden Age in the Renaissance* (Bloomington, Ind., 1969); Eleanor Terry Lincoln, ed., *Pastoral and Romance:
Modern Essays in Criticism* (Englewood Cliffs, N.J. 1969).

pastoral romance (in so far as pastoral can have heroes) leaves a corrupt court and finds order and harmony in uncorrupted nature. He returns to society not with the carcass of a dragon but with a richer and more coherent idea of order and beauty, which in turn enriches society itself.

Chivalric romance, then, depends upon guidance, on forward movement through a perilous countryside. Pastoral romance depends upon redemption, the healing powers of the natural world, on passivity in the midst of plenty, the circle of the enclosed garden. Clearly, this first stanza of the sixth book holds these two ideals in an uneasy and paradoxical reconciliation. We would be justified in recognizing in these conflicting concerns another attempt to reconcile the force of nature with the force of history, natural virtue with social virtue. We are dealing here once again with the dynamics of Spenser's poetry of reconciliation.[23]

> Such secret comfort, and such heavenly pleasures,
> Ye sacred imps, that on *Parnasso* dwell,
> And there the keeping have of learnings threasures,
> Which doe all worldly riches farre excell,
> Into the mindes of mortall men doe well,
> And goodly fury into them infuse;
> Guyde ye my footing, and conduct me well
> In these strange waies, where never foote did use,
> Ne none can find, but who was taught them by the Muse.
>
> (vi. proem. 2)

The reader will remember that the Well of Life into which Redcross fell in Book I could 'aged long decay / Renew, as one were borne that very day' (xi. 30). Faeryland has a very similar effect on the poet: his use of the word 'well' suggests that the strength derived from Faeryland is like the strength derived from Hippocrene, the well of the Muses, the 'sacred imps, that on Parnasso dwell'. The poet is on a quest, like Guyon and Redcross and the rest. Redcross was put to school in the House of Holiness; Artegall learned the nature of justice at Mercilla's court; Guyon was educated in temperance at the Castle of Medina—the poet must be taught by the Muse if he is to find his way through Faeryland.

---

[23] Cf. Berger's important and valuable distinction between 'antique' and 'primitive': Harry Berger, Jr., 'Two Spenserian Retrospects: the Antique Temple of Venus and the Primitive Marriage of Rivers', *TSLL*, 10 (1968), 5–25; 'The *Mutabilitie Cantos*: Archaism and Evolution in Retrospect', in *Spenser: a Collection of Critical Essays*, ed. Berger (Englewood Cliffs, N.J., 1968), pp. 146–76.

But whereas the chivalric hero must select from the host of horrors and ambushes that single transcendent horror which is his
special objective, the poet must choose among the pleasures and
delights of the Faery world that special treasure which is virtue
itself. 'Treasure' is really the wrong word: it is important that
virtue is a growing plant—a part of the natural world which in
chivalric romance produces only monsters, like Orgoglio, made
of wind and earth, or witches, like Acrasia.

> Revele to me the sacred noursery
> Of vertue, which with you doth there remaine,
> Where it in silver bowre does hidden ly
> From view of men, and wicked worlds disdaine.
> Since it at first was by the Gods with paine
> Planted in earth, being deriv'd at furst
> From heavenly seedes of bounty soveraine,
> And by them long with carefull labour nurst,
> Till it to ripenesse grew, and forth to honour burst.
>
> (VI. proem. 3)

Through the world of poetry, with the assistance of the Muses,
it is possible to reach the nursery of virtue itself—not *simply* a
place in which plants grow, though that is the meaning which the
latter part of the stanza follows up, but also the place in which
children are tended. The link between the two sorts of nursery is
important to Spenser's imagery. Pastorella, who is likened to a
flower, and even bears one on her breast, is raised in the countryside hidden from men's view and from the evils of the wicked
world. The fact that Calidore brings her back to civilization suggests a kind of parallel between his quest and the poet's quest for
the flower of courtesy. Of the child whom he rescues from the
bear, Calepine says, 'Therefore some thought, that those brave
imps were sowen / Here by the Gods, and fed with heavenly sap.'
This is precisely what happens here in this silver bower (silver
like the bower of Venus in the *Hymn of Love*, the bower of Cynthia
in Book VI, the bowers of the angels themselves in Book II). There
is an obvious logical connection between the child growing to
maturity and the plant growing to ripeness—a connection which
Spenser also exploits (VI. ii. 35) in the story of Tristram, the young
man whom Calidore comes upon in the forest and makes his
squire.

The flower of virtue, Spenser tells us, is derived 'from heavenly seeds of bounty soveraine'. The line is ambiguous since it suggests both that the flower originates from the heavenly stock of sovereign virtue, and also that it is so derived *because* of God's sovereign bounty. The careful ambiguity simultaneously suggests a continuity between the supreme virtue of God himself and the individual virtue of the good man, and also a sense of the free working of God's love towards mankind. Of course, the term virtue suggests first and foremost the *virtus* of the active man and the valorous hero—he who seeks honour in mighty deeds, like Tristram. But the cradle of this virtue lies not in the world of action but in the world of poetry.

> Amongst them all growes not a fayrer flowre,
> Then is the bloosme of comely courtesie,
> Which though it on a lowly stalke doe bowre,
> Yet brancheth forth in brave nobilitie,
> And spreds it selfe through all civilitie:
> Of which though present age doe plenteous seeme,
> Yet being matcht with plaine Antiquitie,
> Ye will them all but fayned showes esteeme,
> Which carry colours faire, that feeble eies misdeeme.
>
> (VI. proem. 4)

The fact that the flower of courtesy is one of a number of flowers of virtue (the singular plant of the previous stanza has here become plural) reminds us that we have encountered such flowers before. The description of the flower of chastity, in Belphoebe's custody (III. v. 52), is strikingly similar to this description of the flower of courtesy. The flower of chastity, associated particularly with women ('Of woman kind it fayrest Flowre doth spyre'), bore 'fruit of honour'—both the public honour of honourable deeds performed by her knight and also the private honour of the woman herself. Courtesy, too, than which there is no flower fairer, spreads its influence through all society. It bowers on a lowly stalk, perhaps because its position in hierarchies of virtues was by no means as secure as that of some of the other virtues which Spenser chose to describe, perhaps because fundamental to courtesy is a sense of modesty.

The simple beginnings of this natural virtue imply an artlessness which bodes ill for Spenser's own poem. Can art so imitate nature as to reproduce its inherent goodness? Behind the poet's reference to the habits of decadent courtiers there is implied a deeper reservation about his own art of imitation.

> But, in the triall of true curtesie,
> Its now so farre from that, which then it was,
> That it indeed is nought but forgerie,
> Fashion'd to please the eies of them, that pas,
> Which see not perfect things but in a glas:
> Yet is that glasse so gay, that it can blynd
> The wisest sight, to thinke gold that is bras.
> But vertues seat is deepe within the mynd,
> And not in outward shows, but inward thoughts defynd.
>
> (VI. proem. 5)

The word 'pass' carries not only its modern sense but also the sense of 'care'. Casual passers-by find the counterfeit imitations of courtesy attractive, and the only perfection in their own images in the mirror. One thinks instinctively of Lucifera's courtiers, who were so busy prinking themselves that they had no time to be polite to the newly arrived Red Cross Knight and Duessa. But, the world being what it is, even those who *care* can see only the reflection of perfect things, not the things themselves.

Yet Spenser's poem is itself such a reflection—'Yet is that glasse so gay, that it can blynd / The wisest sight.' There is a constant danger that the poem will become an end in itself, that the overriding purpose of the work, the reconciliation of poem and society and the projection of virtuous precept into virtuous action, will be lost sight of. What is more, there is the nagging fear that even if the poet can bring about a *poetic* resolution of the dilemmas of his age, such poetic resolutions may have no validity at all outside the realm of poetry. The problem bothered Spenser's age exceedingly, and it is perhaps natural to find one of the era's greatest spokesmen taking up the question in what amounts to a critique of the nature of poetry and the role of the poet in society. In a word, by examining poetry through courtesy and courtesy through poetry, Spenser examines the success and limitations of his own poem.

Since, says the poet, courtesy is now only a memory, it is logical enough to seek it in the past, in the Golden Age before disorder entered the world. The versatility of the image of the Golden Age was not lost on the Renaissance, which adapted it not only to express historical primitivism or to lament present decay, but also to convey other ideas of perfection.[24] The artist and the poet, we are told, seek to create a Golden World of the imagination, an image of perfection. This commonplace of Renaissance aesthetic theory is embedded in Spenser's conception of poetry in Book VI; his pastoral world becomes an emblem of poetry. At the same time, it is an emblem of true courtesy, the courtesy which no longer exists in the modern world. Poetry and courtesy therefore share a common metaphor within the fiction of the legend. This drawing together of art and action suggests the line of argument Spenser's attempt at reconciliation will take.

But if, to borrow an earlier phrase, Spenser's heroes are engaged in a widening of the territory conquered by the perfect order of poetry, the battle must be fought in that borderline territory between the ideal and the real, the absolute and the relative. Spenser's narrative technique constantly juxtaposes the two realms. Malbecco actually *becomes* Jealousy; Guyon comes face to face, not with someone who is simply very shamefast, but with the virtue herself. 'She is the fountaine of your modestee: / You shamefast are, but Shamefastnesse it selfe is shee' (II. ix. 43). In their dealings with such absolutes, Spenser's heroes mediate between art and life; Calidore, riding out on his quest, sets forth, as it were, from the artistic framework represented by Faery Court. His purpose is to do battle with the sinful disorder of our own world lying outside the poem and at its periphery. These knightly heroes, in certain aspects of their characters, are messengers from the realm of ideal art—living representatives of the effect of art on life. Upon their success depends the success of literature to shape and change men.

Mediation between real and ideal requires a very special kind of language. The world of the poem uses concrete, physical objects to describe what is in fact an abstract ideal. Hence poetry itself confuses the two categories. The neo-Platonist, at least, would argue that that is precisely its power; such is the drift of Sidney's argument, for example. Ultimately the result is a kind of explosion; the Dance of the Graces takes place on a level of ideality beyond the range even of Calidore. In consequence, when he approaches, it vanishes. But Pastorella returns from the ideal world of pastoral to the real world of the court—a kind of alchemy. The process of her return is like a miracle; we somehow expect

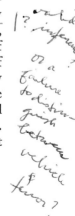

her to cease to be, to be destroyed like the shepherds upon contact with the outside world. A similar encounter between base and beautiful, fallen and unfallen, takes place in Book II. The result there is farce; Braggadocchio confronts Diana–Venus–Belphoebe like a latter-day Chanticleer, or like Aesop's rooster with the pearl.

Spenser's reluctance to be specific about categories has many uses. It allows him to criticize the court for lack of courtesy, at the same time pointing to a court where courtesy does abound—the court of Gloriana. Since Gloriana's court is an idealized pattern of the actual court of Elizabeth, a fairly simple manipulation allows the poet to put Elizabeth herself into his idealized court, thus isolating her from *actual* courtiers, who can be criticized with impunity. Spenser follows a variant of this tactic at the conclusion of the proem to Book VI. Notice how the equivocal formulation of the poet's question leaves doubt whether the court of the 'soveraine Lady Queene' is in antiquity or in modern times. We do not know whether Spenser is saying, 'The ancient world had no court as perfect as this modern one' or 'In all the ancient world the most perfect court was this one.'

> But where shall I in all Antiquity
> So faire a patterne finde, where may be seene
> The goodly praise of Princely curtesie,
> As in your selfe, O soveraine Lady Queene,
> In whose pure minde, as in a mirrour sheene,
> It showes, and with her brightness doth inflame
> The eyes of all, which thereon fixed beene;
> But meriteth indeede an higher name:
> Yet so from low to high uplifted is your name.

> Then pardon me, most dreaded Soveraine,
> That from your selfe I doe this vertue bring,
> And to your selfe doe it returne againe:
> So from the Ocean all rivers spring,
> And tribute backe repay as to their King.
> Right so from you all goodly vertues well
> Into the rest, which round about you ring,
> Faire Lords and Ladies, which about you dwell,
> And doe adorne your Court, where courtesies excell.
>
> (VI. proem. 6–7)

The stanzas strike responsive notes in our memories. Here again is the movement of the river to the sea, emblem of harmony whose presentation formed the core of the canto on the Thames and the Medway. The mirror mentioned here stands in contrast to the courtiers' mirror described earlier; the mirror of the Queen's 'pure minde' reflects perfect courtesy, both dazzling and enlivening (for 'inflame' implies both) those who behold it. The rivers are linked not with a cyclical movement so much as a movement of giving and receiving. This reciprocal action, this orderly co-operation, lies at the very root of courtesy, imitating the natural order. The movement of giving and receiving is complemented by the motif of the ring: the lords and ladies circle their sovereign like the circles of some hierarchy of virtues or representation of the universe.

Just as the figure of concentric circles might serve the Elizabethan theorist as a pattern for the cosmos, or the body politic, or any of the other concepts which the age delighted in arranging hierarchically, so we can perceive a direct link between the cosmos of political order and the functioning of poetry itself. The 'soveraine Lady Queene', the centre of her circling courtiers, is also the source of the poet's inspiration. He renders his poetry back to her in a manner which precisely parallels the rendering of courtly order back to the sovereign.

This further link between the process of poetry and the process of courtesy stresses that the discovery of one may be at least in part the discovery of the other. One might note in passing that logically it follows that criticism of the court is also in this context criticism of the state of Elizabethan letters. Such a connection is hinted at in the episode of the cannibals later in the book, and comes to the fore in the book's conclusion.

It might seem that the distinction between real court and ideal court is clearly established in the proem, but we should not forget that both courts reproduce aspects of the court of Queen Elizabeth and that the very nature of Spenser's argument will involve some deliberate confusion between the two, and a kind of telescoping of time. If Faery Court already has the secret of true courtesy, Calidore's quest is hardly necessary. Accordingly, the fact of Faery Court's virtue is related only to Calidore's *situation*, and not to the nature of Courtesy. Calidore is courteous because he comes from Faery Court; he seeks courtesy because such courtesy

is lacking in the *real* court, and he seeks it in the countryside because it *must* be there if it is missing from court life. In other words,
the argument of Book VI is carried on in terms not of a triangular
relationship between Faery Court and real court and countryside,
but in terms of exclusive dichotomies—Faery court as against real
court, and real court as against countryside.

It is important that we bear this fact in mind, since it determines
the kinds of question we may legitimately ask of Spenser's fiction.
After five books of the *Faerie Queene*, it seems hardly necessary to
point out that the logic of the poem is not the same as the logic
of real life, that illogicalities inevitably arise in situations where
absolutes and relatives jostle one another. The naïve reader may
ask why Una, presumably knowing Archimago's true nature,
allows Redcross to go to Archimago's house, or why Britomart
shows so little sympathy for the predicament of Florimell when
she crosses her path at the beginning of Book III. The answer of
course lies in Spenser's selectivity. In the incident in Book I he is
concerned with telling us something about error in relation to
Redcross, and in Book III he is concentrating on steadfastness in
relation to *Britomart*. Allegory is based upon a broad illogicality—
the suggestion that relatives and absolutes can coexist on the same
philosophical level and even interact in a state of logical equality.
The action of Book VI, as we have seen, takes place not in the
here-and-now, but in the shadowy logical area between the ideal,
the absolute (or Faery Court), and the real, the relative (the corrupt court which Spenser criticizes). Interestingly, the central
question in the Legend of Courtesy is not whether the knight will
complete his quest (that becomes a matter of almost minor importance), but whether the ideal courtesy can have its influence on
this debased version of courtesy which is juxtaposed with the ideal
in the proem. This seems a long way from the relatively simple
quest theme of Book I, for example. Normally the chivalric hero
fights to preserve the standards of his society against the unruly
powers of nature, but the hero of Book VI is the product of one of
two sets of courtly standards; the book deals not only with the
confrontation of nature and society but with the confrontation of
two societies, one corrupt and the other a mirror of perfection.

This confusion of real and ideal is a basic piece of equipment in
Spenser's poetic workshop. On occasion he holds the two apart—
launching a scathing attack on court corruption through the

House of Pride in Book I (for example), yet in Book III saying of
Belphoebe:

> Well may I weene, faire Ladies, all this while
> Ye wonder, how this noble Damozell
> So great perfections did in her compile,
> Sith that in salvage forests she did dwell,
> So farre from court and royall Citadell,
> The great schoolmistresse of all curtesy.   (vi. 1)

This is exactly the paradox of the Salvage Man, but it is only a
paradox as long as we maintain that the court *is* the schoolmistress
of courtesy. Clearly the two episodes make use of different points
of reference, and Spenser ends up having his cake and eating it too.

On other occasions real and ideal commingle. Of course, were
it not for modern depravity, appearance and reality would be one
and the same. As it is, values have become fluid and confusing:

> Then beautie, which was made to represent
> The great Creatours owne resemblance bright,
> Unto abuse of lawlesse lust was lent,
> And made the baite of bestiall delight:
> Then faire grew foule, and foule grew faire in sight,
> And that which wont to vanquish God and man,
> Was made the vassall of the victors might;
> Then did her glorious flowre wex dead and wan,
> Despisd and troden downe of all that overran.
> (iv. viii. 32)

The use of real flower as metaphor for ideal virtue is common
Spenserian practice. We have noticed it already in the passage
describing the 'glorious flowre' of chastity (III. v. 51–2). Its use
is more elaborate in the proem to Book IV, where 'naturall affection' is described as the root of 'honor and all vertue', which
'brings forth glorious flowres of fame, / That crowne true lovers
with immortall blis'. The delicate metaphorical progression, from
root to flower to garland to heavenly translation, parallels the
effect of virtue in the individual or in society: a progressive and
spontaneous burgeoning which eventually 'crowns' its possessors
with heavenly bliss.

In Book VI the flower appears again. It forms the basis of the
working definition of courtesy presented in the proem, and it is

again both abstract and concrete, an ideal and its practical realization. The passage is more complicated than the image of root, flower, and crown in Book IV, since it involves a promise not only to describe the evolution of the flower, but also to trace its source and to distinguish it from imitation. More than most of the other books, Book VI will concentrate on the *definition* of its titular virtue. Its emphasis on origins is very important; the simple progress of the quest theme will be counterbalanced by a quasi-historical search into the past, where the archetypal virtue will be found with Venus and the Graces on Mount Acidale. To some degree this division of attention is present in all the books of the *Faerie Queene*. There is always some pre-existent archetype of the titular virtue by which the hero is educated, or we ourselves are educated (sometimes the reader comes close to occupying the role of hero—in Books III and IV for example). Hence there always is a simultaneous movement towards the quest and a return to the springs of virtue. The reconciliation of these contradictory movements is, of course, merely another expression of the central motif of reconciliation found throughout Spenser's poem. The *Faerie Queene* is a perfectly serious attempt to rescue certain qualities and attitudes from a half-historical, half-idealized past and to register their eternal validity. Spenser is hardly alone in such an endeavour; we find something very similar in Hooker's attempts to create a respectable theological tradition for the Church of England, in Chapman's revitalization of the *Iliad* and the *Odyssey*, in Sidney's *Arcadia*, perhaps in Shakespeare's history plays. This motivation lay behind much of Elizabethan historiography.

But Book VI is the only book to build this division into its fictional structure. As we have seen, pastoral romance, which involves a return to an ideal past, is balanced against chivalric romance with its assurance of the future through the success of the knight's quest. The pastoral world's vision of Perfect Courtesy becomes prerequisite, as it were, to the defeat of the Blatant Beast.

The key to the flower passage lies in the final two lines: 'But vertues seat is deepe within the mynd, / And not in outward shows, but inward thoughts defynd.' Perhaps this is why Calidore, alone of Spenser's heroes, goes on his quest companionless (VI. ii. 37). The true glory of knighthood, the true honour of the courteous man, lies not in the praise of his fellows but in selfless devotion to the common good. Calidore's quest will have no audience —'although good Fortune me befall, / Yet shall it not by none be testifyde.' The very terms in which the quest is set up seem to suggest that courtesy will be somehow unlike the virtues we have seen before, somehow more personal, even though more social. Indeed one might say that Book vi is the crisis book of the *Faerie Queene*, the book widest in its concerns, yet narrowest in its introspection, the book which points back to beginnings yet brings the published poem to an end. It is curious, and yet fitting, that Spenser should return to pastoral. Just as the Red Cross Knight's quest begins all over again at the end of Book I, so the quest of the poet for poetry is never-ending and ever renews itself.

The drawing apart of elements and the need to effect resolutions, so bound up with the problem of initiating action from precept and approximating the real to the ideal, makes Spenser's poem a poem of reconciliation. We might almost say that the overriding purpose of the work is to bring together Garden and Quest, circle and line, self and community. When Socrates wished to define the qualities of a just man, he chose to describe a just society, for, he said, 'We may find that the amount of justice in the larger entity is greater, and so easier to recognize.'[25] Spenser, less convinced of the validity of such a procedure, and more circumspect than the Greek philosopher, begins with the self and moves gradually outwards toward the society. The path of his argument is studded with contrasts and conflicts, and with their corresponding resolutions. The power which makes an achievement imperfect, which negates every ending, and which tells us that no victory is a total victory, is also the power which gives us Art. By definition, poetry seeks to achieve the impossible. The power also gives us love, 'begotten by Despair / Upon Impossibility', as Marvell puts it. Spenser's poetry of reconciliation will not eliminate conflicts, but it can point the way to the creative use of our very imperfections.[26]

[25] Plato, *The Republic*, trans. H. D. P. Lee (Harmondsworth, Middx., 1955), p. 102 [368E].

[26] The term 'poetry of reconciliation' has recently, and coincidentally, been used by William H. Halewood in his study *The Poetry of Grace* (New Haven, Conn., 1970), but his purpose, to explain the dominant characteristic of early seventeenth-century poetry, is quite different from my own.

II

Calidore's Courtesy

1. *Crudor*

CALIDORE, the last of Spenser's heroes, is also the closest to the perfect pattern of a knight. 'Well approv'd in batteilous affray', 'full stout and tall', well-spoken, mild-mannered, he is the very darling of the knights and ladies of Faerie court.

> Ne was there Knight, ne was there Lady found
> In Faery court, but him did deare embrace,
> For his faire usage and conditions sound,
> The which in all mens liking gayned place,
> And with the greatest purchast greatest grace:
> Which he could wisely use, and well apply,
> To please the best, and th'evill to embase.
> For he loathd leasing, and base flattery,
> And loved simple truth and stedfast honesty.　　(vi. i. 3)

This picture of knightly grace seems a far cry from the green naïvety of the first hero of the *Faerie Queene*, the gauche Red Cross Knight, a 'tall clownishe younge man' who had never before borne arms. The contrast suggests that the succession of virtues stretching between Redcross and Calidore is not so much an equal series as a continuous growth in experience. The knights themselves are educated through their own quests, but they also form an ascending scale of accomplishment and skill. Such a pattern accords well with the ostensible purpose of the *Faerie Queene*. While it may *depict* the education of its princely hero, the young Arthur, its *aim* is to educate a gentleman in gentlemanly discipline. The heroes' growth in experience parallels the growth in experience of the ideal reader of Spenser's poem. Like Redcross setting out on his quest, the reader begins his journey through the moralized landscape of Faeryland ignorant and inexperienced. As the knights learn through physical combat, Spenser's reader learns through moral instruction.

The links between the virtues, and the relative status of their heroes, are made plain to us at the narrative level through the meetings between the principals with which several of the books open. Artegall and Calidore have such a meeting at the opening of Book VI. Their encounter is most like that of Redcross and Guyon at the opening of Book II. Through his behaviour there, and in his dealings with Amavia immediately afterwards, Guyon points up the distinctiveness of temperance, at the same time making it quite clear through the story of Ruddymane that holiness and temperance tread common ground. Guyon begins his struggle against intemperance ready equipped with the virtue passed on to him by this symbolic meeting with Redcross. Book III opens with encounters between Britomart and Guyon, and Britomart and Redcross. In the process, Britomart's martial superiority to the other two is made evident. The relationship between Britomart and Artegall (Book IV, for all practical purposes, is hero-less) requires almost half the *Faerie Queene* for its definition, but there is surely no question but that justice builds upon the virtues which have preceded it.

If a meeting between Artegall and Calidore is likely, altogether less likely is an encounter between the hero of one book and the villain of another. But Artegall's meeting with the Blatant Beast does more to define the difference between justice and courtesy even than the coming together of the two heroes. Although the Knight of Justice is immune to the snarlings and backbitings of the Beast (so immune, in fact, that the Beast seems almost to have strayed out of the adjoining book through some literary accident, the leaving ajar of some allegorical gate), the vicious abuse which its thousand tongues let fly makes us wonder about the relation between Justice and civil society. If Justice is independent of public opinion, what role does public opinion play in the ordering of society? Are there larger and more subtle forces in society promoting or destroying harmony? It is these questions, and the related questions of Reputation, so dear to the Elizabethan heart, that Spenser raises in Book VI. In attempting to rid the world of the Blatant Beast, Calidore embarks on an undertaking which both complements and surpasses the narrow concerns of Law and Justice. Without social disharmony there would be no need for laws.

To equate the Blatant Beast with social disharmony is neverthe-

less to extend its province beyond its apparent physical characteristics. The Blatant Beast, we learn from Calidore's conversation
with Artegall, was born of Cerberus and Chimaera (hence Calidore's quest is a Herculean labour at one remove—a fact which
will later turn out to be important). With its 'thousand tongues...
That all in spight and malice did agree', it is remarkably like some
of the agents of disorder whom we have met earlier in the *Faerie
Queene*—especially in Book IV. It has been suggested, with some
justification, that the central theme of Book IV is concord;[1] accordingly the major disruptive element is deceit and discord. Até,
sower of discord between friends, and ringleader in Book IV, in
turn has a predecessor in Atin, the squire of Pyrochles in Book
II who incites and slanders Guyon.

Whereas Book IV centres on discord between two people (just
as Book II deals with discord within the individual), Book VI has
to do with discord in society. But the frame of reference is not
markedly different. The richly disgusting description of Sclaunder
in Book IV (viii. 24–5) could be applied to the Blatant Beast with
little significant change. The Beast, says Calidore, was sent into
the world

> To be the plague and scourge of wretched men:
> Whom with vile tongue and venemous intent
> He sore doth wound, and bite, and cruelly torment.
>
> (VI. i. 8)

While the Blatant Beast might be a very fitting representative of
slanderous tongues and stirrers up of scandal, such activities seem
hardly the opposite of courtesy, at least as courtesy ultimately
becomes defined. The fact is that Courtesy and the Blatant Beast
are not perfect opposites, in the way in which the Dragon is the
opposite of Holiness, Acrasia is the opposite of Temperance, or
even Grantorto the opposite of Justice. Simply by being virtuous
and forgiving and understanding in his relationships with other
people, Calidore will not necessarily destroy scandal. The antidote
to sin is holiness, the antidote to intemperance is temperance, but
the antidote to scandal is not necessarily courtesy, in the narrow

---

[1] See Charles G. Smith, *Spenser's Theory of Friendship* (Baltimore, Md., 1935), esp.
pp. 1–14; Kathleen Williams, *Spenser's 'Faerie Queene': The World of Glass* (London,
1966), pp. 79–150.

sense in which Calidore seems to exemplify it. As we learn more about the nature of courtesy, we come to understand that this foul dog with its tongues and its fangs is not always beast enough to do the job.[2]

This in itself is disturbing, for it suggests that the neat dichotomy between virtue and villain which is so essential to the chivalric quest is missing here. If that is so then the forward movement of the education in virtue, which began with the untutored Red Cross Knight and ends with the accomplished Calidore, is checked or undermined by the failure of the metaphor in whose terms it is described. In Book vi the chivalric context itself is questioned. Not only is the Beast limited in its range of reference, but so is Calidore, for all his worldly sophistication. In these early cantos we learn that his courtesy is devoted too much to externals, and that it is too cramped and confined a virtue. What we discover about Calidore contrasts rather sharply with the proem's emphasis on the personal nature of courtesy. Calidore comes to understand these inward qualities only slowly and rather painfully.[3] In the process, he renders the Blatant Beast almost irrelevant to the central concerns of the book. Book vi becomes not so much a tale of derring-do as a moral pilgrimage—but not the kind of moral pilgrimage immediately expressible through the chivalric metaphor, as Book i is. This movement away from the chivalric framework may well be a questioning of the work's own efficacy as a means of gentlemanly education. Perhaps our own long journey through the virtues has given us only a superficial acquaintance with them.

In this chapter we shall discover and define Calidore's weaknesses beneath his strengths, and trace the double movement of Spenser's story, simultaneously towards success and towards

[2] On the Beast's background, see Jane Aptekar, *Icons of Justice* (New York, 1969) pp. 201–14. By reference to emblem literature, Mrs. Aptekar demonstrates the Beast's connection with Envy and with Guile. Envy and Detraction, like the 'forged guile' and 'open force' of the crocodile in Isis Church, assault the reputation from different directions. Their characteristics are contained within the Blatant Beast, who is also associated with the Hydra, commonly considered emblematic of envy and evil-speaking because every time Hercules cut off one of its heads another grew. Despite these impressive credentials, the Beast proves a rather inflexible representative of evil. See also T. K. Dunseath, *Spenser's Allegory of Justice in Book Five of 'The Faerie Queene'* (Princeton, N.J., 1968), pp. 229–35.

[3] Cf. Artegall and Justice in Book v. Artegall is also too limited in the early episodes and must learn through personal suffering.

failure. Artegall sends Calidore on his way with the customary warning and blessing:

> Now God you speed (quoth then Sir *Artegall*)
> And keepe your body from the daunger drad,
> For ye have much adoe to deale withall.   (vi. i. 10)

We are reminded of the Palmer's 'God guide thee, Guyon!' with which Guyon begins his quest in Book ii. Just as the Palmer, as a holy man, was fit to utter such a blessing, so it is appropriate that Artegall should point out where the Beast of slander and detraction is to be found: his historical equivalent, Lord Grey, suffered mightily from its thousand tongues.[4]

Calidore's journey actually accounts for only part of Book vi. The first two and a half cantos, the subject of the present chapter, follow his quest closely, but the central portion of the book does not concern Calidore, the titular hero, at all. He does not finally reappear until the ninth canto, with his stay among the shepherds and subsequent rescue of Pastorella from the clutches of the brigands. Since these episodes have little to do with the quest, the greater part of the book ignores the quest altogether: only at the beginning and end are we directly involved with the pursuit of the Blatant Beast.

While it would be exaggerating to claim that the book's first section constitutes a total coherent and simple argument, the common critical assumption that it is merely a series of examples of courtesy in action by no means does justice to Spenser's careful narrative. The various incidents are carefully juxtaposed to show the Knight of Courtesy dealing with a succession of problems each more difficult than its immediate predecessor, until finally he is involved in a situation which is beyond even his powers of control. A somewhat similar pattern of decline can be traced not only in Book v but also in Books i and ii.

Books v and vi both open with object-lessons in their respective virtues. Canto i of Book v, it is clear, is a re-enactment of the judgement of Solomon, with Artegall as judge and a disputed girl in place of a disputed child. While Artegall's justice may not be as harsh as its Old Testament provenance might imply, the opening of Book vi, also a simple and familiar story, does seem

---

[4] See *Variorum*, 5: 172–4, 258–9, 265–8. See also A. C. Judson, *The Life of Edmund Spenser* (Baltimore, Md., 1945), 84–109.

to stress mercy and reform to a far greater degree than its predecessor. The narrative of Crudor and the mantle of hair is derived from a well-known Celtic legend, available to Spenser in several literary versions.[5] As a piece of medieval legend, the story is bound to stand in sharp contrast to the Old Testament beginning of Book v. While such Celtic material is by no means unusual in the *Faerie Queene*, its presence here serves to differentiate the world of Book vi from that of Book v. In the earlier book, history, with all the security of orientation that springs from the depiction of actual historical events, is never too far away. Even though the events are heavily allegorized and even though modern scholarship has shown that there is much more to Book v than historical allegory, many of these events are shaped and controlled by a sense of incontrovertible fact. Book vi swings to the opposite extreme. The certainty of event and consequence—of cause and effect—which makes Book v sometimes reassuring and sometimes rather frightening, is replaced by obscurity and uncertainty. The points of reference in Book vi seem shifting and imprecise. Things happen by chance and not design. We are repeatedly given hints of the vulnerability and weakness of courtesy in a fallen world, and the Book puts inordinate stress on the vagaries of fortune. The squire whom Calidore finds bound to a tree declares,

> My haplesse case
> Is not occasiond through my misdesert,
> But through misfortune, which did me abase
> Unto this shame, and my young hope subvert,
> Ere that I in her guilefull traines was well expert.
>
> (VI. i. 12)

Spenser is making an important distinction here. The squire's plight results not from something intrinsically wrong with him, but from simple inexperience. So innocent a fault with so drastic a consequence argues an especially perilous world. It implies that innocence can easily suffer the ill effects of evil without itself being corrupted—a situation only questionably possible in the logical framework of Book I or Book v. Notice particularly that the squire

[5] It seems most likely that his source was the French prose romance *Perlesvaus*, which was available to him in a printed edition of 1521. Failing that, the most likely source is Malory's *Morte d'Arthur*, though the story there lacks certain details found in the *Perlesvaus* version. See Edgar A. Hall, 'Spenser and Two Old French Grail Romances', *Variorum*, 6: 365–71.

is defenceless. Strength affords the best protection against misfortune and the best means of saving others from its effects. Self-
sufficiency and aid to others are part and parcel of courtesy; both
have their place in this first adventure of Calidore's quest. Indeed,
his very first fight, with Maleffort, makes clear that there is more
to courtesy than simply being virtuous: the virtuous man must be
active in his virtue.

The seneschal, as his name implies, is both strong and weak. He
is *male fortis*, badly strong—strong in the service of evil rather
than good—and he is also un-strong, since *male* frequently has the
force of a negative in classical Latin. Certainly he is a poor tacti-
cian; Calidore conserves his energies until he feels his opponent
weaken. Then he suddenly lashes out

> Like as a water streame, whose swelling sourse
> Shall drive a Mill, within strong bancks is pent,
> And long restrayned of his ready course;
> So soone as passage is unto him lent,
> Breakes forth, and makes his way more violent.
> Such was the fury of Sir *Calidore*.   (vi. i. 21)

The simile is derived from Virgil, but it has undergone an important change. Whereas Virgil's stream, in Book ii of the *Aeneid*,[6]
bursts its banks and overflows the surrounding countryside in uncontrolled fury, Spenser's stream was artificially restrained and
now runs along its natural channel. An emblem of anarchy in
Virgil becomes an emblem of powerful natural energy in Spenser.
The sense of controlled power is precisely what Spenser seeks to
convey; there is nothing ill-disciplined about Calidore's victory
over Maleffort. On the contrary, the energy which allows Calidore's sword arm to flail like a water-mill is tempered with prudence. We shall find the twin qualities of prudence and strength
fundamentals of courtesy, at least as it is displayed in the early
cantos of Book vi.

As the strength drains from Maleffort his very name and nature
drain too. In desperation he flees the field.

> They from the wall him seeing so aghast,
> The gate soone opened to receive him in,
> But *Calidore* did follow him so fast,
> That even in the Porch he him did win,

---

[6] Lines 496–9. Cf. Ralegh, *The Ocean to Cynthia*, lines 221–9.

And cleft his head asunder to his chin.
The carkasse tumbling downe within the dore,
Did choke the entraunce with a lumpe of sin,
That it could not be shut, whilest *Calidore*
Did enter in, and slew the Porter on the flore. (VI. i. 23)

The seneschal becomes a mere shapeless mass, his body 'Did choke the entraunce with a lumpe of sin'. The arresting image reminds us that sin wars against itself and is ultimately self-defeating; this 'lumpe of sin' blocks the gate and allows Calidore entrance.

Calidore's controlled and prudent energies are different from those of Talus. Point Talus in the right direction and he will mow down all opposition without so much as a by your leave. Not so with Calidore. Spenser goes out of his way to stress that courtesy operates differently from justice. The repeated echoes of Book v in the sixth book (Calidore's entry into Briana's castle is one of many)[7] serve simply to emphasize the extent of the differences. Justice was based on retribution (duly tempered, later, with mercy); courtesy is based on rehabilitation. It is not therefore appropriate to strike Briana down (as Munera, for example, was struck down), when she plays fast and loose with semantics:

False traytor Knight, (sayd she) no Knight at all,
But scorne of armes that hast with guilty hand
Murdred my men, and slaine my Seneschall;
Now comest thou to rob my house unmand,
And spoile my selfe, that can not thee withstand?

(VI. i. 25)

Briana accuses Calidore of being a walking paradox—a knight who is no knight.[8] In other words, she accuses him of discourtesy, of failure to live up to the ideals and the rules of chivalry, for this is how Calidore and Briana would understand the term. This is irony indeed, since Calidore's reason for fighting in the first place was to defend courtesy. The hero, initially 'abashed' at such an accusation, replies with a stronger paradox: 'No greater shame to man then inhumanitie'. More important than knighthood is our

[7] Arthur gains entry to Belge's city because a corpse prevents the closing of the gate, v.x.37. Note also that Briana's giving a ring to her dwarf as a token, while a commonplace of romances, is also an echo of Book v, where Radigund gives a ring to Clarinda so that she might have access to the imprisoned Artegall (v.v.34).

[8] Cf. the strong emphasis on integrity of personality in Book v.

humanity: we are men first, and a man should behave like a man. At the same time he concedes that the forces of detraction would have reason to attack him were he guilty of the cowardice of which Briana accuses him. Of course, we know that Maleffort was the coward: he fled in terror from Calidore's blows.

Crudor's name derives from the Latin *crudus* and *crudelis*, cruel. He is cruel not only to questing knights and other travellers, but cruel also to Briana, since his love for her depends upon her making a mantle of hair gathered by force from passers-by. His love is based, in fact, upon discourtesy. His assailant, however, shows such observance of the niceties of knighthood that he seems for a moment to put his own life in special danger. Given a chance to kill Crudor, whom he has knocked unconscious, he refuses to deliver the blow until Crudor is on his feet again. In consequence, he must bear the brunt of a second, more savage, attack, which is ended only when Calidore is able to get inside Crudor's defences and beat him to the ground.[9]

How different from similar episodes in Book v this episode turns out to be! Artegall's principal aim in a situation like this would be the proper administering of justice and the adequate punishment of those who had transgressed. But once Crudor is finally subdued we are given striking indication that the Knight of Courtesy does not do things Artegall's way. Far from destroying Crudor, he listens to his plea for mercy. His reply emphasizes rehabilitation:

> With that his mortall hand a while he stayd,
> And having somewhat calm'd his wrathfull heat
> With goodly patience, thus he to him sayd;
> And is the boast of that proud Ladies threat,
> That menaced me from the field to beat,
> Now brought to this? By this now may ye learne,
> Strangers no more so rudely to intreat,
> But put away proud looke, and usage sterne,
> The which shal nought to you but foule dishonor yearne.
>
> For nothing is more blamefull to a knight,
> That court'sie doth as well as armes professe,
> How ever strong and fortunate in fight,
> Then the reproch of pride and cruelnesse.

---

[9] Note Spenser's use of superlatives to describe this fight. Crudor is neither weak nor a coward, whatever else he may be.

In vaine he seeketh others to suppresse,
Who hath not learnd him selfe first to subdew:
All flesh is frayle and full of ficklenesse,
Subject to fortunes chance, still chaunging new;
What haps to day to me, to morrow may to you.

Who will not mercie unto others shew,
How can he mercy ever hope to have?
To pay each with his owne is right and dew.
Yet since ye mercie now doe need to crave,
I will it graunt, your hopelesse life to save;
With these conditions, which I will propound:
First, that ye better shall your selfe behave
Unto all errant knights, whereso on ground;
Next that ye Ladies ayde in every stead and stound.

(vi. i. 40–2)

I have quoted this passage at length because it is crucially important. Calidore stays his *mortal* hand—mortal not simply because it is death-dealing but also because it is subject to death: 'All flesh is frayle and full of ficklenesse.' What is more, a knight professes not merely arms but also courtesy, and the one should be used in the service of the other. He must be temperate ('In vaine he seeketh others to suppresse / Who hath not learnd him selfe first to subdew'), he must temper his justice with mercy, he must respect ladies and love them in chastity and friendship, he must avoid pride and cruelty.

Calidore's speech seems almost to exceed the requirements of the situation. Of course, he is actually speaking to us; his comments on the fickleness of fortune and the need for mutual help and respect extend beyond the narrative metaphor of medieval chivalry and relate to the needs of our own world. We know that knights are supposed to respect ladies; medieval romances tell us so time and again. But the story of Crudor's cruelty to Briana is the story of all men's cruelty to all women—the incessant demand for the external indications of love whose display often inflicts cruelty on others. We know that knights aid the unfortunate, but the almost aphoristic statements about the tyranny of fortune strike home to us independently of the narrative in which they are uttered.

The lesson, with its parabolic simplicity and unequivocating truth, is not lost on Crudor and Briana either. We have seen how important Maleffort's name is to his behaviour. Crudor's decision to reform seems to do violence not only to what we know of his character thus far, but also to the terms of Spenser's allegory; Cruelty ceases to be cruel. This forcible conversion, which shatters even the logic of the allegory, is the more remarkable thereby. It is as though Calidore has perpetrated a miracle—a success in a world whose very terms militate against success.

In meting out justice to Crudor and Briana, Calidore takes the lessons of Artegall a stage further. Not only does he punish: he also saves. Not only does he set right: he also recompenses, for the squire also has his due. And so justice and mercy and courtesy all receive their proper respect, and for a moment a discourteous world becomes courteous. Of course, Lord Grey could hardly have been expected to show mercy to the Irish (though Briana's name is as solidly Irish as a name could be); that particular situation touched rather too many raw nerves among the Elizabethans. But the story of Crudor contains just the element of wishful thinking which any story of social goodness has to contain if it is to be accepted in our cynical world. Calidore *is* a kind of magician:

> That well in courteous *Calidore* appeares,
> Whose every act and word, that he did say,
> Was like enchantment, that through both the eares,
> And both the eyes did steale the hart away.   (vi. ii. 3)

The lesson is simple: he who shows courtesy will receive it in return. Courtesy, like love, is all-powerful—or it would be all-powerful were it not for the machinations of the Blatant Beast and his allies. Perhaps the word 'enchantment' is merely wishful, but one thing is certain: in Spenser's eyes courtesy means far more than simple social graces. The proem to Book vi was not simply empty words.

2. *Tristram*

The story of Crudor and Briana was derived from medieval romance. Perhaps to give further stress to the movement away from the political bias of Book v, Spenser selects for his second canto another episode which relies heavily on the romances—Calidore's encounter in the forest with a handsome young man, Tristram, who lives there in exile to avoid the wrath of his kinsman.

Rosemond Tuve's timely study of medieval influences on the

sixteenth century, and especially on Spenser,[10] has blurred the
traditional and often erroneous distinction between the Italianate
romance of the Renaissance and the Arthurian variety of the
English and French Middle Ages. While the two idioms may not
be markedly different, it is still worth noting that Spenser goes to
great lengths to give his poem an intellectual framework remarkably like Arthurian romance, even if it is more eclectic and more
consciously intellectual than the Matter of Britain. Later Arthurian
romance, especially Malory's *Morte*, is pervaded with a sense of
futility and a feeling that the chivalric ideal has become an anachronism. Of course, from the very beginning chivalric romance was
backward-looking, nostalgic. Born with soldiers' tales of the
Crusades, and grafted on to an older heroic tradition, it looks with
longing to a time when issues were clear-cut, standards were maintained, and heroism in God's service was a reality. In the later
Middle Ages, especially where the theme of love is strong, the
world of chivalric romance takes on many of the characteristics of
the world of adolescence recollected from the vantage point of
adulthood. Malory questions this vision: the standards of romance
endure into the world of full-grown men, and their attempts to
live by a sense of values left over from their adolescence lead to a
collision between camaraderie and personal loyalties, and turn
marital chastity into irresponsible adultery.[11]

Spenser seeks to avoid the cynicism of Malory by making his
world emphatically youthful. This is the story of Arthur 'before
he was king', when Britain stood on the brink of mighty deeds,
just as Elizabeth's England stood constantly in anticipation of
greater and more glorious achievement. With great skill, Spenser
forges a link between the youthfulness of chivalry and the fortunes
of his own age. The crude realities of sixteenth-century politics,
so important in Book v, caused this link to recede into the background. The introduction of Tristram—a youthful Tristram—
acts as a firm reminder of the poem's frame of reference at a point
where we are in danger of forgetting it.

The noble, handsome Tristram, like so many of the characters
in the central section of Book vi, is living in the forest far from

[10] *Allegorical Imagery* (Princeton, N.J., 1966).
[11] See Charles Moorman, *A Knyght There Was* (Lexington, Ky., 1967), esp.
pp. 96–112. On Spenser's use of the narrative techniques of romance, see Arnold
Williams, *Flower on a Lowly Stalk* (Michigan State University, 1967), pp. 3–5.

society. It will be best to consider Tristram's importance as a 'forest-dweller' in connection with my discussion of the other forest dwellers. Here we can look at his story simply in the context of Calidore's adventures.

Seeing Tristram, who has not taken the vows of chivalry, in combat with a knight, Calidore is surprised and alarmed. Tristram should show more respect.[12] Calidore's first reaction to this seeming aggression is to chide him much as Briana chided Calidore himself in Canto i—for his 'unknightly' behaviour:

> What meanes this, gentle swaine?
> Why hath thy hand too bold it selfe embrewed
> In blood of knight, the which by thee is slaine,
> By thee no knight; which armes impugneth plaine? (VI. ii. 7)

But invocation of the laws of chivalry against Tristram is hardly adequate in this situation. Tristram killed the knight because of the *knight's* failure to observe these laws; he was the first to offend against the law of arms by his ill-treatment of his lady. The deceptiveness of first impressions tells us that courtesy cannot be judged by simple externals. Calidore defeated Maleffort and Crudor because he showed restraint and patience. Such qualities are needed here too. Because Calidore is calm and restrained, uses reason and asks questions, he is able to judge fairly. The episode also has a second lesson for us. Implicit in Calidore's dealings with Tristram is the suggestion that true courtesy transcends the law—that failure to observe the law of chivalry is no fault if this higher principle is at stake.

Calidore is agreeably surprised by the youth's replies to his questions. Like the hypothetical reader of the proem, he expects to find courtesy at court, not in the country. Indeed his own experience is more limited than ours, since at Faery Court courtesy *can* still be found. But in the fallen world we cannot trust appearances: 'Vertues seat is deepe within the mynd / And not in outward shows, but inward thoughts defynd.' Crudor was knight outside and no knight inside. Tristram, on the other hand, has not taken the vows of knighthood and so is without the outward trappings of a knight, but his spirit is filled with knightly virtue. His be-

---

[12] Cf. *Don Quixote*: 'For he suddenly remembered that he had never received the honour of knighthood, and so, according to the laws of chivalry, he neither could nor should take arms against any knight' (trans. J. M. Cohen (Harmondsworth, Middx., 1950), p. 36).

haviour actually parallels Calidore's. Calidore came to the rescue
of a squire and his lady in the previous canto, and did battle with
a knightless knight. Now Tristram has come to the rescue of a
lady whose knight ill-treats her. He displays natural courtesy,
derived not from an education in courteous expertise, but from
the natural accident of birth.

The question whether courtesy and noble birth go together,
or whether the first is possible without the second, occupied the
attention of most of the authors who wrote on courtesy in the sixteenth century. This was the great era of the courtesy book—
handbooks on good manners and gentlemanly conduct designed
to make the parvenus of the Elizabethan meritocracy into respectable citizens, or to preserve standards which were gradually being
eroded. We shall return to this question at a later stage. Here it is
enough to observe that on two occasions (stanzas 5 and 24) Calidore concludes Tristram nobly born—even before he has heard
his ancestry.

The association of courtesy and noble birth is hardly an attractive notion in our egalitarian society. But we must be wary of
adopting too rigidly doctrinaire an attitude towards Spenser's
exploration of the question. We must remember first that this *is*
an allegorical narrative. The story can be read on its own terms,
as a simple tale of chivalry, but it can also be read in terms of the
society of Spenser's contemporaries. The machinery of knighthood and chivalry and derring-do functions as an extended metaphor, a kind of microcosm displaying in little the social pressures
and conventions of the Elizabethan age. To these two alternative
approaches (not, I hasten to add, 'allegorical levels') we should
perhaps add a third—a more general exploration of the nature of
morality in which even the preoccupations of Spenser's own day
are merely the particulars affording an approach to the general
discussion. While we should not underestimate the importance of
the question of noble birth and its attributes to the lively yet conservative society of the sixteenth century, we can discern in
Spenser's raising of the issue an attempt to discover the guiding
principles of human society, the cohesive forces which work
against social and political disruption. These forces, as we shall
see, are in essence what Spenser means by courtesy.

Beyond the chivalric metaphor, Tristram's story has several
simple moral lessons to add to our store. First of all selfishness

does not pay; as Calidore points out to Crudor, 'In vaine he seeketh
others to suppresse, / Who hath not learnd him selfe first to subdew.'[13] Second, selflessness is a virtue which ultimately serves a
man's better interest.

> Sayd then Sir *Calidore*; Neither will I
> Him charge with guilt, but rather doe quite clame:
> For what he spake, for you he spake it, Dame;
> And what he did, he did him selfe to save.   (VI. ii. 14)

Selflessness is also a social responsibility, 'For knights and all men
this by nature have, / Towards all womenkind them kindly to
behave.' Calidore's words emphasize the naturalness of generosity:
the verb 'have' implies that such conduct is the result of a kind of
general gift of nature, and that to behave otherwise is a wilful act
of defiance against nature's laws. The pun on 'kind' and 'kindly'
serves to underline the connection between natural behaviour and
goodness. Perhaps more important, the addition of the phrase
'and all men' reminds us that the moral issues here touched on are
universal. 'No greater shame to man then inhumanitie', said
Calidore in Canto i. The stories of knights and knighthood which
Spenser tells in the *Faerie Queene* are not concerned with the moral
and ethical problems of a particular aristocracy (which in any case
probably never existed) but with the problems of ordinary educated Elizabethans and ordinary social beings.

We must, then, keep in perspective the question whether courtesy is an aristocratic monopoly. Even here in Canto ii, it seems
equally evident that natural courtesy needs developing. If the seed
of courtesy is to grow, it requires the right training. Tristram
explains that he has not 'lewdly spent' his time in the forest, 'Nor
spilt the blossome of my tender yeares / In ydlesse' (VI. ii. 31).
The image is arresting, both because of its reminder of the flower
of courtesy in the proem, and because it is not the kind of language
a person normally uses about himself. In fact, Tristram is not so
much a person as a kind of emblem of youthful goodness—a
characteristic made the clearer when Calidore dubs him squire.
Tristram blossoms forth

> Like as a flowre, whose silken leaves small,
> Long shut up in the bud from heavens vew,
> At length breakes forth, and brode displayes his smyling hew.
>
> (VI. ii. 35)

---

[13] Note that Artegall had to learn a rather similar lesson, v. vi–viii.

The squire, in short, is like the flower of courtesy, hidden from men's view but destined to grow to ripeness and 'forth to honour burst'. While his logical connection with the incidents around him may be slight, he helps to remind us, in this pastoral book, of the purity of youth. Perhaps his example, brief though his appearance may be, helps us to judge Aladine and Priscilla aright, and to sympathize with their efforts to keep their love alive in the face of parental opposition.

3. *Aladine and Priscilla*

Both of these early episodes in the Legend of Courtesy—the story of Crudor and the story of Tristram—help to provide an empirical definition of the virtue, and they delineate very clearly the strengths of Calidore himself. In the first episode, his skill as fighter and debater succeeds triumphantly in convincing a knight who abuses knighthood of the error of his ways. The second episode is less simple, since it involves not only a knight who abuses knighthood, but also a non-knight who takes upon himself the authority of knighthood. Whereas the first episode involves a simple offence, the second involves two transgressions which must be weighed one against the other.

The third story in Book vi—that of Aladine and Priscilla—presents a greater dilemma. Aladine has been wounded by the knight whom Tristram kills. He was with his lady, Priscilla, on a secret rendezvous in the forest, when the knight broke in on them and attempted to carry Priscilla off, wounding Aladine in the process. The reason for the secrecy is the fact that Priscilla's parents disapprove of her friendship with Aladine, who, though he is himself a knight, does not measure up to the social standards of Priscilla's family.

Now if we accept, as I think we must, that the love of Aladine and Priscilla is worthy of respect (the narrator gives no explicit indication to the contrary, and the whole tenor of the narrative suggests this), then two standards come into total collision. On the one hand, the pair's love is precious—a small emblem of harmony amid hostility. On the other hand, Priscilla's parents have a right to determine whom she may marry. If Calidore supports the young lovers (and surely Courtesy must defend Harmony), then he comes in conflict with Priscilla's parents and, behind them, the normal standards of society. If he fails to support them, he destroys love. The dilemma is really an extension of the conflict hinted at in the episode of Tristram. Tristram offended against knightly law (in itself an offence), but there was a reason for doing so. Social propriety and personal virtue collided. Aladine and Priscilla perhaps present Calidore with a miniature version of the old conflict between love and society. But at this stage Calidore cannot effect a very meaningful reconciliation between these opposing forces.

Calidore comes upon Aladine wounded, with Priscilla lamenting over him. While we might question the morality (and the prudence) of the couple's dalliance in the woods, clearly the present accident was hardly their fault. Nor can we wholly blame Aladine for ill-advisedly doffing his armour; he is not a Redcross equipped with the armour of a Christian man. Thus far we have already discovered, from the explanation given by the lady whom Tristram rescues, that Aladine offers to meet his opponent in armed combat, but the knight is too impatient for that. Unlike Calidore, who refused to do injury to Crudor when he lay on the ground unhorsed and swooning, the marauder throws the laws of knighthood to the winds and attacks Aladine as he lies defenceless under the trees. His action shows lack of respect for love, lack of respect for ladies, and a complete disregard for the knightly rules calling for equality of combat. If Aladine and Priscilla lack prudence in dallying in the woods, their offence pales into insignificance beside the knight's.

Even in these desperate straits, social pressures reveal themselves in unexpected ways. Priscilla must be gently reminded that there is nothing demeaning in carrying her lover to his home, nor in asking Calidore to help. 'My selfe will beare a part, coportion of your packe', says Calidore, demonstrating his selflessness and desire to help.

Two issues come to prominence at the castles of Aldus (Aladine's father) and Priscilla's parents. First there is the question of birth and parental approval. Second, there is the question of honesty. In order to protect Priscilla from her parents' wrath, Calidore must tell her parents what is for all practical purposes a lie. The first issue seems at first sight more relevant to the idea of courtesy than the second; it is directly involved with the conventions governing the ordering of society. It is easy to misinterpret Spenser here: his argument is by no means egalitarian. We should note the order in which he presents his material. We learn at the opening of Canto iii,

> a man by nothing is so well bewrayd,
> As by his manners, in which plaine is showne
> Of what degree and what race he is growne.
> For seldome seene, a trotting Stalion get
> An ambling Colt, that is his proper owne:
> So seldome seene, that one in basenesse set
> Doth noble courage shew, with curteous manners met.

> But evermore contrary hath bene tryde,
> That gentle bloud will gentle manners breed. (VI. iii. 1–2)

At first sight, this remark seems directed against Aladine, who is of meaner birth than Priscilla. But in fact Aladine's background is also honourable. Himself a knight, he is the son of a knight. His father, the narrator tells us, 'Was to weete a man of full ripe yeares, / That in his youth had beene of mickle might, / And borne great sway in armes' (VI. iii. 3). The term 'meaner', we should remember, is comparative. This episode is not a grand confrontation of Love and Degree, but a much lesser problem of True Love versus Parental Approval—at least as far as Priscilla and Aladine are concerned. It is worth remembering, though, that a very similar difference of degree between Pastorella's parents, and *their* parents' disfavour, leads to Pastorella's exposure and her childhood among the shepherds. When love and society find themselves in conflict, the consequences can be cosmic. Perhaps aware of this fact, Calidore agrees to help:

> He passed forth with her in faire array,
> Fearelesse, who ought did thinke, or ought did say,
> Sith his own thought he knew most cleare from wite.
> So as they past together on their way,
> He can devize this counter-cast of slight,
> To give faire colour to that Ladies cause in sight.
>   (VI. iii. 16)

It is hard to ignore an echo of the proem's criticism of 'fayned showes . . . which carry colours faire, that feeble eies misdeeme'. But this is, we note, a *counter*-cast—a manœuvre designed to thwart some previous manœuvre by another party. The attitude of the parents of Priscilla was responsible for this present turn of events. Calidore is merely countering the effects of an evil already perpetrated.

While we may be aware of larger dilemmas lurking behind an innocuous narrative, it is hard to avoid the feeling that Calidore's lie somehow trivializes himself and his virtue. Is it really the function of courtesy to go round sorting out teenage love problems? Is a hero who makes up stories really believable? In this respect, discussion of the legitimacy of white lies, a topic which seems to have preoccupied commentators on this story, seems somewhat beside the point.[14] The episode does serve the useful purpose of emphasizing once again the need for selflessness in the face of injustice or hardship, and there can be no doubt that Calidore's intervention *does* preserve harmony, temporarily at least, but as we move on to Calidore's next encounter we are surely almost as troubled as Calidore himself—

> and then most carefully
> Unto his first exploite he did him selfe apply.   (vi. iii. 19)

4. *Calepine and Serena*

We found that the episode of Crudor and that of Tristram owed a great deal to one another. The episode of Aladine and Priscilla and that of Serena and Calepine also form a pair, the second in large measure dependent on the first. What is more, this fourth episode is the final stage of a descending series, from total success with Crudor, to momentary confusion with Tristram, to a dangerous commitment with Priscilla, to failure with Calepine. Put in other terms, the first incident (with Crudor) carried few risks to reputation; the second (with Tristram) some risks; the third (with Priscilla) many risks; and the fourth (with Calepine) such risks

---

[14] A. C. Judson quotes Guazzo, *La Civile Conversatione* 1.97: 'I denie not, but that it is commendable to coyne a lye at some time, and in some place, so that it tend to some honest ende.' ('Spenser's Theory of Courtesy', *Variorum* (6: 340–5).) Artegall's use of guile in Book v, and Arthur's use of such tactics in both books, implies that there is no stigma attached to such sleights. Note that the grounds of Burbon's deception are different (see v.xi.56) because they involve a compromise with Catholicism—the decision of Henry of Navarre that Paris is worth a mass, a decision which to Spenser, or any loyal English Protestant, can only be interpreted as selling out to the Whore of Babylon (see also Angus Fletcher, *The Prophetic Moment* (Chicago, 1971), pp. 209–10). In view of earlier points of contrast with Book v, we are perhaps intended to notice the parallel in the two events and yet to conclude that their burden is different. Charles E. Mounts ('Virtuous Duplicity in *The Faerie Queene*', *MLQ*, 7 (1946), 43–52) singles out five examples of such 'virtuous duplicity' in Book vi.

that the Blatant Beast is able to break through and spread his poisonous scandal.

We should remember the circumstances in which Aladine's attacker came upon Aladine and Priscilla. In Priscilla's words, 'that discourteous knight . . . them in that shadow found, / Joying together in unblam'd delight.' Calidore comes upon Calepine and Serena in much the same way:

> So as he was pursuing of his quest
> He chaunst to come whereas a jolly Knight,
> In covert shade him selfe did safely rest,
> To solace with his Lady in delight:
> His warlike armes he had from him undight;
> For that him selfe he thought from daunger free,
> And far from envious eyes that mote him spight.
> And eke the Lady was full faire to see,
> And courteous withall, becomming her degree.
>
> (VI. iii. 20)

What is more, Calidore comes upon them as he is 'pursuing of his quest'. It is an ominous detail, for it implies that the Beast may be near. Calepine, at least, is unaware of the danger. Like Mars under the spell of Venus, 'His warlike armes he had from him undight.' The lesson of self-defence, as we discover later, is slow in coming to Calepine. Thinking himself 'far from envious eyes that mote him spight', he is pathetically unprepared for the vicissitudes which Calidore's intrusion plunges him into. His lady may be 'courteous' but she is no match for the 'envious' Blatant Beast.

Of course, Calidore cannot *help* his intrusion.

> Yet since it was his fortune, not his fault,
> Him selfe thereof he labour'd to acquite,
> And pardon crav'd for his so rash default,
> That he gainst courtesie so fowly did default.
>
> (VI. iii. 21)

But this does not alter the consequences. We are reminded of the Squire's plea of misfortune in Canto i. Even if Calidore is not directly culpable, he has shown himself the dupe of fortune, and that is quite enough to allow the Blatant Beast entry. In Book VI we are concerned less with apportioning guilt than with assessing the outcome of given social acts.

The problems do not end with Calidore's intrusion. Faced with the resultant disharmony, he does not prove eminently capable in the task of restoring order. As the Knight of Courtesy he should surely show courtesy in his every action. We have discovered already that courtesy involves more than proper public behaviour: it embraces also proper private conduct, selflessness, ability to understand and assist other people. But Calidore is also a knight on a quest, and matters knightly are clearly uppermost in his mind. For a moment 'professional' matters win out. Calidore's talk of courtesy is of *knightly* courtesy pure and simple; he engages Calepine in conversation about knightly deeds. There can be no part for Serena in such a conversation. She wanders off. Far from bringing the two together again, Calidore actually separates them by discussing affairs of chivalry:

> Of which whilest they discoursed both together,
> The faire *Serena* (so his Lady hight)
> Allur'd with myldnesse of the gentle wether,
> And pleasaunce of the place, the which was dight
> With divers flowres distinct with rare delight,
> Wandred about the fields, as liking led
> Her wavering lust after her wandring sight,
> To make a garland to adorne her hed,
> Without suspect of ill or daungers hidden dred.
>
> (VI. iii. 23)

We can feel the approaching evil: the vocabulary is loaded with it—'allur'd'; 'rare delight'; 'wandred'; 'wavering lust'; 'wandring sight'; the long-drawn-out last line, 'Without suspect of ill or daungers hidden dred.' We recall the similar situation of Amoret when, on Britomart's falling asleep, she wandered in the forest:

> The whiles faire *Amoret*, of nought affeard,
> Walkt through the wood, for pleasure, or for need;
> When suddenly behind her backe she heard
> One rushing forth out of the thickest weed.   (IV. vii. 4)

Once again, unprotected beauty is wandering alone. The folk-tale element, never far away in Book VI, seems to manifest itself here. Any country girl might have told Serena that she was running a risk. Wandering alone (like Proserpine or Eurydice) to pick flowers, or lying unprotected beneath some tree, is tantamount to an invitation to the fairy folk to carry her off.[15]

[15] Cf. Stith Thompson, *The Folktale* (New York, 1961), p. 247.

> All sodainely out of the forrest nere
> The *Blatant Beast* forth rushing unaware,
> Caught her thus loosely wandring here and there,
> And in his wide great mouth away her bare. (VI. iii. 24)

Calidore forces the Beast to let go of his victim ('For he durst not abide with Calidore to fight'), but Serena already bears the Beast's festering bite.

The story, of course, carries its immediate lessons, about the dangers of frank behaviour in defiance of social norms, about the need for vigilance, about the need for unity among the positive elements in society. This unity is missing, since the strength of Calidore is in a sense in opposition to the delight of Calepine and Serena; Action does not support Pleasure. The very fact that Calidore seems somehow unable to grasp the import of his own behaviour does suggest a fatal weakness in his idea of courtesy. It also suggests (this is perhaps even more important) that the metaphor of knightly deeds and chivalric adventure is somehow inadequate to deal with the complexities of modern social order and human values. Calidore's enthusiastic swapping of stories with Calepine is, in a way, pathetically anachronistic beside the horrors lying in wait for Serena and for Calepine. The old values no longer serve.

The misfortunes which Calidore has now set in motion do not touch him directly. Just as courtesy manifests itself in a man's relations with his fellows, so the ill effects of discourtesy are revealed first in those against whom the discourtesy is aimed. Hence our attention is directed in the book's second section not at Calidore's quest but at Calepine's sufferings. In the earlier cantos we saw courtesy in action, strength united with harmony. Now we shall see harmony and strength divided from one another, Calepine unable to defend himself or Serena from the physical attacks which stand metaphorically for the detraction and back-biting of society's hostility.

The larger implications of the story of Calepine and Serena prompt us to look back over the ground we have covered. The four principal episodes contained in these two and a half cantos clearly form a picture of diminishing success, each episode more difficult than its predecessor, each episode less clear-cut in its outcome. We might add that the series presents a spectacle of increasing triviality, from the fierce battle against Cruelty in the name of courteous love, to the sorting out of domestic troubles and an unfortunate intrusion on a sunny afternoon. Interestingly, none of these problems could be solved by the out-and-out fighting which the reader of the *Faerie Queene* has become fairly used to by the time he reaches Book VI. The Blatant Beast is best kept at bay not by violence but by prudence. There is more to championing Courtesy than fighting—a truth which Calidore himself seems to forget in his cheerful conversation with Calepine.

There is also more to the Beast than simply discourtesy. The Beast hints at, or should hint at, a much larger conception of social disharmony. As I pointed out earlier, there is a dislocation between quest and virtue here. Spenser resolves the problem at this point by dispensing temporarily both with his hero and with his hero's adversary. But he continues to deal with the qualities they represent, choosing to unify the book not simply through the quest, but also through its allegorical preoccupation —courtesy and its antithesis, harmony and disharmony.

The quest, then, is not so much forgotten as supplemented. Spenser has found a rather different solution to the narrative problem he faced in Books III and IV. In those two books his desire to concentrate on the virtue rather than the virtue's adversary led him to move the quest away from his hero and towards his reader. Books III and IV require our active participation in the discovery and definition of the virtue in a way in which Books I and II do not. Since the first two books present us with fairly clearly defined virtues with a good deal of tradition behind them, we are largely concerned with what might *stop* our heroes from reaching these virtues. In Books III and IV the virtues are not clearly defined, and our main concern is with definition—or perhaps with realizing the very extent of what seemed to us fairly limited virtues. *We* are educated, as well as our hero.

In certain respects, Book VI is a lot more like Books III and IV than it is like Book I—though, as always when one makes such generalizations about the structure of the *Faerie Queene*, such an observation will not pass without substantial qualification. Certainly there is a breadth of subject in Book VI which we do not find in the Legend of Holiness. Throughout the *Faerie Queene*, each book is set off against the others, each virtue playing upon and illuminating its neighbours, each formal structure adding to the richness of those around it. But there is a broad tendency in the work towards all-inclusiveness rather than exclusive definition. The effect of the *Faerie Queene* is cumulative: Spenser (in a sense like Arthur) is in search of the grand virtue which will include them all. Thus he hints at the all-inclusive amalgam, the central emblem of all virtue, of all harmony, of concord, of love, which will point outwards and radiate into the very corners of his huge work—a work which has the lineaments and the extent of life itself. The 'Mutabilitie Cantos' are such an amalgam; so is the Temple of Venus; so are the Gardens of Adonis and Mount Acidale. And each amalgam builds (if that is the right word) on its predecessors. I should add that the question as to whether Books III and IV were written before Books I and II has little to do with this general proposition. We are concerned with the balance of the work as we have it, regardless of the order in which it was put together.[16]

Books III and IV, then, recognizing the limitations of the quest theme, come close to abandoning it in favour of a more generalized treatment of virtue—a quest by the reader, if you like. In Book VI, Spenser seeks to avoid the limiting effect of the quest not by its abandonment, but by holding vice and virtue apart. This solution avoids the restrictions of the quest theme while retaining that coherence of plot which is so conspicuously lacking in the central portion of the *Faerie Queene*. Spenser is able to give the virtue of courtesy a breadth which could not be accommodated within the theme of the knightly quest (which postulates the defeat of a kind of photographic negative of the virtue). But this somehow renders the quest itself irrelevant, and that and its attendant problems will become more strongly evident later in the narrative. We now turn away from the quest, towards a broader exploration of courtesy and discourtesy and their effects.

16 The most extensive study of Spenser's method of composition is Josephine Waters Bennett, *The Evolution of 'The Faerie Queene'* (Chicago, 1942). W. J. B. Owen showed the limitations of her argument in 'The Structure of *The Faerie Queene*', *PMLA*, 68 (1953), 1079–1100.

III

Forest Folk

1. Turpine

Book VI is readily divisible into three sections, the first extending to the point in Canto III where the Beast bites Serena, the second occupying the centre of the book as far as the end of Canto viii, the third concerned with Mount Acidale and the completion of the narrative. There is ample justification for treating these three sections as separate units. The disappearance of Calidore from the narrative forms a significant turning-point in the action, when our attention moves away from the representative of courtesy itself to a kind of surrogate, the less accomplished and less fortunate Calepine. Calepine's adventures follow the general course of Calidore's adventures from Canto ix on, so that the central portion of the book raises several of the issues which the final portion explores in greater depth.

Whereas Calidore leaves Faery court with honour and the good wishes of his fellows, Calepine is driven out into the countryside, first because of love (his love for Serena) and second because the ensuing scandal cuts off any hope of return. The scandal, precipitated all unwittingly by Calidore, is represented by the Blatant Beast's biting of Serena and the subsequent attacks of the cowardly Turpine. Despite his initial experiences, harried through the wilderness with the wounded Serena by his adversary Turpine, he ultimately learns that the natural world offers strengths as well as dangers, and patterns for social living as well as savageries. The remainder of his story concerns his gradual re-assertion of his knighthood and his rescue of Serena from the clutches of the vicious part of nature. Their return to society, he as knight, she as lady cured of her former faults, never takes place in the narrative as we have it; it is perhaps subsumed in the return of Calidore and Pastorella in the final cantos of the work

The principal unifying element in the second section, unlike the clearly delineated sequence of episodes with which the book begins, is not so much event as character. The story of Turpine and Blandina and their outrageous behaviour towards Calepine and Serena shows us the consequences of an attack by the Blatant Beast, particularly on the psychology, the mental fortitude, of those attacked. Spenser spares no pains to show us just how drastic and humiliating the Beast's ravages are. The 'jolly knight' Calepine, who 'solaced with his lady in delight' is reduced to a pitiful and friendless creature bearing his wounded lady on his back, sleeping in the open, even hiding behind her to escape Turpine's onslaughts. The picture of the dejected Calepine and his wounded lady is pitiful and moving, after the colour of the episode of Tristram and the success of Calidore's aid to Priscilla. We drop here into a lower key: these figures are intensely human and helpless.

> Then up he tooke her twixt his armes twaine,
> And setting on his steede, her did sustaine
> With careful hands soft footing her beside,
> Till to some place of rest they mote attaine.
>
> (VI. iii. 28)

Sir Turpine's refusal to help them is an interesting and surprising echo of Priscilla's reservations about helping Aladine (VI. ii. 47):

> Perdy thou peasant Knight, mightst rightly reed
> Me then to be full base and evill borne,
> If I would beare behinde a burden of such scorne.
>
> (VI. iii. 31)

Calidore, we remember, was prepared to use his shield, symbol of his knighthood, to help Priscilla bear the wounded Aladine home to his father. But Turpine will not even take a knight's lady on to his horse.

Critics have suggested that Turpine and Blandina, his lady, represent the extremes lying on either side of the Aristotelian virtue of 'near friendliness'.[1] This ingenious interpretation helps explain the

---

[1] W. F. De Moss, 'Spenser's Twelve Moral Virtues "According to Aristotle"', *Variorum*, 6: 325–7. I do not agree with De Moss's general thesis, that throughout Book VI Spenser's idea of courtesy corresponds to that of Aristotle's 'near-friendliness' (or 'likeability', as J. A. K. Thomson calls it in his translation of the *Nicomachean Ethics*), but in this particular instance Spenser does seem to have had Aristotle in mind. In view of my later discussion of Grace, note that Huloet's *Dictionarie* (see Chapter IX, n. 33) lists *Blande* as a possible translation of *Graciously*.

rather puzzling behaviour of Blandina—though of course there are many methods of getting one's way besides Turpine's own speciality, bullying. One hardly needs the support of Aristotle to see Blandina as *blanda*, flattering, and Turpine as *turpis*, churlish and base.[2] Turpine is another example (like Mirabella, still to come) of defiant pride, of one who seeks to rise above, or abuse, his due station. He is representative of that cruel and selfish world which Crudor was converted from—a world whose members invariably persecute those less fortunate than themselves and make a virtue out of doing so. In just such a world the Blatant Beast flourishes. Indeed, the Beast epitomizes the kind of social cruelty of which Turpine is a notable practitioner. One is reluctant to dub Spenser the champion of the common man (there is plenty of evidence that he wasn't), but Turpine and Blandina are disquietingly like the archetypal capitalist and his charity-giving wife. If the poor are poor it is their own fault; if a man is in need of help we must find some good reason why we cannot give it.

The total debasement of Calepine sets the story of Priscilla in a new perspective. Was it consequences of this kind that Calidore sought to save Priscilla from? Such are the ill effects of scandal that the accused can do nothing to defend himself against the accuser. Having lost his reputation, he can neither make people believe his protestation of innocence nor back up his words with action—

> The dastard, that did heare him selfe defyde,
> Seem'd not to weigh his threatfull words at all,

[2] The passage, which is partly based on Ariosto, *Orlando Furioso*, xx.110ff. (see *Variorum*, 6: 200–1), and partly Spenser's own invention, presents several puzzles besides Blandina. There are strange narrative problems. Does Calepine have a horse, for example? In stanza 28, he apparently does, but in 31 he evidently does not, hence his request to Turpine 'to take him up behind upon his steed'. In stanza 32 Turpine directly alludes to Calepine's lack of a mount, and in stanza 33 Calepine wades through the stream apparently with Serena wading beside him—horseless. By stanza 46 we find the situation changed again: 'he goth on foote all armed by her side, / Upstaying still her selfe upon her steede.' Not only is there the curious fact that a horse has reappeared, but now Calepine is 'all armed', while we have already been told in stanza 27, that, 'his weapons soone from him he threw away'. By stanza 34 he has acquired a spear. Certainly he makes no attempt to use the weapons, if he has them, when Turpine attacks him a few stanzas later. The editors of the *Variorum* edition (6: 201) take the rare step of suggesting that 'perhaps a stanza is missing' between stanzas 33 and 34. In the face of such a riot of discrepancies, the major crux in stanza 49, with which I deal below, recedes in importance. Perhaps we should conclude that Spenser's intention in much of this passage has become so obscured by a corrupt text as to render consistent explanation impossible.

> But laught them out, as if his greater pryde
> Did scorne the challenge of so base a thrall. (vi. iii. 36)

Hardly surprisingly, the word *courtesy* springs to Calepine's lips time after time, always to be ignored. The wounded Serena must sleep under the stars 'Cover'd with cold, and wrapt in wretchednesse, / Whiles he him selfe all night did nought but weepe, / And wary watch about her for her safegard keepe' (iii. 44). When Turpine attacks again, Calepine's first consideration is to keep out of his way.

> Therefore misdoubting, least he should misguyde
> His former malice to some new assay,
> He cast to keepe him selfe so safely as he may.
>
> (vi. iii. 47)

Such opportunistic avoidance of trouble has struck many readers as somewhat less than honourable. Spenserian commentators show a strange reluctance to admit that in the *Faerie Queene* even the good guys do not always keep the requisite chivalric stiff upper lip. Calepine has been brought to this pass by the suffering and exposure and sorrow inflicted upon him by the accident of the Blatant Beast's attack and by the subsequent harassment by Turpine. He is a man stripped of his manhood, totally humiliated —'But his best succour and refuge was still / Behinde his Ladies backe.'

Literalist readers of this story of Calepine's succumbing to Turpine's baseness may well raise an objection. If the answer to Calepine's retreat is so simple, why doesn't Turpine simply dispatch Serena? How can she *protect* Calepine? The answer lies, I think, in a rather important distinction between the Beast and Turpine. Whereas Serena's offence (her risking of her reputation, her wandering off) was an active transgression, Calepine's offence is only a *lack* of strength and prudence. The Beast has more courage than Turpine, even if he does fear Calidore. He bites those members of society who go wrong, who lay themselves open to his attacks. Even the strongest men may fall victim to him. Turpine, however, attacks those who are subsequently implicated in the transgression, or whose lack of strength makes them vulnerable. Turpine's victims are innocent do-nothings, or at most sinners of omission; the Beast's victims are sinners of commission.

Later developments in Calepine's story seem to bear this view out.[3]

The wound is now inevitable. Turpine strikes Calepine through the shoulder. Barring miracles, there is no way of avoiding death. The miracle, of course, happens, and it is a miracle with an obvious logic. If the Beast and Turpine hold sway in society, if the law of the jungle rules the court, might it not be that the law of the court rules the jungle? The sudden arrival of the Salvage Man makes it seem so.

2. *The Salvage Man*

The discovery that the chivalric landscape can be good as well as evil, that the natural world contains strengths relevant to the world of men, may seem to give the book a new direction, but it is in the nature of a confirmation rather than a shift in the book's emphasis. Tristram has already shown us that an education in the forest may inculcate virtue rather than wild indiscipline, and the fact that two pairs of lovers retreat into the countryside for their mutual solace may be an indication of its suitability for the pursuit of love as well as a warning that the natural world harbours dangers. The introduction of the Salvage Man will be followed by the appearance of further forest dwellers—the baby whom Calepine rescues from Matilda, the Hermit with whom Calepine and Serena lodge and finally, of course, the shepherds, who may not dwell in the forest but are country folk nonetheless. Even Timias had his stay in the forest earlier in the *Faerie Queene*.

The first of these forest figures, Tristram, evokes surprise from Calidore, who is as startled as we are to find a young man of such polished manners so far from the court.

> Him stedfastly he markt, and saw to bee
> A goodly youth of amiable grace,
> Yet but a slender slip, that scarse did see
> Yet seventeene yeares, but tall and faire of face
> That sure he deem'd him borne of noble race.
> All in a woodmans jacket he was clad
> Of Lincolne greene, belayd with silver lace;

---

[3] Were it not for these later developments—above all the curability of Turpine's wounds—it would be attractive to read the Blatant Beast as a specialist in Envy, Turpine a specialist in Detraction. Calepine, we remember, immediately before the arrival of the Blatant Beast, thought himself 'far from *envious* eyes that mote him spight'.

And on his head an hood with aglets sprad,
And by his side his hunters horne he hanging had.

(VI. ii. 5)

Chivalric romance is full of aristocrats who have taken to the
forest to escape, or enjoy, the effects of love. The illustrious company includes Malory's Lancelot, Ariosto's Orlando, Chrétien's
Yvain and, in the *Faerie Queene* itself, the squire Timias. Naturally
Calidore supposes that this is the reason for Tristram's presence
so far from city and court. But Tristram, he discovers, is in retreat
from the injustices of society: his uncle has usurped the throne
and the forest provides a place of safety for him. His story derives
its essential details, with one or two minor changes, from Malory.[4]
Tristram himself has the traditional attributes associated with
him in Gottfried von Strassburg, Malory, and elsewhere.[5] He is
the very epitome of aristocratic breeding, he hunts 'the salvage
chace', he hawks,[6] and he is splendidly attired. Gottfried's elaborate description, however, is not so much a description specifically
of Tristan as a variation on the description of the handsome young
squire, whoever he may be, which appears so frequently in
romance.[7] Descriptions of folk-heroes, like Robin Hood, follow

---

[4] See *Variorum*, 6: 194–5. Cf. the story of *Guillaume de Palerne*, cited by Richard
Bernheimer, *Wild Men in the Middle Ages* (Cambridge, Mass., 1952), p. 164. In this
late twelfth-century poem, Guillaume is brought up in the woods by a werewolf,
to escape being poisoned by his wicked uncle.

[5] See Gottfried, *Tristan*, trans, A. T. Hatto (Harmondsworth, Middx., 1960).
When Tristan, immediately after his abduction, is abandoned on the coast of Cornwall, he comes upon two palmers: 'He had his speech and bearing under such fine
restraint that these grey and venerable sages ascribed it to heavenly favour, and
studied his ways and demeanour and his handsome person, too, with ever keener
interest. His clothes held their attention, for they were very splendid and of marvellous texture' (p. 77). See also Gottfried's description of Tristan's clothes (p. 74)
and the meeting between Tristan and King Mark, esp. p. 85.

[6] He was particularly associated with hunting and hawking. See Malory: 'And
after, as he growed in might and strength, he laboured ever in hunting and in hawking, so that never gentleman more, that ever we heard read of. And as the book
saith, he began good measures of blowing of beasts of venery . . . and all these
terms we have yet of hawking and hunting. And therefore the book of venery, of
hawking and hunting, is called the book of Sir Tristram. Wherefore, as meseemeth,
all gentlemen have and use, and shall to the day of doom, that thereby all men of
worship may dissever a gentleman from a yeoman, and from a yeoman a villain'
(*Morte d'Arthur* VIII.3). Sir Thomas Cokaine's *Short Treatise of Hunting* (1591; STC.
5457) refers to Tristram as the first hunter and includes 'Sir Tristrams measures of
blowing'.

[7] Sometimes the connection with Tristan is explicitly stated. Chrétien de Troyes,
for example, using superlatives to describe Cligés, states that 'He knew more of

the same pattern; the appearance of Chaucer's Yeoman is strikingly reminiscent of Spenser's Tristram.[8] Interestingly enough, the details of Tristram's dress (VI. ii. 5-6) remind us of Belphoebe's, in Book II, and of Radigund's in Book V (where the images are clearly a deliberate parody of Book II even as they echo Virgil).[9]

Many associations, then, gather round the figure of Spenser's Tristram. The whole is a kind of mingling of folk-tale and romance—of Robin Hood, of country yeomen, of Tristan lost in Cornwall and Tristan in exile in France. We may well ask ourselves why a figure with such complicated associations should be introduced here and, above all, why nothing more is made of his story. Certain reasons for his introduction will be obvious (I have touched on them already): first, he is a model of courtesy; second, his introduction helps establish the tone of Book VI by reminding us of traditional romance narratives.

---

fencing and of the bow than did Tristan, King Mark's nephew, and more about birds and hounds than he.' (*Arthurian Romances*, trans. W. Wistar Comfort (London, 1914), p. 127.)

[8] See the Prologue to the *Canterbury Tales*, lines 101ff. On Robin Hood and other folk heroes, see Maurice Keene, *The Outlaws of Medieval Legend* (London, 1961); Christina Hole, *English Folk Heroes* (London, 1948); the two Robin Hood plays in *Chief Pre-Shakespearean Dramas*, ed. Joseph Quincy Adams (Cambridge, Mass., 1924), pp. 345-9; and Evelyn Kendrick Wells, *The Ballad Tree* (New York, 1950), pp. 11-40. In later stories Robin Hood was often described as a man of noble birth, though his identification with the dispossessed Earl of Huntingdon dates only from 1601, in the play by Munday and Chettle, *The Downfall of Robert, earle of Huntington, afterwards called Robin Hood of Merrie Sherwoode*. The stories that gathered round Robin Hood's name told of his exploits as a flouter of authority, particularly in defiance of the unpopular Forest Laws and the King's officers appointed to enforce them. Note that it is three fosters (foresters) whom Timias chases and overcomes (*F.Q.*, III.v).

[9] See Gough's note, *Variorum*, 5: 200. Radigund, as an amazon warrior, is naturally associated with Diana, but just as Belphoebe is a curious mixture of Diana and Venus when she appears in Book II, so Radigund's description is based on the description of Venus in the *Aeneid* but involves the characteristics of Diana. Radigund is clad 'all in a Camis light of purple silke' which is 'woven uppon with silver', the metal customarily associated with Diana. She wears, like Mars, 'a mayled habergeon', and on her shoulder bears a shield, a symbol of Mars which Spenser ingeniously makes at the same time a symbol of Diana:

> And on her shoulder hung her shield, bedeckt
> Uppon the bosse with stones, that shined wide,
> As the faire Moone in her most full aspect,
> That to the Moone it mote be like in each respect. (v.v.3)

The irony of it all is that Radigund is the very opposite of a Diana figure in her sexual behaviour. Parallels with the description of Tristram will be found in v.v.2. Belphoebe is likened to 'that famous Queene / Of Amazons' in II.iii.31.

Yet one is still left with the impression that the stanzas devoted to the description of Tristram are surprisingly elaborate, all for the somewhat limited purpose of adding another illustration of courtesy to the first third of the book. The answer, I think, lies in the type of narrative strategy which earlier caused Spenser, equally unexpectedly, to have Belphoebe suddenly appear from the undergrowth before that ramshackle pair Braggadocchio and Trompart —hence the echoes, here in Book vi, of this other miraculous visitation. Belphoebe's presence in Book ii seems in any case to have something of the supernatural about it—as though she has broken out of the twelve-canto structure designed to contain her. Perhaps Aeneas's exclamation 'O dea certe!' is all that need be said. Spenser's universe is populated with many such indefinable figures—vicious characters who may begin as particularized figures of vice, but who soon merge into a kind of general sense of evil; and virtuous characters the strength of whose goodness extends beyond their specific definition. These composite, generalized figures often serve to right the balance—to establish good over against evil, or evil over against good. Tristram belongs in such a line. He stands as a positive figure of virtue, a focus of our attention, contrasting with the Blatant Beast, who makes his appearance in the very next canto. Insulated from the Beast, Tristram demonstrates what courtesy might be were it not for the evils of scandal, discourtesy, and slander. He is a much bigger figure in the overall structure of the book than he is in the narrative—and in himself a fine example of Spenser's endless variety and ingenuity.

The arrival of the Salvage Man has therefore in some measure been prepared for in the appearance of Tristram. Like Tristram, the Salvage Man is very much a forest type—the kind of creature one would expect to find in a romantic narrative set in the forest. To Spenser's readers he would be immediately recognizable, with his shaggy clothing, his inability to speak, and his savage unflinching strength. Not only is he a common figure of literature, but Spenser has used the motif of the wild man on previous occasions in the *Faerie Queene*.[10] There is Sir Satyrane, a mediating

---

[10] See Robert N. Goldsmith, 'The Wild Man on the English Stage', *MLR*, 53 (1958), 481–91; Thomas P. Harrison, Jr., 'Aspects of Primitivism in Shakespeare and Spenser', *Texas Studies in English*, 20 (1940), 39–71; Roy Harvey Pearce, 'Primitivistic Ideas in the *Faerie Queene*', *JEGP*, 44 (1945), 139–51; Herbert Foltinek, 'Die Wilden Männer in Edmund Spensers *Faerie Queene*', *Die Neueren Sprachen*, 10 (1961), 493–512; H. Janson, *Apes and Ape Lore* (London, 1952). Cf. Mircea Eliade, 'The

figure who leads Una back from the world of nature and its unreasoning Salvage Nation, and who is the son of a human mother
raped in the forest by a satyr.[11] There are the satyrs among whom
Hellenore takes up her abode in Book III, an oversexed but likeable
crew. In fact as we begin reading with wild men and wild man
variants in mind, they spring up from all parts of the *Faerie
Queene*. Even Artegall is acting the part of a wild man when he
comes to Satyrane's tournament disguised as a version of the
Green Knight and bearing on his shield the motto *salvagesse sans
finesse* (IV. iv. 39). Orgoglio, too, is a wild man, carrying in his
hand the wild man's customary weapon, an uprooted tree, like the
Salvage Man when he defends the sleeping Arthur against Turpine's murderous designs.

The Salvage Nation in Book I seems representative of an inherent goodness in nature, just as Orgoglio symbolizes its opposite, the subversive power which causes nature to lose its
harmony and its communion with God. Spenser is clearly of
Hooker's persuasion: nature is itself good, though it is open to
subversion as a result of the Fall.

In his fascinating study of the wild man in the Middle Ages,
Richard Bernheimer distinguishes three types of wild man which
span this division of nature between beneficent and hostile elements. Corresponding to the hostile universe of the medieval
heroic romances (*Sir Gawain and the Green Knight*, for instance) is
the first type, a savage creature whose origin may lie in the
personification of natural upheavals—storms, earthquakes, and
thunder.[12] A second type is good, amiable, and friendly to the
peasants.[13] He is related to some varieties of fairy. A third type is
the 'temporary' wild man, perhaps sired by a wild man but born

---

Myth of the Noble Savage', in *Myths, Dreams, and Mysteries* (New York, 1960),
pp. 39–56.

[11] Bernheimer (*Wild Men*, p. 71) points out that by the sixteenth century wild
men and satyrs had become inextricably confused—hence the so-called satyrs' dance
in *The Winter's Tale*, which in reality is probably a dance of wild men.

[12] *Sir Gawain and the Green Knight*, 720–3, mentions 'wodwos, that woned in the
knarres' among the creatures Gawain fights. S. K. Heninger, Jr., 'The Orgoglio
Episode in *The Faerie Queene*', *ELH*, 26 (1959), 171–87, argues that Orgoglio (like
Typhon) is an earthquake.

[13] See, for example, Arthur Dickson, *Valentine and Orson* (New York, 1929),
p. 115. Cf. the Wild Herdsman, mentioned by Dickson, and the various types of
benevolent tree-spirit—see J. G. Frazer, *The Golden Bough*, abridged edition (London,
1922), p. 541.

of a human mother (like Satyrane) or running mad in the forest because of love and remorse (like Timias).

Spenser's Salvage Man appears to belong to the second category, but there are at least hints that he should be classified with the third, though his history is never actually recounted. Certainly the third type abounds in the romances. Tristram wild in the woods around Tintagel or in the forest of Morrois; Ariosto's Orlando; Yvain, his promise to his lady broken, crazy with grief; Lancelot, who in the *Morte d'Arthur* several times takes to the woods in fits of madness—these are examples of the 'temporary' wild man. In a slightly different situation are those like Orson, brought up in the forest by animal foster-parents. The story of Orson is especially interesting as it combines on the one hand the themes of the exposure of children (cf. Pastorella) and their carrying off by beasts (cf. Matilda's babe) and on the other hand the well-known theme of the human mother/beast father.[14] Orson, like Spenser's Salvage Man, is incapable of speech. He is also not aware of his parentage or of the fact that he has a twin brother Valentine, with whom, of course, he fights and is recognized. Both Orson and Yvain are eventually brought back to civilization and tidied up—an astonishingly simple process.[15]

Spenser's Salvage Man shows a distinct resemblance to Orson. Spenser tells us:

> O what an easie thing is to descry
> The gentle bloud, how ever it be wrapt
> In sad misfortunes foule deformity,
> And wretched sorrows, which have often hapt?
> For howsoever it may grow mis-shapt,
> Like this wyld man, being undisciplynd,
> That to all vertue it may seeme unapt,
> Yet will it shew some sparkes of gentle mynd,
> And at the last breake forth in his owne proper kynd.
>
> That plainely may in this wyld man be red,
> Who, though he were still in this desert wood,
> Mongst salvage beasts, both rudely borne and bred,
> Ne ever saw faire guize, ne learned good,

---

[14] On connections with the *Bärensohn* theme see Dickson, *Valentine and Orson*, p. 117. Orson's foster-parents were bears.

[15] Cf. the legend of the hairy anchorite, who, on being loved by a lady, is transformed into a handsome young man; see Thompson, *Folktale*, p. 259.

> Yet shewd some token of his gentle blood,
> By gentle usage of that wretched Dame.
> For certes he was borne of noble blood,
> How ever by hard hap he hether came;
> As ye may know, when time shall be to tell the same.
>
> (VI. v. 1–2)

This is the only reference to the Salvage Man's background we are
given, and it leaves us with another loose end in the narrative. It
is, of course, dangerous to speculate whether Spenser might
have given us the promised sequel in a subsequent book, and if
so, how. But I think he may have had in mind something similar
to the Orson story—for such themes were clearly uppermost in
his mind as he wrote this central portion of Book VI.[16]

The suggestion that this unkempt hairy creature may somehow
represent courtesy in retreat from its natural habitat rather im-
probably links him with Tristram and adds a new dimension to
Tristram's story. 'Vertues seat is deepe within the mynd / And
not in outward shows, but inward thoughts defynd.' Tristram at
least *looked* the part; the Salvage Man does not. The fact that we
meet the elegant Tristram first perhaps serves to soften the shock,
and render more probable the fact of finding a seed of true courtesy in this mumbling denizen of the forest.

Not only does the Salvage Man suggest to us the third type of
wild man; he also possesses the skills which we associate with the
second type. He is skilled in matters medicinal, and 'from his
mothers wombe, which him did beare, / He was invulnerable made
by Magicke leare.' This last touch, a common feature of folk-tales
and sometimes of romances,[17] is particularly appropriate. We

---

[16] I do not think this possibility is ruled out by the phrase 'both rudely borne
and bred'. Todd (*Variorum* 6: 201) also mentions the possibility of a connection with
Orson. For a full listing of the Salvage Man's various characteristics, see Osgood's
note, *Variorum* 6: 201–2. In view of the next episode—that of Matilda and the bear—
it is interesting to find close association between wild men and bears, in the Orson
story and elsewhere. The bear is the animal closest in lineage to the wild man:
Bernheimer cites several instances in folk customs where the two figures have become confused (*Wild Men*, pp. 53–5, and p. 198, n. 12).

[17] See J. A. MacCulloch, *The Childhood of Fiction* (London, 1905) and, for instance,
The Seege of Troye, ed. M. Barnicle (London: EETS, 1927), lines 121ff. Note that
bears were supposedly skilled in the art of healing. In the twelfth-century Latin
bestiary translated by T. H. White we read: 'Nor do they neglect the healer's art.
Indeed, if they are afflicted with a serious injury and damaged by wounds, they
know how to doctor themselves by stroking their sores with a herb whose name is
Flomus, as the Greeks call it, so that they are cured by the mere touch.' (*The Bestiary*
(New York, 1957), pp. 45–6.)

might expect a country dweller far removed from the court to
be invulnerable to the wounds of discourtesy and slander. Hence
the Salvage Man easily rescues Calepine and Serena from Turpine,
leading them off to his dwelling

> Farre in the forrest by a hollow glade,
> Covered with mossie shrubs, which spredding brode
> Did underneath them make a gloomy shade;
> There foot of living creature never trode,
> Ne scarse wyld beasts durst come. (vi. iv. 13)

This spirit of the forest lives there in a simplicity which, for all its
ruggedness, is much like Ovid's picture of the Golden Age. The
Salvage Man does not plough or sow, nor does he hunt. He lives
in the open air on forest fruits, 'obaying natures first beheast'.

Such surroundings are ideal for Calepine's peace of mind. Like
a courtier out of favour, he bides his time in exile from the court,
until the tale-carrying which first drove him out has died down—
until, in other words, the wound inflicted by Turpine has healed,
thanks to the Salvage Man's knowledge of herbs,

> So as ere long he had that knightes wound
> Recured well, and made him whole againe:
> But that same Ladies hurts no herbe he found,
> Which could redresse, for it was inwardly unsound.

(vi. iv. 16)

It is Serena herself who is 'inwardly unsound'; her physical dis-
ability springs from a moral disorder. Clearly the Salvage Man,
who has no knowledge of the court, can hardly advise her on its
cure.

3. *Matilda and the Bear*

Calepine is separated from Serena in one of the most curious
episodes in Book vi—the story of Matilda and the bear child. It is
curious primarily because it is such a strange mixture of materials,
for which no single source has ever been found, nor is it likely to
be found. But in a way it is a suitable episode for the most fanciful
book of the *Faerie Queene*, the most multicoloured assemblage of
popular and literary components. We do not generally associate
Spenser with whimsy—or at least only in recent years have scholars
begun to realize that the poet of sage seriousness was capable of
cracking a smile. But to approach Spenser's works in general, and

the *Faerie Queene* in particular, as a kind of Victorian Sunday-school tract is surely wildly mistaken. The evident humour of the 'Pouke' and the 'unpleasant quire of frogs' in the *Epithalamion* is matched by the comedy of Hellenore and Malbecco in Book III or by the quiet incredibility of this story of Matilda in Book VI.[18]

Calepine himself, or at least his name, is a product of the Spenserian whimsy. He surely is derived from Friar Ambrogio Calepino, author of the famous *Dictionarium*, the first edition of which was published in 1502. Although we cannot be sure that Spenser owned a copy of the book, it could be that he lighted on the name at random in looking round his study, and allotted it to Serena's knight. Certainly he, or E. K., knew the work, since it was undoubtedly used for the *Shepheardes Calendar*. We also know that Spenser's school, Merchant Taylors', had a copy in its library.[19]

Perhaps Spenser's eye next lighted on Mirabellius's *Polyantheae* (1503), a less well-known but influential dictionary which he may also have used. This would give him a very suitable name for the proud Mirabella. And if his copy of Calepino was one of several such editions (including the edition of 1581), he would find that it was printed in Venice by the famed press of Aldus Manutius, and at once he would have a name for Aladine's father. As Professor Nelson has pointed out,[20] to call one of your characters Aldus is rather like naming him the Clarendon Press.[21]

It is hard to argue that these strange names, for all that they might have other explanations, are merely coincidentally related to the products of Italian publishers. It looks as though the fancifulness is Spenser's, not mine. Add to this the repeated touches of

---

[18] See Judith P. Clark, ' "His Earnest unto Game": Spenser's Humor in *The Faerie Queene*', *Emporia State Research Studies*, 15, no. 4 (1967), 13–27; Robert O. Evans, 'Spenserian Humor: *Faerie Queene* III and IV', *Neuphilologische Mitteilungen*, 60 (1959), 288–99.

[19] See DeWitt T. Starnes and E. W. Talbert, *Classical Myth and Legend in Renaissance Dictionaries* (Chapel Hill, N.C., 1955), pp. 17, 77–80; Donald Cheney, *Spenser's Image of Nature* (New Haven, Conn., 1966), p. 202. Arnold Williams rejects this identification (*Flower on a Lowly Stalk* (Michigan State University, 1967), p. 70).

[20] In a paper delivered to the International Spenser Colloquium, New Brunswick, Canada, 1969.

[21] On possible echoes of Mirabellius in Spenser, see Starnes and Talbert, *Classical Myth and Legend*, pp. 88–91. For other meanings of Mirabella's name see Williams, *Flower*, p. 69. She is both *mirabile* and *bella*, perhaps *una bella*, perhaps also *una bella mira*. Williams's explanation of the name of Aldus (p. 69) seems strained. For earlier occurrences of the name Mirabel, see Ernest Langlois, *Table des noms propres dans les chansons de geste* (Paris, 1904), pp. 453–4.

realism in Book VI—Calepine's enjoyment of the thrush's song,
the unfortunate lady 'thumped forward' and 'punched' with her
knight's spear, Calepine's embarrassment with a squalling baby—
and you see very clearly one aspect of the book's atmosphere.[22] It
is lighter, in every sense, and more sparkling.

The lightness of tone so evident in much of Book VI adds credence to my suggestion that the episode of Matilda and the Bear
is a product of Spenser's own fancy, a texture of half-remembered
associations and vaguely recollected reading. The particular combination of material sets the reader's own association going in half
a dozen directions at once. Calepine comes upon the Bear when
walking in the forest 'to take the ayre and heare the thrushes song',
as countless convalescents have done before and since. He is un-
armed 'as fearing neither foe nor frend'. His success in subduing
the huge beast is heroic indeed, but it is the heroism of the pastoral,
the destruction of fierce animals who somehow threaten the
balanced existence of a shepherd society. In this case, though,
there is no pastoral, only the fear of future chaos in the realm of
Sir Bruin (is this name too merely coincidental?) if an heir is not
found.

Calepine makes a gauche nursemaid.

> Then tooke he up betwixt his armes twaine
> The litle babe, sweet relickes of his pray;
> Whom pitying to heare so sore complaine,
> From his soft eyes the teares he wypt away,
> And from his face the filth that did it ray,
> And every litle limbe he searcht around,
> And every part, that under sweathbands lay,
> Least that the beasts sharpe teeth had any wound
> Made in his tender flesh, but whole them all he found.
>
> (VI. iv. 23)

We share Calepine's relief when he meets Matilda, hears her
unfortunate story and ('Lo how good fortune doth to you pre-
sent/This litle babe, of sweete and lovely face') gives the babe to
her.

> Right glad was *Calepine* to be so rid
> Of his young charge, whereof he skilled nought:
> Ne she lesse glad, for she so wisely did,

---

[22] Respectively: VI.iv.17; VI.ii.10; VI.ii.22; VI.iv.25.

> And with her husband under hand so wrought,
> That when that infant unto him she brought,
> She made him thinke it surely was his owne.   (VI. iv. 38)

By accepting the child, Matilda fulfils a prophecy (again a common topos of pastoral romance):[23]

> Yet was it sayd, there should to him a sonne
> *Be gotten, not begotten*, which should drinke
> And dry up all the water, which doth ronne
> In the next brooke, by whom that feend shold be fordonne.
>
> (VI. iv. 32)

The 'feend' is a 'great gyant, called Cormoraunt', whom Sir Bruin overcame

> by yonder foord,
> And in three battailes did so deadly daunt,
> That he dare not returne for all his daily vaunt.
>
> (VI. iv. 29)

Clearly the story places in sharper relief the issues already raised by Priscilla and Aladine. The harmony of the family, personal harmony, can only be preserved by a lie—in this case telling Sir Bruin that the child is his own. Upon this personal harmony depends the continuity of Sir Bruin's government and the protection of his gains against the incursions of a giant whom Spenser's readers would recognize as belonging with the monsters at fords who so frequently appear in Arthurian romance. Cormoraunt, of course, is not merely a giant but a fiend, defeated in three battles like the dragon in Book I and as clearly a representative of the powers of darkness as the Blatant Beast himself.[24]

All this seems to justify the untruth. The child is a fulfilment of the prophecy and, what is more, a future practiser of courtesy. Matilda, we are told,

---

23 *Variorum*, 6: 377–8.

24 We can trace the giant Cormoran to a story of Walter Map, apparently first taken from a French chronicle. Geoffrey of Monmouth (1.16), perhaps working from the same source, confuses it with the story of Goëmagot, the legendary anarchic figure who dominated the south-western part of England and was destroyed by Corineus, the first Cornishman. The name Cormoraunt is eminently suited for Spenser's giant, associated on the one hand with 'Goëmot' (as Spenser calls him in II.x.10) and so with anarchy, and on the other hand with the cormorant, traditional symbol of greed. On possible associations with the Hydra, see below, p. 270.

it in goodly thewes so well upbrought,
That it became a famous knight well knowne
And did right noble deedes, the which elswhere are showne.

(vi. iv. 38)

Wherever 'elsewhere' may be, it is not the *Faerie Queene*. Like Tristram's, Matilda's narrative is unfinished.

4. Arthur, Timias, and the Hermit

The story of Matilda's babe leaves us with a strange sense of moral ambiguity, a feeling that perhaps the very principles of social order sometimes get in the way of its preservation. The natural world, or perhaps heaven itself, comes to the rescue of Sir Bruin; the babe is taken from a fierce bear and given to Bruin, a pacific one. In his care, the babe will grow up, like Orson, to do mighty deeds.[25]

If stories of the *enfance* of heroes, like Tristram and Matilda's babe, bring promise of future prosperity and social order, and if Matilda's babe saves Matilda from a difficult situation, Serena is

[25] A story somewhat analogous to that of Matilda and the bear can be found in a German version of the well-known French romance *Pierre de Provence*: 'The epic recounts how a king's son met a princess who enthralled him and who also returned his love, and how the two succeeded in eloping together. . . . They ride through the forest in sweet unison on the prince's horse, until they decide to dismount and rest. The princess, tired from the day's events, falls asleep with her head on the prince's lap, while he looks at her ring which he has pulled from her finger. Suddenly a buzzard swoops down from the heavens and snatches the trinket away. As he pursues the bird, trying in vain to hit it with sticks and stones, the prince penetrates deeper and deeper into the forest and loses his way. It dawns upon him after a frantic search that he cannot find his beloved. . . . He becomes violent and demented, tears off his fine clothes . . . and proceeds to roam the woods, beastlike, on all fours, as a wild man' (Bernheimer, *Wild Men*, pp. 15–16). He is subsequently taken by hunters, brought back to the court where the princess is staying *incognita*, cleaned up and recognized. The story departs from the French in involving a wild man. In the French versions the bird which carries off the ring is a seabird, and in chasing it Pierre falls into the hands of Moorish pirates. Did Spenser have some version of the German plot, with its wild-man associations, in his mind as he wrote the story of Matilda? For the French version of the romance, see *Pierre de Provence et la Belle Maguelonne*, ed. Adolphe Biedermann (Paris, 1913). Gaston Paris (*Romania*, 18 (1889), 510–11), describing an Italian analogue, identifies the following as a recurrent theme: 'Two lovers are separated as a result of the carrying off of a jewel by a bird, which the young man pursues; after long adventures, they end by reuniting and are happy' (my translation). Alessandro d'Ancona (*Poemetti popolari italiani* (Bologna, 1889)) studies all the variants and analogues of this story. They include the story of Prince Kamaralzaman in the *Thousand and One Nights*, and also *Guillaume d'Angleterre, Die Gute Frau, Die Historie vom Graf von Savoien, Syr Isambrace, Escoufle* and *Ottinello e Giulia*.

only rendered more helpless than ever. Calepine lost, she is left in the custody of a creature friendly perhaps, but ultimately of little use to her. At this point, when Serena is close to despair, Arthur and Timias enter the action. Arthur is perhaps the most puzzling of all the major figures in the *Faerie Queene*. Perhaps because he appears and disappears at intervals throughout the work, most commentators on Spenser's poem make stabs at defining his function without attempting to trace a pattern in his actions which would justify the rather exalted terms in which he is presented in the Letter to Ralegh:

By ensample of which excellente Poets [Ariosto and Tasso], I labour to pourtraict in Arthure, before he was king, the image of a brave knight, perfected in the twelve private morall vertues, as Aristotle hath devised, the which is the purpose of these first twelve bookes. . . . To some I know this Methode will seem displeasaunt, which had rather have good discipline delivered plainly in way of precepts. . . . But such, me seeme, should be satisfide with the use of these dayes, seeing all things accounted by their showes, and nothing esteemed of, that is not delightfull and pleasing to commune sence. For this cause is Xenophon preferred before Plato. . . . So much more profitable and gratious is doctrine by ensample, then by rule. So have I laboured to doe in the person of Arthure: whome I conceive after his long education by Timon . . . to have seene in a dream or vision the Faery Queen, with whose excellent beauty ravished, he awaking resolved to seeke her out, and so being by Merlin armed, and by Timon throughly instructed, he went to seeke her forth in Faerye land. . . . In the person of Prince Arthure I sette forth magnificence in particular, which vertue for that (according to Aristotle and the rest) it is the perfection of all the rest, and conteineth in it them all, therefore in the whole course I mention the deeds of Arthure applyable to that vertue, which I write of in that booke.

The Letter, whose ambiguous syntax and arcane allusions seem to invite it, has been subjected to a veritable deluge of commentary, the merits and limitations of which I shall not discuss here.[26] The references to Aristotle are particularly confusing, since the first may perfectly well suggest that Aristotle 'hath devised' 'the image of a brave knight', not 'twelve private morall vertues' at all; while

---

[26] For references, see above, p. 2. The importance of imaginative literature as moral example is constantly stressed by sixteenth-century writers and critics and has a direct bearing on the courtesy literature examined below (Chapter VI). Cf. Bruce Dearing, 'Gavin Douglas's *Eneados*: a Reinterpretation', *PMLA*, 67 (1952), 845–62.

the second is so imprecise and offhand ('Aristotle *and the rest*') as to raise questions about the seriousness of the whole argument. It may seem unlikely that Spenser should imagine Aristotle presenting a picture of perfect knighthood through his *Ethics*, but it is less so if we remember that Spenser's work is neo-medievalist in spirit, and that at least before 1550 or so it was perfectly usual for the historian or moralist to apply the terminology of chivalry to the example of ancient history. Chivalry was a more culturally contemporaneous, if romanticized, mode of right conduct than classical modes of virtue, and it had the advantage of being associated with Christian morality. Thus medieval historians made Alexander the Great a knight in shining armour, thereby giving his example an immediacy whose importance outweighed any question of historical accuracy.[27] The reader will understand at once that the *Faerie Queene* is heir to this conception of the past, but he may still wonder why Spenser is so insistent that Arthur is his hero. There seems no consistency to his exploits, which give the appearance of bridging awkward narrative gaps when a *deus ex machina* seems especially necessary, and can seldom be construed as figuring forth that 'magnificence' to which Spenser alludes in the Letter.

In Book 1, of course, Arthur does play an important role, identifiable perhaps with Spenser's notion of Magnificence—depending on how we define that quality. His arrival on the scene suggests God's providence, and the exchange of gifts which prefaces his departure implies a connection with grace. He also serves the useful narrative function of drawing off some of the apocalyptic associations of the Red Cross Knight's climatic fight with the dragon, a function which helps make the dragon fight a less definitive, more tentative victory. We can, of course, see his actions in Book 1 as 'applyable' to the virtue of Holiness. Whether

[27] Of course, the justification for the study of history lay above all in its value as example. See F. J. Levy, *Tudor Historical Thought* (San Marino, Calif., 1967); Louis B. Wright, *Middle-Class Culture in Elizabethan England* (Chapel Hill, N.C., 1935); Geoffrey Shepherd, ed., *An Apology for Poetry*, by Sir Philip Sidney (London, 1965), pp. 36–42. On the popularity of history during Elizabeth's reign see also H. S. Bennett, *English Books and Readers 1558 to 1603* (Cambridge, 1965), pp. 214–20. Arthur B. Ferguson discusses the medievalizing of classical heroes in *The Indian Summer of English Chivalry* (Durham, N.C., 1960). See also Rosemond Tuve, 'Ancients, Moderns, and Saxons', *ELH*, 6 (1939), 165–90; J. E. Housman, 'Higden, Trevisa, Caxton, and the Beginnings of Arthurian Criticism', *RES*, 23 (1947), 209–17; Herschel Baker, *The Race of Time* (Toronto, 1967).

Spenser's use of this term in the Letter implies that Arthur will figure forth the titular virtues in each of the books, or whether he has something much vaguer in mind, could be an important question. In a sense Arthur *is* Holiness in Book I, just as his fight with Pyrochles and Cymochles in Book II can be seen as the battle of Temperance against the irascible and concupiscent powers which those two villains represent.[28] His arrival just when they are despoiling Guyon's supposedly dead body does have a providential air, but it is significant that he fights with Guyon's sword, not his own magic one, and that the fight is long and bloody. Commentators who see Arthur's intervention as a bestowal of God's grace on Guyon are probably indulging in wishful thinking, or confusing the angel who watches over Guyon's body before the arrival of the Palmer, with the Briton Prince.[29] Arthur's conquest of Cymochles and Pyrochles accords well with his later battle against the forces of Maleger, since that, too, presents the struggle of the temperate man against the assaults of excess and sin. While Arthur should probably not be read as a surrogate for Guyon, there may well be a connection between his championing of Alma and Guyon's simultaneous destruction of the Bower of Bliss. It is perhaps significant that the two most explicitly allegorical struggles in Book II—the fight against Cymochles and Pyrochles and the defence of Alma—should fall to Arthur, not Guyon. As in Book I (and perhaps again in Book V) Arthur seems to serve as an allegorical buffer between the virtue and its champion.

Book III, however, seems to run counter to this emergent scheme of Arthur's function. His role in the book is relatively small, but is integrated into the narrative in a way which makes him much like any of the other knights who appear in those rather complicated scenes with which the book begins. There is at least the suggestion that Arthur sees in Florimell a glimmering of Gloriana's beauty (III. iv. 54), but that hardly accounts for the enthusiasm of his pursuit. Perhaps she is like the form of beauty itself, yet such a reading seems little congruent with narrative probability.[30] The answer, surely, if there is an answer, is that Arthur recognizes in Florimell the spirit of the generative cycle—

[28] See Hughes, *Variorum*, 2: 462; Harry Berger, Jr., *The Allegorical Temper* (New Haven, Conn., 1957).

[29] See A. C. Hamilton, *The Structure of Allegory in 'The Faerie Queene'* (Oxford, 1961), pp. 98ff.; Maurice Evans, 'The Fall of Guyon', *ELH*, 28 (1961), 215–24.

[30] C. S. Lewis, *English Literature in the Sixteenth Century* (Oxford, 1954), p. 383.

that his pursuit represents a kind of disinterested pity for the vicissitudes and deprivations which are sadly a part of the natural process and which the foster, or the boar, or Busyrane are representative of. If this is so, then Arthur figures forth an almost mystical principle at the very centre of Spenser's conception of chastity—the renewing spirit of chaste generation. Book III, then, dispenses with Arthur in his role of narrative convenience but retains his deeds 'applyable' to the titular virtue.

In certain respects Arthur's function in Book IV is greater than in any of the other books. Fowler has shown us how this book is associated with the tetrad.[31] The struggle of Cambell and Triamond over Canacee is resolved by the intervention of Cambina, the fourth element which turns the warring triad into a harmonious pattern of the three types of love:

> The deare affection unto kindred sweet,
> Or raging fire of love to woman kind,
> Or zeale of friends combynd with vertues meet.
>
> (IV. ix. 1

Cambina's arrival makes possible the establishment of friendship, the mutual respect and affection which is the ground of all love and which leads to concord. The narrator mentions the three types of love in connection with that other tetrad Amyas and Placidas, Poeana and Aemylia, the final establishment of whose harmony is Arthur's doing—an intervention which incidentally has the effect of rescuing Amoret too. In what is for all practical purposes a hero-less book, Arthur's action seems almost to make him the hero,[32] though we should realize that his role here is no different from his role in the earlier books. It bears a distinct resemblance to his function in Book V, where in the later cantos his performance is at least as important as Artegall's.

Book V varies the established pattern in one respect, though. Arthur's arrival bears no sign that he is a *deus ex machina*. The unveiling of his shield is a curious, though not unfitting, response to the Phaeton-like Sol-dan,[33] but it does not immediately identify him with the Arthur of Book I. In Book VI, his arrival

---

[31] Alastair Fowler, *Spenser and the Numbers of Time* (London, 1964), pp. 24-33.

[32] A view suggested by Calvin Huckabay, 'The Structure of Book IV of *The Faerie Queene*', *Studia Neophilogica*, 27 (1955), 53-64.

[33] Jane Aptekar, *Icons of Justice* (New York, 1969), p. 81, citing Angus Fletcher (see his recent study *The Prophetic Moment* (Chicago, 1971), p. 210).

is as convenient as the arrival of Satyrane in the Legend of Holiness. Like Satyrane with Una, he reclaims Serena from the benevolent protection of nature and begins her progress back to society. It is a fitting task, since Arthur has shown before a breadth of vision and imagination which most of Spenser's heroes do not reveal.[34] Above all, it takes us back to Book III, where his affinity for natural process can now be seen as a logical antecedent of his teaming up with the Salvage Man against the social irregularities of Turpine and Blandina.

In each of the six books, Arthur thus demonstrates that he is 'perfected' in the virtues which the books discuss. The question remains as to whether his own career shows a coherent pattern of development, whether we can see in his various adventures the progress of his quest for Gloriana. In a sense, we should not look among Arthur's own deeds for the evidence of this. If there is a logic to Spenser's arrangement of the six virtues, it follows that there is a logic to Arthur's progress, for the movement of the poem's argument is indicative of Arthur's journey towards the Faerie Queene. This fact in itself is not unimportant, for it implies that the education of Prince Arthur is the *raison d'être* of the whole work. Spenser presents, then, not a picture of the perfected state, as Plato had done, but a chronicle of the young man's search for perfection, which Xenophon presented in the *Cyropaedia*, the Education of Cyrus. The *Faerie Queene* builds up, block by block, the structure of that all-consuming virtue which is Glory. I have suggested before that the *Faerie Queene* contains within it the whole of the English experience.[35] Arthur's quest for perfection is symbolic of the movement of English, or British, history—Arthur, founder of the Tudor line, seeks Elizabeth, its last and greatest representative. We may object that Arthur is hardly the hero of the *Faerie Queene*, that his role is altogether too subsidiary. But Arthur is perhaps the hero of Spenser's poem rather as Jesus is the hero of Milton's *Paradise Lost*.[36] The pre-existence of the 'promis'd seed' is the intellectual justification for Milton's argument that the Fall is indeed fortunate. British history, and the seed of British glory with which it began, stands behind Gloriana–Elizabeth as

[34] Consider the contrast between his reactions and Artegall's at the trial of Duessa.

[35] See above, p. 6.

[36] For this parallel I am indebted to Miss Virginia George.

the intellectual justification for Spenser's celebration of his sovereign. Arthur is the redeemer of British history, the sordid march of which was chronicled for us in all its detail in Book II.[37] Legend had it that he would return.[38] The *Faerie Queene* outlines the promise of this return and looks forward to a kind of Second Coming when beginning and end, alpha and omega, will be gathered into a final vision of glory.

This view of Arthur puts his adventures in a new perspective, a perspective given support quite recently in Rosemond Tuve's investigation of the virtues and vices of the *Faerie Queene*. She has shown that the *magnificentia* of Arthur, far from being a rather poor copy of Aristotle's Magnanimity, is a kind of fusion of elements Christian and classical, a medieval virtue of eminent lineage, thoroughly suitable as Arthur's special attribute.[39] His status as British saviour accords well with his intervention in Book I, a book which may present the history of the English church[40] in a manner which reproduces in little the movement of the whole poem. But while his intervention there quite logically seems to present the intervention of God's grace, the congruence is almost fortuitous: Arthur dispenses not a theological grace so much as a historical grace; the two are conflated in Book I because in the history of the church they are the same thing. In later books we see above all Arthur's progress through the virtues: his function as bringer of grace is muted. Book v is perhaps an exception: the unveiling of Arthur's shield strikes terror and confusion into England's enemies since it prefigures the apocalyptic light of Tudor glory.[41] In Book VI, Arthur demonstrates the power of courtesy not by recourse to the supernatural but by knightly skill. His 'baffling' of Turpine allies Nature and Grace, Salvage Man and Briton Prince, thereby hinting at Calidore's own vision of courtesy which will follow on Mount Acidale, and showing that Arthur has already learned what Calidore must still learn so painfully.

[37] See Berger, *Allegorical Temper*, pp. 89–114.

[38] T. D. Kendrick, *British Antiquity* (London, 1950), pp. 36ff.; Roger Sherman Loomis, 'The Legend of Arthur's Survival', in *Arthurian Literature in the Middle Ages*, ed. Loomis (Oxford, 1959), pp. 64–71.

[39] *Allegorical Imagery* (Princeton, N. J., 1966), pp. 57ff.

[40] J. F. Kermode, '*The Faerie Queene*, I and v', *BJRL*, 47 (1964), 123–50.

[41] The Souldan clearly represents Philip II of Spain. See René Graziani, 'Philip II's *Impresa* and Spenser's Souldan', *JWCI*, 27 (1964), 322–4. On Arthur's role in general see Merritt Y. Hughes, 'The Arthurs of *The Faerie Queene*', *EA*, 6 (1953), 193–213.

This rather elaborate preface to Arthur's arrival in our synopsis of the Legend of Courtesy will go some way towards accounting for his presence, and will open up one vista through which the work as a whole may be viewed. He is accompanied by Timias, another figure whom we have met before. Timias has been distinguished in earlier episodes in the *Faerie Queene* by an almost fatal impetuosity. In Book IV we learned how he came to lose the favour of Belphoebe—by succumbing, or seeming to succumb, to Amoret's charms.[42] His reunion with Belphoebe is an object-lesson in prudence, presented to us specifically as an exemplum of concord.

> To happie blisse he was full high uprear'd,
> Nether of envy, nor of chaunge afeard,
> Though many foes did him maligne therefore,
> And with unjust detraction him did beard;
> Yet he himselfe so well and wisely bore,
> That in her soveraine lyking he dwelt evermore.

> (VI. v. 12)

In line with the advice given Serena by the Hermit, Timias exercises self-restraint, the quality he had failed to exercise with Amoret.

In pursuing the Blatant Beast, employed as a decoy by the trio of enemies Despetto, Decetto, and Defetto, Timias falls back into his old impetuous ways. The fact that the Beast bites him indicates that he has transgressed as Serena transgressed. The ambush in the forest is a kind of re-enactment of his fight with the three foresters in Book III. The earlier fight, in which Timias is desperately wounded (perhaps by lust—hence the wound in the thigh), ultimately brings about his meeting with Belphoebe. If we conclude that he lays himself open to accusation again by his attentions to Amoret, this third fall and the bite by the Blatant Beast are logical enough. In this new context, of course, the mishap has a new significance; Defetto, Decetto, and Despetto stand in the same relationship to the Blatant Beast, I think, as Turpine does.[43]

Timias and Serena find cure for their injuries at the Hermit's cell.

---

[42] The result, as we have already noticed, is that he takes to the woods like a wild man. See IV.vii.39–41.

[43] They also parody the Platonic triad. See below, pp. 235–6, 257–8.

Small was his house, and like a little cage,
For his owne turne, yet inly neate and clene,
Deckt with greene boughes, and flowers gay beseene.
Therein he them full faire did entertaine
Not with such forged showes, as fitter beene
For courting fooles, that curtesies would faine,
But with entire affection and appearaunce plaine.

(VI. v. 38)

The final lines of the stanza are important; this man has very special qualities, since he is a knight who has retired from the court after a life of chivalry, and therefore combines knowledge of the ways of the court with a life in which 'forged showes' are totally unnecessary and in which he has access to higher knowledge. He is the active man turned contemplative—the chivalric man turned to the pastoral life.

The Hermit belongs to that large literary category of knights who have adopted the life of contemplation out of weariness with the fast-moving, deceitful, and vapid life of the court,[44] retiring to the supposed honesty and simplicity of the countryside.[45] Aldus

[44] The figure of the knight who has retired to the forest to pass his last days in contemplation is comparatively common in chivalric works, the best-known example probably being Caxton's *Book of the Ordre of Chivalry* (ed. Alfred T. P. Byles (London: EETS, 1926)), a handbook on chivalry, furnished with a narrative introduction involving an old knight who has retired from the court. The knight is versed in the ways of chivalry, and, through the volume of instructions to knights which he possesses, a fountainhead of courtesy. Cf. Chaucer's *Book of the Duchess*. Caxton's work was translated from Ramón Lull. On the supposed merits of the life of retirement and its classical precedents, see E. M. W. Tillyard, *Myth and the English Mind* (New York, 1962), and the fuller account, primarily dealing with the seventeenth and eighteenth centuries, Maren-Sofie Røstvig, *The Happy Man* (Oslo, 1954–8). Bernheimer gives a detailed exposition of the connection between the myth of retirement, the myth of the Golden Age, and wild men, *Wild Men*, pp. 102–20. See also Pauline M. Smith, *The Anti-Courtier Trend in Sixteenth-Century French Literature* (Geneva, 1966); Charles Weaver, *The Hermit in English Literature from the Beginnings to 1660* (Nashville, Tenn., 1924).

[45] While such a belief owes a great deal to direct classical precedent, it is worth bearing in mind such instances as the retreat of Tristan and Iseult into the forest of Morrois, and the rather unusual idea of the wild man perpetrated by Hans Sachs. Sachs, whose home town of Nuremberg had a long wild man tradition, conceived of the wild man as an ordinary human who had intentionally chosen forest life over corrupt city life, he and his kind living in colonies in the wilderness (Bernheimer, *Wild Men*, pp. 113–14). Cf. the poem, probably by Antony Munday, in *Englands Helicon*:

> Through a faire Forrest as I went
>   upon a Sommers day,
> I met a Wood-man queint and gent,
>   yet in a strange aray.   *Footnote continued on page 78*

represented a lesser example of the same type. As a literary *topos*,
the retired knight and his country cell were frequently associated,
in the sixteenth century and before, with attacks on court living.
They lead directly to the pastoral bias of Horatian satire, so
popular in the succeeding century. His knowledge of both court
and country equips the Hermit to cure the bite of the Blatant
Beast. Not only does he know the court well, but he is also in a
sense superior to it. This gives him unique powers. The narrator
has already told us,

> No wound, which warlike hand of enemy
> Inflicts with dint of sword, so sore doth light,
> As doth the poysnous sting, which infamy
> Infixeth in the name of noble wight:
> For by no art, nor any leaches might
> It ever can recured be againe.   (VI. vi. 1)

The word 'art' is, I think, loaded. The wound's cure lies in living
according to man's nature—in self-control: avoidance, we conclude, of both 'wavering lust' and 'daunger of defame'. The
wound needs discipline

> With holesome reede of sad sobriety,
> To rule the stubborne rage of passion blinde:
> Give salves to every sore, but counsell to the minde.
>
> (VI. vi. 5)

The reasons for the drastic effects of the Beast's bite lie in his
character and ancestry—an ancestry, we note, similar to that of
the Sphinx.[46] Of his mother Echidna, we read:

> Yet did her face and former parts professe
> A faire young Mayden, full of comely glee;
> But all her hinder parts did plaine expresse
> A monstrous Dragon, full of fearefull uglinesse.
>
> (VI. vi. 10)

The woodman has visited court, city and country, but found them all morally want-
ing. He finally abandons them for the forest whence he came. Munday engages in
mild satire directed not simply against the court but against all human society:
'But Lord how Country-folks can glose' (*Englands Helicon*, ed. Hugh Macdonald
(London, 1925), p. 190).

[46] See Henry Gibbons Lotspeich, *Classical Mythology in the Poetry of Edmund
Spenser* (Princeton, N.J., 1932), p. 108. Cf. v.xi.23.

This is one of the two possible manifestations of evil—that of Lucifera (the seductive, insidious manifestation) as against that of Orgoglio (where evil can be recognized as evil and overcomes by brute force). If we compare the experience of Serena and Timias, we see that the Beast can adopt either of these tactics. Serena fell victim because she followed her inclinations: behind the attractive appearance lay the terrifying reality. Timias fell victim because he did not realize the power of the evil he was facing: it was too strong for him. 'Of that commixtion', in the Hermit's words, is the Blatant Beast. The best way of curing and avoiding his bite 'is to avoide the occasion of the ill'.

> If therefore health ye seeke, observe this one.
> First learne your outward sences to refraine
> From things, that stirre up fraile affection;
> Your eies, your eares, your tongue, your talk restraine
> From that they most affect, and in due termes containe.
>
> (VI. vi. 7)

It is the same lesson that Calidore taught Crudor in Canto i: 'In vaine he seeketh others to suppresse / Who hath not learnd him selfe first to subdew.' In short, the best defence against the Beast is prudence and self-restraint.

The moralistic severity of the Hermit's advice has proved uncongenial to many readers of Spenser, so it is worth adding a word about the spirit in which it is offered. We accept with a certain degree of equanimity the suggestion that man must go out and fight the dragon of Original Sin, perhaps because the advice touches our secular world less, and because Redcross is so obviously a hero to be judged by a hero's standards. Calepine, on the other hand, is not a hero; he is very much one of us. The average sixteenth-century courtier, with Spenser's new book on his knee, must have appreciated immediately the applicability of the Hermit's advice to his own situation. For every fortune made at court, a dozen were lost or never made.[47] If the Hermit seems almost to suggest that it is hopeless to look for prosperity at court, that the avoidance of compromising positions is in the nature of the case almost impossible, that is in line with much Elizabethan thinking. Even the Hermit's specific suggestions are reminiscent of similar

---

[47] See, for example, A. L. Rowse's observations, *Ralegh and the Throckmortons* (London, 1962), pp. 273ff.

advice given by similar people all through medieval and Renaissance literature. We may feel that the Hermit is unduly optimistic in his supposition that there exists a way of avoiding courtly backbiting, that there *is* an ideal conduct which will find its reward in the sovereign's bounty, but by voicing such sentiments he protects his author from any accusation of disrespect for the Queen. She is the ideal, her court a rather depressing reality.[48]

5. Turpine's defeat

The first defeat of Turpine is complementary to Calepine's sufferings at his hands. Arthur's tactics bring out in Turpine his particular vice of cruelty to those weaker than himself. Only by feigning weakness can Arthur persuade Turpine to attack him at all. Such deceit is therefore perfectly justified. The parallels with Calepine's story are close. For instance, the insults which Turpine and his porter directed at Calepine are repeated in the insults which Turpine and his groom direct at Arthur. The Salvage Man's reaction, interestingly enough, is as severe as that of Talus might have been under the same circumstances; he simply tears the groom to pieces.

As before, Turpine's accusations are echoes of his own faults:

> Art thou he, traytor, that with treason vile,
> Hast slaine my men in this unmanly maner,
> And now triumphest in the piteous spoile
> Of these poore folk, whose soules with black dishonor
> And foule defame doe decke thy bloudy baner?
>
> (VI. vi. 25)

It is Turpine who is 'unmanly' (again we are reminded of the preliminary exemplum of courtesy in Canto i), and it is Turpine who attacks 'poore folk', adopting in the process tactics which are neither honourable nor fair. On this occasion he attacks, like Achilles and his Myrmidons, with 'forty yeomen'—thereby vastly outnumbering Arthur and the Salvage Man just as Despetto,

---

[48] Cf. Plato's discussion of 'Discipline', *The Republic*, trans. H. D. P. Lee (Harmondsworth, Middx., 1955), p. 178. Essentially the Hermit is seeking to establish a proper balance between freedom and self-control—one of the principal thematic concerns of Book VI; see William V. Nestrick, 'The Virtuous and Gentle Discipline of Gentlemen and Poets', *ELH*, 29 (1962), 357–71, and Kathleen Williams, *Spenser's 'Faerie Queene': the World of Glass* (London, 1966), pp. 190–1.

Decetto, and Defetto had outnumbered Timias. The parallel with Timias is brought out in the similes. Timias, we are told, fought

> Like a wylde Bull, that being at a bay,
> Is bayted of a mastiffe, and a hound,
> And a curre-dog; that doe him sharpe assay
> On every side, and beat about him round;
> But most that curre barking with bitter sownd,
> And creeping still behinde, doth him incomber.
>
> (VI. v. 19

Arthur, too, fights like a bull:

> And evermore that craven cowherd Knight
> Was at his backe with heartlesse heedinesse,
> Wayting if he unwares him murther might:
> For cowardize doth still in villany delight.

> Whereof whenas the Prince was well aware,
> He to him turnd with furious intent,
> And him against his powre gan to prepare;
> Like a fierce Bull, that being busie bent
> To fight with many foes about him ment,
> Feeling some curre behinde his heeles to bite,
> Turnes him about with fell avengement.
>
> (VI. vi. 26–7

These two similes are important for a number of reasons, not least in reminding us that Calepine's hiding behind his lady's back corresponds very closely to Turpine's behaviour—thereby supporting the assumption that Calepine's actions betoken his falling into baseness, his becoming 'Turpine-like'. The 'curre-dog' of Canto v, what is more, was Defetto, 'the third nor strong nor wise, but spightfullest'. He signifies Detraction, 'backbiting', a word we have already used in connection with Turpine and which is embodied, so to speak, in this simile. There can surely be little doubt left in our mind that the relationship of Turpine to the Beast is similar to that of the three ruffians and the Beast. The way in which the two stories are mutually illuminating can be called typical of Spenser's narrative technique. He uses a very similar technique in the story of Faunus, which illuminates the larger story of Nature's court surrounding it, and in the story of Fradubio, which is emblematic of Redcross's relationship with Duessa. These examples are strikingly indicative of the way in which the apparent extravagance of parallel incidents is in fact a means of achieving economy. The two similes I have just quoted are typical of such economy.

As if to remove from our mind any doubt about the existence of parallels, Spenser has Turpine do his share of hiding behind his lady. Driven off by Arthur, he takes to his heels, seeking refuge in Blandina's chamber.

> She starting up, began to shrieke aloud,
> And with her garment covering him from sight,
> Seem'd under her protection him to shroud.
>
> (VI. vi. 31)

Clearly we are to conclude that Turpine has himself fallen into baseness. Such allegorically typical conduct evokes the obvious criticism from Arthur:

> That both thy love, for lack of hardiment,
> And eke thy selfe, for want of manly hart,
> And eke all knights hast shamed with this knightlesse part.
>
> (VI. vi. 33)

But while the allusions to 'want of manly hart' and 'knightlesse part' obviously echo Calidore's defeat of Crudor in Canto i, the differences between these two incidents are as instructive as the similarities. Both Crudor's cruelty and Turpine's baseness are offences against courtesy, but cruelty is courtesy misdirected, whereas baseness is simply lack of any courtesy at all. Thus Crudor's offence can be corrected by simple redirection, but Turpine remains incorrigible. Turpine is a coward, and cowardice has no part in courtesy, any more than the flattery and honeyed language (Blandina) which generally accompanies it.

Crudor's aberration is described in that part of the book before the arrival of the Blatant Beast. This is important. The Beast does not simply offend against courtesy, as Crudor does, but symbolizes *dis*courtesy. It cannot be reformed, only destroyed. While we should not go so far as A. C. Hamilton,[49] who declares that Turpine '*is* the Blatant Beast in human form', we are justified, I think, in seeing Turpine's activities as extensions of the Beast's. Like the ruffians, Turpine turns the Beast's attacks to his own purposes and preys on others' misfortunes.

[49] *Structure*, p. 196.

Although Turpine, we are told, has engaged in a 'wicked custome', just as Crudor did (Turpine's custom, strangely, is not mentioned elsewhere in his story), Spenser goes out of his way to differentiate the two. Arthur's somewhat surprising declaration to Turpine makes this difference clear:

> For oft it falles, that strong
> And valiant knights doe rashly enterprize,
> Either for fame, or else for exercize,
> A wrongful quarrell to maintaine by fight;
> Yet have, through prowesse and their brave emprize,
> Gotten great worship in this worldes sight.
> For greater force there needs to maintaine wrong, then right.
>
> (VI. vi. 35)[50]

The passage is one of the most interesting in the book. Although perverted knighthood is in a sense 'knightless', it is in a quite different category from simple cowardice. Spenser's extensive use of superlatives in describing the fight with Crudor now becomes functional: Crudor and Calidore were an equal match; it was only Calidore's prudence and sagacity (because he had right on his side) that brought about his success.

There are several other parallels with the story of Crudor. One very simple one deserves mention: Cantos i and vi end very similarly—

> There he remaind with them right well agreed,
> Till of his wounds he wexed hole and strong,
> And then to his first quest he passed forth along.
>
> (VI. i. 47)

> The morrow next the Prince did early rize,
> And passed forth, to follow his first enterprize.
>
> (VI. vi. 44)

But the difference is that Turpine is unrepentant: Arthur has used the same method as Calidore, but with such material as Turpine mercy simply does not work: he is incurably corrupt and deceitful.

He is also like Até: he stirs up discord. By enlisting the help of

---

[50] Cf. Chrétien de Troyes, describing Count Angrés of Windsor, who defies the royal authority in *Cligés*: 'But the count was a powerful man and a good and hardy knight, whose match it would have been hard to find, had he not been a base traitor.' (*Arthurian Romances*, p. 116.)

two knights (we are reminded of Braggadocchio's similar ruses) he
is able to attempt revenge on Arthur without risking his own life.
The knights 'both combynd, what ever chance were blowne, /
Betwixt them to divide, and each to make his owne'. By the time
Turpine has finished with them, one is dead and the other corrupted (he fought for reward—a breach of the knightly code).[51]
Sir Enias, the survivor, falls victim to Turpine's wiles largely because he lacks prudence. Once he is made aware of his own folly,
he shows admirable circumspection in leading Turpine astray in
turn and bringing him to Arthur. Turpine first fell into Arthur's
power through a trick: Arthur feigned weakness. Sir Enias uses
the same tactics, tricking Turpine into a confrontation with
Arthur. But Arthur meanwhile is sleeping:

> Wearie of travell in his former fight,
> He there in shade himselfe had layd to rest,
> Having his armes and warlike things undight,
> Fearlesse of foes that mote his peace molest;
> The whyles his salvage page, that wont be prest,
> Was wandred in the wood another way,
> To doe some thing, that seemed to him best,
> The whyles his Lord in silver slomber lay,
> Like to the Evening starre adorn'd with deawy ray.
>
> (VI. vii. 19)

Like the stories of Priscilla and Matilda, this passage presents a
further picture of moral ambiguity which has sometimes proved
misleading. The *Variorum* editors are surely far too categorical
when they write, 'The Prince seems to have forgotten that he sent
away the knight to fetch Turpine. He placed himself in great
danger by thus carelessly going to sleep.'[52] This is not Redcross in
a drugged stupor before Orgoglio's attack, nor is it even Guyon
in a faint after his passage through the Cave of Mammon. What
is essential here is that though Arthur has decided to deal with
Turpine, he is not equipped when Turpine arrives: his 'salvage
page' is somewhere off in the woods. Arthur's previous success
against Turpine had been carried out with the assistance of the
Salvage Man: courtesy and nature were allied. Once again, Arthur
can only defeat Turpine if he is helped by the natural world.

So questions concerning Arthur's irresponsibility in going to

---

[51] Cf. Mammon's temptation of Guyon, II.vii.10.
[52] 6: 218.

sleep are really beside the point. Rather than turning back to Books I and II, we should be better advised to look at precedents in Book VI—the pairs of lovers in the opening cantos, for instance. They were menaced by a danger for which they were momentarily ill prepared: this was the sum total of their offence. Thus concord, the state courtesy seeks to maintain, was brought into sharp and painful juxtaposition with the senseless violence of their attackers. Here in Canto vii, this is not an imperfect Guyon, but another pacific figure set upon by malicious and cunning evil. Of course Arthur's situation might be interpreted as a warning to us; the precedents are there. But the movement of the verse throughout the canto (not least in the imagery, which is particularly rich and beautiful when referring to Arthur and the Salvage Man) is directed towards differentiation of the motives and behaviour of Turpine and Arthur—the one cunning and treacherous, the other peaceful, restrained, courteous, and transparently honest. Through the medium of Sir Enias, Spenser is even able to insulate Arthur's honesty: although Turpine is ensnared through a trick, it is no longer Arthur's trick.

At the conclusion of Turpine's story (whether he is dead or merely discomfited we are never told) we are in a better position to understand Arthur's role in Book VI. There is no doubt that Turpine's defeat is in the nature of a climactic episode. Customarily, Spenser moves his narrative forward through a kind of retrospective progression. Key episodes draw together echoes from their predecessors to form a new texture of meaning and prepare the ground for forward progress in the development of theme. Turpine's defeat is such an episode. We have seen how it reverberates much of the book's earlier narrative, and perhaps reorganizes our thoughts about episodes already completed. Although Arthur has nothing directly to do with Calidore's vision of courtesy on Mount Acidale, his victory over Turpine plays a vital part in the defeat of the forces of discord set over against the harmonious dance of the Graces. Arthur disposes of the main ally of the Blatant Beast, just as he disposed of the main allies of the dragon in Book I—Orgoglio and Duessa. Arthur is, in fact, the hero of a kind of sub-plot in Book VI.

Of course, in Book I Arthur's fight was part of the first book's central plot: not only did it figure forth the defeat of the allies of Evil but it also served the practical purpose of freeing Redcross.

SCP—G

Arthur's victory over Turpine anticipates Calidore's victory over the Beast, but there is no stated suggestion that Turpine's defeat has anything to do with the defeat of the Beast, at any rate on the level of plot. This is appropriate enough, for it would not be seemly that Calidore receive assistance in his quest. None the less, the logic of argument in Book VI surely makes it clear that with the defeat of Turpine Calidore's task is made easier and his enemy weakened. Arthur's role in Book VI is major.

IV

$\mathcal{N}$ature Subverted

1. Mirabella

MATERIAL from the most diverse sources finds a place in the spaciousness of Faeryland; Spenser's great amalgamation of themes in Book VI is matched by the eclecticism of his plot. His story of Mirabella is unlike any other episode in the book and opens up for us an entirely new area of analogues and allusions.[1] The debt for the tone and atmosphere of this episode lies primarily with Spenser's master, Chaucer. Its sources can be traced back through the well-known literary topos the court of love,[2] and through the specific story of the Purgatory of Cruel Beauties, of which there are a number of instances in the literature of the late Middle Ages.[3]

We first meet Mirabella in Canto vi, where Timias and Serena

[1] This need not lead us to conclude that the episode is in any sense an interpolation. Identification of this story with Spenser's lost *Court of Cupide*, for instance, seems pointless, since the passage must have been so revised as to lose its original shape, even if we could make the identification. Cf. Helen E. Sandison, 'Spenser's "Lost" Works and their Probable Relation to his *Faerie Queene*',*PMLA*, 25 (1910), 134–51.

[2] On the court of love, see W. A. Neilson's illuminating study of the poem of that name, *The Origins and Sources of the 'Court of Love'* (Cambridge, Mass., 1899); E. B. Fowler, *Spenser and the Courts of Love* (Menasha, Wis., 1921), and C. S. Lewis, *The Allegory of Love* (Oxford, 1936). Cf. A. J. Denomy, *The Heresy of Courtly Love* (New York, 1947). The topos continued in popularity through the sixteenth century and even into the seventeenth (e.g. Massinger's *Parliament of Love*, 1624, and the parliament of love in Marston's *Parasitaster*, 1606). A late example of some interest is *The Amorous Contention of Phillis and Flora*, attributed to Chapman but probably by Richard Stapleton. Published as a separate volume in 1598, the poem includes a Court of Cupid and a dance of the Graces (see *The Poems of George Chapman*, ed. Phyllis Brooks Bartlett (New York, 1941), p. 435).

[3] See W. A. Neilson, 'The Purgatory of Cruel Beauties', *Romania*, 29 (1900), 85–93. E. Margaret Grimes's article on *Le Lay du Trot*, *Romanic Review*, 26 (1935), 313–21, adds a further analogue. Among English versions of the Purgatory are episodes in Gower, *Confessio Amantis*, and Douglas, *The Palace of Honour*. It originates in Andreas Capellanus's *Art of Courtly Love*. Cf. the story of the cruel mistress Lidia, *Orlando Furioso*, XXXIV.11–43.

come upon her after leaving the Hermit, but at this point Spenser
interpolates his narrative of Arthur's revenge on Turpine and
does not resume her story until Canto vii. We learn that she is 'led
by a Carle and a foole' and ill-treated by them as she rides. She is
a 'Ladie of great dignitie' though lowly born, 'deckt with
wondrous gifts of natures grace' and thoroughly 'proud and
insolent':

> Through such her stubborne stifnesse, and hard hart,
> Many a wretch, for want of remedie,
> Did languish long in lifeconsuming smart,
> And at the last through dreary dolour die:
> Whylest she, the Ladie of her libertie,
> Did boast her beautie had such soveraine might,
> That with the onely twinckle of her eye,
> She could or save, or spill, whom she would hight.
> What could the Gods doe more, but doe it more aright?
>
> (VI. vii. 31)

Our first reaction—surely the correct one—is that Mirabella is
the physical embodiment of the cruel lady of so many Elizabethan
and Italian sonnet sequences.[4] She is proud, unyielding and
imperious. In fact she goes beyond the traditional hard-hearted
mistress in actually attempting to usurp the power of the gods,
like Lucifera before her, and Mutabilitie later on. What is more,
instead of meeting the fate traditionally wished upon cruel
mistresses—creeping old age—she falls victim to the wrath of the
gods themselves.[5]

---

[4] M. Pauline Parker, *The Allegory of the 'Faerie Queene'* (Oxford, 1960), p. 242.
There is not a shred of evidence to support the contention that in Mirabella we have
a picture of the poet's own Rosalind, as A. C. Hamilton suggests (*The Structure of
Allegory in 'The Faerie Queene'* (Oxford, 1961), p. 197), and others deny (*Variorum*,
6: 220-1). The idea seems to originate with John Upton, ed. *Spenser's 'Faerie Queene'*
(London, 1758), 2: 657. On the historical identity of Rosalind, see the lively series of
exchanges beginning with W. H. Welply's article in N & Q, 180 (1941), 58-9.

[5] Poems telling of punishment in store for cold damsels are, of course, frequent
enough. Within the court of love tradition are such poems as Alain Chartier's *La
Belle Dame Sans Merci* and its successor *Le Parlement d'Amour* (probably not by Alain).
See Edward J. Hoffman, *Alain Chartier: His Work and Reputation* (New York, 1942);
Arthur Piaget, 'La Belle Dame Sans Merci et ses imitations', *Romania*, 30 (1901),
22-48, 317-51; 31 (1902), 315-49; 33 (1904), 179-208; 34 (1905), 375-428, 559-602.
English poems include a translation of *La Belle Dame* (*Political, Religious and Love
Poems*, ed. F. J. Furnivall (London: EETS, 1866)) and hosts of lyrics, songs, and
ballads. See, for example, the Lady Margaret ballads, *English and Scottish Popular
Ballads*, ed. F. J. Child (Boston, Mass., 1882-98), 1: 425-31. Cf. *Variorum* 6: 223-4.

Mirabella's offence is that she has persistently ignored her responsibilities towards love. She has subverted Cupid's rule and placed his authority in jeopardy. Consequently, she is arrested and brought before him, tried and sentenced:

> The damzell was attacht, and shortly brought
> Unto the barre, whereas she was arrayned:
> But she thereto nould plead, nor answere ought
> Ever for stubborne pride, which her restrayned.
> So judgement past, as is by law ordayned
> In cases like, which when at last she saw,
> Her stubborne hart, which love before disdayned,
> Gan stoupe, and falling down with humble awe,
> Cryde mercie, to abate the extremitie of law.
>
> The sonne of *Venus* who is myld by kynd,
> But where he is provokt with peevishnesse,
> Unto her prayers piteously enclynd,
> And did the rigour of his doome represse;
> Yet not so freely, but that nathelesse
> He unto her a penance did impose,
> Which was, that through this worlds wyde wildernes
> She wander should in companie of those,
> Till she had sav'd so many loves, as she did lose.
>
> (VI. vii. 36–7)

The first of these two stanzas presents, on one level, a picture of a proud and haughty woman falling in love. That, traditionally, is what Cupid's judgement means. Her penance involves a reversal of her former situation: she will become a kind of female courtly lover, afflicted with the same kind of love-longing as she has caused in others, and meet with the same rebuffs as she has previously dealt her suitors. We note in passing that Cupid's sentence emphasizes rehabilitation rather than punishment.

Disdain ('sib to great Orgolio') and Scorn are responsible for carrying out the sentence. The description of Disdain's giant figure takes us back to his previous appearance in the seventh canto in Book II, which Spenser clearly had in mind as he wrote. In Book II, Disdain stands at the gate of the palace of Philotime, who sits 'in glistring glory' dispensing her favours to a throng of suppliants. Guyon is led to her palace, symbolic of the acquisition of wealth for worldly gain, by her father, Mammon, who explains

that 'honour and dignitie' and 'all this worldes blis' are derived
from her (II. vii. 48), and offers Guyon her hand in marriage.
Guyon, predictably, refuses, realizing that with her golden
chain, symbol of ambition, she parodies God himself, to whose
throne is attached the Chain of Being. The figure of Disdain
is an appropriate addition to this palace of the representative of
worldly wealth, of those who have bought their positions in the
world.

Now in the story of Mirabella the allegory is redeployed. Just
as disdain accompanies newly acquired riches, so it accompanies
refusal to love. But whereas Disdain was Philotime's servant, now
in the topsy-turvy situation of Mirabella's punishment he is
Mirabella's persecutor. In fact, Mirabella in a sense goes beyond
Philotime. She combines the pride of social position (Philotime
or Lucifera, after whom Philotime is partly modelled) with the
sensual pride of perverted love (Duessa–Orgoglio). It is therefore very appropriate that the Disdain of Book VI combines
characteristics both of his namesake in Book II and of Orgoglio
in Book I.[6]

Timias, rash as ever, leaps to Mirabella's defence, when he
comes upon her, dishevelled and miserable, buffeted by Disdain
and prodded with Scorn's whip. His intervention is a mistake, not
only because it shows a failure to appreciate the situation (Mirabella is only getting what she deserves) but also because he has to
abandon Serena—temporarily, as he thinks. Serena's unfortunate
experiences have already involved two abandonments, first by
Calepine and Calidore, and second by Calepine in his pursuit of
the bear. In both cases the consequences for Serena were dire. On
this third occasion they will terminate in what is almost her ritual
murder at the hands of the Salvage Nation.

Interestingly, the central simile in Timias's fight with Disdain is
similar to that employed in his previous fight:

> Like as a Mastiffe having at a bay
> A salvage Bull, whose cruell hornes doe threat
> Desperate daunger, if he them assay,
> Traceth his ground, and round about doth beat,
> To spy where he may some advantage get;

---

[6] On Disdain see F. M. Padelford, *Variorum*, 6: 224–5. Disdain is a not unusual
figure in court of love poems. See, for example, the charming poem of Eustache
Deschamps, 'Le Lay Amoureux' (*Oeuvres Complètes* (Paris, 1880), 2: 193–203).

The whiles the beast doth rage and loudly rore:
So did the Squire, the whiles the Carle did fret,
And fume in his disdainefull mynd the more,
And oftentimes by Turmagant and Mahound swore.

(VI. vii. 47)

On the two occasions when Spenser employed this simile before, the hero played the part of the bull, the villains that of the dogs. It seems at first that the roles are here reversed. But a more careful reading of the episode reveals that Timias is not the hero after all. Disdain and Scorn are the means by which Cupid is exercising his authority over Mirabella. For once, they are put to orderly use. The result, for Timias, is that he once again falls victim to Cupid's law. Could it be that his encounter with Mirabella stirs again the love-longing of his encounter with Amoret? Certainly he seems taken in by the metaphor which Mirabella represents. Slave to the tradition of courtly love, he fails to recognize the extent or the danger of Mirabella's offence.

With Timias forced to 'forward fare', captive to Disdain and Scorn, Serena is helpless. Scorn alternately beats Timias with his whip and (much worse) taunts him and pours scorn on him—'words sharpely wound, but greatest griefe of scorning growes'.[7] The squire, assailed on all sides by taunts and blows, is helpless before another kind of discourtesy—the cruelty of female scorn. Mirabella can only look on powerlessly, unable to assist Timias and only adding to his discomfort by her pleas to his captors.

The arrival of Sir Enias and Arthur causes Scorn and Disdain to redouble their cruelty 'As if it them should grieve to see his punishment'. This is good psychology: a heartless woman pours scorn upon her lover most abundantly when she has an audience, preferably male. Sir Enias, like so many men under such circumstances, finds himself attracted to this hypothetical woman, imagines that he will be able to turn such scorn into love, but ends up scorned himself. In other words, he too is overcome and falls captive to Disdain and Scorn.

Mirabella's cruel fate requires the infliction on her of that frustration which she has inflicted on others. She must acquiesce in the sentence imposed by Cupid, and must speak out against the well-intentioned efforts of other people to interfere with Cupid's justice. Arthur, hardly surprisingly, is flabbergasted

---

[7] Church conjectured 'swords' for 'words'. See *Variorum*, 6: 474.

when Mirabella calls upon him 'for love of God' to refrain from killing a creature against whom the very heavens themselves, he thinks, would rise up. Mirabella explains her situation to him (note that the flower of the first line leads only to the blight of the last; Mirabella's conduct is the very reverse of courtesy):

> In prime of youthly yeares, when first the flowre
> Of beauty gan to bud, and bloosme delight,
> And nature me endu'd with plenteous dowre,
> Of all her gifts, that pleasde each living sight,
> I was belov'd of many a gentle Knight,
> And sude and sought with all the service dew:
> Full many a one for me deepe groand and sight,
> And to the dore of death for sorrow drew,
> Complayning out on me, that would not on them rew.
>
> (VI. viii. 20)

Arthur's final reaction to Mirabella's story is to declare the justice of Cupid's laws, 'For were no law in love, but all that lust / Might them oppresse, and painefully turmoile, / His kingdome would continue but a while.' In this context, of course, Crudor's evil practice constitutes an attack on Cupid's kingdom. So, in a sense, does Turpine's. Love involves a sense of responsibility, and a sense of responsibility implies acceptance of certain standards:

> Ye gentle Ladies, in whose soveraine powre
> Love hath the glory of his kingdome left,
> And th'hearts of men, as your eternall dowre,
> In yron chaines, of liberty bereft,
> Delivered hath into your hands by gift;
> Be well aware, how ye the same doe use,
> That pride doe not to tyranny you lift;
> Least if men you of cruelty accuse,
> He from you take that chiefedome, which ye doe abuse.
>
> (VI. viii. 1)

There is no reason to suppose that the narrator is anything but sincere in granting 'maisterie' to the woman. This is the position he has already taken in the Temple of Isis in Book v, where Britomart accepted the crocodile when it came to her submissively, and reaffirmed in the conclusion of the story of Radigund, where it is surely evident that Radigund's fault was not so much her assertion of 'maisterie' as her failure to respect masculine prerogatives. Mirabella, like Radigund, delights in dealing out public humiliations to her lovers. By contrast Spenser presents us with a picture of Mars chained to the throne of Venus[8] ('In yron chaines, of liberty bereft') as an emblem not of women's tyranny but of women's responsibilities and of the power of love. It is important that Venus's power be used to create harmony—that it be not abused, as when Duessa, for instance, caused Redcross to remove his armour only to ensnare him, or Crudor abused Briana's love.

Perhaps the most fascinating question in connection with the episode of Mirabella concerns this so-called Petrarchan convention. Are we justified in reading this strange story as a kind of parody, a literalization, of the conventions of the Elizabethan love sonnet, at least as some of its practitioners use it?[9] Of course, this part of the *Faerie Queene* was probably written when the vogue for sonnets was at its height. Certainly the whole episode is consciously literary.[10] A consideration of its formidable literary background is outside the range of my concerns, but there can be no doubt that Spenser's average reader would recognize the furniture of this episode as distinctly similar to dozens of poems of his own and earlier times. Such treatments of the court of love might vary in details (Spenser makes several innovations), but the overall situation was stock poetic material. Spenser's reader would also understand that Mirabella herself is a kind of walking fiction.[11]

This, of course, is something which Timias has difficulty in understanding. It is interesting that his reunion with Arthur is reminiscent of the recognition which follows the Prince's rescue

[8] See Edgar Wind, *Pagan Mysteries in the Renaissance*, 2nd edn. (Harmondsworth, Middx., 1967), p. 89 and Fig. 77.

[9] See also Donald Cheney's remarks, *Spenser's Image of Nature* (New Haven, Conn., 1966), pp. 108–16, and Lu Emily Pearson's extensive discussion of Petrarchanism, in *Elizabethan Love Conventions* (Berkeley, Calif., 1933). Cf. Rosemond Tuve *Elizabethan and Metaphysical Imagery* (Chicago, 1947), p. 420.

[10] Harry Berger, Jr. ('A Secret Discipline: *The Faerie Queene*, Book vi', in *Form and Convention in the Poetry of Edmund Spenser*, ed. William Nelson (New York, 1961)) argues that 'in the Court of Cupid *topos* Spenser presents a totally artificial world which, with its carefully sustained legal metaphor, smacks of oversophistication'. This view, I think, springs from a misunderstanding of Cupid's role here. Spenser is using a well-worn *topos*, to be sure, but he does so in order to identify the *benevolent* rule of love (as opposed to the tyrannous Cupid of Book iii, for example). Arthur, we might note, is ultimately persuaded of the rightness of Cupid's sentence.

[11] Her story is even a sonnet writ large: see *Amoretti* x.

of his squire from the clutches of Despetto, Decetto, and Defetto. The reunion follows a similar pattern—Arthur's joy and Timias's silence and sorrow. But in this second case Timias's conduct is directly linked with his inability to read the significance of what is almost an emblematic scene—Mirabella under the blows of Scorn and Disdain. The virtue of prudence is here equated with a sense of the fictional. The point of the lesson is driven home by the literalist Salvage Man's behaviour during this reunion. Seeing Scorn ill-treating Enias, he seizes his whip and 'would with whipping, him have done to die'. His behaviour is really indistinguishable from Timias's and equally self-defeating. Arthur must intervene to stop the Salvage Man just as he intervened to rescue Timias.

On a more general level, Mirabella's story and the narrator's comments on it present a view of the responsibilities of womankind obviously applicable to the social and political orders. The woman's role is here roughly analogous to the widely held view that the sovereign has a responsibility towards his subjects and is in turn subject to a higher power. A proper awareness of these responsibilities leads to political and social stability. In the state and in society, failure to play one's allotted part, failure to act courteously, leads to social and moral disintegration.

We have observed that Mirabella's story is drawn from two medieval themes, the Court of Cupid and what Neilson calls the Purgatory of Cruel Beauties. Spenser is the only poet, to my knowledge, to combine these two themes. In the process he transforms them, dovetailing one into the other in such a manner that the superfluities in each are abandoned and the two form a perfect fit.[12] He adds echoes of other episodes in the *Faerie Queene* which help to define the meaning of Mirabella's story. The allusion to the story of Orgoglio links it firmly with the two vices of pride and perverted love. The theme of perverted love receives further emphasis through allusions to the masque of Cupid in Book III. This link, which we shall examine later, is particularly

[12] The reader will find the details of the two *topoi* in the studies of Neilson and others cited above (n. 2). The Court of Cupid is customarily set in a dream vision, but Spenser renders this setting unnecessary by placing the Court in a flashback: the trial before Cupid has already taken place before we meet Mirabella. The usual literary setting of the Purgatory—the troops of ladies, the elaborate explanation of their significance—is also unnecessary because the Court of Cupid provides adequate explanation for Mirabella's punishment.

important, since we shall find that it provides a key to our understanding of the stories of both Serena and Mirabella.

These stories really form a separate section in Book VI, with certain rather specific themes, and prompt a division of the action up to the end of Canto viii into three sections. First comes the series of adventures involving Calidore. Each of his adventures brings him closer and closer to failure, and hence closer and closer to the Beast, who is, so to speak, only looking for a gap in Calidore's courteous defence to leap in and spread destruction. The principal attribute of Calidore in addition to his courtesy is his prudence. His name itself probably reinforces this emphasis.[13] This first section of the book comes to an end when Calidore fails to exercise the necessary prudence, setting in motion the train of events leading to Serena's downfall. The main lesson to be drawn from this section is that Calidore's courtesy is in important respects inadequate. The second section is taken up with the story of Turpine. He represents backbiting society, and his story shows the consequences of lack of prudence (in this instance, Serena's). His story ends with his extermination by Arthur and the Salvage Man. In a society where backbiting and destruction are rife, moral standards become debased. This is the subject of the third section. Hypocrisy, a 'holier-than-thou' attitude, secret lust, all are given a chance to flourish. Above all, human relationships are perverted, sex is used as a weapon, cruelty and scorn hold sway. Values go awry. Mirabella scorns love; Serena is sacrificed to false gods. The flower of womanhood is perverted into sterility.

We shall understand this third section better by turning back to a series of episodes in the extended study of love contained in the central books of the *Faerie Queene*. One of the major themes of these books, especially Book III, is the perversion of love, either

---

[13] Upton (*Variorum*, 6: 187) suggests the Greek *kalliodoros* as the derivation of his name—which 'leads us to consider the many graceful and goodly ornaments that heaven peculiarly gave him'. It may indeed be that the first syllable of his name is derived from the Greek *kallos* (beauty), but that is about as far as we can go. A much more likely derivation is from the Latin *callidus*, which means 'clever by reason of experience', 'dexterous', 'skilful', and 'cunning'. From the beginning, these qualities of Calidore are repeatedly emphasized: he is 'well approv'd in batteilous affray' (ii.2), 'well skild in fight' (i.20), 'wondrous practicke in that play' and 'passing well expert in single fight' (i.36). He is also not above subterfuge. Josephine Waters Bennett (*The Evolution of 'The Faerie Queene'* (Chicago, 1942), p. 215) suggests a connection with *calidus*, but that seems less likely (cf. Cheney, *Image of Nature*, p. 204). Arnold Williams, *Flower on a Lowly Stalk* (Michigan State University, 1967), p. 67, follows the Greek derivation.

by rejecting it entirely, as Marinell does, or by turning it to
lustful ends, as, for example, the Foresters do. These three
Foresters, one of whom pursues Florimell, should be read as
perverters of order—specifically of the sexual order which provides the principal frame of reference for the book. Their attack,
and the subsequent cure of Timias by Belphoebe, provides a
close parallel with the fight against Despetto, Decetto and Defetto,
the Beast's wound, and the cure by the Hermit.

Later in the book, the delicate, fleeting figure of Florimell
reappears, still in flight:

> Like as an Hynd forth singled from the heard,
> That hath escaped from a ravenous beast,
> Yet flyes away of her owne feete affeard,
> And every leafe, that shaketh with the least
> Murmure of winde, her terror hath encreast;
> So fled faire *Florimell* from her vaine feare,
> Long after she from perill was release:
> Each shade she saw, and each noyse she did heare,
> Did seeme to be the same, which she escapt whyleare.
>
> (III. vii. 1)

This, too, has its parallel in Book VI. When Timias falls victim to
Disdain and Scorn, Serena's reaction is very similar to Florimell's.
We read that she

> When first the gentle Squire at variaunce fell
> With those two Carles, fled fast away, afeard
> Of villany to be to her inferd:
> So fresh the image of her former dread,
> Yet dwelling in her eye, to her appeard,
> That every foote did tremble, which did tread,
> And every body two, and two she foure did read.
>
> (VI. viii. 31)

Florimell, rushing from one misfortune to another, finally throws
herself upon the mercy of an old fisherman in a boat by the sea
shore. Roche comments as follows:

She is driven farther and farther away from the norms and protection
of society and escapes into the apparent protection of the fishing boat.
Like the symbolism of her former escape [from the Forester] on the
palfrey, this boat is a symbol that Florimell has subjected herself to

the realm of fortune and the vagaries of this mutable life as represented by the sea.[14]

At this point in Book III Spenser does something very unusual. He turns from the narrative to address the knights of Faerie court:

> But if that thou, Sir *Satyran,* didst weet
> Or thou, Sir *Peridure,* her sorie state,
> How soone would yee assemble many a fleete,
> To fetch from sea, that ye at land lost late;
> Towres, Cities, Kingdomes ye would ruinate,
> In your avengement and dispiteous rage,
> Ne ought your burning fury mote abate;
> But if Sir *Calidore* could it presage,
> No living creature could his cruelty asswage.
>
> (III. viii. 28)

This allusion to Sir Calidore is the only one outside Book VI. Ultimately, it is not he but Sir Satyrane who comes to Florimell's rescue, for all that he cannot reach her. Equally at home both in the world of nature and in the court, he is in some senses an appropriate rescuer. Nevertheless, Roche's comment (p. 157) is perceptive: 'Sir Calidore the knight of courtesy is certainly the proper champion to avenge Florimell's ill-usage, but at this point Spenser wants to emphasize not the wrong to society but the wrong to nature.' That of course, is perfectly in accord with the private, personal nature of Book III's titular virtue.

Immediately following Florimell's attempted escape by water come two examples of love perverted—the nymphomaniac giantess Argante and the lady of the Squire of Dames. Spenser is interested in the offence of these two against nature, but Roche's observation suggests that there could be another way of looking at the same series of events. The story of Mirabella, which is decidedly reminiscent of the story of the Squire of Dames, deals not so much with Mirabella's *sexual* offence as with the *social* consequences of the offence. In the same way, Timias's unfortunate treatment at the hands (and the teeth) of the Blatant Beast and his accomplices is a retelling in social terms of the earlier story of the Foresters. Book VI, then, while it is concerned also with the

---

[14] *The Kindly Flame* (Princeton, N.J., 1964), p. 156. My indebtedness to Roche in this excursion into Books III and IV will be obvious.

use and abuse of love, looks at such matters from a social point of view. Essentially the same material is used to illustrate a somewhat different theme.

The story of Florimell, with her vain attempts to find succour in a world increasingly hostile and foreign to her, is in certain respects a parallel of Amoret's story. In his presentation of Serena, Spenser draws freely on echoes of both. Perhaps Serena is rather like Amoret—a young girl seeking emotional security amidst all manner of psychological or social difficulties.[15] In Books III and IV at issue are Amoret's character and the nature of her marital relationship. In Book VI at issue are the *social* consequences of Serena's conduct.

At the opening of Book IV, Amoret is under the protection of Britomart, who has just rescued her from the House of Busyrane, where she was subjected to a kind of nightmare world in which her sexual fantasies and fears became real. Britomart successfully protects her from the knights of Castle Joyous, where love is a somewhat unsavoury game. The theme of Castle Joyous is repeated in Britomart's unhorsing of Blandamour (love-as-a-game) whom she finds with Paridell (love-as-destruction) and the two hags Duessa and Até. All these characters are bent upon upsetting the proper framework of concord in their various ways, for the irresponsible Blandamour represents as great a threat as the destructive Paridell, just as Blandina, who is always pleasant regardless of circumstances, only helps Turpine perpetrate his various outrages.

---

[15] The parallels between the stories of Serena and Amoret are numerous. The passage describing Serena in flight, already quoted, should be compared with the description of Amoret's escape from Lust:

> Full fast she flies, and farre afore him goes,
> Ne feeles the thorns and thickets pricke her tender toes.

> Nor hedge, nor ditch, nor hill, nor dale she staies,
> But overleapes them all, like Robucke light,
> And through the thickest makes her nighest waies. (IV.vii.21–2)

Of Serena's flight, we read:

> Through hils and dales, through bushes and through breres
> Long thus she fled, till that at last she thought
> Her selfe now past the perill of her feares. (VI.viii.32)

The picture of a girl in flight through clinging undergrowth has a history going back at least to Ovid. (Cheney, *Image of Nature*, pp. 108–9, also draws attention to parallels between Serena and Amoret.)

Até sets the tone for the whole book. She is the 'mother of all debate / And all dissention, which doth dayly grow / Amongst fraile men', and she makes a fitting companion for Paridell, counterpart of Paris, whose rape of Helen brought all Troy to destruction. She is accorded one of the most extensive presentations of any of Spenser's characters. In the course of the eleven stanzas devoted to a description of her character and attributes, we are told:

> So much her malice did her might surpas,
> That even th'Almightie selfe she did maligne,
> Because to man so mercifull he was,
> And unto all his creatures so benigne,
> Sith she her selfe was of his grace indigne:
> For all this worlds faire workmanship she tride,
> Unto his last confusion to bring,
> And that great golden chaine quite to divide,
> With which it blessed Concord hath together tide.
>
> (iv. i. 30)

This power of discord is the essential enemy in a book devoted to the praise of concord. Até's pride (and this is one point where Book iv touches Book vi) extends as far as a challenge against the Almighty himself—like Mirabella's refusal to knuckle under to Cupid. Até, like her counterpart Sclaunder, represents a very similar power to the Blatant Beast.

In Book iv Spenser emphasizes the power of love properly directed and the consequences of its misdirection or subversion. The book's great emblem of concord is the Temple of Venus. But the terms of Book iv are readily applicable to Book vi. The offence of Mirabella involves the acting out of love-as-a-game, just as Serena falls victim to love-as-destruction. If these negative qualities help by exclusion to define the nature of Friendship in Book iv, they work equally effectively to define social harmony in the wider context of Book vi. Mirabella's treatment of love as an unfeeling and cruel game reminds us of the element of falsity, of play-acting in her behaviour. Roche's masterly analysis of the Busyrane episode in Book iii establishes quite conclusively that Busyrane's castle and the destructive quality of the masque of Cupid are essentially figments of Amoret's imagination—pieces of fiction which demonstrate the literalism of Amoret's response much as Mirabella's behaviour also demonstrates a fatal literalism, an inability to understand metaphor. For Amoret, the innocent-looking wedding entertainment causes terrifying psychological disorders. What is essentially a figure of speech becomes an actual design for conduct; Amoret begins to *believe* a work of art as though it were not a fiction at all.[16] Amoret's view of the masque of Cupid is in total contrast to the omnipotent yet merciful presentation of Cupid in Book VI. The metaphor itself is not so very different but is given a slightly different slant. It is, of course, still open to misinterpretation, as Timias's attack on Disdain and Scorn makes evident, and as the conduct of the Salvage Nation in the very next canto, by association, makes clearer still.

Amoret, innocent and naïve, fails to understand the metaphor of art and is plunged into despair and fear. Mirabella attempts to go through life behaving like the subject of a sonnet. These two examples of aesthetic obtuseness are only a part of a much wider treatment of the nature of poetic response which runs all the way through the *Faerie Queene*.[17] The landmarks which dot the countryside of Faeryland are literary as well as physical: Faeryland is a model, a geography, of the world of poetic fiction. Maurice Evans has argued that the Bower of Bliss should be regarded as a lie, a piece of unnatural fiction;[18] Britomart's dream in Isis Church raises similar questions about the nature of fantasy; so does Malbecco's metamorphosis. What is more, we are continually meeting, and entering, known *topoi*—pageants of sins, lists of trees, paradises—which make our own journey through the *Faerie Queene* a constant exercise in the reassessment of the familiar. Our own aesthetic response is constantly on trial—but so is that of Spenser's characters.

2. *Serena*

We might call Mirabella a person 'lacking in imagination'. But if Mirabella is crassly unresponsive to the artistic use of language, the Salvages form a whole nation of anti-poetic boobs who cannot understand even the fundamentals of Petrarchan language but

---

[16] *Kindly Flame*, pp. 72–88. See also Millar MacLure, 'Nature and Art in *The Faerie Queene*', *ELH*, 28 (1961), 1–20, esp. p. 11.

[17] Paul J. Alpers, The Poetry of '*The Faerie Queene*' (Princeton, N.J., 1967) touches on some of these issues, *passim*. See also Cheney's discussion of poetic language at the opening of Book I, *Image of Nature*, pp. 18ff.

[18] 'Guyon and the Bower of Sloth', *SP*, 61 (1964), 140–9.

insist on living it out as though it were real life.[19] Serena, like Alice, strays into a world where the creatures of the literary imagination take on the embodiment of flesh and blood.

These enemies of poetry, understandably, live in a wilderness quite unlike the golden world of the imagination. Into this wilderness, abandoned by Timias, Serena strays:

> In these wylde deserts, where she now abode,
> There dwelt a salvage nation, which did live
> Of stealth and spoile, and making nightly rode
> Into their neighbours borders; ne did give
> Them selves to any trade, as for to drive
> The painefull plough, or cattell for to breed,
> Or by adventrous marchandize to thrive;
> But on the labours of poore men to feed,
> And serve their owne necessities with others need.
>
> Thereto they usde one most accursed order,
> To eate the flesh of men, whom they mote fynde,
> And straungers to devoure, which on their border
> Were brought by errour, or by wreckful wynde.
> A monstrous cruelty gainst course of kynde.
>
> (VI. viii. 35–6)

The inhabitants of 'these wylde deserts' are a kind of anti-natural force, their life a kind of parody of the Golden Age. They know neither trade nor ploughing, not because (like the shepherds) they are self-sufficient without these occupations, but because they live off everyone else; they are akin to the brigands who, in the next episode, will destroy the shepherds' society.

There is no naïve unreasoning primitivism about this nation of wild men. We need only compare them with the people among whom Una finds herself in Book I, or even the satyrs with whom Hellenore lives in Book III. This nation practises an advanced, if repulsive, form of religion; it even attributes the arrival of Serena in its midst to heavenly grace:

> Soone as they spide her, Lord what gladfull glee
> They made amongst them selves; but when her face
> Like the faire yvory shining they did see,
> Each gan his fellow solace and embrace,
> For joy of such good hap by heavenly grace.

---

[19] See Cheney's observations, *Image of Nature*, pp. 104ff.

> Then gan they to devize what course to take:
> Whether to slay her there upon the place,
> Or suffer her out of her sleepe to wake,
> And then her eate attonce; or many meales to make.
>
> (VI. viii. 37)

The whole episode is grotesque, funny and disgusting by turns.
An elaborate physical description of Serena serves only to describe what particular portions of her anatomy are likely to provide
the tastiest morsels; it forms a preliminary for a still more
elaborate catalogue containing all the conventional Renaissance
metaphors:

> Her yvorie necke, her alablaster brest,
> Her paps, which like white silken pillowes were,
> For love in soft delight thereon to rest;
> Her tender sides, her bellie white and clere,
> Which like an Altar did it selfe uprere,
> To offer sacrifice divine thereon;
> Her goodly thighes, whose glorie did appeare
> Like a triumphall Arch, and thereupon
> The spoiles of Princes hang'd which were in battel won.
>
> (VI. viii. 42)

The conventional imagery of the love sonnet is grotesquely out
of place; the only altar relevant here is the altar built for Serena's
sacrifice.[20] The irony is compounded by the fact that the sum of
the alternatives facing Serena at this moment consists of the loss
of her honour or her being eaten by the Salvages. Salvage society
may have set limits to lust, but its 'civilized' way of behaving is
simply to consume, to destroy Beauty; its conventions call for
destruction rather than desecration. The priest makes this clear
when he rebukes the lustful members of the group, declaring that
the 'sacred threasure' is 'Vow'd to the gods'—'Religion held
even theeves in measure.' Decking himself with 'finest flowres',
the priest prepares his vessels for the sacrifice. Serena is taken to
the flower-strewn altar as night falls; the priest stands over her,
his arms bare and his knife poised. What follows is a kind of
infernal parody of the Dance of the Graces—the dance on Mount

---

[20] Israel Baroway, *Variorum*, 6: 234-5, analyses the lines not as grotesquerie but
as examples of the Oriental style.

Acidale transferred, as it were, to the darkness of the brigands' cave:

> Then gan the bagpypes and the hornes to shrill,
> And shrieke aloud, that with the peoples voyce
> Confused, did the ayre with terror fill,
> And made the wood to tremble at the noyce:
> The whyles she wayld, the more they did rejoyce.
>
> (VI. viii. 46)

The final line adds to the nightmarish quality. Mirabella besought Disdain and Scorn to spare Timias, but her words helped not at all, 'For aye the more, that she did them entreat, / The more they him misust, and cruelly did beat.' So it is with Serena.

Calepine's intervention, 'by chaunce, more then by choyce', incorporates a commonplace of romance, the so-called Rescue at the Stake.[21] It also constitutes an assertion of knightly prowess which serves to cancel out Calepine's former weakness and which provides a prefiguration of Calidore's progress in the following cantos. As if to emphasize the continuity in Calepine's career, the narrator picks up a simile he used once before, when Calepine gave chase to the bear—that of a hawk:

> With that he thrusts into the thickest throng,
> And even as his right hand adowne descends,
> He him preventing, layes on earth along,
> And sacrifizeth to th'infernall feends.
> Then to the rest his wrathfull hand he bends,
> Of whom he makes such havocke and such hew,
> That swarmes of damned soules to hell he sends:
> The rest that scape his sword and death eschew,
> Fly like a flocke of doves before a Faulcons vew.
>
> (VI. viii. 49)

The metaphorical thrust of the stanza emphasizes the way in which Calepine's intervention sets all to rights. Those who before had been bent on sacrificing Serena are now themselves sacrificed 'to th'infernall feends', and 'swarmes of damned soules' are sent to hell where they belong. The topsy-turvy society of the Salvage

---

[21] For a collection of examples, see C. Boje, *Über den altfranzösischen Roman von Beuve de Hamtone* (Halle, 1909), p. 116. See also Dickson, *Valentine and Orson*, pp. 78–9. The most readily available source for Spenser would be Malory's *Morte d'Arthur* (xx.8), where Launcelot rescues Guinevere.

Nation, with its social restraints and its vicious religion, receives the reward it deserves.

But while we might expect a tender reconciliation to follow Calepine's grand victory over the Salvages, it is not to be. The canto ends enigmatically and inconclusively. Calepine unbinds Serena, still unaware of her identity (it is dark), and questions and encourages her, 'But she for nought that he could say or doe, / One word durst speake, or answere him a whit thereto.'

> So inward shame of her uncomely case
> She did conceive, through care of womanhood,
> That though the night did cover her disgrace,
> Yet she in so unwomanly a mood,
> Would not bewray the state in which she stood.
> So all that night to him unknowen she past.
> But day, that doth discover bad and good,
> Ensewing, made her knowen to him at last:
> The end whereof Ile keepe untill another cast.
>
> (VI. viii. 51)

The inconclusiveness of the episode is, of course, reminiscent of that point in Book IV where Scudamour and Amoret are reunited following a fight involving Arthur, Scudamour and Britomart, a fight in which the forces of love-as-a-game and love-as-destruction—'To weet, sterne Druon, and lewd Claribell, / Love-lavish Blandamour, and lustfull Paridell'—are resisted by an alliance of Scudamour and Britomart, a faithful husband and the figure of chaste love. Despite the fact that Scudamour and Amoret are together in the same spot and despite the fact that Scudamour talks about her—indeed spends the whole of the next canto doing so—there is no mention of a reunion. In the *Faerie Queene* stories repeatedly end inconclusively, to be sure, because the poem is like life, and because one episode is subsumed in another in an endless series, but in the case of Serena the uncertainty is especially puzzling and frustrating.

Why, we ask, will she not talk to Calepine? Mere shame at her nakedness hardly seems reason enough. Why is her mood 'unwomanly'? The use of the term suggests that somehow Serena has failed to play the role which society demands of her; just as a knight must be knightly, so women must be womanly. We linked the narrator's references to the role of women with which this canto opened not to Serena but to Mirabella, yet they apply with equal force to Serena. Serena has evidently fallen short of her responsibilities. Since the book lays repeated emphasis on the fulfilment of one's social obligations, this is failure indeed. To understand what it means, we need to retrace her story.

She first falls into trouble as a result of her wandering at will after Calidore has interrupted her with Calepine. Calepine protects her, but finally, by a series of accidents, comes to desert her, leaving her in the hands of the Salvage Man. At the home of the Hermit she is cured by adjusting her attitude to the outside world, by keeping her passions under control, bridling her outward senses. Timias becomes embroiled with Mirabella and, in consequence, Serena is left totally friendless and, as she judges, in extreme danger. She takes flight. In so doing she compounds her misfortunes, since she thereby misses Arthur who arrives on the scene soon afterwards. By fleeing from the sight of Cupid's just punishment she puts herself in the hands of those who repudiate Cupid by offending against the laws of love.

Calepine saves Serena, destroying the Salvages and turning their religion against themselves. In the past, his love had represented a kind of haven for Serena from the cruelties and backbiting of the world.[22] But during her flight from Scorn and Disdain, in despair she repudiated Calepine, blaming him for her misfortunes. Her repudiation of his love, based on his supposed faithlessness, leads to her capture by the screaming Salvages. Denying love, she is seized by fiends.

In the stillness after Calepine's battle with the Salvages, when the hysteria of the previous terrifying minutes has had a chance to abate, Serena is suddenly bitterly ashamed. Though Calepine does not know her, there is no indication that she does not recognize him. At the same time she realizes that not only has she repudiated Calepine but she has repudiated love as well. Naked on the altar of perversion and lust, Serena remembers the teachings of the Hermit and is ashamed at her wilful disregard of his words. Such is her shame that nothing Calepine can do will win her over. It is almost as though she now sees in Mirabella's fate the pattern of her own. Her shame at her nakedness is shame at her own sin. Spenser's choice of the word 'disgrace' to describe her predicament is suggestive. Like Adam and Eve, she has fallen from grace.

[22] On the significance of Serena's name, see Cheney, *Image of Nature*, pp. 200-1.

So it is that she is 'in so unwomanly a mood': she has misused her womanliness.[23]

I can see the objections mounting up. How, if Serena is so clearly the *captive* of the Salvages, can we speak of her giving herself up to the qualities they stand for? She surely opposes them. How, if her behaviour is manifestly shameless, can she represent unprotected beauty? The answer to the first question is very simple: the technique is common in Spenser. Amoret captive to Busyrane is 'captive' to the fears he represents, just as Serena captive to the Salvage Nation is 'captive' to the perversions they stand for. In each case, therefore, the logic of the allegory identifies the heroines with their antagonists. In fact, Spenser normally depicts good characters as captive or assailed at those points where they have fallen or are falling into evil. Problems only arise at those points where the evil is truly external. Amoret, for example, is the victim of the character Lust but seems not to fall victim to the vice he represents.

Regarding the second question, unprotected beauty may indeed be assailed and perverted. That is the point of Spenser's argument. It is not a question of attributing praise or blame. In this world of disorder, men may fall through no immediate fault of their own, beauty may be attacked just because it is beautiful. If there is a certain sadness in this reunion of lovers, the darkness obscuring their identities even from themselves, it is the tragedy of all art—of beauty almost captured, of Orpheus almost reunited with his Eurydice. Perhaps Serena and Calepine cannot find happiness until Calidore has brought the Flower of Courtesy back into the world and thus repaired that first injury which set their whole sad story in motion. Perhaps only when it is safe to pick flowers and the song of the thrush no longer causes men to lose their ways can their love flourish. But one thing is certain: Calepine's defeat of the false love of the Salvages symbolically lays the way open for Calidore's discovery of true love.

---

[23] Walter F. Staton, Jr., 'Italian Pastorals and the Conclusion of the Serena Story', *SEL*, 6 (1966), 35–42, takes a completely opposite view, attributing Serena's silence to her ungratefulness: 'Though her reputation is healed through self-restraint, her basic character remains unchanged: her blaming of the faithful Calepine for her misfortunes shows this very neatly.' Staton's argument that she remains fatally self-centred seems hard to justify except by reference to analogues outside the poem. It may be, of course, that Spenser wishes to show her at the opposite extreme from her state when she dallied with Calepine in the woods.

3. Cupid

Serena's capture by the Salvage Nation when she has wandered from the protection of Timias, terrified by the spectacle of Cupid's power, takes us back to her previous ill-starred encounter with the Blatant Beast. It also has its parallels with Amoret's story, since Amoret wanders off from the protection of Britomart, the ideal of marital chastity, and falls into the clutches of Lust. The parallels with Amoret's situation are instructive and I think Spenser expects us to take them into account.[24] One parallel with Serena's story, the crucial one, we have so far noticed only in connection with Mirabella—the House of Busyrane. Both involve a familiar romance motif: the rescue from a magician, like the rescue at the stake, is common in romance.[25] In both instances, a girl has fallen into the clutches of evil forces who intend putting her to death.

Before Roche's notable study, most scholars saw Busyrane simply as a figure of lust, and the masque of Cupid as a representation of the fierceness and unreason of that god. There *was* a tradition which made Cupid fierce and cruel,[26] but an equally strong tradition associated with the courts of love depicted him as reasonable, dignified, and often merciful.[27] The Cupid of the masque *seems* fierce and cruel to Amoret and to us, but we forget that there is another way of looking at Cupid. Roche's contribution to the debate centring on the House of Busyrane has in a sense pointed out to Spenser's readers that the poet is deliberately playing off one tradition (the reasoning Cupid of the courts of

[24] There is also a general parallel between the flights of Florimell and Serena. Apart from verbal echoes, the situations themselves are remarkably similar. Florimell escapes from perverted love only to be assailed by the same thing in another shape, as she floats at sea with the fisherman (finally the same thing appears in *every* shape: Proteus carries her off). Serena escapes from what she thinks is dangerous, only to fall victim to something far worse, and much further from ordered society than where she was before.

[25] See Edwin Greenlaw, 'Britomart at the House of Busyrane', *Variorum*, 3: 359–66. He identifies striking parallels in *Amadis of Gaul*, the Vulgate Lancelot, *Arthur of Little Britain*, and others.

[26] See C. S. Lewis, 'Spenser's Cruel Cupid', in *Studies in Medieval and Renaissance Literature* (Cambridge, 1966), pp. 164–8; Neilson, *Origins*, pp. 24–6. On the Triumph of Cupid see Fowler, *Courts of Love*, pp. 111ff. Cf. W. L. Renwick, *Variorum*, 3: 301.

[27] Erwin Panofsky's chapter 'Blind Cupid', *Studies in Iconology* (New York, 1939), pp. 95–128, does not cover this category of representations of Cupid. This Cupid frequently takes on the appearance of a feudal ruler. He may still be called a god (as in Nicole de Margival's *Panthère d'Amours*: see Neilson, *Origins*, pp. 69ff.), or he may become simply a King of Love (see Lewis, *Allegory of Love*, pp. 120ff.).

love) against the other (the unreasoning triumph of Cupid).
Amoret is as confused as we are. That the procession is indeed
ambiguous can be established fairly easily. Take this stanza, for
instance:

> The whiles a most delitious harmony,
> In full straunge notes was sweetly heard to sound,
> That the rare sweetnesse of the melody
> The feeble senses wholly did confound,
> And the fraile soule in deepe delight nigh dround:
> And when it ceast, shrill trompets loud did bray,
> That their report did farre away rebound,
> And when they ceast, it gan againe to play,
> The whiles the maskers marched forth in trim aray.
>
> (III. xii. 6)

Amoret makes the mistake of seeing only *discordia* in the *discordia
concors*. She forgets that there is a martial element even in love—
that the 'shrill trompets' play their part in creating harmony as
well. Instead of seeing the triumph of love (with herself as the
spoil surrendered to her victor knight) as a figure of convention,
she accepts it as the literal truth. As a result, she retreats into
herself, or into the clutches of Busyrane, the 'abuse' of marriage.
Spenser, then, is investigating the metaphorical presentation of
love—one aspect of poetic language in fact. In Book VI he picks
up this same investigation again. Exploring the misapprehensions
of Mirabella, who is set on living out the role of the hard-hearted
mistress, and of Serena, who does not understand the justice of
Cupid's sentence, he goes on to consider the effects of a whole
nation acting out the metaphors of love as war and destruction
and depredation.

Mirabella and Amoret oppose Cupid for different reasons, but
with similar results. In Amoret opposition to love springs from
fear. In Mirabella it springs from defiance. In Amoret, the opposition manifests itself in her own personal reaction to love: very
little attention is given to its effects on Scudamour. In Mirabella,
as we have seen, the point at issue is not the girl's *natural* development, but the *social* effects of her conduct. Put in other terms,
Amoret's inability to understand metaphor may have had
unfortunate psychological results, but Mirabella's misunderstanding calls the whole convention into question. The House of
Busyrane is itself a powerful argument against a particular conven-

tional treatment of love—love as war—even though Spenser does not choose to emphasize this aspect of the affair at this stage. But when Mirabella starts behaving like ladies she has read about in books, one begins to wonder whether the books themselves are really worth while, or at least one wishes that Mirabella's education were more than skin-deep, so that she could understand what she read. When the Salvage Nation abuses sonnet metaphors, the same pious hopes spring to the reader's mind. At first sight such language seems out of place, but its suitability soon becomes apparent. As the alliance of Blandamour and Paridell in Book IV makes clear, love-as-destruction may often ally itself with love-as-a-game. The 'love' of the artificial sonnet is both. The game of love becomes destructive through the metaphors it employs: the altar, the triumphal arch, the 'spoiles of Princes . . . which were in battel won'.

Now I do not think Spenser is saying that we should not write sonnets like that. After all, what is the *Faerie Queene* itself if not an attempt to describe life in terms of chivalric metaphor? But we make a fatal mistake if we expect literally to find St. George riding through the streets of London, or Britomart a commissioned officer in Elizabeth's army. If we confuse literature with life, we are bound to end either by condemning literature as a lie and a fraud, or by living out a set of standards which have no place in the everyday world of here-and-now. The Salvage Nation suffers from the latter confusion. Confusing the image with the reality it represents, they are guilty of a kind of idolatry. The satyrs of Book I, in a similar confusion, sought to worship Una. The dance of the Salvages becomes a dance of blood-lust. The wood, the realm of nature, trembles at the noise. These mad philistines, I suggest, are a parody of the society of the court which Spenser knew, and from which he retired. Significantly, Spenser will turn next to a society of men in touch with nature, presenting us with a vision of the perfect harmony which is sought by so few.

From an investigation of the social aspects of love, the focus has shifted again. It is not the perversion of *love* which interests Spenser so much as the perversion of what one can only describe as sensibility (an alien and anachronistic notion but one which will serve our turn). Behind love lies beauty, and beauty, its perfection beyond the reach of fallen man, can only find expression in metaphor, the imperfect approximation of perfect form. It is the poet's task to create metaphor, to shape the golden world of poetry. Spenser alluded to it at the opening of the book. He will return to the same topic at the end, alluding to the Blatant Beast:

> So now he raungeth through the world againe,
> And rageth sore in each degree and state;
> Ne any is, that may him now restraine,
> He growen is so great and strong of late,
> Barking and biting all that him doe bate,
> Albe they worthy blame, or cleare of crime:
> Ne spareth he most learned wits to rate,
> Ne spareth he the gentle Poets rime,
> But rends without regard of person of of time.
>
> Ne may this homely verse, of many meanest,
> Hope to escape his venemous despite,
> More then my former writs, all were they cleanest
> From blamefull blot, and free from all that wite,
> With which some wicked tongues did it backebite,
> And bring into a mighty Peres displeasure,
> That never so deserved to endite.
> Therfore do you my rimes keep better measure,
> And seeke to please, that now is counted wisemens threasure.
>
> (VI. xii. 40–1)

And suddenly Spenser's argument falls into place. Mirabella, the Salvage Nation, ultimately Turpine and the Blatant Beast—these are enemies of art, of *his* art, and of the world of the *Faerie Queene*. Book VI dramatizes the battle against the enemies of poetry.

V

The Flower of Courtesy

1. A pastoral oasis[1]

IF literary greatness consists in complexity to a purpose, profundity of thought and language, and rich patterns of ideas, we approach in the final cantos some of the greatest poetry Spenser ever wrote. These cantos have a complexity and a richness which make them a fitting and impressive conclusion to that part of Spenser's great plan actually brought to completion. While there are intrinsic reasons for this superiority, the structure of the book also tends to shift the thematic weight towards the concluding episodes. Calidore, long out of the action, reappears in Canto ix, and his return draws together the book's loose ends and half-finished narratives, leading us into what C. S. Lewis would have called the 'allegorical core'.[2] Not only does Book vi seem to abound in incomplete stories but it also exploits to an exceptional degree the method of cumulation which is so much a part of Spenser's technique. Throughout the *Faerie Queene* we are continually asked to evaluate episodes in terms of other episodes, to notice parallels and absorb their significance; we are constantly doubling back on our tracks as we read. The technique is based less upon precedent, the application of old lessons to new situations, than upon revaluation, the reassessment of old lessons in the light of changed circumstances. A recent critic,[3] in a felicitous phrase, has described Spenser as 'the poet of second thoughts'. In the *Faerie Queene* events repeat themselves, always in slightly different configurations and often with strikingly different signification. These techniques are employed in Book vi to two ends—first, to present through the poetry of reconciliation a new

---

[1] The term is Renato Poggioli's: 'The Oaten Flute', *Harvard Library Bulletin*, 11 (1957), 147–84.

[2] *The Allegory of Love* (Oxford, 1936), p. 353.

[3] William Blissett, 'Florimell and Marinell', *SEL*, 5 (1965), 87–104.

vision of harmony; second, to explore the nature of poetry and poetic response. The two themes are developed and resolved in the book's final cantos.

With the beginning of the pastoral episode, at Canto ix, there is a significant change in the mood of the book and the rhythm of its argument. A movement predominantly linear is replaced by a movement primarily circular, spiralling out from the Dance of the Graces in the centre of the three pastoral cantos. This new quality of the verse and the allegory, a kind of added dimension, presents special problems of critical method, especially when combined with a tightly knit fabric of ideas. I am not suggesting that in the earlier part of the book this dimension is lacking. The constant echoes and reverberations and ironies with which Spenser interrupts the linear movement of his verse are present there too. But it is in the final cantos that these complexities multiply, ultimately spreading out, like ripples from a stone thrown in a stream, to form a pattern. And since the final cantos bring the book's principal concerns into focus, our analysis of Book vi, and especially our examination of the ideas in Book vi, must be centred there.

To speak of a work in spatial terms, to allude to circles and lines, is to invite accusations of impropriety. I shall not attempt to defend my terms here, but let my argument be their defence. Any discussion of literary *form* must in itself beg questions about space and volume, and what we mean when we say that a work has *shape*. I shall suggest that the Dance of the Graces is itself a representation of artistic form, that what Calidore sees is the embodiment of formal order in the art of the dance. It is significant that Spenser chooses the dance for such a representation: the shifting patterns of the dance are held and contained within the perimeter of the dancers, much as the shifting relationships of meaning are contained within the stanzas and books of Spenser's own poem.

We shall find as we examine the Dance of the Graces that Book vi is built upon paradox. That, too, hardly comes as a surprise; the technique is fundamental to Renaissance sensibility, especially in its neo-Platonic strain, and it certainly forms an essential part of Spenser's method.[4] Indeed, all of the *Faerie Queene* expresses a paradox, summed up in the personage of Mutability, 'For all that

4 See above, p. 8.

moveth, doth in *Change* delight: / But thence-forth all shall rest eternally'. In the figure of Pastorella, too, the paradox of time and eternity finds a momentary embodiment. Behind this great central dilemma of the human condition stand lesser questions—man's conduct in society, the meaning of social order, the nature of human love. The book itself does not resolve all the problems it raises, but no work of literature ever does. Perhaps, though, it provides us with the mythic equipment to make our own resolutions, or to face their incompletenesses.

Some inkling of the complexity of what is to follow is expressed, paradoxically, in the very simplicity of the plot. So many are our questions by the time we reach Canto ix that the ease with which Spenser begins this new story seems to foretell a larger structure of argument. To leave the shadowy world of the cannibals and to enter on this new canto is to imagine ourselves suddenly in sunlight and on well-known ground. Not only is the outline of the plot familiar to us from its countless pastoral predecessors,[5] but Canto ix moves through a symmetrical series of events, in the centre of which are Meliboe's criticism of court life and Calidore's decision to remain in the shepherds' world.

The opening of a new canto often sums up or repeats the argument of the canto before it. We need not be surprised, then, that Canto ix opens with a direct allusion to the process of composition itself. There is a certain reassurance in the use of the familiar image of the poem as field, the poet as ploughman—a sense of method and control:

> Now turne againe my teme thou jolly swayne,
> Backe to the furrow which I lately left;
> I lately left a furrow, one or twayne
> Unplough'd, the which my coulter hath not cleft:
> Yet seem'd the soyle both fayre and frutefull eft,
> As I it past, that were too great a shame,
> That so rich frute should be from us bereft;
> Besides the great dishonour and defame,
> Which should befall to *Calidores* immortall name.

But even in the disciplined and abundant fields of poetry we must not be lulled into a false sense of security. The gentle ambiguity of the final lines (do these furrows hold Calidore's honour or his

---

[5] On the pastoral background to the work, see *Variorum*, vol. 6, *passim*, W. W. Greg, *Pastoral Poetry and Pastoral Drama* (London, 1906), and Chapter x below.

dishonour?) reminds us that we must read attentively, and perhaps announces in Calidore's role an ambiguity ultimately insoluble. Calidore enters the shepherds' world in pursuit of the Blatant Beast, whom he has pursued 'from court . . . to the citties . . . to the townes . . . from the townes into the countrie . . . And from the country back to private farms'.

> From thence into the open fields he fled,
> Whereas the Heardes were keeping of their neat,
> And shepheards singing to their flockes, that fed,
> Layes of sweete love and youthes delightful heat:
> Him thether eke for all his fearefull threat
> He followed fast, and chaced him so nie,
> That to the folds, where sheepe at night doe seat,
> And to the litle cots, where shepherds lie
> In winters wrathfull time, he forced him to flie.
>
> (VI. ix. 4)

Calidore's arrival in the pastoral world is not the result of a turning aside from the quest. It is an accident: his pursuit of the Blatant Beast by chance brings him to the shepherds. 'There on a day as he pursew'd the chace, / He chaunst to spy a sort of shepheard groomes, / Playing on pypes, and caroling apace.' Like Don Quixote among the rustics,[6] Calidore, being 'nothing nice', does not disdain the shepherds' offer of hospitality. To pause is not to neglect his quest; he stops only to refresh himself. But even as he does so, he catches sight of Pastorella in the midst of the shepherd swains.

Arranged like the pattern of some dance, the shepherds sit in circles, the men on the outside, the women in the middle. And in the very centre sits the damsel, like 'some miracle of heavenly hew', 'environ'd with a girland . . . of lovely lasses'. Serena, we remember, seemed like a heavenly gift to the savage cannibals. But the standards of the shepherds are not the lopsided standards of the Salvage Nation. In certain senses, Pastorella really has 'descended' to the shepherds, not simply as a miraculous visitant from paradise (though she may be that), but also as a person of noble blood among the peasants, a fact hinted at just a few

---

[6] *Don Quixote*, trans. J. M. Cohen (Harmondsworth, Middx., 1950), p. 84. The closest parallel to the whole episode and perhaps one of its sources is of course Erminia's stay among the shepherds, *Gerusalemme Liberata*, Canto vii. Note especially the parallels between the speeches of Calidore and Erminia, and see my discussion of Fortune, Chapter ix, below.

stanzas later. And we know, from his encounter with Tristram, that Calidore is well able to recognize noble blood when he sees it. Pastorella's principal suitor is Coridon, 'Yet neither she for him, nor other none / Did care a whit . . . Though meane her lot, yet higher did her mind ascend' (vi. ix. 10). The poet seems to be drawing a rather audacious parallel between Pastorella and Mirabella, the girl whose refusal to bestow her love on her suitors called down the wrath of Cupid upon her head. But the differences in Pastorella's situation are instructive, and they incidentally remind us that pastoral is actually the least egalitarian of literary modes. Coridon is an unsuitable match for Pastorella both because he is a coward and also, more importantly, because he is of humble birth. Pastorella, with the help of God and nature, unwittingly preserves the purity of her aristocratic blood. Mirabella, on the other hand, of humble birth herself, tyrannizes over her aristocratic suitors, thus making a mockery of precedence and orderly hierarchy.

The effect of Pastorella's beauty on Calidore is electric:

> So stood he still long gazing thereupon,
> Ne any will had thence to move away,
> Although his quest were farre afore him gon;
> But after he had fed, yet did he stay,
> And sate there still, untill the flying day
> Was farre forth spent, discoursing diversly
> Of sundry things, as fell, to worke delay;
> And evermore his speach he did apply
> To th'heards, but meant them to the damzels fantazy.
>
> (vi. ix. 12)

Clearly his stay among the shepherds may prove longer than he expected. His skill in conversation, directed at the shepherds, is nevertheless meant for Pastorella. The quest seems far away. As we read of Meliboe's family and their guest gathering round the fire in the evening, the words of Despair, that other great rhetorician, come back to our memory, with their promises of 'sleep after toil, port after stormy seas, ease after war . . .'.

2. *Meliboe and Coridon*

The process of Calidore's downfall is documented for us in the fifteen or so stanzas devoted to his conversation with Meliboe. They are important stanzas, not because they suggest to us

Calidore's true motives for remaining among the shepherds—
which they clearly do not—but because they show the ease with
which a man experienced in the affairs of the world, loyal to his
sovereign, impeccable in his conduct, may talk himself into
believing anything for the sake of love. The conversation of
Meliboe and Calidore does not provide us with a profound
philosophy of pastoral; it is a slightly mocking, somewhat
sympathetic treatment of human foibles. The narrator can afford
this moral laxity, since ultimately Calidore's actions will be
vindicated in a somewhat unexpected way.[7]

Calidore takes up the conversation:

> How much (sayd he) more happie is the state,
> In which ye father here doe dwell at ease,
> Leading a life so free and fortunate,
> From all the tempests of these worldly seas,
> Which tosse the rest in daungerous disease;
> Where warres, and wreckes, and wicked enmitie
> Doe them afflict, which no man can appease,
> That certes I your happinesse envie,
> And wish my lot were plast in such felicitie.   (VI. ix. 19)

His final words here may state very plainly that his lot is *not* that
of Meliboe, but the seeds of temptation are already present. The
stanza reads like a set speech. Wars, wrecks, freedom, felicity—
we have heard all these things before in so many eulogies of the
country life and criticisms of the city, and they come rolling off
Calidore's tongue with just a little too much facility, just a little
too much glibness. The stanza *is* a set speech; the previous stanza
implies as much:

> The gentle knight, as he that did excell
> In courtesie, and well could doe and say,
> For so great kindnesse as he found that day,
> Gan greatly thanke his host and his good wife;
> And drawing thence his speach another way,
> Gan highly to commend the happie life.
>
> (VI. ix. 18)

---

[7] Harry Berger, Jr. ('A Secret Discipline: *The Faerie Queene*, Book VI', in William
Nelson, ed. *Form and Convention in the Poetry of Edmund Spenser* (New York, 1961))
maintains that 'Melibee's "morality" is in fact the same kind of excuse for laziness
used by the moral pastors of the *Shepheardes Calender*; it is a recreative withdrawal
from care.' This judgement is in my opinion far closer to the truth than the common
view which makes Meliboe's way of life wholly good.

'And now there will follow A Speech in Praise of the Good Life.'
It is almost like some rhetorical exercise. Calidore *draws* his speech
another way, the words come readily. As in his encounter with
Calepine and Serena, his ease of conversation is both a major
asset and a liability. One begins to fear that he might deceive
himself with his own eloquence. Certainly a man worn out by the
trials and misfortunes of a difficult quest is, as we learned from
the Red Cross Knight's experiences, easy prey to specious
rhetoric, perhaps even his own.[8]

Meliboe, as his reply tells us, is content with his simple lot,
'so taught of nature, which doth litle need / Of forreine helpes
to lifes due nourishment'.

> Sometimes I hunt the Fox, the vowed foe
> Unto my Lambes, and him dislodge away;
> Sometime the fawne I practise from the Doe,
> Or from the Goat her kidde how to convay;
> Another while I baytes and nets display,
> The birds to catch, or fishes to beguyle:
> And when I wearie am, I downe doe lay
> My limbes in every shade, to rest from toyle,
> And drinke of every brooke, when thirst my throte doth boyle.
>
> (VI. ix. 23)

Even Meliboe is given to superlatives. He drinks of *every* brook
and rests in *every* shade. There is a grand and improbable profusion, more fitting to literature than to life, in the daily round
which he describes. As with Serena and her Salvages, and Mirabella and her suitors, a nagging suspicion lingers in our minds
that something is not quite right, that somehow fact and fiction
have become muddled, that Calidore has stepped into the pages
of a pastoral romance and that Meliboe and the rest are really
characters from books, not people.

The old shepherd turns to the court, where he spent ten useless
years and, as he puts it, 'did sell my selfe for yearely hire'. Calidore
hangs on his every word, for he has found his arcadia, and all his
efforts will be to remain. 'All this worlds gay showes, which we
admire, / Be but vain shadowes to this safe retyre', he declares,
looking for 'meanes to worke his mind, / And to insinuate his
harts desire'. It is not arcadia pure and simple that attracts him:

[8] See Ernest Sirluck, 'A Note on the Rhetoric of Spenser's "Despair" ', *MP*, 47
(1949), 8–11.

in fact his arcadia, his 'harts desire', is really the girl. For the sake of Pastorella he rides roughshod over logic, ignoring the lessons of his quest, talking himself into an obviously false position. Meliboe takes up the argument:

> In vaine . . . doe men
> The heavens of their fortunes fault accuse,
> Sith they know best, what is the best for them:
> For they to each such fortune doe diffuse,
> As they doe know each can most aptly use.
> For not that, which men covet most, is best,
> Nor that thing worst, which men do most refuse;
> But fittest is, that all contented rest
> With that they hold: each hath his fortune in his brest.
>
> It is the mynd, that maketh good or ill,
> That maketh wretch or happie, rich or poore:
> For some, that hath abundance at his will,
> Hath not enough, but wants in greatest store;
> And other, that hath litle, askes no more,
> But in that litle is both rich and wise.
> For wisedome is most riches; fooles therefore
> They are, which fortunes doe by vowes devize,
> Sith each unto himselfe his life may fortunize.
>
> (VI. ix. 29–30)

And so it is that Calidore reaches his decision:

> Since then in each mans self (said *Calidore*)
> It is, to fashion his owne lyfes estate,
> Give leave awhyle, good father, in this shore
> To rest my barcke, which hath bene beaten late
> With stormes of fortune and tempestuous fate,
> In seas of troubles and of toylesome paine,
> That whether quite from them for to retrate
> I shall resolve, or backe to turne againe,
> I may here with your selfe some small repose obtaine.
>
> (VI. ix. 31)

The one important point to bear in mind throughout this remarkable conversation is that Pastorella is the constant object of Calidore's attentions. He sees and admires Pastorella before his final decision to remain among the shepherds. The rest is rationalization. The process of this rationalization can be traced through Calidore's constant refusal to take account of Fortune. The picture of self-sufficiency which Meliboe paints may be all well and good for literary shepherds but it clearly has no application in the world outside. Book VI has shown us very clearly that men are not self-sufficient, that the vagaries of Fortune can destroy a man or save him at will. 'My haplesse case / Is not occasiond through my misdesert, / But through misfortune'—the words of the captive squire might stand as a kind of epigraph to the whole book. Calidore came upon Calepine and Serena because 'it was his fortune, not his fault', but the fact of the Beast's bite was equally a fact, regardless of its causes. It is fortune which preserves Pastorella among the shepherds, which brings Calepine to Serena's rescue, causes the discovery of Pastorella. This same power is destined to destroy the shepherds' world, Meliboe along with it. Perhaps Meliboe's mention, pastoral commonplace though it is, of the capture of birds and fish and the luring of offspring from the beasts should strike us as a warning of greater entrapments to come. Certainly Calidore himself is mistaken. His suggestion that Meliboe and his comrades do not fear 'foes, or fortunes wrackfull yre' is ironic indeed in the light of subsequent events. Sidney's Basilius made the same mistake.

Calidore's most revealing utterance is his last, since it is based on a complete misunderstanding of Meliboe's earlier remarks.[9] 'In vaine', Meliboe had said, 'doe men / The heavens of their fortunes fault accuse.' One cannot blame the heavens for one's own misfortunes (which is just what Calidore earlier seemed inclined to do) since they know best what each man is suited for. Meliboe is of course expressing the idea, so eloquently set forth by Boethius, that what imperfect man construes as capricious fate is in fact the working of God's providence, invisible to man in its totality, and that to rail against it is both foolish and blasphemous. But when Meliboe goes on to declare that 'each hath his fortune in his breast', he is by no means denying his earlier statement. He is simply suggesting that each person is free to pursue his life as he himself decides, with the unstated qualification 'subject to the preordained pattern already mentioned'. Calidore, impatient to turn the conversation his way, ignores this qualification, and turns Meliboe's tentative endorsement of free will into something resembling a free for all. 'Since the decision

---

[9] Cf. William Nelson's introduction to his edition *Selected Poetry of Edmund Spenser* (New York, 1964), p. xxvii.

rests with me, since I am altogether self sufficient,' he seems to say, 'I'll stay.'

'It is the mynd, that maketh good or ill, / That maketh wretch or happie, rich or poore', says Meliboe. His remark, in which the terms 'rich or poore' are in fact grammatically in apposition but rhetorically in a metaphorical relationship to 'wretch or happie', is too close to Calidore's experience of the court to allow him to see 'rich or poore' as anything but literal statements: to him the rich are wretched, the poor happy, which of course is not what Meliboe means at all. So the whole sense of the stanza becomes perverted. Instead of the simple, age-old statement 'wisdome is most riches',[10] Calidore understands that worldly riches are a bar to happiness and a bar to wisdom. Thus he is faced with a choice between worldly ambition and spiritual enrichment, his misinterpretation of the final line of the earlier stanza leading him to suppose that the choice is entirely within his power. Is not knowledge, wisdom, the way to heaven?

But even the Hermit, who finally chose the life of the spirit, had once done noble deeds. So had Aldus. For a knight, contemplation can only be a reward for action, not its substitute. Calidore, by deciding to remain among the shepherds, is forced into denying his social responsibilities and with them his vow to the Faerie Queene.

Meliboe's subsequent rejection of Calidore's gold is not only a familiar repetition of a literary commonplace, but also a quietly ironic comment on the level of Calidore's understanding of the old man's remarks.[11] The reason for his stay is obvious enough; it is not Meliboe's philosophy but Pastorella's beauty that causes him to stay,[12] and little by little to forget the customs of the

---

[10] Osgood (*Variorum*, 6: 241) cites Proverbs 3: 3–16; 8: 18–21; 24: 3–4.

[11] The paradox of the term 'Golden Age' itself did not escape the attention of commentators. See Harry Levin, *The Myth of the Golden Age in the Renaissance* (Bloomington, Ind., 1969), pp. 22–4. Some instances of the poets' ambivalence towards money have been usefully assembled by Irving D. Blum, 'Money Imagery in English Renaissance Poetry', *SRen*, 8 (1962), 144–54.

[12] Meliboe's philosophy has application only in a world not subject to Fortune. His remarks, a compendium of classical opinion (see *Variorum*, 6: 240–1, where Upton mentions Homer, Plato, Juvenal and Plautus), are based largely on Juvenal's tenth satire: 'Is there nothing then that men shall pray for? If you ask advice, you will allow the heavenly powers themselves to appraise what is profitable for us and useful for our interests. For not delights but what is most meet for us will the gods bestow, they love man better than he loves himself. . . . Still, that you may also prefer some prayer and [sacrifice] . . . you must petition for a sound mind in a sound

court. Each day, 'feeding on the bayt of his own bane', he goes
to the fields with Pastorella, 'During which time he did her
entertaine / With all kind courtesies, he could invent',

> But she that never had acquainted beene
> With such queint usage, fit for Queenes and Kings,
> Ne ever had such knightly service seene,
> But being bred under base shepheards wings,
> Had ever learn'd to love the lowly things,
> Did litle whit regard his courteous guize,
> But cared more for *Colins* carolings
> Then all that he could doe, or ever devize:
> His layes, his loves, his lookes she did them all despize.
>
> (VI. ix. 35)

Calidore's action in putting aside his knightly armour brings us
face to face with the central moral dilemma of the whole quest.
In the context of Calidore's quest, the action is culpable in the
most obvious of senses: abandonment of the badge and trappings
of knighthood is moral cowardice of the worst kind, constitutes
an affront to Gloriana, and implies that Calidore has forgotten all
about his quest. Our memories inevitably carry us back to Book 1
and Redcross and Duessa. They also, of course, carry us back to
Aladine and Priscilla, and Calepine and Serena, whose imprudent
behaviour formed a pair of emblematic prefigurations of the
larger pastoral episode. Aladine and Calepine were less at fault
than Calidore, since no quest was involved. Yet they suffered
mightily.

If the removal of his armour is attributable to Calidore's fault,
his arrival among the shepherds may be laid to his fortune. One
aspect of his arrival seems to escape the attention of commentators. This is the inescapable fact that, willy-nilly, Calidore himself

---

body. Pray for a brave spirit that stands not in fear of death, that reckons length
of life as the least among nature's blessings, that can bear any toils, that knows not
anger, is stirred not by desire, and holds the sufferings of Hercules and his cruel
labours to be better than all a despot's joys of love and feasts and quilt of eiderdown.
I prescribe only what you can give yourself. For assuredly the one road to the life
of peace lies through virtue. If we are but wise, O chance, thy potency is vanished;
it is we that make thee a goddess, and throne thee in the sky.' (Lines 346–66, in
Thirteen Satires of Juvenal, trans. S. G. Owen (London, 1903).) I have quoted this
passage in order to emphasize Meliboe's omissions. A more powerful argument in
favour of Calidore's continuing his quest could scarcely be imagined: 'Semita
certe tranquillae per virtutem patet unica vitae.' Calidore, it seems, is seeking a
short cut.

chases the Blatant Beast into this idyllic pastoral. Spenser says so, in so many words. Calidore arrived in arcadia, we are told, 'as he pursew'd the chace'. The turn of phrase is an almost exact repetition of one used on the occasion of an earlier intrusion, on Calepine and Serena. Here are the two passages:

> So as he was pursuing of his quest
> He chaunst to come whereas a jolly Knight,
> In covert shade him selfe did safely rest.   (VI. iii. 20)

> There on a day as he pursew'd the chace,
> He chaunst to spy a sort of shepheard groomes,
> Playing on pypes, and caroling apace.   (VI. ix. 5)

Calidore's arrival, echoing the earlier tragedy of Serena and Calepine, seems somehow to sully the beautiful paradise he has found and to expose it to the outside world.

But while the Knight of Courtesy is in a way to blame for the ensuing disasters, and while his removal of his armour is in some sense a symbol of his error, at the same time we are aware of the fact that this armour is merely the *outward* sign of his role as the Knight of Courtesy. We have learned to beware of mere appearances. Courtesy often reveals itself in the least likely places, unheralded and without the benefit of comely exterior. Conversely, an attitude which links courtesy with mere politeness has already been called in question, especially when Calidore interrupts Calepine and Serena in the third canto. Clearly Calidore is not equipped to do battle against the enemies of courtesy if he himself does not know what true courtesy is. Guyon went to the Castle of Alma to learn temperance; Redcross visited the House of Holiness.

As the reader must already sense, Pastorella possesses the secret of true courtesy. It is through love for her that Calidore will be vouchsafed knowledge. While we may blame him as much as we like for abandoning his quest in this fashion, it is evident that in putting off his armour Calidore also repudiates courtly superficialities and prepares himself to discover the truth. Lear, in conclave with the Fool and Poor Tom, must first slough off the state of moral confusion in which we first found him before he can be invested with a new set of moral beliefs, a new view of the world. In entering the world of the shepherds, Calidore abandons his quest for the Beast but begins his quest for the positive element which the Beast is attacking—the true flower of courtesy. In this context the heroic quest becomes an irrelevancy, and the train of events bringing evil into the Garden becomes a triumphant *felix culpa*. Calidore is wrong to abandon his quest; he has an obligation to his sovereign and to the knightly code. But as a result he woos and wins Pastorella and he is vouchsafed the vision on Mount Acidale—a vision of harmony which must inevitably include also his Queen, indeed the universe itself. In winning the flower of courtesy, Calidore brings the power to combat the Blatant Beast into an exhausted and uneasy world. He gains the power to complete his quest even as he abandons the quest itself.

Meanwhile, Calidore goes out of his way to preserve the shepherds' harmony. He praises Coridon, he defers to him in the dance. We see (or think we see) in Calidore's behaviour the mark of true and guileless friendship, similar to the exchange of honours between Cambell and Triamond during Satyrane's tournament. By contrast, Coridon is like the ridiculous and stupid witch's son who brought gifts to Florimell.[13] Even after Coridon has failed to worst Calidore in a wrestling match, even after he had lost Pastorella to his rival, harmony is still preserved by Calidore's prudence and courtesy. Having obtained the love of Pastorella, Calidore, we are told, 'menaged so well, / That he of all the rest, which there did dwell, / Was favoured, and to her grace commended'. As Spenser, following Guazzo, takes care to point out, 'courtesie amongst the rudest breeds / Good will and favour.'[14]

[13]   Then all with one consent did yeeld the prize
      To *Triamond* and *Cambell* as the best.
      But *Triamond* to *Cambell* it relest.
      And *Cambell* it to *Triamond* transferd;
      Each labouring t'advance the others gest,
      And make his praise before his owne preferd. (IV.iv.36)

      Oft from the forrest wildings he did bring,
      Whose sides empurpled were with smiling red,
      And oft young birds, which he had taught to sing
      His mistresse prayses, sweetly caroled,
      Girlonds of flowres sometimes for her faire hed
      He fine would dight; sometimes the squirell wild
      He brought to her in bands, as conquered
      To be her thrall, his fellow servant vild. (III.vii.17)

[14] See *Variorum*, 6: 244.

3. The Graces

Condemnation of Calidore's behaviour is given explicit expression at the opening of Canto x, in one of those 'semi-official' statements by the narrator.

> Who now does follow the foule *Blatant Beast*,
> Whilest *Calidore* does follow that faire Mayd,
> Unmyndfull of his vow and high beheast,
> Which by the Faery Queene was on him layd,
> That he should never leave, nor be delayd
> From chacing him, till he had it attchieved?
> But now entrapt of love, which him betrayd,
> He mindeth more, how he may be relieved
> With grace from her, whose love his heart hath sore
> engrieved.

But even at this juncture the narrator's blame strikes a somewhat ironic note. The love of Pastorella, the corruption of court living, the promise of peace and tranquillity—these are compelling reasons for choice of the pastoral life. We might add that Pastorella, as we discover later, is not really a country girl at all. Surely, then, the case is altered. 'Ne certes mote he greatly blamed be', says the narrator,

> For who had tasted once (as oft did he)
> The happy peace, which there doth overflow,
> And prov'd the perfect pleasures, which doe grow,
> Amongst poore hyndes, in hils, in woods, in dales,
> Would never more delight in painted show
> Of such false blisse, as there is set for stales,
> T'entrap unwary fooles in their eternall bales. (VI. x. 3)

In these lines we hear something of the tone of *Colin Clouts Come Home Again*, and behind the poem we perhaps catch sight of the poet himself in Ireland. It is not my purpose to interpret Spenser's work in terms of his own life, but the feeling that Book VI is in some sense the *apologia* of an Elizabethan intellectual who could not quite stomach the London life and London ambition seems to me inescapable. Just as in *Colin Clouts Come Home Again* the contrast between the glory of the sovereign and the despicable behaviour of her courtiers makes the court a centre simultaneously of good and of evil, so Spenser moves freely from praise of the quiet life to praise of his sovereign. The transition moves via

Pastorella, one glance at whom would dazzle those brought up on the 'false blisse' of the court,

> That never more they should endure the shew
> Of that sunne-shine, that makes them look askew.
> Ne ought in all that world of beauties rare,
> (Save onely *Glorianaes* heavenly hew
> To which what can compare?) can it compare.   (VI. x. 4)

The Queen and Pastorella are *compared*: the reiterated word in the final line drives the point home. The effect of the comparison, of course, is to lessen the extent of Calidore's transgression. In a sense, Spenser seems to say, Calidore has abandoned the quest in order to pursue something markedly similar to Gloriana's beauty. (We are reminded of Arthur's pursuit of Florimell perhaps, as some critics have suggested, because her beauty is like that of Gloriana.) The light imagery which now begins to gather round Pastorella[15] reminds us of the light imagery commonly employed in tributes to the Queen.[16]

At this point Spenser presses his advantage home. The whole context of his argument changes. The action moves directly into the Dance of the Graces, a complete redefinition of all that has gone before and a glorious vindication of Calidore's decision.

> He chaunst to come, far from all peoples troad,
> Unto a place, whose pleasaunce did appere
> To passe all others, on the earth which were:
> For all that ever was by natures skill
> Devized to worke delight, was gathered there,
> And there by her were poured forth at fill,
> As if this to adorne, she all the rest did pill.
>
> It was an hill plaste in an open plaine,
> That round about was bordered with a wood
> Of matchlesse hight, that seem'd th'earth to disdaine,
> In which all trees of honour stately stood,
> And did all winter as in sommer bud,
> Spredding pavilions for the birds to bowre,
> Which in their lower braunches sung aloud;
> And in their tops the soring hauke did towre,
> Sitting like King of fowles in majesty and powre.
>
> (VI. x. 5-6)

[15] E.g. VI.ix.9.

[16] For an example, see Sir John Davies, *Hymnes of Astraea*, XIV, in Elkin Calhoun Wilson, *England's Eliza* (Cambridge, Mass., 1939), pp. 266-7.

The violence of the word 'pill' might surprise us, but this, we gather, is pillage in a very good cause. It is a Golden Age scene where everything is hyperbole: the trees are taller than everywhere else, the birds are kings among birds, the season is always at its richest, everything 'at fill'.

In Ovid's picture of the Golden Age the earth gives up its fruits in spontaneous richness, no plough wounds the soil, the trees exude honey and it is always spring: 'ver erat aeternum'.[17] Interestingly, Spenser's version of this same Golden Age largely involves definition by exclusion. When it is winter elsewhere it is nevertheless summer here.[18] Indeed, the reference to pillage almost implies that *because* it is winter elsewhere it is summer here. At the foot of the hill a stream flows, 'Unmard with ragged mosse or filthy mud, / Ne mote wylde beastes, ne mote the ruder clowne / Thereto approch, ne filth mote therein drowne: / But Nymphes and Faeries by the bancks did sit'. This stream is the traditional dividing line between the fallen world and the vision of paradise, the River of Paradise of the *Divine Comedy* or *Pearl*. Mount Acidale itself is related to a well-known *topos*, the hill of the Muses— 'That pleasant Mount', says Spenser in Book I (x. 54), 'that is for ay / Through famous Poets verse each where renound, / On which the thrise three learned Ladies play.' Renwick cites Ovid and Claudian,[19] but to these we might add poets nearer home, among them Gavin Douglas, whose Muses dance in 'ane meid quhair alkin flouris grew' and 'schaddowit with Ceder treis'—a place where all the works of nature are gathered together in unequalled abundance.[20] It is the same scene Keats was to employ, with his own modifications, three hundred years later in the 'Ode to Psyche', though with one significant difference. Whereas the 'windless bowers' of Keats and Shelley, like the pastoral world of 'Vivamus mea Lesbia atque amemus', represent a withdrawal

---

[17] Levin, *Golden Age*, pp. 19–25. The Greek background of the myth is illuminatingly discussed by W. K. C. Guthrie, *In the Beginning* (Ithaca, N.Y., 1957), pp. 63–79.

[18] The substitution of summer for spring is perhaps a concession to the English, or Irish, climate. Levin, p. 66, cites a similar example from Drayton's *Muses' Elysium*. Note that Spenser's choice of imagery here brings pastoral and heroic together: the Golden Age scene is depicted as a knightly tournament, with 'trees of honour', 'spredding pavilions' with their spectator birds, and the hawk 'like King of fowles' looking on from his raised vantage point.

[19] *Variorum*, 6: 245.

[20] *Palace of Honour*, lines 1140, 1146, in *Shorter Poems*, ed. Priscilla J. Bawcutt Edinburgh, 1967).

from the cruelties of the world, Spenser's Earthly Paradise reaches upwards towards a new truth. Keats, characteristically, sets his paradise in a valley, Spenser on a hilltop.

> And on the top thereof a spacious plaine
> Did spred it selfe, to serve to all delight,
> Either to daunce, when they to daunce would faine,
> Or else to course about their bases light;
> Ne ought there wanted, which for pleasure might
> Desired be, or thence to banish bale:
> So pleasauntly the hill with equall hight,
> Did seeme to overlooke the lowly vale;
> Therefore it rightly cleeped was mount *Acidale*.   (VI. x. 8)

On Mount Acidale, we learned in Book IV (v. 5), Venus was 'with the pleasant Graces wont to play'. We may not have imagined her playing anything so unclassical as a variant of prisoner's base, but this is only one of many surprises which the vision of the Graces holds for us and for Calidore. In fact, our first inkling of the dance is more reminiscent of fairies than of Graces—those midnight revels which Milton's 'belated Peasant' sees.[21]

> him seemed that the merry sound
> Of a shrill pipe he playing heard on hight,
> And many feete fast thumping th'hollow ground,
> That through the woods their Eccho did rebound.
>
> (VI. x. 10)

Of course, these are not midnight revels, though the last line (reminiscent of the *Epithalamion*) does call to mind what is really a parody of Acidale—the dark and fearsome dance of the cannibals round Serena, which 'made the wood to tremble at the noyce' (VI. viii. 46).[22]

In keeping with the rustic setting, the ladies dance to a shepherd's pipe—as the shepherds themselves had danced to this same pipe in the previous canto. The fact that they 'fast thump' the hollow ground also seems more fitting for a rustic dance

---

[21] *Paradise Lost*, 1.781–4. There is an episode remarkably similar to Spenser's Dance of the Graces in Boiardo's *Orlando Innamorato*, II. 15–43ff., in which Ranaldo comes upon a dance of Cupid and the three Graces. The name Acidale is related to Acidalia, a surname of Venus.

[22] Cf. Charles G. Osgood, '*Epithalamion* and *Prothalamion*: "and theyr eccho ring" ', *MLN*, 76 (1961), 205–8.

than a celestial visitation.[23] Calidore, perhaps remembering his
folklore as well as us, looks on.

> He nigher drew, to weete what mote it be;
> There he a troupe of Ladies dauncing found
> Full merrily, and making gladfull glee,
> And in the midst a Shepheard piping he did see.
>
> He durst not enter into th'open greene,
> For dread of them unwares to be descryde,
> For breaking of their daunce, if he were seene;
> But in the covert of the wood did byde,
> Beholding all, yet of them unespyde.
> There he did see, that pleased much his sight,
> That even he him selfe his eyes envyde,
> An hundred naked maidens lilly white,
> All raunged in a ring, and dauncing in delight.
>
> All they without were raunged in a ring,
> And daunced round; but in the midst of them
> Three other Ladies did both daunce and sing,
> The whilest the rest them round about did hemme,
> And like a girlond did in compasse stemme:
> And in the middest of those same three, was placed
> Another Damzell, as a precious gemme,
> Amidst a ring most richly well enchaced,
> That with her goodly presence all the rest much graced.
>
> Looke how the Crowne, which *Ariadne* wore
> Upon her yvory forehead that same day,
> That *Theseus* her unto his bridale bore,
> When the bold *Centaures* made that bloudy fray
> With the fierce *Lapithes*, which did them dismay;
> Being now placed in the firmament,
> Through the bright heaven doth her beams display,
> And is unto the starres an ornament,
> Which round about her move in order excellent.
>
> (VI. X. 10–13)

Afraid that by stepping into the glade he will cause the dance to
disappear, he remains hidden, watching the naked maidens (like

[23] Spenser is echoing Horace, *Odes*, 1. 4: 'Iam Cytherea choros ducit Venus
imminente Luna, / iunctaeque Nymphis Gratiae decentes / alterno terram quatiunt
pede' (Now Cytherean Venus leads the dance, the moon hanging over, and the
Nymphs and comely Graces, linked together, beat the ground with alternate foot).

the Faunus of the 'Mutabilitie Cantos') with the air and the sentiments of an intruder. Interestingly, we see the scene through Calidore's eyes, our own understanding following his as he picks out and places the various performers in this magical vision.[24] First, there are the hundred naked maidens dancing in a ring. Then he sees that within the ring are three other ladies, the rest of them hemming the three around so that they 'like a girlond did in compasse stemme'. The word 'stem', with its associations of limiting and holding in place, and especially alluding to the encircling stems of a garland, accords well with the general atmosphere of the dance: the maidens seem almost a part of the rich natural abundance of the Mount. How different this is from the uncouth savagery of the dance around Serena! The enraptured Calidore, his mood expressed in a conceit worthy of the Metaphysicals, wishes he were all eyes.

But at this point Calidore notices another damsel, and the imagery shifts again. This damsel, who, we are told, is in the 'middest' (in the centre of the three other damsels?) is like a gem, her three companions forming a ring on which this gem is set. The images move from the mutable realm to the celestial, from garlands to jewels. The change is given further stress by the mention of grace, link between earth and heaven, and our first inkling of the dancers' identity.

From jewels, with their astrological associations, we move to the heavens themselves. Ariadne received her crown not from Theseus but from Bacchus, after Theseus had abandoned her; and the battle of the Lapiths and Centaurs took place at the wedding of Pirithous and Hippodamia, not of Theseus and Ariadne.[25] But this *contaminatio*,[26] this confusion of myths, far

[24] See William V. Nestrick, 'Virtuous and Gentle Discipline of Gentlemen and Poets', *ELH*, 29 (1962), 57–71. Nestrick also cites Hamilton's similarly perceptive comment, *The Structure of Allegory in 'The Faerie Queene'* (Oxford, 1961), p. 362.

[25] See *Variorum*, 6: 251; Henry Gibbons Lotspeich, *Classical Mythology in the Poetry of Edmund Spenser* (Princeton, N.J., 1932), p. 39. Spenser's inspiration for this passage is very possibly Lodge's *Scillaes Metamorphosis* (1589). Lodge's poem opens with a delicately handled scene in which the speaker, mourning the loss of his love, sees Glaucus rise from the river and come to comfort him. Glaucus speaks of mutability: 'With secret eye looke on the earthe a while, / Regard the changes Nature forceth there.' In fact, changes of a *super*natural kind now take place:

> But (loe) a wonder; from the channels glide
> A sweet melodious noyse of musicke rose,
> That made the streame to dance a pleasant tide,

Footnote continued on page 130

from detracting from the effectiveness of the passage, only heightens it.[27] Ariadne's crown is 'placed in the firmament', for all time, a gently circling ring of stars round which the night sky moves in perfect order. The tumult of the Centaurs' bloody fray, and the rout of gods and goddesses and mythological stories which seem to fall over one another in a kind of grand literary disorder, give an air of transcendence to the beautiful simplicity of Ariadne's crown. It is as though the dark diabolism of the cannibals' dance round Serena is obliterated for all time in this single image, the image whose referent is the Graces' Dance itself.

We shall later examine the way in which Calidore's understanding of the scene he sees before him remains limited and imprecise. At a certain point in the description of the dance—the point at which the ring is described—the language becomes ambiguous, these linguistic ambiguities reflecting Calidore's own lack of comprehension. The studied vagueness which Spenser so carefully builds up throughout this passage, not only in terms of language but also through his mythology, gives the scene a visionary and cloudy imprecision which yet has the sharpness of a dream. We see, yet we do not wholly understand; we understand, yet our sight is somehow obscured. This poetic rarefication, if I might coin a term to describe it, is amazingly rapidly built up. We move

> The weedes and sallowes neere the bancke that groes
> Gan sing, as when the calmest windes accorde
> To greete with balmie breath the fleeting forde.
>
> Upon the silver bosome of the streame
> First gan faire Themis shake her amber locks,
> Whom all the Nimphs that waight on Neptunes realme
> Attended from the hollowe of the rocks.
>   In briefe, while these rare parragons assemble,
>   The watrie world to touch their teates doo tremble.
>
> Footing it featlie on the grassie ground,
> These Damsels circling with their brightsome faires
> The love-sicke God and I, about us wound
> Like starres that Ariadnes crowne repaires:
>   Who once hath seene or pride of morne, or day,
>   Would deeme all pompe within their cheekes did play.

(*Elizabethan Minor Epics*, ed Elizabeth Story Donno (London, 1963), p. 23.)

[26] Enid Welsford, ed. *Fowre Hymnes and Epithalamion* (Oxford, 1967), p. 183.

[27] See Donald Cheney, *Spenser's Image of Nature* ((New Haven, Conn., 1966), pp. 232–6. Kathleen Williams's observations (*Spenser's 'Faerie Queene': the World of Glass* (London, 1966), pp. 217–18), while she does not examine the complexities of Spenser's allusions, are perhaps more immediately helpful.

from thumping feet to constellations, and from garlands to the heavens, in a matter of a few lines. Even the images seem somehow to run together. We are told, not to *think* of Ariadne's crown, but to 'Looke'.[28] The mythological stanza does not announce that it is a simile but carries us forward *into* the simile itself. Simile and referent are blended in a single transcendent poetic experience. It is a perfect union of subject-matter and form; our sense of multitudinous implications, their contradictions merely reinforcing one another, is precisely the mood which Spenser needs to build up if we are properly to understand the relation of the Graces to Calidore's world, and of this climactic episode to the Legend of Courtesy as a whole.

That it *is* a climactic episode there can be no doubt. Quite apart from its poetic qualities, the Dance, with its circles and its shining centre, seems to mirror the movement of the book as a whole. As Calidore moves from outside world to pastoral retreat to Acidalian Mount, the description of the dance moves us from naked maidens to the three maidens to the single damsel in their midst. But the mysterious damsel is at once the centre, the focal point, of the dance, and also its least perceptible figure, just as Mount Acidale stands at the topographical centre of the book, yet is somehow vague and unknowable.

4. Folk-tale

Several critics, faced with the problem of bringing critical logic to bear on the haunting, folk-tale atmosphere of Book VI have described it as 'Celtic'.[29] The term is not entirely satisfactory, because mysterious dances[30] and strange woodland figures and savage customs are not peculiar to Celtic culture, though we perhaps associate folk-tale with distant corners of the British Isles

[28] See Paul Alpers' penetrating analysis of these stanzas, *The Poetry of 'The Faerie Queen'* (Princeton, N.J., 1967), pp. 12–14.

[29] See M. Pauline Parker, *The Allegory of the 'Faerie Queene'* (Oxford, 1960), p. 253; Douglas Bush, *Mythology and the Renaissance Tradition*, 2nd edn. (New York, 1963), pp. 109–10. Cf. Howard Rollin Patch, *The Other World According to Descriptions in Medieval Literature* (Cambridge, Mass., 1950), p. 173.

[30] Bands of dancing ladies are also common features of court of love poems. See W. A. Neilson, *The Origins and Sources of the 'Court of Love'* (Cambridge, Mass., 1899), esp. pp. 115–16, 126, 149, 163. Note, too, that to speak of the beloved's beauty in terms of dancing graces, or her goodness as rings of virtues, was commonplace. See Spenser's own *Amoretti*, 40; *F.Q.*, II.iii.25; *Shepheardes Calender*, June. Cf. Jonson's 'Elegie on the Lady Jane Pawlet', lines 39–42, in *Poems*, ed. G. B. Johnston (London, 1954), p. 235.

simply because there was more of it there more recently. The one passage which may owe something to folk-tale is the Dance itself, since it is reminiscent of a number of legends and literary treatments of fairy dances.

There are many such folk-tales involving fairy dances. In fact, fairies are remarkable for an inordinate love of dancing: they very seldom move about in any other way. It is perhaps natural enough that the rings of darkened grass sometimes found in meadows should be associated with them, though surprising that the problem of their origin should occupy so many learned minds even as late as the nineteenth century[31] (their cause is nothing more supernatural than a variety of fungus). The fairy ring is enchanted. There the fairies dance, generally at night but sometimes during the daylight, always in an ordered ring.[32]

Fairy lore and particularly fairy dances caught the imagination of the Elizabethans.[33] Their appearance in plays and pageants was frequent, and folk-tales concerning fairies were common everywhere, though especially in Celtic areas. In these tales, two motifs are particularly relevant to Spenser's dance—human participation in the dance and the disappearance of the dance at the approach of mortals.[34] Dances in which humans are involved are among the most frequent occurrences in fairy tales. The results are generally disastrous. Humans wandering alone in the countryside are lured into a fairy dance. As a result they lose all track of time: one hour among the fairies is equivalent to one year here on earth. They often return to find their homes in ruins and their families long since dead.[35] On other occasions, the fairies are gratified by such

[31] Connoisseurs of such matters will find a long discussion in *The Gentleman's Magazine*; see *The Gentleman's Magazine Library*, ed. George Laurence Gomme (London, 1885), pp. 59–61, for a summary. Cf. Lewis Spence, *The Fairy Tradition in Britain* (London, 1948), pp. 316–17; Désiré Monnier, *Traditions Populaires Comparées* (Paris, 1854), pp. 386–7.

[32] Spence sees its origin in 'frenzied and orgiastic' rituals to promote growth. But the more decorous dance which we associate with fairy stories was the one more commonly depicted in Spenser's day. See also W. Y. Evans Wentz, *The Fairy Faith in Celtic Countries* (London, 1911), pp. 405–6.

[33] See Minor White Latham, *The Elizabethan Fairies* (New York, 1930); K. M. Briggs, *The Anatomy of Puck* (London, 1959). Typical perhaps is Humfrey Gifford's poem 'A delectable Dreame' (*A Posie of Gilloflowers*, 1580; *STC.* 11872), in which the speaker breaks up a dance of fairies, led by a harper, who sings a song against women and one in favour of them.

[34] See, for instance, Wentz's account from Cornwall, p. 181.

[35] Thomas Keightley, *The Fairy Mythology* (London, 1850), pp. 124–5; Edwin Sidney Hartland, *The Science of Fairy Tales* (London, 1891), pp. 161–70.

human participation and reward the participant generously. This is particularly so when a human provides music for their dance[36] —as Colin Clout does here in Book VI.

The two motifs, gratefulness and disappearance, coalesce in Spenser's story. The mortal Colin Clout makes music; the mortal Calidore intrudes. But a third element is also added. When a mortal intrudes on a fairy dance he sometimes learns some magical wisdom. This, we remember, is what happened in Chaucer's Wife of Bath's Tale. Chaucer's knight, condemned to the task of finding out what women desire most, has met with total failure in his efforts. His time-limit running out, he faces death on his return.

> The day was come that homward moste he tourne.
> And in his wey it happed hym to ryde,
> In al this care, under a forest syde,
> Wher as he saugh upon a daunce go
> Of ladyes foure and twenty, and yet mo;
> Toward the whiche daunce he drow ful yerne,
> In hope that som wysdom sholde he learne.
> But certeinly, er he cam fully there,
> Vanysshed was this daunce, he nyste where.
> No creature saugh he that bar lyf,
> Save on the grene he saugh sittynge a wyf—
> A fouler wight ther may no man devyse.[37]

It is this old woman, of course, who provides the knight with his answer. Calidore's intrusion follows a somewhat similar pattern and has the same motivation: he intervenes in order to understand.

It is tempting to identify the passage in Spenser as a 'fairy induction' linking two episodes in the story and making the transition between natural and supernatural. This is how one scholar, quite wrongly I think, explains Chaucer's fairy dance. In

---

[36] See Wentz, pp. 207–8. Note Lewis Spence, *British Fairy Origins* (London, 1946), p. 179: 'Frequently the fairies seem to adopt the style of dancing engaged in by the natives of the country they inhabit. . . . Thus in Britain we may expect to find them engaging in our native "hornpipes, jigs, strathspeys, and reels", and country dances generally, and the best proof of this is that they frequently employ local pipers or fiddlers as their musicians, who would normally be ignorant of any other species of melody.'

[37] *The Works of Geoffrey Chaucer*, ed. F. N. Robinson, 2nd edn. (London, 1957), *Canterbury Tales*, III. 988–99.

fact the fairy induction normally involves not merely narrative transition but also physical transition: a lure to persuade the mortal into some trap or tempt him away from his responsibilities. It is true that the latter explains the broad situation in Spenser, but there is no lure as such. The only situation reminiscent of such a transition is Calepine's chase after the bear—and in that instance there is no movement into a fairy world. With Chaucer there is no case to be made at all—and this is even more so with an episode from Walter Map which the same scholar then refers to.[38] This episode is, however, interesting for other reasons:

> Welshmen tell us of another thing, not a miracle but a marvel. They say that Gwestin of Gwestiniog waited and watched near Brecknock Mere . . . which is some two miles around, and saw, on three brilliant moonlight nights, bands of dancing women in his fields of oats, and that he followed these until they sank in the water of the pond; and that on the fourth night he detained one of the maidens.[39]

Gwestin subsequently marries the girl and remains happily with her until he violates a taboo she has laid upon him and she flees from him. The story is a very common one and introduces us to a further folk-tale motif related to Spenser's episode, that of the fairy bride. It will be observed that Gwestin succeeds in gaining his wife by boldly going into the dance and seizing her. Walter goes on to tell another story rather similar to the first:

> Not unlike this story is that of Edric Wilde, that is, the man of the woods, so called from the agility of his body and the charm of his words and works. . . . When he was returning late from the hunt, he wandered in doubt about the ways until midnight, accompanied only by one boy. He chanced upon a great house on the edge of a grove. . . . When he drew near . . . and looked in, he saw a great band of many noble women. . . . The soldier [i.e. Edric] noted one among them far excelling the others in face and form, more to be desired than all the darlings of kings. . . . At the sight of her, the soldier received a wound in his heart, and he could scarcely endure the fires kindled by Cupid's dart. . . . He had heard of the wanderings of spirits, and the troops of demons who appear by night . . . and he had learned of the vengeance inflicted by offended divinities upon those who came upon them

---

[38] Lilla Train, 'Chaucer's "Ladyes Foure and Twenty" ', *MLN*, 50 (1935), 85–7. On the Fairy Induction, see Lucy Allen Paton, *Studies in the Fairy Mythology of Arthurian Romance* (Boston, Mass., 1903), pp. 15–19.

[39] Walter Map, *De Nugis Curialium*, trans. Frederick Tupper and Marbury Bladen Ogle (London, 1924), II.11 ('Of the Appearance of Phantoms').

suddenly. He had heard, too, how they preserve themselves undefiled and how they secretly inhabit unknown places apart from men and how they detest those who strive to explore their counsels that they may expose them and pry into them that they may publish them, and with how great care they conceal themselves lest, being once visible, they should lose their value.[40]

Nevertheless he seizes the woman and escapes with her, though only after being attacked and injured by her sisters. She remains silent for three days but on the fourth declares that she will remain with him until he makes some allusion to her sisters or the place of her abduction. This, of course, he later does—in anger. She at once disappears and he pines away and dies.

Leaving on one side the remarkable interest of the passage in connection with other episodes in Book VI, we can notice three possible points of similarity between this and Spenser's dance: the spectator sees one girl whom he especially desires; he brings her back to the world only after a fight and after suffering injury; these supernatural beings are in possession of certain mysteries which they keep from prying mortals.

The third point we have already seen borne out in the passage from Chaucer. I would suggest, though, that the first and second might also be in our minds as we read Canto x. The girl in the Dance is not Calidore's bride, to be sure, and his intrusion on the dancing figures does not lead to his seizing one of the participants. But the broad similarities between Map's story (and there are many others like it) and Spenser's are inescapable. Calidore does ultimately bring Pastorella back to society, through many difficulties. We shall find that her coming is clearly associated with the myth of Proserpine—the return of new life and strength to the world. The figure in the Dance *is* associated with Pastorella, through two passages in Canto ix which we shall cast a glance at in a moment. Such associations run through our minds as we watch the Dance, not as explanations of what we see so much as resonant possibilities. And the spectacle of the ruined cottages of the shepherds which Calidore later confronts perhaps also reminds us that the enchanted world which he has entered plays cruel tricks with time and causes unexpected turns of events.[41]

[40] *De Nugis*, II.12 ('Likewise concerning the Same Apparition').
[41] The episode of the tiger, of course, comes between the Dance and this event, but the general observation holds good.

The precise sources of Spenser's story would perhaps be hard to identify, though they are probably not folklore, any more than Chaucer's tale is derived from folklore.[42] More interesting than the episode's sources is the atmosphere Spenser creates. His decision to include obvious allusions to common beliefs about fairies in the middle of his Legend of Courtesy not only widens the dimensions of courtesy but also, in this case, creates a feeling of continuity between the simple reality of the pastoral Colin Clout's love for a particular woman and the spectacle of transcendent love and perfect courtesy in the Dance of the Graces.[43]

The fairy ring provides a simple and easy transition from the human to the divine. Dances of the Graces have nothing to do with mortals; fairy rings are linked to the pastoral world; the Graces are pastoral only peripherally, if at all. Fairy dances are connected with the winning of a wife; the Graces are not. Fairies involve mysterious and hidden meaning, but they are more lowly, more rustic, more linked to simplicity and simple people than are the Graces. By making the Dance of the Graces a fairy ring transformed, Spenser brings the Dance closer to us, invests it with human relevance and yet does not detract from its transcendence or its sublimity. The result is the creation of a symbol infinitely and wonderfully complex.

5. Acidale: order and disorder

The Dance of the Graces is the intellectual and poetic centre of the Legend of Courtesy. We have already traced the gradual 'rarefication' of Spenser's story—from the cruelties of the outside world, to the shepherds' country, to the Golden World. Within this Golden World, we move swiftly from fairy dance, to Dance

---

[42] No literary analogues or sources for the dance are cited in G. H. Maynadier, *The Wife of Bath's Tale, its Sources and Analogues* (London, 1901), or J. W. Beach, 'The Loathly Lady: a Study in the Popular Elements of the Wife of Bath's Tale' (unpublished dissertation, Harvard University, 1907), or W. F. Bryan and G. Dempster, *Sources and Analogues of Chaucer's 'Canterbury Tales'* (Chicago, 1941), though Maynadier's assumption that the tale's sources are principally popular and Celtic has been refuted by Margaret Schlauch, 'The Marital Dilemma in the Wife of Bath's Tale', *PMLA*, 61 (1946), 416–30, who finds them to be principally learned and classical.

[43] Note, too, the connection with the chivalric quest into the other world and the knight's return with some token of his triumph—an obvious link between folklore and chivalry. See Charles Moorman, *A Knyght There Was* (Lexington, Ky., 1967), p. 56. Moorman cites *Le Bel Inconnu* and *La Mule Sanz Frain*.

of the Graces, to the central, all-important figure of the shepherd maid who is both Colin Clout's mistress and also has the appearance and the substance of a goddess. Everything in Spenser's poetic repertoire contributes to make this almost schizophrenic vision credible. Even the dance itself does not exist in isolation, but at the top of an ascending series. Early in Canto ix, Pastorella sits in the centre of the shepherds' 'rout' just as the central figure of the Dance of the Graces is surrounded by the circling dancers. In both cases the ladies surrounding the central figure are likened to a garland. Later, the shepherds dance to Colin Clout's pipe and again Pastorella is the foremost dancer. While it may be illegitimate categorically to associate the figure of Pastorella with the figure in the centre of the circling dancers on Mount Acidale, such parallels make the Dance of the Graces an all-inclusive vision which embraces and contains these lesser emblems of order. The range of association which the Dance embodies is well expressed in the stanzas describing the Graces and explaining Colin Clout's role.

> Those were the Graces, daughters of delight,
> Handmaides of *Venus*, which are wont to haunt
> Uppon this hill, and daunce there day and night:
> Those three to men all gifts of grace do graunt,
> And all, that *Venus* in her selfe doth vaunt,
> Is borrowed of them. But that faire one,
> That in the midst was placed paravaunt,
> Was she to whom that shepheard pypt alone,
> That made him pipe so merrily, as never none.
>
> She was to weete that jolly Shepheards lasse,
> Which piped there unto that merry rout,
> That jolly shepheard, which there piped, was
> Poore *Colin Clout* (who knowes not *Colin Clout*?)
> He pypt apace, whilest they him daunst about.
> Pype jolly shepheard, pype thou now apace
> Unto thy love, that made thee low to lout;
> Thy love is present there with thee in place,
> Thy love is there advaunst to be another Grace.
>
> (VI. x. 15–16)

The introduction of the author's own *persona* into the world he creates is of course a convention of pastoral. Even in its simplest form the convention has a far-reaching effect on the relation of author and reader to the work, since it blurs the distinction between the poet and his own creation much as the comments of a character on the play he is a part of change the relationship between audience and play. Sometimes (as in Sidney's *Arcadia*, for instance) the author's *persona* plays only a very minor role. But in Spenser's poem the poet's fictional self is piping not for some minor shepherds' dance but for the dance which sums up and epitomizes many of the principal themes of the work—just *how* principal we shall see as this study progresses. The dancers dance to Colin's music: it is he who orders and controls them. In a sense, the relation of the dance to Colin is like the relation of the poem to Spenser. We are confronted in this beautiful scene with the spectacle of the poet creating, the poem coming into being. But, paradoxically, the poem which here comes into being is the poem which contains that poem: the whole is contained in the part.

This, though, is not the end of the complexity. Colin does not pipe to an abstraction or a vision, but to an earthly girl, to his own mistress. She and the shepherd are the two static figures amidst, or beside, the swirling dancers. While we are told that she is an earthly girl, she is nevertheless as ethereal as the other dancers: she disappears as they do, thereby suggesting not only that poetic inspiration is elusive and obscure, but that love, too, is uncertain and fleeting. Or perhaps just as Colin is a fictional Spenser, Colin's love for the girl is a fictional representation of the poet's relation to the controlling idea of his poem, round which he shapes and orders the subsidiary images and themes. If this is so, then the girl in the centre of the dance is the flower of courtesy itself.

The final line of the passage, 'Thy love is there advaunst to be another Grace', introduces another dimension to the paradox. Not only does the dance revolve round the central figure, the poem round the central emblem, but there is also a mysterious relationship between the various revolving circles. This was suggested to us in the stanzas immediately preceding those I have just quoted. Somehow, we know not how (but we believe it), a simple shepherd girl *is* another Grace, *is* the flower of courtesy. Spenser deliberately keeps her position ambiguous (the whole dance depends on such ambiguity): she is another Grace and more than another Grace and worthy to be another Grace. The remark 'And all, that Venus in her selfe doth vaunt / Is borrowed of them' has, I think, an intentional double meaning: either Venus borrows her grace from the Graces, or we borrow from Venus grace *through* the Graces. In other words, we are either watching a dance of four Graces (who epitomize the grace of Venus, since Venus borrows grace from them) or watching a dance of three Graces with Venus in the centre (in which event Venus's grace is passed down to us through the three Graces who surround her).

This ambiguity is mirrored in the visual ambiguities which confront us early on in the episode. I asserted that we see the Dance through Calidore's eyes. Calidore is able to follow and understand the pattern of the hundred maidens who hem the central dancers, but the precise configuration of these central damsels escapes him. When we are told that Colin's mistress was 'as a precious gemme, / Amidst a ring most richly well enchaced', what precisely does this mean in visual terms? Are the three Graces smaller stones surrounding the greater (in which event Colin's mistress is in the centre) or do they correspond to the circle of the ring (in which event Colin's mistress is a fourth member of the same circle)? Is she, in other words, Venus or a fourth Grace? The ambiguity is visual as well as conceptual. By associating Colin's mistress with Venus, Spenser makes the Graces (emblems of courtesy, according to Colin) her handmaids; by associating her with a fourth Grace, he makes her the means by which Venus's powers descend to us. She is thus both the epitome of courtesy and the source of courtesy; and the dance becomes the dance of courtesy, bound together by the love which emanates from Venus.

At stanza 17 the enchantment evaporates. Calidore steps into the ring and the dancers vanish 'all away out of his sight'. This is the climax of Calidore's intrusions—the third and most cataclysmic. One would like to think that Calidore had learned from his previous intrusions. But at first there is precious little evidence that he has. His manner is inappropriately hearty: 'Haile jolly shepheard, which thy joyous dayes / Here leadest in this goodly merry make, / Frequented of these gentle Nymphes alwayes.' As Colin Clout, recovering his composure, explains, regrettably things are not quite as simple as that: the Graces only come when they, and not we, choose. You can't have miracles to order.

Calidore's reaction is again curiously inappropriate. As with Calepine and Serena, he blames the whole incident on 'my ill fortune', and presses Colin for an explanation. The figures Calidore has seen, says Colin, are the Graces, who 'on men all gracious gifts bestow / Which decke the body or adorne the mynde'—

> As comely carriage, entertainement kynde,
> Sweete semblaunt, friendly offices that bynde,
> And all the complements of curtesie:
> They teach us, how to each degree and kynde
> We should our selves demeane, to low, to hie;
> To friends, to foes, which skill men call Civility.
>
> (VI. X. 23)

All this has been made clear to us in the preceding sections of the book, especially in those episodes involving Calidore. But Colin's attention now shifts to the central figure. Again Spenser avoids precise definition:

> So farre as doth the daughter of the day,
> All other lesser lights in light excell,
> So farre doth she in beautyfull array,
> Above all other lasses beare the bell. . . .
>
> Another Grace she well deserves to be,
> In whom so many Graces gathered are,
> Excelling much the meane of her degree;
> Divine resemblaunce, beauty soveraine rare,
> Firme Chastity, that spight ne blemish dare;
> All which she with such courtesie doth grace,
> That all her peres cannot with her compare,
> But quite are dimmed, when she is in place.
> She made me often pipe and now to pipe apace.
>
> (VI. X. 26–7)

The final line is both a comment on the poem and a suggestion about its inspiration. The romantic reader, anxious to read the poem as a kind of confessional, might choose to call this 'Grace' Spenser's own Elizabeth Boyle. Others, taking their cue from the *Shepheardes Calender*, may call her Rosalind. But perhaps it would be both truer to the spirit of the poem and more immediately relevant to its theme to call her that inspiration which brought the poem into being, the '*Idea* or fore-conceit' out of which the poet fashioned the work of art.

Almost in the same breath, Spenser turns to the Queen. Perhaps (he seems to say), even so all-embracing and transcendent a vision as this might be misconstrued in a poem ostensibly in praise of the Queen herself. The central figure of the dance, an all-inclusive symbol of virtue, has usurped the position normally allotted the sovereign, who cannot by any stretch of the imagination be incorporated into the dance as Spenser has described it. In turning to the Queen, the poet employs the traditional idea that thus Gloriana's handmaid will be eternized in verse. If Colin's mistress is indeed another Grace, then the Queen is her Venus.

Calidore's reply to Colin's explanation is both illuminating and perplexing. For the first time, he is driven to an admission not simply of 'lucklessness' but of imperfection. He has, he says, 'rashly sought that, which I mote not see'. What is this thing which Calidore 'mote not see', and what effect will it have upon him? Colin's explanation of the significance of the Graces may only be a kind of rationalization of a vision essentially irrational, a quality which somehow lies outside the range of the questing knight, the man of action. If so, then there remains a further question, ultimately the most important. Can this vision be translated into action? To this question we must return.

In the presence of such strange knowledge, and overcome by the beauty of the place in which it was vouchsafed him, Calidore is reluctant to leave—'Thence, he had no will away to fare / But wisht, that with the shepheard he mote dwelling share.' This chance remark reminds us that it was actually the sight of beauty that kept Calidore among the shepherds: he saw Pastorella and he elected to stay. Soon the shepherds' world will disappear as the vision of the Graces disappeared. In each case Calidore stands before these creations of the imagination much as the reader stands before the work of art. If Colin is the poet and the dance is his poetry, Calidore represents ourselves, the readers, in our fumbling efforts to understand the incomprehensible and our insistence on pat answers.

The perceptive reader will recognize that this puts Spenser's audience uncomfortably close to Mirabella and the Salvage Nation, or to Amoret in the House of Busyrane. Like Calidore, these characters did not understand the nature of poetic truth.

Their inability to understand metaphor is linked with Calidore's inability to comprehend the nature of the dance. Thus, not only is Spenser's own *persona*, Colin Clout, brought within the scope of the poem, but so are we. The Dance of the Graces is the most important statement of a persistent theme in Book vi, the relation between poetry and society. Behind that stand two other related themes: the nature of fiction and our response to art. Book vi is a poem talking about itself.

Though Calidore does appear to learn from his conversation with Colin Clout, his incursion on the Golden World of Mount Acidale destroys the vision. Not only must we recognize the limitations of Calidore in ourselves, but we must also understand that Calidore, all unwittingly, repeatedly does what the Beast does intentionally: he breaks in and destroys. Book vi is the only book the object of whose quest is all around us. We must travel to Canto xii to meet Acrasia or Grantorto, but the Blatant Beast races through the world of the Legend of Courtesy like an ever-present and vulgar philistinism—not merely outside us but within us all.

6. The Brigands

Several critics, taking the lead from Lewis, have remarked on the 'chaste' quality of the Dance of the Graces.[44] The sense of sexual violence so pervasive in the dance around Serena is wholly lacking here. In fact the 'chastity' of Mount Acidale arises in part from its very juxtaposition with the Salvages' dance. But more important than the contrast with this earlier dance is a certain generalized quality in Calidore's vision. To speak of chastity is to suggest, despite the lessons of Book iii, a quality of exclusion, as though discordant elements are shut out of Acidale. On the fictional level this may be true, but on the symbolic level the vision transcends, rather than excludes, the sexual. It is a triumphant example of Spenser's poetry of reconciliation: all the paradoxes and contradictions of experience seem somehow to be brought together in the harmony of the dance. The fact that this is a

---

[44] Lewis, *Allegory of Love*, pp. 331. Alpers, *Poetry*, p. 13, takes issue with Lewis on this passage, but I am not at all sure why, since Alpers' observation that we are not supposed to *visualize* a naked human body at this point in no way invalidates Lewis's assertion that 'the Graces symbolize no sexual experience at all' while the ladies in Acrasia's fountain do. In the context of Lewis's argument the contrast is a very useful one.

vision not only of Beauty but of Colin Clout's mistress (and one can hardly become more specific than that) only makes it the more universal—so universal, in fact, that the figure of Pastorella is inevitably associated in our minds, and, I think Spenser suggests, in Calidore's, with the dancing figures. The vision becomes a vision of Pastorella's beauty too.

With Calidore back in the shepherds' country, Coridon finally loses the initiative. The turning-point is the attack by the tiger. The fact that fierce beasts are so traditional a part of pastoral romance (and, incidentally, sometimes cause similarly cowardly behaviour on the part of the shepherds) has tended to divert critics' attention from the tiger's attack, which is dismissed with a mere remark as to its appropriateness in pastoral. In fact, the attack has the effect of distinguishing nobility from self-interest. Coridon's flight is in keeping with Meliboe's doctrine of self-sufficiency, whereas Calidore, nurtured in a crueller world than this, practises self-effacing unselfishness in accordance with the dictum 'What haps to day to me, to morrow may to you.' It is important that the tiger 'chaunst' to come upon them. Meliboe's philosophy works well in a world where fortune has no power, but is useless against natural catastrophe, unlooked-for danger or aggressive cruelty. Faced with ill fortune, the foolish Coridon turns tail and runs.

The tiger is of a piece with the other interrupters of harmony. Unlike Una's lion, who leapt out at the disconsolate Una but was won over by her beauty, the tiger is a perverter of harmony, not a representative of benevolent nature. Its mouth gapes like hell gate as it comes upon Pastorella 'full of fierce gourmandize'. The latter phrase takes us back to the perverted cannibals, and the picture of destruction through gaping jaws even reminds us of the Blatant Beast himself.

The allusion to hell gate also carries us forward to the attack by the Brigands. The tiger gives us the first hint of this attack by showing us that the shepherds' world is not immune to destruction. The brigands plunder and destroy the shepherds' community, wrecking their houses, carrying off their possessions and plunging the shepherds themselves, inhabitants of a green and sunlit world, into the wintry darkness of their anti-society beneath the earth.

The attack is not simply an attack on the shepherds' way of

life, but a frontal assault on the idea of courtesy itself, as symbolized by Pastorella—

> Faire *Pastorella*, sorrowfull and sad,
> Most sorrowfull, most sad, that ever sight,
> Now made the spoile of theeves and *Brigants* bad
> Which was the conquest of the gentlest Knight,
> That ever liv'd, and th'onely glory of his might.
>
> (VI. X. 40)

The metaphor of conquest, in itself a dangerous one if the metaphor is mistaken for the reality, is set against the truly violent
conquest inflicted on Pastorella by the diabolical Brigands. The
metaphor places Calidore and Brigands in direct opposition, with
Pastorella as prize: she is 'th'onely glory of his might'. Perhaps
we should conclude that upon her will depend the whole of
Calidore's success against discourtesy.

Calidore's situation was foreshadowed in Calepine's. Calepine
rescued Serena from a society whose behaviour closely parallels
that of the Brigands,

> That never usde to live by plough nor spade,
> But fed on spoile and booty, which they made
> Upon their neighbours, which did nigh them border.
>
> (VI. X. 39)[45]

The Brigands live deep within the bowels of the earth, 'Through
hollow caves' whose entrances are concealed with shrubs.
Within, there is no light but a 'continuall candlelight, which
delt / A doubtfull sense of things, not so well seene, as felt'.

> Now when faire *Pastorell*
> Into this place was brought, and kept with gard
> Of griesly theeves, she thought her self in hell,
> Where with such damned fiends she should in darknesse dwell.
>
> (VI. X. 43)

Her beauty fades 'like to a flowre, that feeles no heate of sunne'.
It is as though the flower of courtesy itself wilts and decays.

The story of the Brigands is a kind of infernal parody of the
story of the shepherds and Mount Acidale. Calidore ascended the
mount to learn the meaning of courtesy; he must now descend to
the bowels of the earth to rescue the flower of courtesy from the

---

[45] Cf. VI.viii.35.

hands of despoilers. The Brigands live in a community under the ground just as the shepherds lived in a community amid the green fields; the Captain of the Brigands is made the dupe of Pastorella just as Calidore did not hesitate to exploit Coridon's friendship; the Captain himself shows a strange and surprising loyalty towards Pastorella, eventually dying to protect her from the onslaught of his companions, who seek to wrest her from him in order to sell her into slavery:

> Like as a sort of hungry dogs ymet
> About some carcase by the common way,
> Doe fall together, stryving each to get
> The greatest portion of the greedie pray;
> All on confused heapes themselves assay,
> And snatch, and byte, and rend, and tug, and teare;
> That who them sees, would wonder at their fray.
>
> (VI. xi. 17)

The image of hungry dogs is a particularly appropriate one. The recurrent simile of the curs and the bull showed us that the curs' attack is used to symbolize the attack of disorder against order. Here again Spenser uses substantially the same metaphor, but now he omits the bull; this is total anarchy, there *is* no order.

The outbreak of savagery results in the death of all the shepherds, with the exception of Coridon, who, true to character, escapes death by running away, and Pastorella herself, who is wounded and prudently feigns death. But if Pastorella has learned the value of prudence, the same can hardly be said of Calidore, whose reaction on returning from the hunt and finding the shepherds' huts laid waste is hardly that of a prudent man. In fact it borders on hysteria:

> Ne wight he found, to whom he might complaine,
> Ne wight he found, of whom he might inquire;
> That more increast the anguish of his paine.
> He sought the woods; but no man could see there:
> He sought the plaines; but could no tydings heare.
> The woods did nought but ecchoes vaine rebound;
> The playnes all waste and emptie did appeare:
> Where wont the shepheards oft their pypes resound,
> And feed an hundred flocks, there now not one he found.
>
> (VI. xi. 26)

Calidore's lament expresses, with a psychological realism which is at once characteristic of Spenser and sparingly employed in his works, all the despair of a man who has been vouchsafed a vision of beauty and finds it now in ruins. It is a highly stylized lament, perhaps owing most to Ovid, but its full force can only be appreciated in relation to all the events of the tenth canto and to the sheer wonder of the vision of the Graces. At this point Coridon brings news of Pastorella's supposed death.

> When *Calidore* these ruefull newes had raught,
> His heart quite deaded was with anguish great,
> And all his wits with doole were nigh distraught,
> That he his face, his head, his brest did beat,
> And death it selfe unto himselfe did threat;
> Oft cursing th'heavens, that so cruell were
> To her, whose name he often did repeat.   (vi. xi. 33)

But as Meliboe had pointed out to Calidore, there is little point in railing against the heavens, which do what is best for mankind though mankind may not realize it at the time. If Calidore momentarily capitulates to the tyranny of fortune, he soon recovers himself. He and Coridon set out for the robbers' den: 'So forth they goe together (God before).'

That the shepherds' world is a thing of the past is underlined for us in the methods Calidore employs to persuade Coridon to return: 'Yet Calidore so well him wrought with meed, / And faire bespoke with words, that he at last agreed.'[46] So much for Meliboe's spurning of gold; Coridon, base creature that he is, is won with the money the shepherds repudiated, and with fair words. This second commodity, too, is now very much discredited; fair words did not prevent Serena from being wounded, neither did they bring back Colin Clout's dance, nor did they impress Pastorella. Courtesy is more than fair words, but eloquence has its uses for gentlemen obliged to do business with obtuse rustics. If more proof were needed of the rustic Coridon's self-interest, his advice to Calidore on their coming upon their stolen flocks would provide it. Coridon is for driving the flocks away while the shepherds sleep, but Calidore has other ideas. By winning the herdsmen's confidence he gains access to the Brigands' lair—a further lesson that prudence brings its rewards.

[46] Cf. Turpine's bribery of the two knights who attack Arthur, vi.vii.4–5. The opening stanza of Canto vii seems to depict Turpine as a kind of anti-Calidore.

The Calidore who frees Pastorella from her hellish imprison-ment is no longer the shepherd Calidore who wooed the shepherd maiden. But neither is he the noble knight who pursued the Blatant Beast. Part way between the two, he is still clad in shepherd's weeds, but he bears with him also the weapons of war. The very inadequacy of his 'sword of meanest sort' adds to the valour of his single-handed fight with a cave full of brigands, but it is also an indication that the knight is still only partly a knight, that there is still a long way to go before his quest can continue.

So, in a scene of quiet and human tenderness, Calidore is re-united with Pastorella, who 'Knowing his voice although not heard long sin . . . sudden was revived therewithall'.

> Like him that being long in tempest tost,
> Looking each houre into deathes mouth to fall,
> At length espyes at hand the happie cost,
> On which he safety hopes, that earst feard to be lost.
>
> (VI. xi. 44)

Calidore's decision to remain among the shepherds represented, among other things, an attempt to discover a haven from the storms of misfortune—a haven evidently not to be found by the simple exclusion of evil, an impossibility in a fallen world. But there *is* an end, or at least hope of an end, to such storms. From 'deathes mouth' Calidore conducts Pastorella back 'to the joyous light, / Whereof she long had lackt the wishfull sight'.

The return to the light is in the nature of a miracle. Calepine had similarly comforted Serena on rescuing her from the canni-bals, but she remained silent until the daylight came back. The conclusion of her story seems to merge into the conclusion of Pastorella's. Both concern lost identity and identity restored, and both involve heroines of singular beauty. The first is repeatedly called 'the fair Serena'; and around Pastorella, in image after image, light itself seems to gather. Perhaps we have here a reason for the inconclusiveness of Serena's story; her story becomes Pastorella's. The daughters of light are returned to the light, and great rejoicing will follow. 'For this thy brother was dead, and is alive again; and was lost and is found.'

note that both Serena & Pastorella are welcome el.

7. Conclusion

Canto xii opens with a return to the image of the ship:

> Like as a ship, that through the Ocean wyde
> Directs her course unto one certaine cost,
> Is met of many a counter winde and tyde,
> With which her winged speed is let and crost,
> And she her selfe in stormie surges tost;
> Yet making many a borde, and many a bay,
> Still winneth way, ne hath her compasse lost:
> Right so it fares with me in this long way,
> Whose course is often stayd, yet never is astray.

One can discern here a coalescence of two different images, separate until now. The image of the ship driven hither and thither by circumstances but now returning to its right course is both the ship of the poet's narrative and the ship tossed by Fortune.[47] Certainly the sense of wanderings ended pervades this final canto. The narrative, which has followed a meandering path through many characters and events, draws to a close. Calidore, who has wandered far from his quest for the Blatant Beast, returns to the chase. And, in circumstances miraculous, Pastorella, so long lost among the shepherds, is brought back to her parents as if returned from the dead.

Bellamour and Claribell are not merely the parents of Pastorella; they seem representative of all the trials and triumphs of the book's lovers. Claribell's marriage to Bellamour involves secrecy and imprisonment and ill-treatment, like the fate of Pastorella, rescued ultimately by *her* lover Calidore. The love of Pastorella's parents, in the face of parental disapproval, reminds us of Aladine's for Priscilla. Bellamour's retirement from knightly pursuits is reminiscent of Aldus's retirement. Bellamour and Claribell, after years of suffering, regain their lost birthright and with it the Castle of Belgard—as Tristram hopes to regain his and as Pastorella regains hers.

We can read the love of Bellamour and Claribell as justification of the love of Aladine and Priscilla. The circumstances are precisely parallel. Claribell's father

> through the wealth, wherein he did abound,
> This daughter thought in wedlocke to have bound

[47] See III.iv.9.

Unto the Prince of *Picteland* bordering nere,
But she whose sides before with secret wound
Of love to *Bellamoure* empierced were
By all meanes shund to match with any forrein fere.

(VI. xii. 4)

The fact that Pastorella was the fruit of this union is both a vindication of their conduct and a warning. Defiance of authority in the name of love augurs hardship and suffering—just as loyalty to the art of poetry perhaps brings scorn and opprobrium. Pastorella must be removed from sight and 'fostred under straunge attyre'. But the myth itself, of exposed infants reared by a favourable natural world which does not pass judgement as society passes judgement—this provides assurance that Pastorella will not perish. The maid who leaves the child to her fate in the fields notices 'Upon the litle brest like christall bright . . . a litle purple mold, / That like a rose her silken leaves did faire unfold'.

The flower, it seems almost unnecessary to add, is another manifestation of the flower of courtesy, associated with Pastorella both in the shepherds' world, with its garlands, and in the Brigands' cave. It proves the means of recognition. Claribell's maid 'Chaunst to espy upon her yvory chest / The rosie marke, which she remembred well',

> Which well avizing, streight she gan to cast
> In her conceiptfull mynd, that this faire Mayd
> Was that same infant, which so long sith past
> She in the open fields had loosely layd
> To fortunes spoile, unable it to ayd.
> So full of joy, streight forth she ran in hast
> Unto her mistresse, being halfe dismayd,
> To tell her, how the heavens had her graste,
> To save her chylde, which in misfortunes mouth was plaste.

(VI. xii. 16)

With the benevolent relish of a Plautus or a Molière, Spenser fits his recognition episode together piece by piece. The child, abandoned 'to fortunes spoile', has been reunited by 'chance' (stanza 20) with her own mother. She had been placed (the metaphor is arresting) 'in misfortunes mouth'—like Matilda's babe, perhaps. And indeed Pastorella *had* been in misfortune's mouth: she had been even in the jaws of hell.

Then her embracing twixt her armes twaine,
She long so held, and softly weeping sayd;
And livest thou my daughter now againe?
And art thou yet alive, whom dead I long did faine?

(VI. xii. 19)

But in the world of the *Faerie Queene* few triumphs are total. Seemingly inevitably, Calidore is no longer at Belgard to join in the rejoicing at Pastorella's return: he has departed on his quest, 'Asham'd to thinke, how he that enterprize, / The which the Faery Queene had long afore / Bequeath'd to him, forslacked had so sore'. Afraid 'least reprochfull blame / With foule dishonour him mote blot therefore' and courteously striving to reassure Pastorella, he sets off to find the Beast. His reunion with Pastorella, like so many reunions in the *Faerie Queene*, is fated never to take place. He finds the Blatant Beast attacking the Church:

Through all estates he found that he had past,
In which he many massacres had left,
And to the Clergy now was come at last;
In which such spoile, such havocke, and such theft
He wrought, that thence all goodnesse he bereft,
That endlesse were to tell. The Elfin Knight,
Who now no place besides unsought had left,
At length into a Monastere did light,
Where he him found despoyling all with maine and might.

(VI. xii. 23)

We have seen the effects of the Beast's activities upon the Lords Temporal at court, and, if the Brigands can be considered the Beast's lieutenants, on the common people as well. The attack on the Lords Spiritual takes the form of the despoiling of a monastery —at first sight a rather surprising location to be described by the Protestant Spenser.[48]

Into their cloysters now he broken had,
Through which the Monckes he chaced here and there,
And them pursu'd into their dortours sad,
And searched all their cels and secrets neare;
In which what filth and ordure did appeare,
Were yrkesome to report; yet that foule Beast

48 Warton, *Variorum*, 6: 265, suggests that Spenser is here following Erasmus.

Nought sparing them, the more did tosse and teare,
And ransacke all their dennes from most to least,
Regarding nought religion, nor their holy heast.

From thence into the sacred Church he broke,
And robd the Chancell, and the deskes downe threw,
And Altars fouled, and blasphemy spoke,
And th'Images for all their goodly hew,
Did cast to ground, whilest none was them to rew;
So all confounded and disordered there. (VI. xii. 24-5)

The passage has caused a good deal of disagreement among Spenser scholars. Some see it as representing Henry VIII's dissolution of the monasteries, with its attendant wholesale destruction, in which the good was lost along with the bad. They read the passage as Spenser's antiquarian lament over the loss of valuable manuscripts or beautiful works of art,[49] and they point to passages in the *View* which indicate that its author respected the Catholic Church as an institution even though he was bitterly opposed to it as a political force.[50] Others, taking their cue from Jonson's famous remark that in the Blatant Beast Spenser represented the Puritans, have suggested that he is here commenting on the evil effects of Puritan extremism.[51] Upton tends in the other direction, by stressing 'the scandalous behaviour' of the popish clergy.[52]

All these interpretations seem to me to express truth in their various ways. The choice of a monastery as the scene of the Beast's desecration is in fact very logical. We must not forget that the *Faerie Queene* was conceived and executed as an exercise in the revival of the past; Spenser peoples his romance with characters and situations which formed the stock-in-trade of medieval writers. Just as he quite naturally turns to the House of Holiness

[49] Warton, *Variorum*, 6: 267-8. On the havoc wrought, see T. S. Dorsch, 'Two English Antiquaries: John Leland and John Stow', *ES*, 12 (1959), 18-35.

[50] See Editor's note, *Variorum*, 6: 265-6. There is no inconsistency here with the Kirkrapine episode in Book I, which is principally concerned with the exploitation of the wealth of the English church (Kirkrapine) and the problem of absenteeism (Abessa). Hardly surprisingly, in view of contemporary opinion, such evil practices are associated with popery. On Irish religion in the *View*, see *Variorum*, 9: 221ff., and notes pp. 423ff.

[51] See *Variorum*, 6: 266-7. On the general background of Puritan asceticism, see M. M. Knappen, *Tudor Puritanism* (Chicago, 1939), pp. 424-41.

[52] *Variorum*, 6: 267.

as a means to describe the spiritual regeneration of the Red Cross Knight, so he uses a monastery to epitomize the institution of the Church in Book VI. Monasteries and monks are perfectly accepted features of medieval romance, so Spenser makes use of them too.

The monastery has the additional advantage that it is an ambiguous symbol. We might well have reason and justification to disband monasteries, but the Blatant Beast seems little interested in righting wrongs. While in the 'cels and secrets nere' of the monks' living quarters he unearths 'filth and ordure', 'yet' (and the word in itself suggests a lack of regard for putting things right) he continues his rampage without so much as pausing, having regard for neither religion nor the vows of the monks. In the church itself, the Beast robs the chancel, overturns the choirstalls, fouls the altars, blasphemes, and breaks down images.

This suggests another way of looking at the incident. The incident points out the dangers of religious controversy, the brood of Error. Squabbles over doctrine may well be quite distinct from the underlying respect due to religion itself, but the first leads to neglect of the second. Disagreements over the temporal organization of the Church or details of liturgy or belief have led to the full-scale destruction of those elements in religion which really *do* matter—love of God and respect for his will. The poet is pleading not for Puritanism or Catholicism but for justice and respect, 'which skill men call Civility'.[53] We might also read the episode as an expression of regret over the philistinism of Puritan fanatics. The Beast's destruction of the monastery shows a disregard for beauty (and hence for Grace), which is merely a premeditated and malicious version of Calidore's accidental intrusion on Mount Acidale.

But, above all, the incident stresses the all-encompassing evil of the Blatant Beast, suggesting, too, that the unprotected monastic life, cut off from the normal protection afforded by a properly functioning social system, is a natural prey for a force which thrives on isolation. The main protection against the Blatant Beast is mutual respect and love of one's neighbour—along with the moral strength to resist the assaults of evil when they come. Calepine and Serena lacked this strength; so did the shepherds, isolated in a second Eden. So does the monastic discipline, which

<hr>

[53] See Hughes's judicious comments, *Variorum*, 6: 386–8.

the Elizabethans considered an unwarranted escape from life quite out of tune with the Protestant ideal of active virtue.

In the next three stanzas Spenser drives home the point that the Beast's principal evil is his indiscriminate destruction. The climactic description of Calidore's adversary tells us that his tongues are those of dogs and cats, bears and tigers, and human beings who speak 'reprochfully, not caring where nor when' (stanza 27). Dogs, bears, and tigers, of course, all play a part in the imagery or action of Book vi. The description is therefore a kind of summation of the book. Hardly surprisingly, the description proves to be largely a catalogue of the Beast's oral attributes, 'appearing like the mouth of Orcus griesly grim'. Our memories recall earlier instances of the image—the mouth of the tiger 'gaping like hell-gate', Pastorella expecting to fall 'into deathes mouth' and placed in 'misfortunes mouth', and, most obviously, Matilda's babe in the jaws of the bear.

Calidore overcomes the Beast by holding him down with the mark of his knighthood, his shield. The Beast, also in character, 'fared like a feend'—'Or like the hell-borne Hydra, which they faine / That great Alcides whilome overthrew'. The reference to Hercules and the Hydra is particularly appropriate, not only because of Hercules' mythological significance (a point to which I shall return) but also because the Beast has a great deal in common with the Hydra. The Renaissance associated it particularly with evil-speaking and blasphemy. Equally appropriate is the allusion to Cerberus, whose attributes are markedly similar to those of the Hydra.[54]

Thus Calidore chains and muzzles the Beast,

> Like as whylome that strong *Tirynthian* swaine,
> Brought forth with him the dreadfull dog of hell,
> Against his will fast bound in yron chaine,
> And roring horribly, did him compell
> To see the hatefull sunne, that he might tell
> To griesly *Pluto*, what on earth was donne.   (vi. xii. 35)

The contrast with Pastorella is total. Pastorella returned to the joyful light after her sojourn in the hellish cave of the Brigands; the Beast is led out into the world like Cerberus reluctant to leave

---

[54] On the iconographical attributes of both creatures see Jane Aptekar, *Icons of Justice* (New York, 1969), pp. 205–12.

his native darkness. And from all around the people flock to view him, just as they had come to see the body of the Dragon slain by Redcross.

But even amid the glory of the Red Cross Knight's success, Archimago makes a final bid for authority. In the same way, the everyday and paradoxical problems of social life being more immediate and perplexingly insoluble, the ending of Book vi is even less conclusive than the final canto of Book i. In this imperfect world, where Slander is evidently at large, it seems hardly appropriate allegorically to have the Blatant Beast in bondage. 'Whether wicked fate so framed, / Or fault of men' he escapes again, and begins his ravages once more with greater violence. Perhaps this is Spenser's final pessimistic comment: the more the Beast is chased, the fiercer it becomes.

It may also be that the more one attacks court abuses, the more one is made their victim. The final two stanzas round out not only Book vi but the whole poem. They also bring its subject, with startling explicitness, back to Spenser himself. The Blatant Beast, says Spenser, attacks all people indiscriminately, 'Albe they worthy blame, or clear of crime . . . ',

> Ne spareth he most learned wits to rate,
> Ne spareth he the gentle Poets rime,
> But rends without regard of person or of time.
>
> (vi. xii. 40)

We are reminded that Book vi is also a poem about poetry, and a poem about Spenser, and a poem about literary patronage in the court of Queen Elizabeth.

> Ne may this homely verse, of many meanest,
> Hope to escape his venemous despite,
> More then my former writs, all were they cleanest
> From blamefull blot, and free from all that wite,
> With which some wicked tongues did it backebite,
> And bring into a mighty Peres displeasure. (vi. xii. 41)

We can interpret this much disputed passage either as a plaintive request for better consideration or as a dare to find fault, to behave like the Blatant Beast. Spenser makes no claim for his poetry; his reference to 'homely verse' is particularly appropriate at the conclusion of a pastoral episode. Cryptically, he calls on his rhymes to 'seeke to please, that now is counted wisemens threasure'. Men are so short-sighted that they destroy those who criticize them, without considering the justice of the criticism, and they heap honours on those who praise them, without considering whether the praise is merited. To avoid the fate of the first and the dishonesty of the second, the best recourse is silence. This was the advice given to Serena. But Spenser is a poet with a poet's job to do. He has seen the glory of true courtesy and of true art, and he knows the nature of their enemies. To speak is to lay himself open, but he can only speak and hope.

It is a sad and cynical ending to the most beautiful of the six books. The Beast is free, the reunion of Calidore and Pastorella has not taken place. Even the poet himself is exposed to the censures of a hostile public. But Calidore's vision of the Graces and Pastorella's subsequent return to her parents suggest another dimension through which to view the tribulations of the active life. If the Graces, and their earthly manifestation in Pastorella, can be made a part of man's struggle to govern himself and others, if art and poetry and beauty can truly move men to action, then Spenser's poetry of reconciliation will be vindicated and his own life's work justified.

As I anticipated at the outset, this analysis has left many questions unanswered. Even as a method such close examination of the text from incident to incident is suspect. But the alternative is to treat Spenser as principally a poet of ideas by defining these ideas and showing how they are developed in his poetry. In my opinion it is better to start with the known—the text—and to answer questions with the material at hand before launching into the generalized statement. While Spenser is indeed a poet of ideas (though not a great philosopher) he is first a poet, and among poets he is a master of form. The particular order of his materials, above all their intricate and unspeakably complex interaction, these are his greatest strengths. All critics of Spenser face this problem of where to begin—with poetry or with generalities. Most critics compromise. I have done my best to avoid doing so.

We are now faced with the bare outline of a pattern. Now we must step back, fill the pattern in with the colouring of ideas, and perceive its overall shape, its completeness as a work of art.

VI

Courtesy

1. The origins of courtesy

In one respect the Dance of the Graces is analogous to Mercilla's Court in Book v, the House of Holiness in Book i, and perhaps the Castle of Alma in Book ii. Each of these episodes is the allegorical climax of its book, containing a definition of the titular virtue and drawing the argument together. The parallels between Books i and vi are particularly striking: what Redcross learns about Holiness in the House of Holiness, Calidore learns about Courtesy on Mount Acidale. Yet such parallels only serve to point up a fundamental difference in approach. Redcross, we remember, begins his quest as a raw, untrained youth—'tall, clownish younge man', the Letter to Ralegh calls him. Calidore, on the other hand, is an accomplished and experienced knight, an outstanding example of the book's virtue. The reason for this difference is not far to seek. In Book i there is little doubt in the reader's mind as to what Holiness *is*. In fact, the gradual unfolding of the Red Cross Knight's story will strike the reader as a remembrance rather than a discovery. The interest of the quest springs from the difficulty of achieving holiness, not the difficulty of defining it. But whereas Book i describes a virtue known to Spenser and known to his readers, achieved by a man whose limitations are palpably apparent, Book vi describes a virtue which Spenser's readers do not understand when they set out, sought by the most competent of Spenser's heroes. In Book i, we find ourselves with the author looking in on Redcross; in Book vi we are with Calidore looking out on Spenser. We *think* we know what courtesy is; Spenser even uses the first three cantos to present us with some familiar images of it. But he undercuts his presentation. By the time the book is through, Courtesy turns out to be a virtue far greater than we had anticipated.

The emphasis in Book vi, then, is on definition. The present chapter will examine those aspects of the definition already familiar to Spenser's readers, glancing at the literature of courtesy from which they are derived and finally concentrating on the book's early episodes. Later we shall go on to examine what is new about Spenser's idea of courtesy. The book in fact opens with a definition. Virtue, the proem states, was planted in the earth from heavenly seeds, which grew to ripeness and 'forth to honour burst' . . .

> Amongst them all growes not a fayrer flowre,
> Then is the bloosme of comely courtesie,
> Which though it on a lowly stalke doe bowre,
> Yet brancheth forth in brave nobilitie,
> And spreds it selfe through all civilitie:
> Of which though present age doe plenteous seeme,
> Yet being matcht with plaine Antiquitie,
> Ye will them all but fayned showes esteeme,
> Which carry colours faire, that feeble eies misdeeme.
>
> (VI. proem. 4)

Four phrases might be singled out as aspects of Spenser's argument: 'brave nobilitie', 'all civilitie', 'plaine Antiquitie', and 'fayned showes'. The image of the flower branching forth in 'brave nobilitie' reminds us of family trees, the notion that there is a connection between a family's history and its claim to moral perfection. 'All civilitie' implies a breadth in the power of courtesy, which will later prove crucial to its definition in Book VI. The contrast of today's 'fayned showes' and the 'plaine Antiquitie' of times gone by is the context in which all of the argument not only of Book VI but of the *Faerie Queene* as a whole takes place. The fine plainness of ancient courtesy is replaced with 'forgerie',

> Fashion'd to please the eies of them, that pas,
> Which see not perfect things but in a glas:
> Yet is that glasse so gay, that it can blynd
> The wisest sight, to thinke gold that is bras.
>
> (VI. proem. 5)

The mirror is but a reflection of a reality which the courtier copies, himself constantly aping himself in a sterile and slavish mimicry. Behind the word 'glas' there lurks, of course, a pun, connected with the common Elizabethan usage of the terms 'glass' and 'mirror' to mean 'example'. *Antiquity*, like Spenser's poem, does indeed present an *example*, but the courtier's mirror is made of glass pure and simple. The courtier is trapped by his own comeliness, utterly preoccupied with himself. Such perversion leads to the slavish and destructive lust of the cannibal-courtiers for Serena, and the unyielding tyranny of the hard-hearted Mirabella.

Yet, ironically, it is precisely within the individual that the true universality, the metaphysical principle lies—'But vertues seat is deepe within the mynd.' The point, of course, is that this inner principle, the pre-existent *Idea*, shapes and fashions its external manifestations. When these externals do not derive from such a principle, the result is the mere pretence of virtue, an imitation of an imitation. Sidney gives a pregnant rendering of the implications behind such a notion in his discussion of poetry in the *Apology*, distinguishing between mere outward ornament and ornament shaped by the '*Idea* or fore-conceit of the work'. The true poet creates a kind of golden world. Spenser, in his allusion to gold in the passage just quoted, has the same thing in mind.

Spenser moves from consideration of the courtesy of antiquity to the courtesy of his sovereign,

> In whose pure minde, as in a mirrour sheene,
> It showes, and with her brightnesse doth inflame
> The eyes of all, which thereon fixed beene. (vi. proem. 6)

The mirror image is here turned to good account, the aping mirror of the courtier set beside the mirror of the Queen, revealing the true copy of virtue. As we have already discovered, two standards are therefore set up: a hypothetical ideal court (Gloriana's) set beside a corrupt court; an ideal court set in antique times beside a present-day debased court. Such, indeed, is the operation of Fairyland: it provides an ideal world to play off against the real world, and it gives a hint that perhaps the ideal may in some way revive and change the actual. It provides perfect patterns of virtue, like the Queen herself. Spenser introduces the motif of giving and receiving, central to the book, at the very outset:

> Then pardon me, most dreaded Soveraine,
> That from your selfe I doe this vertue bring,
> And to your selfe doe it returne againe:
> So from the Ocean all rivers spring,
> And tribute backe repay as to their King.
> Right so from you all goodly vertues well

> Into the rest, which round about you ring,
> Faire Lords and Ladies, which about you dwell,
> And doe adorne your Court, where courtesies excell.
>
> (VI. proem. 7)

Thus the motif of the dance is introduced to give the pattern of a perfect court, the sovereign rendering virtue to her subjects, the subjects rendering virtue to their sovereign. As we move into the book the main images and the central ideas have already been rapidly and surely established.

The perfect court, figured forth in the Proem, provides the opening for the first canto. 'Courtesy' is firmly identified with 'court'—

> And well beseemeth that in Princes hall
> That vertue should be plentifully found,
> Which of all goodly manners is the ground,
> And roote of civill conversation. (VI. i. 1)

The statement in fact hides a sleight of logic. It is fitting that virtue be found in the court; virtue is the ground of all goodly manners and civil conversation. Our natural tendency is to insert 'because' between the two statements, but to do so is to act on precisely those preconceived notions which Spenser intends to examine. It is part of his purpose to keep the two mutually incompatible alternatives alive: the ideal court where courtesy is to be found, and the corrupt court from which courtesy has been driven out.

In the ideal court, Calidore reveals the ideal combination, gracefulness of body turned to virtuous account. In the first canto, appropriately, he scores his most unequivocal victory, against Crudor. In the later narrative, as a decline in his fortunes sets in, the definition of courtesy grows more complicated. 'Brave nobilitie', the question of nature and nurture, is obliquely introduced as an issue in the second canto:

> Thereto great helpe dame Nature selfe doth lend:
> For some so goodly gratious are by kind,
> That every action doth them much commend,
> And in the eyes of men great liking find;
> Which others, that have greater skill in mind,
> Though they enforce themselves, cannot attaine.
> For everie thing, to which one is inclin'd,

> Doth best become, and greatest grace doth gaine:
> Yet praise likewise deserve good thewes, enforst with paine.
>
> (VI. ii. 2)

The word 'thewes' is used primarily in its old meaning of 'manners' or 'behaviour'. The syntax of this important stanza is not as
clear as it might be.[1] The poet emphasizes that some people have
a natural superiority (like Tristram or Calidore), but he does not
rule out the possibility that others may deserve praise for their
great efforts.[2] He does not specify in what sense these naturally
superior people are so, but the ambiguity of the word 'thewes',
coupled with the electric effect which such courtesy apparently
has on those exposed to it, makes clear that in large measure it is a
question of comeliness of body and of speech. It is noble birth
which forms the subject of the opening of Canto iii, Spenser using
the parallel of horses to emphasize the fact that normally good
breeding produces good qualities.[3] However, he immediately proceeds to tell the story of Aladine and Priscilla, thereby stressing
that good breeding does not necessarily mean best breeding and
that courtesy depends on more than simply noble birth. Its *full*
development, in fact, comes from the cultivation of outward
appearances to supplement inner virtue, as is made plain to us in
the introduction to the fifth canto:

> O what an easie thing is to descry
> The gentle bloud, how ever it be wrapt
> In sad misfortunes foule deformity,
> And wretched sorrowes, which have often hapt?
> For howsoever it may grow mis-shapt,

---

[1] Paraphrased, the stanza reads: 'Dame Nature herself lends great assistance in this
matter, since some people are naturally so good and gracious that every one of their
actions serves to recommend them to others, and in men's eyes they achieve great
popularity. Others, though they are cleverer and more adept, cannot achieve such
popularity even if they take great pains; for everything to which this first group
turns its attention comes out superior and gains greater recognition. However,
good manners achieved through great pains also deserve praise.'

[2] Cf. the categories in the *Institucion of a Gentleman* (1555): 'gentle gentle' (men of
noble birth and noble character); 'gentle ungentle' (men of noble birth and base
character); 'ungentle gentle' (men of base birth and noble character); 'ungentle
ungentle' (men churlish in birth and disposition). See John E. Mason, *Gentlefolk in
the Making* (Philadelphia, 1935), p. 37. Cf. A. Smythe-Palmer, ed. *The Ideal of a
Gentleman or a Mirror for Gentlefolks* (London, 1908), pp. 171–205.

[3] The parallel derives from Castiglione. See *Variorum*, 6: 330. Note also Charles
G. Smith's references, *Spenser's Proverb Lore* (Cambridge, Mass, 1970), p. 268.

Like this wyld man, being undisciplynd,
That to all vertue it may seeme unapt,
Yet will it shew some sparkes of gentle mynd,
And at the last breake forth in his owne proper kynd.

(VI. v. 1)

The words refer to the Salvage Man, who displays those sparks of courtesy, which might nevertheless 'breake forth' under the right conditions. We are reminded of Spenser's likening of Tristram to a flower.

A complete contrast to this is provided by the description of Turpine at the opening of Canto vii. His behaviour, we are told, reveals his 'base kind', his 'vile donghill mind'. Turpine is a stirrer up of trouble, of confusion and disorder. He is an enemy of benevolent nature[4] and hence not endowed with nature's gifts. We can conclude that he is 'basely born'—Arthur says as much—but he is also without any merit to compensate for this. Thus he is the logical opposite of Calidore: dishonest, basely born, cowardly.

The poet's own utterances at the beginnings of cantos do very little actually to redefine courtesy, concentrating mostly on the single subject of noble birth. Here, as we have seen, Spenser's views are less than clear. The stress on noble birth seems not to be a simple theory of aristocratic superiority, and there is certainly no direct connection established between the almost mystical qualities of courtesy and the rather more mundane process of aristocratic generation. If the court were what it should be, the poet seems to imply, then such a connection *could* be discovered. As it is, the seed of courtesy is implanted in men by a benevolent nature. Nature seems still to favour the aristocracy, for the old line lives on amidst the corruption of modern times, but the flowering forth of courtesy may be attributable as much to the opportunity for heroic action which the court provides as to the noble birth of the courtiers. Matilda's babe seems to exemplify the powers of nurture rather than nature, and yet . . . we do not actually *know* that he is not of noble or miraculous birth. Nevertheless, he provides a total contrast with Turpine, whose knightly calling (presumably, therefore, 'nurture') is no antidote against his appallingly plebeian behaviour, as sure a sign of his bad birth as Tristram's behaviour bespeaks his nobility. From the example of Turpine, Tristram, and Matilda's babe we can perhaps establish

---

[4] See below, pp. 182ff.

that courtesy presupposes natural accomplishment, that birth is an overwhelming advantage, but that Spenser is not enough of an optimist to espouse the view that the aristocracy possesses out-and-out moral superiority.

Indeed, the action of Book VI is determined by the fact that backbiters in profusion cause dissension in the court. In *Mother Hubberds Tale* Spenser calls such backbiters 'common courtiers'—

> For though the vulgar yeeld an open eare,
> And common Courtiers love to gybe and fleare
> At everie thing, which they heare spoken ill,
> And the best speaches with ill meaning spill;
> Yet the brave Courtier, in whose beauteous thought
> Regard of honour harbours more than ought,
> Doth loath such base condition, to backbite
> Anies good name for envie or despite.   (713–20)

Unfortunately, there is little connection between beauteous thought and general popularity anywhere but in Faerie Court. The ape in *Mother Hubberds Tale*, of whom this passage was written, is all too successful in his efforts to gain an entrée into court. What he lacks in natural comeliness he makes up for by an extravagant and wheeling strangeness—'his behaviour altogether was / *Alla Turchesca*'. And a 'kindly aptnes of his joynts' (appropriately enough for an ape) makes him skilled in all that 'pertaines to reveling'.

With this accomplished exponent of counterfeit courtesy Spenser contrasts the true courtier, devoting a long passage of some seventy lines to a description of proper courtly conduct which includes a correct sense of order (he 'unto all doth yeeld due courtesie'), a dislike of lying and deceit, an avoidance of idleness, skill in knightly deeds and in hunting, and the practice of running, wrestling, and archery. To these are added musical ability, delight in love and, above all, a liking for learning. The true courtier does noble deeds not for personal gain, but out of a sense of duty to his sovereign. He acts as administrator and adviser. Above all, he aims at honour.

Some of these qualities are mentioned again in Book VI,[5] though Spenser chooses above all to emphasize the moral aspects of courtesy. There is no mention of learning except in connection

[5] See also the description of Sidney, in *Astrophel, Variorum*, 7: 179ff.

with Matilda's babe, no mention of skill in arms except in its application; ability to run (Calepine) and wrestle (Calidore) are mentioned in passing but they are nothing more than incidentals. Far more important than any of these is a widening and deepening of the meaning of courtesy: Spenser sets out not merely to describe his idea of the perfect courtier but to explain the origin of courtesy itself.

2. Courtesy as a moral quality: Stefano Guazzo and others

Colin Clout's explanation of the meaning of the Graces would offer few surprises to the Elizabethan reader acquainted with the literature of courtesy.

> These three on men all gracious gifts bestow,
> Which decke the body or adorne the mynde,
> To make them lovely or well favoured show,
> As comely carriage, entertainement kynde,
> Sweete semblaunt, friendly offices that bynde,
> And all the complements of curtesie:
> They teach us, how to each degree and kynde
> We should our selves demeane, to low, to hie;
> To friends, to foes, which skill men call Civility.
>
> Therefore they alwaies smoothly seeme to smile,
> That we likewise should mylde and gentle be,
> And also naked are, that without guile
> Or false dissemblaunce all them plaine may see,
> Simple and true from covert malice free:
> And eeke them selves so in their daunce they bore,
> That two of them still froward seem'd to bee,
> But one still towards shew'd her selfe afore;
> That good should from us goe, then come in greater store.
>
> (VI. X. 23–4)

Defining the intellectual background to stanzas like these is, however, as complex an undertaking as any we are likely to touch on in this study.[6] The courtesy books of the later sixteenth century are

[6] Mohinimohan Bhattacherje (*Variorum*, 6: 328–33) shows the similarities between the views of Castiglione and Spenser. H. S. V. Jones (*Variorum*, 6: 333–40) adds some English sources. A. C. Judson (*Variorum*, 6: 340–5) augments the English sources and adds Guazzo. See also Leonard R. N. Ashley, 'Spenser and the Ideal of the Gentleman', *BHR*, 27 (1965), 108–32; H. C. Chang, *Allegory and Courtesy in Spenser* (Edinburgh, 1955), 171–220; Virgil B. Heltzel, 'Haly Heron: Elizabethan Essayist and Euphuist', *HLQ*, 16 (1952), 1–21.

a curious and sometimes unwieldy mixture of material traceable to the chivalric manuals of the fifteenth century,[7] classical works on education and good government, Christian doctrine, Italian humanism, and contemporary treatises on education or political theory. Essentially, this passage expresses views commonly found in the courtesy books of Spenser's day.

The history of the Renaissance courtesy book has already been effectively documented in a number of modern studies, to which my reader can refer for more detailed information.[8] Scholars point out that fifteenth-century England was still dominated by military might. The nobility maintained its political position by its ability to fight: the nobleman's authority was measured in terms of the soldiers at his command and the strength of his alliances. Learning profited him little: it was better left to the Church, which continued to dominate education, producing what few secular administrators were required by a system of government largely decentralized and diffuse. The situation in some other countries, notably Italy, was slightly different. The growth of the city-state and the parallel growth in trade led to the early emergence of an administrative class economically independent and in some measure relieved of the constant necessity of defending itself against, or contributing to, military adventures of various kinds. The particular skills required of it were organizational rather than military, and called for the kind of education which was not neces-

---

[7] Books on chivalry and courtesy books really form separate categories, but there is a general similarity of intention and a degree of historical continuity. Strictly speaking, civility books likewise make up a separate category, especially popular in the fifteenth century. See Mason, *Gentlefolk*, Chapter 1. Civility books deal with questions of precedence, fitting behaviour for various social classes, and so on.

[8] The fullest study, which includes a bibliography of courtesy books published in Europe before 1625, is Ruth Kelso, *The Doctrine of the English Gentleman in the Sixteenth Century* (Urbana, Ill., 1929). See also the informative chapter in Joan Simon, *Education and Society in Tudor England* (Cambridge, 1966), pp. 333–68; Fritz Caspari, *Humanism and the Social Order in Tudor England* (Chicago, 1954); Kenneth Charlton, *Education in Renaissance England* (London, 1965). R. S. Pine-Coffin has a useful note in his translation of Della Casa's *Galateo* (Harmondsworth, Middx., 1958), pp. 105–31. There are relevant chapters also in Mason, *Gentlefolk*; Elbert N. S. Thompson, *Literary Bypaths of the Renaissance* (New Haven, Conn., 1924), and William Harrison Woodward, *Studies in Education During the Age of the Renaissance 1400–1600* (Cambridge, 1906). Cf. W. L. Wiley, *The Gentleman of Renaissance France* (Cambridge, Mass., 1954). Smythe-Palmer brings together a large collection of excerpted passages especially from Renaissance courtesy books in *The Ideal of a Gentleman*. On educational books in general, see H. S. Bennett, *English Books and Readers 1558 to 1603* (Cambridge, 1965).

sary for the military leader. Out of such a social environment there emerged the notion of the *optimo cittadino*, the ideal citizen described in Palmieri's *Della Vita Civile* and elsewhere, well educated, skilled in public affairs, and (the point is important) deserving of respect for his own merits, not those of his ancestors.[9] Such discussion of the qualities and merits of the active life was paralleled by the development of that second ideal figure, *il cortegiano*, and a third, *il principe*.

In England the old order was changing. The revival of interest in chivalry, so well documented by Arthur Ferguson,[10] constituted a reaction to this change. Works like Caxton's revived *Boke of the Ordre of Chyvalry* (1484) and those many works of instruction in manners which were so much a feature of the fifteenth century alternately advocated training in horsemanship, feats of arms, and bodily skills and deplored the decline of such marks of nobility and 'gentleness'.[11] The new courtesy books on the Italian model which later gained currency in England did not discount the importance of these accomplishments, but they became merely a part of a larger conception of the nobleman more in key with the changing times. The new 'governor' who emerged from the currents of thought represented by Castiglione's *Courtier* on the one hand and Erasmus's *Education of a Christian Prince* on the other was a man versed in classical learning, industrious, and, above all, dedicated to the service of his country. Such selflessness had its beginning in Italian works on public service, while the classical learning belongs to the new humanist educational tradition exemplified in the circle of More's friends, of whom Sir Thomas Elyot, author of *The Governor* (1531), was one.[12]

Elyot's principal work is different in tone from the less obviously practical *Cortegiano* of Castiglione. Both betray the influence of Plato, to be sure, and both stress the importance of learning, but

[9] See Hans Baron, *The Crisis of the Early Italian Renaissance* (Princeton, 1966), *passim*.

[10] *The Indian Summer of English Chivalry* (Durham, N.C., 1960).

[11] Charlton, *Education*, pp. 75ff. Fifteenth-century books of manners (see n. 7, above) present a concept of 'courtesy' almost wholly dependent on sets of external rules. See Frederick J. Furnivall's collection *Manners and Meals in Olden Time* (London, EETS, 1868). Among later examples is Hugh Rhodes, *The Boke of Nurture* (1577), in Furnivall.

[12] On Elyot, see Caspari, *Humanism*, pp. 76–109; Stanford E. Lehmberg, *Sir Thomas Elyot: Tudor Humanist* (Austin, Tex., 1960); and Pearl Hogrefe, *The Life and Times of Sir Thomas Elyot, Englishman* (Ames, Iowa, 1967), esp. pp. 129–56.

while Castiglione's subject is a courtier, Elyot's is a lawyer and administrator. The English writer's totally serious purpose is to propose a model education for the creation of a governing class. Castiglione, more conservative, is concerned wholly with the restricted world of the court. It is significant that it was not until 1561, with Hoby's translation, that the Italian work was widely read in England.[13] By that time, men were in many cases more interested in consolidating positions gained than in advancing up the ladder of administrative preferment. The social fluidity of the early part of the century was less pronounced in the later part.

The difference in social status of the subjects of Castiglione and Elyot reflects the particular situation of Tudor England. The landed gentry, the minor administrators, the teachers, the monied burghers, formed the backbone of the nation in the days of Elizabethan peace and relative prosperity soon to follow. For these men Elyot wrote. The notion of a privileged class midway between the sovereign and the bulk of his subjects is probably as old as kingship. The definition of this class is, of course, a problem not only for the historians of later ages but for the citizens of the day. The question 'What is a gentleman?' echoes through all the vast collection of handbooks on courtesy which the London printing presses produced in the second half of the century.[14] From the anonymous *Institucion of a Gentleman* (1555) and Lawrence Humfrey's *The Nobles or of Nobilitie* (1561) to such works as the translation of the Italian Nenna, *Nennio, or a Treatise of Nobilitie* (1595), for which Spenser contributed a commendatory sonnet, we find attempts to arrive at a definition of such terms as 'noble', 'gentle', 'gentleman', 'courteous', and so on. Essential to the thinking of all their authors, and of Spenser too, is that there *is* such a person as a gentleman, who has special responsibilities to society and to his fellow men. Whether he is a gentleman *born* or a gentleman *bred* is no clearer to many of the authors than it is to the Clown in *The Winter's Tale*, who declares he has been gentleman born 'these four hours'.[15] Nevertheless, all seem agreed that it is possible to abuse one's gentle or noble rank, and all are of the opinion that virtue, even if it comes of right, requires cultivation. The gentleman, declares Humfrey, acts to uphold the

[13] Kelso, *Doctrine*, p. 50.   [14] See Kelso, *Doctrine*, pp. 18–41.
[15] *Winter's Tale*, v. ii.

protestant religion. Thereby 'both the tyranny of princes is bridled, and the rage of the common people repressed, and the pride of prelates tamed'.[16] His remarks, in a sense typical, are interesting forerunners of the sentiments of Spenser. As for the populace, it is a many-headed beast—surely kin of Spenser's Blatant Beast.[17]

Humfrey puts relatively little emphasis on the question of lineage, and in this respect he is representative of the freer sort of courtesy writer. Nenna's view is perhaps typical: 'So is he worthy of far more greater glorie who of himselfe becommeth noble, then hee who is simplie borne noble.'[18] Nenna's volume is almost exclusively given over to the question of what makes a man noble. Pierre de la Primaudaye, in his sophisticated and influential conduct book *The French Academie*, touches on 'Nature and Education' only as one of a large number of topics, but his conclusion is similar.[19]

Lawrence Humfrey takes care to explain that his gentleman has nothing to do with chivalry, but by the end of the century interest in chivalric practices revived sufficiently to sustain works like Richard Robinson's *Auncient Order, Societie, and Unitie Laudable, of Prince Arthure, and his Knightly Armory of the Round Table* (1583),[20] which contains an elaborate history of archery in verse, and Sir William Segar's *Booke of Honor and Armes* (1590). Segar's work, which ran to a second and more elaborate edition in 1602, is a curious compilation. It details the various kinds of challenges a knight might issue, how to write such a challenge as well as deliver it orally, under what circumstances a challenge is to be accepted and how victory is to be gained, 'What sorts of men ought not bee admitted to triall of Armes', types of nobility, which

---

[16] Simon, *Education and Society*, p. 339.

[17] M. M. Knappen, *Tudor Puritanism* (Chicago, 1939), p. 177.

[18] *Nennio, or a Treatise of Nobilitie*, trans. William Jones (1595), Cc4*v*. (Reprinted Jerusalem and London, 1967).

[19] Trans. T. Bowes. There were editions in 1586, 1589, 1594, etc. Among the reasons for its success one would like to reckon its prose style, which is particularly fine. On Nature and Education, see Chapters 16 and 66. In the latter we read: 'Many make three kinds of Nobilitie: one that is bred of vertue & of excellent deeds: the second that proceedeth from the knowledge of honest disciplines and true sciences: and the thirde that commeth from the scutchions and Armes of our auncestors, or from riches. But to speake truelie, there is no right Nobilitie, but that which springeth of vertue, and good conditions.' Cf. Madalene Schindler, 'The Vogue and Impact of Pierre de la Primaudaye's *The French Academie* on Elizabethan and Jacobean Literature', *DA*, 21 (1960), 192 (University of Texas).

[20] *STC*. 800. The greater part of the volume is devoted to heraldry.

pieces of armour it is most dishonourable to lose, and so on. Knotty and hardly relevant problems like 'whether a bastard may challenge a gentleman to combat' and 'whether a quarrell betweene two Emperours may be decided by particular combat' are carefully debated, and the book also devotes attention to the Accession Day tilts and other neo-chivalric goings-on of the sixteenth century. But despite this apparent conservatism, Segar's conclusion about nobility accords with the others we have noticed: 'I say that the true nobilitie of men is Vertue, and that he is truelie noble that is vertuous, bee he borne of high or of lowe Parents.'[21]

With works like Robinson and Segar behind him, Spenser finds himself able to resurrect the chivalric order as a viable metaphor for gentlemanly conduct. The result is a widening of the ground normally covered by courtesy books and a corresponding deepening of the virtues with which he deals. The definition of courtesy in Book VI draws on the full range of courtesy books but does more besides. Nenna is only one of the Italian authors so popular among English readers, and his work is less clearly illustrative of a shift in the Italians' attentions from the courtier of Castiglione to the middle-class citizen of a writer like Stefano Guazzo,[22] whose *Civil Conversatione* appeared in 1574.[23] With Guazzo, the study of courtesy assumes a distinctly moral tone. It is significant that Spenser seems to have drawn more on Guazzo's work than any other among the courtesy books.

Those scholars who find the main concentration of material from courtesy books in the first three cantos of Book VI[24] overlook the fact that much of the moral emphasis in Guazzo finds echoes in the latter parts of the book. Lievsay, in his study of Guazzo, reminds us:

A marked community of interests and premises, a basic sameness of attitude can be seen in the works of the two men [Guazzo and Spenser]. The same high seriousness in the molding of character and the guiding

[21] *STC.* 22163, F1v.

[22] Books along the lines of Erasmus's *Institution of a Christian Prince* do, however, continue to appear. A late example is, of course, James VI's *Basilikon Doron* (1599). For examples, see Mason, *Gentlefolk*, p. 317.

[23] Trans. George Pettie and Bartholomew Young, 1581–6 (ed. Sir Edward Sullivan, 2 vols., London, 1925).

[24] See, for example, Donald Cheney, *Spenser's Image of Nature* (New Haven, Conn., 1966), p. 177.

of conduct, the same basic combination of pagan and Christian ethical idealism run through *La Civil Conversatione* and *The Faerie Queene*.[25]

This high seriousness sets Guazzo somewhat apart from his predecessors. Whereas both Castiglione and Della Casa[26] were at least partly concerned, for all their protestations to the contrary, simply with preventing *faux pas* and winning for their readers influence and popularity in society, Guazzo is quite definitely interested in making his reader a *better person*. Castiglione especially and Della Casa to a lesser extent emphasize the need for keeping up appearances, using *sprezzatura* to make one's fellows think one more accomplished than in fact one is; Guazzo stresses honesty to oneself and to others:

I woulde wishe every one that seeketh to winne credite in companie, to resolve with him selfe above all things (which very fewe folke doe) to followe that excellent and divine counsell of Socrates, who being demaunded what was the readiest way for a man to winne honour and renowne: answered, To indevour, to bee such a one in deede, as hee desireth to seeme to bee in shewe. (1: 147–8)

Sinceritie and playne dealing is especially good, a thing verie commendable and necessarie, not only in deeds, but even in woordes likewise.
(1: 153)

The readers of courtesy books, of course, were not only those anxious to maintain standards but also those wishing to learn how to advance themselves. Perhaps Guazzo's seriousness explains his relative neglect beside Castiglione and Della Casa. Nevertheless, his intention, of defining the qualities of behaviour which bring about harmony in society, is very similar to that in the Legend of Courtesy. Guazzo's title itself betrays this intention. It is later picked up by Spenser in the first canto of Book VI: courtesy, he declares, is 'the ground, / And roote of civill conversation'. Perhaps the nearest modern equivalent to the word 'conversation' here is the word 'intercourse'. As for 'civil', Guazzo defines it not as having to do with cities—for civility is to be found in the country as well—but as an attitude of mind, the quality which brought cities into being, a quality akin to social harmony.[27] 'Too bee shorte,

---

[25] John Leon Lievsay, *Stefano Guazzo and the English Renaissance* (Chapel Hill, N.C., 1961), p. 97.

[26] *Galateo* (1558), trans. Robert Peterson (1576).

[27] *Civile Conversation*, 1: 56. Cf. the title page which, as Lievsay points out, tells a large part of the story: 'The Civile Conversation of M. Steeven Guazzo Written

my meaning is, that civile conversation is an honest commendable and vertuous kind of living in the world.' The last phrase is important: the work, which is in dialogue form, is in part a refutation of the value of the solitary life. Love of such a life, Guazzo declares, arises from an acute and dangerous melancholy.[28] We are reminded of Meliboe, who exists by and for himself, beholden to no one. Solitary pleasures, we learn, are but counterfeit, for true pleasure naturally gives pleasure to others. In other words, man is a social animal and he should concern himself with his conduct in society. Spenser's view seems similar: Tristram will blossom in society, the Salvage Man needs contact with humanity if his natural virtue is to develop, the world of the shepherds is important less for what it is than for what it contains. Only the Hermit's solitariness is commended for its own sake, but even the Hermit is skilled in the ways of society, and is ready to apply this skill.

In keeping with Guazzo's deep concern with social harmony, there is an important discussion of slander in the latter half of his first book, the most notable discussion to appear in any of the courtesy books:

That fault is at this day common throughout the world, and therefore wee must spite of our teeth beare with ill tongues, which swarme in greater number than Bees doe in July: neither is it possible for a man to escape their stinging, do the best hee can. For now adaies men take such pleasure in this vice, that many which are free almost from all other faults, yet they are not able to bridle their blasphemous tongues.
(1: 65)

Two types of slanderers are distinguished—those who 'without feare, without shame, without any respect or difference, whet their

first in Italian, and nowe translated out of French by George Pettie, devided into foure bookes. In the first is contained in generall, the fruites that may be reaped by conversation, and teaching howe to knowe good companie from yll. In the second, the manner of conversation, meete for all persons, which shall come in any companie, out of their owne houses, and then of the perticular points which ought to bee observed in companie between young men and olde, Gentlemen and Yeoman, Princes and private persons, learned and unlearned, Citizens and Strangers, Religious and Secular, men and women. In the third is perticularly set forth the orders to bee observed in conversation within doores, between the husband and the wife, the father and the sonne, brother and brother, the Maister and the servant. . . .'

[28] On the virtues of human company as a cure for misanthropic melancholy, see Lawrence Babb, *The Elizabethan Malady* (East Lansing, Mich., 1951), Chapter 2, 'The Scientific Theory of Melancholy'.

tongues to rent a sunder', and 'those curre dogges, which without barking bite us privily'. Spenser does not give these two types entirely separate roles in his poem; to him, slander is normally insidious. The Blatant Beast attacks Serena when she least expects it; Turpine takes care to attack only those weaker than himself. In contrast to the effect of slander in society, Guazzo tells us that courtesy gives rise to courtesy:[29] 'Therefore it is our partes rather to prevent our friends in salutations, and to goe beyond them in curtesie' (1: 157)—a striking parallel with Spenser's dictum that good should from us go, than come in greater store.[30]

Such similarities between Guazzo and Spenser do not in themselves indicate a direct source. Interest in the social order and its connection with courtesy is part and parcel of the tradition. Nor should the similarities blind us to the differences—Guazzo's view of love, for instance, or his somewhat different emphasis on the question of nature and nurture.[31] On the latter, Guazzo presents the view of Castiglione, which seems to be broadly Spenser's own view ('three sortes of gentrie, the first in respect of blood . . . the other in respect of good conditions . . . the third in respecte of bothe'), and then proceeds to differ from it. His own criteria are perhaps a little more typical of an era of economic progress, since he adds a further yardstick—that of riches. It is instructive that Guazzo, whose middle-class audience would for the most part qualify in none of the other respects, offers them some hope with the last. As the twentieth-century middle class takes vicarious pleasure in the doings of royalty or presidents' wives, so perhaps the reader of Guazzo, like the reader of Spenser, might feel a sense

---

[29] Cf. 'Yet there are some gentlemen of better disposition, who frequenting for the most part, the company of gentlemen, take no scorne when occasion serveth to accept of the company of those which are no gentlemen. . . . The gentleman which useth the companie of his inferiours, giveth, and receiveth, singular pleasure: For that they are marvellous wel apaid when they see a Gentleman, notwithstanding the inequalitie, which is betweene them, to make him selfe their equall. Whereby they are induced to love him, to honor him, and to doe him service: and whereby they themselves winne credite, and are the better esteemed of by their equals' (1: 92). Compare this with Calidore's attitude towards the shepherds. Note also Cligés's remarks concerning the British court, in Chrétien de Troyes' medieval romance: 'And he who wishes to win honour should associate himself with them, for honour is won and gained by him who associates with gentlemen.' (*Arthurian Romances*, trans. W. Wistar Comfort (London, 1914), p. 146.)

[30] See below, p. 252. Cf. La Primaudaye, Chapter 43, 'Of Envie, Hatred, and Backbiting'.

[31] On love, see 1: 235; on nature and nurture, see 1: 175.

of security stemming from the firmly established social hierarchy of which he was a part, and a lingering hope in the possibility of his own betterment.

It is evident from this glance at courtesy literature that behind Spenser's Legend of Courtesy there exists a well-established and complex tradition. Discussion of the role of the educated man in Elizabethan society was widespread, and the debates on nature and nurture prove a particularly convenient jumping-off point for the consideration of poetic truth which, as we shall discover, underlies so much of Book VI.

3. Courtesy defined: Cantos i–viii

The redefinition of courtesy in Book VI, as we have seen, has curious structural consequences. Above all, it leads to a dislocation of plot, as quest goes one way and virtue the other. The actual need for redefinition is conceptualized for us in the moral dilemma of the titular hero's truancy. Calidore abandons his quest, but is rewarded with a mystical or symbolic vision akin to the vision of the New Jerusalem which the Red Cross Knight witnesses in Book I. In the Legend of Holiness the vision is closely bound up with the defeat of the dragon of Original Sin. But in Book VI, despite the direct connection between receiving the power of courtesy to defeat slander and the actual business of defeating it, there is an equally direct antagonism between following the quest and abandoning it. The way out of this curious situation lies in rethinking the very terms of the quest. In Book I, we start out with an untutored knight facing a large monster. The basic problem is how to make him strong enough. In Book VI we begin with a knight skilled in courtesy who must defeat discourtesy. If Calidore is what he is claimed to be, how can the outcome be in doubt? In fact the *quest itself* changes its meaning as the narrative proceeds, and the knight's preparedness is shown to be illusory, depending on too narrow a definition of the virtue. Quest and virtue must in consequence be held apart until the issues crystallize and the reader is able to reorient himself. Spenser is not reiterating a commonly held belief but replacing it with a new one. He changes his reader along with his hero.

The vision of the Graces, in Colin's interpretation, tells us that courtesy consists of 'comely carriage', 'entertainement kynde', 'sweet semblaunt', 'friendly offices that bynde'—various qualities of the body or of the mind. Added to this is the virtue of civility, correct behaviour towards other members of society. The two stanzas in which Colin explains these things tell the reader essentially what he knows already; the redefinition of courtesy comes in the latter part of Colin's speech. We have, then, two explanations of the nature of virtue, the old and familiar, and the redefinition. The opening cantos of the book are taken up with a rehearsal of the old and familiar explanation of courtesy—the knowledge of courtesy with which Spenser's readers come to his work. The poet's purpose is not to demonstrate that his readers' knowledge is wrong, but that it is inadequate. Crudor's main offence, we find, is against 'entertainement kynd'. By forcing Briana to despoil ladies of their hair and men of their beards in order to win his love, he bases this love on the disruption of civil conversation. But though his love is a logical contradiction, in other respects Crudor is brave and skilled, particularly if we bear in mind Arthur's comfortable remark to Turpine (vi. vi. 35), 'For greater force there needs to maintaine wrong, then right'. Calidore, himself skilled in fight, is hard put to overcome him. We have already noticed how, in sharp contrast to somewhat similar episodes in Book v, he shows mercy towards him, aiming to win over rather than to destroy. We have learned that knighthood consists not in the practice of arms alone, but also in courtesy; that it involves self-restraint and treatment of others as we would have them treat us. We have discovered that the very offenders against courtesy are loudest in accusing others of discourtesy. Above all, Spenser makes clear to us that courtesy is a kind of insurance against the caprices of fortune. Mutual courtesy, we conclude, both lessens the effects of misfortune and makes reversals less likely; courtesy and civil order are set over against misfortune, chance, lack of order.[32]

The moral issues in the next episode we found to be less clear-cut. The knight whom the squire Tristram kills has already wounded Aladine and is ill-treating his own lady. His disruption of order in his quest for love (or lust) parallels that of Crudor. Tristram's fight with him demonstrates that the law of arms, which makes it an offence for one not a knight to fight with a knight,

---

[32] Cf. Pamela's defence of chastity in the *Arcadia* (*The Prose Works of Sir Philip Sidney*, ed. Albert Feuillerat (Cambridge, 1912), 1: 402–10). See Douglas Bush, *Mythology and the Renaissance Tradition*, 2nd edn. (New York, 1963), pp. 114–15.

must be applied with due regard to the dictates of courtesy, a
quality existing independently of this law. The knight was the
first to offend; Tristram intervenes to set matters to rights—not
out of self-interest but with complete selflessness, thereby demonstrating that courtesy springs from a sense of responsibility towards others. The emphasis on selflessness is a departure from
certain of the earlier courtesy books (Castiglione for instance),
though others of Tristram's characteristics are more traditional.
He reveals the 'comely carriage' and 'friendly offices' which Colin
mentions, and he is of noble birth. But, we learn, the practice of
civility is not the mere mechanical application of orders of precedence; there are cases where law must yield to understanding, or
(in Book v's terms) Justice to Equity.

The story of Aladine and Priscilla also emphasizes the limitations of the law of degree. Though difference of degree is the
cause of the troubles of the lovers (combined with knightly discourtesy of course), Calidore chooses to support their case, against
Priscilla's parents. As with Tristram's offence against the law of
arms, he does so not for himself but in the interests of harmony.
The episode is a small emblem of 'friendly offices that bind'.
Calidore is prepared to assist the lovers in spite of the disapproval
of society, 'Fearlesse, who ought did thinke, or ought did say, /
Sith his own thought he knew most cleare from wite'.[33]

Just how severe the disapproval can be is shown in the story
of Calepine and Serena. The situation here is perfectly clear.
Whether because of a mistake on his part, or because of fortune
(as he himself explains it), Calidore invades the privacy of Calepine. Calidore does his best to remedy the situation, but his behaviour is a remarkable demonstration of the inadequacy of mere
external courtesy:

> With which his gentle words and goodly wit
> He soone allayd that Knights conceiv'd displeasure,
> That he besought him downe by him to sit,
> That they mote treat of things abrode at leasure.
>
> (VI. iii. 22)

This is hardly realistic. Serena is not likely to be interested in
knightly shop talk. Calidore's reaction to his intrusion is hardly
the result of genuine disinterest or careful prudence; concerned

---

[33] On Guazzo and white lies, see *Civile Conversation* I: 97, and p. 48 above.

for his own shame, he impetuously employs his more superficial talents without regard for what should underlie them. His glib 'entertainement kynd' does nothing for Serena, and she is attacked by the Blatant Beast.[34]

These four initial episodes are generally held to be a series of examples of courtesy in action, but this interpretation must now be accepted only with reservations. They are evidently primarily emblematic not of the strengths but of the shortcomings of the virtue, at least as the court practises it. The court erects rules of chivalry, degree and all manner of similar superficialities, as guides to virtuous conduct. Though in some measure Calidore's imagination can transcend such pettinesses, it fails him with Calepine and Serena. He lacks a conception of courtesy broad enough to make principles out of his occasional insights.

Calidore, and Spenser along with him, is moving in these early cantos towards a radical realignment of the goals of courtesy literature—a realignment which makes his Legend of Courtesy a social as well as a literary phenomenon. We have seen how the late sixteenth century revived an interest in chivalry not unlike that of the late fifteenth century. Writing of the earlier period, the Dutch historian Johan Huizinga points out that the aristocracy, unable to conceive the need for change in a way of life which seemed to them to contain so much that was worth preserving, retreated more and more into the minute observance of their own rules, going through the rather absurd motions of chivalry and courtly love and ignoring the political realities of changing times. Their love of ceremony and high living found willing imitators among the burghers. But there were those of a more sensitive character who could not tolerate this emphasis on externals and the cultivation of double standards. They praised instead the simple life, and longed for the freedom of country living or solitary contemplation.[35] Spenser's conception of courtesy is based

---

[34] Cf. W. L. Renwick's idea of 'typical action': the titular hero acts out the attributes of his virtue in a series of incidents designed to reveal its nature. Renwick sees the opening episodes of Book VI as a series of variations on the nature of courtesy In these terms, Calidore is trapped by the limitations of his virtue in Canto iii: the inadequacy is less *his* inadequacy than it is the *virtue's*. See W. L. Renwick, *Edmund Spenser: an Essay on Renaissance Poetry* (London, 1925), pp. 158–60, and *passim.*

[35] *The Waning of the Middle Ages* (Garden City, N.Y., 1954), *passim,* esp. pp. 128ff. Petrarch's *De Vita Solitaria* might be regarded as an example of such bucolic works.

on an awareness of a similar dichotomy in his own age and a desire to bridge it. In the early episodes Calidore remains bound to his society. Only later does he discover a new set of standards outside the chivalric framework, and this set of standards turns out ultimately to be the true courtesy. But he can find this true courtesy only by bursting the bounds of the quest.

If the first four episodes, moving in ever-widening divergence between society and the protagonists, demonstrate the limitations of the ideas of courtesy generally accepted by Spenser's contemporaries, they also hint at deeper considerations. There are, for example, strange and repeated allusions to fortune. The repeated emphasis on self-control and self-effacement suggests that Spenser sees courtesy as, in some measure, the application of temperance in a social situation. Certainly the lessons the courteous man must learn—bridling of the senses and application of reason—are lessons Guyon learned in his quest for temperance.

The deepening of the definition of courtesy is achieved primarily through Calepine and his adventures and then finally through the story of Pastorella. In the first section of Book VI we see courtesy in action; in the central section we see the effects of discourtesy. Calepine is the typical courtier subjected to typical attacks. Perhaps, as one critic has suggested, Calepine's weakness springs simply from his inability to defend himself, a skill which he finally learns through his stay with the Salvage Man.[36] But along the way he shows how the average courtier is constantly at the mercy of his would-be detractors. Both he and Serena are naïve in supposing themselves immune from the sometimes oppressive moral standards of the court, and it is fitting that the Hermit should tell Serena to take greater care in her conduct, but we should be equally naïve if we supposed that the court applied its moral judgements with an even hand. Men in authority like to attack men who cannot defend themselves; if might does not always make right, weakness always seems to make wrong. Arthur, one of whose main functions is to serve as a contrast to Calepine, backs courtesy with force of arms. He also supports his own strength with the strength of nature, epitomized in the Salvage Man. Calepine must learn to use nature's strength as well as

[36] See Cheney, *Image of Nature*, pp. 195ff. Cheney suggests that as Crudor lacks courtesy to supplement his martial prowess, so Calepine lacks skill in fight to enforce his courtesy and preserve it against attack.

nature's solace; he finally demonstrates his new-found ability in his defeat of the bear.[37]

Natural strength does not, however, reintegrate Calepine into society. But it does allow him to attack the courtly artificiality of the cannibals and rescue Serena from them. Serena, whose very name suggests that she is a lover of the peace and tranquillity of the natural world, is finally saved by Calepine's sword. His victory defines in broad terms the proper relationship between art and nature, strength and mercy, necessary for the courtier. The central section of the book shows that courtesy is not simply a matter of the court, for it involves a feeling of harmony with natural process—a harmony violated in their various ways by both Mirabella and the Salvage Nation. In the event of disharmony, honour and strength are needed to re-establish harmony: the enemies of courtesy must be punished (Mirabella) or destroyed (Turpine). Thus the failure of Calidore's courtesy in the earlier episodes is explained in these central ones. 'Of Court it seemes, men Courtesie doe call', but its roots lie deeper than the court.

[37] Arthur uses the *strength* of nature in his attack on Turpine and he is able to *solace* in nature (he sleeps afterwards) because natural strength, the Salvage Man, is ready to defend him. The solace of Calepine and Serena is not matched with strength (Calepine the city-dweller cannot defend Serena against the Beast), and Calepine's later 'solace' to hear the thrush's song leads only to a largely irrelevant victory and a series of misfortunes.

VII

Nature

1. Nature and the body politic

'Thou Nature art my Goddess!' cries Shakespeare's Edmund;
'God being the author of Nature, her voice is but his instrument',
declares Hooker; 'I therefore hate this trouble-feast reason', Florio
translates Montaigne, 'I follow mine owne naturall inclinations.'[1]
There is not a period in the history of the English language when
the word Nature has not borne a multiplicity of meanings.[2] The
Elizabethan age, a time when the old values and ways of looking
at the world were under constant scrutiny and redefinition, seized
upon the concept of Nature as a way of articulating a philosophy
of man, a means of coming to grips with social change, and a way
of discussing the social order. Hooker, seeking to establish the
theological basis of the English church, finds its justification in
natural law; Puttenham and his fellow-rhetoricians appeal to nature
as the final arbiter of language; William Vaughan praises poets
because they were the first to 'observe the secrete operations of
nature'.[3]

Since in nature the Elizabethans find the root causes of things,
it follows that their writings are much preoccupied with what one
scholar has called the nature of nature.[4] In fact the activity of

---

[1] *King Lear*, I. ii; Richard Hooker, *Of the Laws of Ecclesiastical Polity*, ed. Christopher Morris (London, 1907), I.viii.3 (p. 176); *The Essayes of Michael, Lord of Montaigne*, trans. John Florio, ed. Thomas Seccombe (London, 1908), III. 303.

[2] On the meaning of the word, see C. S. Lewis, *Studies in Words* (Cambridge, 1960), pp. 24–74. Also helpful, though less concerned with the Renaissance, are two essays in Arthur O. Lovejoy's *Essays in the History of Ideas* (Baltimore, Md., 1948), pp. 69–77, 308–38.

[3] G. Gregory Smith, ed., *Elizabethan Critical Essays* (Oxford, 1904), 2: 325.

[4] Hiram Haydn, *The Counter-Renaissance* (New York, 1950), pp. 461–554. On Elizabethan attitudes to nature see also Douglas Bush, *Prefaces to Renaissance Literature* (Cambridge, Mass., 1965), pp. 44–64; John F. Danby, *Shakespeare's Doctrine of Nature* (London, 1961), pp. 15–53; Theodore Spencer, *Shakespeare and the Nature of Man*, 2nd edn. (New York, 1949), pp. 1–50; Eric LaGuardia, *Nature Redeemed* (The Hague, 1966), esp. Chapter 1. Cf. A. Sidney Knowles, Jr., 'Spenser's Natural Man', *Renaissance Papers 1958, 1959, 1960*, pp. 3–11.

defining nature is another way of discussing the qualities of its products. When Elizabethan philosophers quarrel over definitions of nature, they may be using this concept as a kind of metaphor for law, or poetry, or mathematics, or theology. When poets write of nature, nature may well serve as a metaphor for poetry itself. Spenser's use of the concept certainly involves this latter meaning, but at the same time he is concerned with social issues of some importance. In choosing the pastoral mode for Book VI, he makes the book's central theme doubly plain by giving it concrete articulation in the poem's setting. This represents a marked shift in emphasis from Book v.

Every critic of Book VI points to Spenser's change of tone. The change is not so much a relaxation of intellectual activity (as some of the older critics have suggested) as a shift in mood—a movement away from the inexorability of Artegall's justice (with a particularly unsympathetic Irish policy forming its historical equivalent) into a world of mercy and love. The landscape itself changes. From the populated realms of Belge and Irena, the crowds and armies of Book v, we move into the rural setting of Briana's castle and the great expanse of woodland which seems to cover the first two-thirds of Book VI with a great canopy of greenery.

While there is little evidence of courts and cities in the landscape through which Calidore and Calepine pass, we should not forget that the justification for this landscape lies in the very fact that Book VI is a poem *about* courts and cities, even if the redefinition of man's role in society—the practice of courtesy and the knowledge of 'civility'—involves his stepping outside its framework. To claim, as Spenser's narrator claims, that courtesy is no longer to be found at court, is only another way of saying that definition of the proper social order involves a return to first principles. One way of articulating such a return is by adoption of the pastoral mode, a kind of historical jump into the myth of primitivism. The depiction of a world without cities also helps to stress the fact that neither society itself nor the individual within the society is self-sufficient; there must be a continued contact, a giving and receiving, with what lies outside.

Each of the events in the book can be read in terms of the protagonist's relationship to the social order. Crudor, for example, is a case of knightliness gone wrong, and his change of heart is both a reminder of Calidore's eloquence and a startling demonstration of Crudor's innate goodness. This perverted knight seeks to gain by antagonism what can only be gained by harmony. He misunderstands the relationship of war to love. Calidore's intervention re-establishes equilibrium and reshapes Crudor's conduct to make it natural.

The situation of Tristram, on the other hand, demonstrates the effects of disharmony on the members of society whom it afflicts. He has retreated into the forest, the natural world, to escape oppression. While there, like Artegall or Belphoebe or Satyrane, he has turned his exile to good account, becoming an intrepid huntsman and adding the hunter's skill to his natural nobility of bearing. His retreat is paralleled by Aladine and Priscilla, who must meet in secret because of the disapproval of Priscilla's parents. Calidore's task is to create harmony where before there existed antagonism. Seen in this light, his action in bringing the lovers back to their homes is highly commendable and illustrative of his poetic role. His failure with Calepine and Serena demonstrates what is perhaps a natural disinclination on their part to accept their responsibilities in society, and to do their utmost to behave diplomatically. Fenice's reminder in Chrétien's *Cligés* holds good four hundred years later:

> It is well to remember and observe the injunction of St. Paul: if anyone is unwilling to live chaste, St. Paul counsels him to act so that he shall receive no criticism, or blame, or reproach. It is well to stop evil mouths.[5]

Their powerlessness in the face of adversity is at once a criticism of their conduct and a demonstration of the evils inherent in a self-centred and self-destructive society.

Through the book's early episodes Calidore acts as an enlightened member of the imperfect society from which he has come. He is able to teach Crudor the proper relationship of war to love by recourse to the precepts of knightly behaviour. But this same knightly code leads to an initial misunderstanding of Tristram's behaviour. With Priscilla and Aladine Calidore's courtesy is barely adequate. It fails altogether with Calepine and Serena, who are consequently driven out into the realm of nature. There they are

---

[5] Chrétien de Troyes, *Arthurian Romances*, trans. W. Wistar Comfort (London, 1914), p. 160.

assailed by a society which will not readmit them (the base Turpine), and befriended by Arthur, the perfect knight, by the Salvage Man and by the Hermit.

In this excursion into the natural world, Calidore, representative of society, plays no part. This is not to suggest that the logic of Spenser's poem forbids it, but simply that the isolation of Calidore and Calepine from one another helps to emphasize their differences. Arthur adopts a role somewhat similar to Calidore's. The central episodes drive home certain points made earlier in the narrative, among them the need for co-operation to avoid the ravages of discourtesy. One of the examples of such co-operation turns out to have special importance in relation to the final third of the book. The Salvage Man and Arthur form an alliance to overcome Turpine, and later the Salvage Man is instrumental in saving the Prince's life. The alliance suggests a certain identity between the natural world and the world of the court. This is the major discovery of the final cantos: the proper running of society depends on close contact with the natural world.

When Calidore does reach the natural world it is under somewhat different circumstances, in a pastoral episode with formidable literary precedent and only a limited similarity to the world of Calepine, Serena, the Salvage Man, and the rest. Whereas the earlier landscape, inhabited also by Turpine and the cannibals, was in certain respects a metaphor for the life of the corrupt court whose characteristics were first described to us in the proem, the landscape which Calidore enters has nothing to do with the court at all. Its relevance lies in its contrast: it presents us with an idyllic picture of total harmony which stands at the opposite pole from the corrupt standards of Mirabella and the Salvage Nation and proposes a rather different view of courtesy from that presented in Calidore's earlier adventures.

To understand the pastoral episode properly, we must bring to it a wide knowledge of Elizabethan literary and philosophical conventions. We have already begun in an earlier chapter by looking at the background to Spenser's view of courtesy. In the present chapter we shall cast a glance at views of nature, among the Elizabethans in general and in the *Faerie Queene* in particular.

2. *Elizabethan views of nature*

'Now if nature should intermit her course,' writes Hooker in a famous passage,

and leave altogether though it were but for a while the observation of her own laws; if those principal and mother elements of the world, whereof all things in this lower world are made, should lose the qualities which now they have; if the frame of that heavenly arch erected over our heads should loosen and dissolve itself; if celestial spheres should forget their wonted motions, and by irregular volubility turn themselves any way as it might happen; if the prince of the lights of heaven, which now as a giant doth run his unwearied course, should as it were through a languishing faintness begin to stand and to rest himself; if the moon should wander from her beaten way, the times and seasons of the year blend themselves by disordered and confused mixture, the winds breathe out their last gasp, the clouds yield no rain, the earth be defeated of heavenly influence, the fruits of the earth pine away as children at the withered breasts of their mother no longer able to yield them relief: what would become of man himself, whom these things now do all serve? See we not plainly that obedience of creatures unto the law of nature is the stay of the whole world?[6]

This sonorous affirmation of God's providence (the style reinforces the argument) represents what can be described as the orthodox Elizabethan view of nature (we must, though, be wary of affixing labels—or at any rate of allowing our thinking to be confined by them). It is sometimes called the optimistic view. Nature, it claims, is part of an ordered cosmic pattern extending from the very simplest elements in God's creation, through the animals and man, to the angels, and ultimately to God himself. The scheme, Aristotelian in conception, though much altered by philosophers in the Middle Ages, and to some extent by empirical observation in the Renaissance, is well known to every student of the period, and I need not elaborate on it. It is based, of course, on the idea of hierarchy, and it is frequently expressed as a series of concentric circles, a figure which the Renaissance found especially versatile.[7]

[6] *Eccl. Pol.*, I. iii. 2.

[7] E. M. W. Tillyard, *The Elizabethan World Picture* (London, 1943), gives a convenient though over-simplified summary of Elizabethan ideas of order. See also the more satisfactory studies by C. S. Lewis, *The Discarded Image* (Cambridge, 1964), and Hardin Craig, *The Enchanted Glass* (New York, 1936). James Winny brings together the more relevant texts in *The Frame of Order* (London, 1957).

Linking the various parts of the created universe is the Chain of Being, its topmost extremity tied to the foot of God's throne, and its various links descending to the least of God's creatures. In this hierarchical order, man occupies a crucial position, since he stands between the animals, which are devoid of reason, and the angels, who are all intellect.[8] As for man's physical surroundings, they are like a book—the Book of Nature—whose study will help him to understand the supreme reasonableness of God. To the Christian Humanist, man's salvation is dependent upon adequate study of two books—principally the Bible, the Book of God's Word, but also Nature, the Book of God's Works.[9] The study of the order in nature may consequently be construed as a sacred as well as a moral act, in much the same way that the practice of humility, for example, becomes a sacred act when it involves imitation of the humility of Christ.

Governing God's Book of Nature is the Law of Nature, God-given and immutable. It is revealed to mankind through the operations of the universe, through the cosmic pattern and its supreme harmony. But the needs of mankind in society have led to the formation or, more precisely, deduction, of a second law, modelled on the first. This is the Law of Nations, which provides the general principles of man's social living. A third, Civil Law, provides for the particular needs of a particular society, and is modelled in turn on the Law of Nations. Even though each of these bodies of law is separate and distinct, they all emanate from a single source, which is the created universe, tempered by God's word. In a sense, then, any action by a governor or prince with respect to Civil Law or the Law of Nations is an expression of God's will, and even the submission of the individual citizen to the individual law is an acknowledgement of God's supreme authority. Of course, we must remember that the sixteenth century is distinguished by a whole series of attempts to detach secular government from religious dictates. But in important ways the trend in England was in the other direction. Given that the Established Church was firmly in political hands, it was expedient to link political acts with God's providence and to threaten rebels

---

[8] Arthur O. Lovejoy, *The Great Chain of Being* (Cambridge, Mass., 1936).

[9] Ernst Robert Curtius traces the history of the concept in *European Literature and the Latin Middle Ages* (New York, 1953), pp. 319–26. The idea has remained very persistent: note rather similar Romantic attitudes to Nature.

with his thunderbolts. The effects of such thinking, itself a legacy of the medieval world view, ran deep. One might expect such a belief in the cosmic consequences of the individual act to have little hold on an increasingly urbanized society, but surely the Elizabethan love of history, nostalgia, and pastoral points to its reluctance to abandon such notions in the face of their irrelevance to city living. The genius of the Tudors lay in their ability to turn such hankering after the simple life into a political force of great potency. Even the Puritan capitalist of the seventeenth century, with his belief that to make money was to win favour in the sight of the Lord, was only adapting the old ideas to new purposes.[10]

The sense of cosmic harmony, or the sense that there *ought* to be a cosmic harmony, is so much a part of everyday Elizabethan thought that we must be wary of carrying over into an Elizabethan context some of the distinctions which we all too readily make in our twentieth-century ways of thinking. If the exercise of Civil Law is a reflection of the laws of the cosmos, then neat distinctions between temporal and divine, secular and sacred, have little relevance to the Elizabethan mind. This being so, it is disturbing to find critics of the *Faerie Queene* attempting to erect just such distinctions. Many of the arguments over Book II, for example, seem to spring from a conviction that the book must be either secular or religious, as though there is no possibility that it can be both at the same time. What might be called the ideological distinctions which we make as we read the *Faerie Queene* are at best limited in applicability and value. Quite apart from the fact that Spenser is an Elizabethan, we must remember that Spenser is an exceptionally eclectic poet who is specially interested in synthesizing world views, philosophies, ideas, not in compartmentalizing them.

This synthesizing activity is inherently conservative, involving an assimilation of the past into the present. In such an activity, nature turns out to be an ally. For all its abundant nuances, the Elizabethan idea of nature does tend to support the status quo. Pastoral looks backwards in time; the Golden Age sets perfect nature in the past. Elizabethans described noble birth, ancestry,

---

[10] On order in the body politic, particularly in relation to political philosophy see Ernest William Talbert, *The Problem of Order: Elizabethan Political Commonplaces and an Example of Shakespeare's Art* (Chapel Hill, N.C., 1962); W. H. Greenleaf, *Order, Empiricism and Politics: Two Traditions of English Political Thought, 1500–1700* (London, 1964); David Bevington, *Tudor Drama and Politics* (Cambridge, Mass., 1968).

as *natural* superiority; artistic imitation involved the emulation of classical models, which were considered worthy of attention because they followed nature. Hooker's appeal to natural law was also an appeal to the historical primacy of the English church. This conservative tendency in Spenser's thought, so much a feature of his age, allies him with the optimistic view of nature, though there are elements in the *Faerie Queene* which suggest that there is another way of looking at it.

Side by side with the view of an ordered nature there existed in sixteenth-century thought a quite different set of beliefs which saw nature as confused or incomprehensible. The ordered hierarchies of the universe, Man as the noble creation of God, the animals as part of the fulness of nature created for Man's use—all these are hopelessly flawed by Adam's first sin, by Man's fall from grace. As a result of this Fall, death succeeds life, winter succeeds summer, behind every hint of God's bounty there lurks the blinding proof of Satan's subversion. Above all, Man's reason is fatally defective: he can no longer perceive the Good even if it is there. The Book of God's Works may still be open to him but he has lost the ability to read it. In consequence, he can do little or nothing to bring about his own salvation, but will be saved or damned only through the action of God's grace. Unable to perceive the workings of God's providence, Man tends to presume its inscrutability and fall back on a belief in fate, personified in the figure of blind Fortune, an unmerciful goddess of inexorable power. 'If any one falls into the hands of robbers', writes Calvin,

or meets with wild beasts; if by a sudden storm he is shipwrecked on the ocean; if he is killed by the fall of a house or a tree; if another, wandering through deserts, finds relief for his penury, or, after having been tossed about by the waves, reaches the port, and escapes, as it were, but a hair's-breadth from death,—carnal reason will subscribe all these occurrences, both prosperous and adverse, to fortune. But whoever has been taught from the mouth of Christ, that the hairs of his head are all numbered, will seek further for a cause, and conclude that all events are governed by the secret counsel of God.[11]

Such are man's limitations, then, that even if he is aware of the existence of providence he is unable to understand it. The framers of the Anglican Articles of Religion were quick to understand the

[11] *Institutes*, I. xvi. 2, trans. John Allen (Philadelphia, Pa., 1928).

implications of such a doctrine. The seventeenth Article, 'Of Predestination and Election', points out that the condition of helplessness in which the believer in predestination finds himself may have an admirable effect on the godly but is unlikely to be therapeutic for the sinner:

For curious and carnal persons, lacking the Spirit of Christ, to have continually before their eyes the sentence of God's Predestination, is a most dangerous downfall, whereby the Devil doth thrust them either into desperation, or into wretchlessness of most unclean living, no less perilous than desperation.

But we should not presume, as so many historians of ideas do, that Calvin viewed the *universe* as totally depraved. In fact, part of the irony of man's situation lies in the very fact that he is unable to avail himself of the positive strengths which God's creation affords. In the same way, while his awareness of God is built into him, he is equally aware that he is unworthy of any part in salvation.

The difference between the optimistic and the pessimistic views of nature is, then, less a question of fundamental differences of data than of differences in interpretation. The optimistic view tends naturally toward a belief in the efficacy of Good Works, and a Thomistic emphasis on right reason; the pessimistic view stresses man's helplessness but puts an Augustinian and Pauline stress on the power of God's redeeming grace. In terms of dogma this is an extremely important difference, but for both sides of the argument the premises are essentially the same. There *were* those, of course, who acknowledged no benevolent natural order at all, and this belief later found its apologist in Hobbes, just as the orthodox Anglican view received its greatest statement half a century before him in Hooker. But many of those who at first sight appear anarchists are nothing of the sort. The much-emphasized early seventeenth-century preoccupation with charnel houses, for example, recedes in importance when we realize that the emphasis on death and judgement is as old as Christianity, and that the theme of the decay of the world in itself presupposes the existence of order in the universe.[12] Even Donne's *First Anniversary* proves

[12] But see Don Cameron Allen, 'The Degeneration of Man and Renaissance Pessimism', *SP*, 35 (1938), 202–27; Douglas Bush, 'Science and Literature in the Seventeenth Century', in *Engaged and Disengaged* (Cambridge, Mass., 1966), pp. 180–206; H. B. Parkes, 'Nature's Diverse Laws: the Double Vision of the Elizabethans', *Sewanee Review*, 58 (1950), 402–18.

to be a stylized religious meditation rather than a spontaneous expression of despair, and is too close to Platonism to provide the nihilists with much ammunition. In many respects it is a very traditional poem, not least in its assumption that there is a direct link between the individual and the universe surrounding him.[13] One of the consequences of Adam's sin is, of course, the fact that disorder in the universe becomes a pattern for disorder in mankind and vice versa—hence the much-quoted speech of Ulysses (in Shakespeare's *Troilus and Cressida*), a compendium of Elizabethan ideas on order which has been much drawn upon by modern historians.[14]

We would do well to mark the occasion of Ulysses' speech. It comes in response to Agamemnon's deploring the defeatism of those who give themselves over to 'fortune's love' and in consequence give up whenever things seem against them. In a sense, we are faced with a situation similar to that in Book VI; the central problem, as Ulysses defines it, is how to engender in the Greek army the strength to *resist* fortune, to rise above it. We might also notice the unconcerned ease with which the speaker passes from Law of Nature to Law of Nations, and moves up and down the scale of creation, viewing disorder as a turning from the natural ascent towards God, in the direction of will, and appetite, and the behaviour of beasts. This turning aside negates the Reason upon which the universe itself is founded. Hardly surprisingly, the optimistic, humanist view scarcely distinguished between Reason and Nature, the latter being in a sense the outward manifestation of the former.

My use of the term 'unconcerned ease' was deliberate. We have to read Ulysses' speech in context. He is perhaps the greatest opportunist of them all, and certainly the most orotund speechifier. But the fact that he is something of an old windbag does not necessarily invalidate the principles he enunciates, any more than

---

[13] On the poem's background see especially Louis L. Martz, *The Poetry of Meditation* (New Haven, Conn., 1954), pp. 211–48, and Frank Manley's introduction to his edition of *The Anniversaries* (Baltimore, Md., 1963).

[14] *Troilus and Cressida*, II. iii. On its relevance to the history of ideas, see, for instance, Tillyard's analysis in *The Elizabethan World Picture*, but note Harry Levin's important reservations in 'English Literature of the Renaissance' in Tinsley Helton, ed., *The Renaissance: a Reconsideration of the Theories and Interpretations of the Age* (Madison, Wis., 1964), pp. 125–51. On its dramatic significance, see Robert Kimbrough, *Shakespeare's 'Troilus and Cressida' and its Setting* (Cambridge, Mass., 1964), pp. 138–71.

Polonius's advice to Laertes need be rejected as atypical of Shakespeare's age just because it is pronounced by a fool. There are many who agree with Kipling that it is commendable to keep your head when all about you are losing theirs and blaming it on you, without necessarily endorsing the spirit in which the advice was first offered. Certainly, the more sophisticated writers of the 1590s were apt to look askance at the rhetoric of such sonorous statements of cosmic order. Ben Jonson found the opening of Davies's *Orchestra* outrageously funny, apparently failing to realize that Davies has the last laugh: Antinous's paean of praise for the order of the universe is in fact a subterfuge to win Penelope—as utilitarian an enunciation of the divine order as any in the love poetry of Donne.

A great deal of the old way of thinking died with Elizabeth, and it is perhaps somewhat unhistorical to set up contrasts between Hooker and Hobbes. But it is worth emphasizing that the tradition of Christian humanism inhibited empirical observation a good deal less than we might suppose. In fact, as Bacon points out, and as we have already observed, the process of free inquiry can be seen as an attempt to make sense of a universe whose meaning, because of the Fall, is not immediately apparent. Hence it is inquiry in the service of God.

But further, it is an assured truth, and a conclusion of experience, that a little or superficial knowledge of philosophy may incline the mind of man to atheism, but a further proceeding therein doth bring the mind back to religion. For in the entrance of philosophy, when the second causes, which are next unto the senses, do offer themselves to the mind of man, if it dwell and stay there it may induce some oblivion of the highest cause; but when a man passeth on further, and seeth the dependence of causes, and the works of Providence, then, according to the allegory of the poets, he will easily believe that the highest link of nature's chain must needs be tied to the foot of Jupiter's chair. To conclude therefore, let no man upon a weak conceit of sobriety or an ill-applied moderation think or maintain, that a man can search too far, or be too well studied in the book of God's word, or in the book of God's works, divinity or philosophy.[15]

It is commonly supposed that Bacon's separation of divinity and philosophy was a device to free the latter from the former. We forget that Sidney did the same, that Copernicus believed as firmly

[15] *Advancement of Learning*, ed. Thomas Case (London, 1951), p. 11 (1.i.3).

in the order of the universe as any medieval, that even Newton was a devout, perhaps over-devout, Christian, that Boyle wrote not only on chemistry but also on seraphic love. The clue perhaps lies in Bacon's seemingly innocuous phrase 'according to the allegory of the poets'. We cannot investigate Bacon's views on figurative language here,[16] but his remark does perhaps remind us that the literal, empirical truth of a given statement has little or no effect on its value as a metaphor. When Spenser declares in Book v that 'the world is runne quite out of square', not only does he base his picture of a disordered universe on a presupposed image of order; he also adds strength to the picture of an ideal age long ago which he sets up in opposition to such disorder. Like Bacon (especially in the *Wisdom of the Ancients*) Spenser is at pains to emphasize the value of figurative language, but he insists that it *is* figure. This is the reasoning underlying his treatment of Busyrane and of the Salvage Nation. The issue is a very important one for Spenser's contemporaries, and one which particularly preoccupies literary theorists. It also has relevance to political life. There were surely not very many people who thought that Elizabeth was *literally* the *primum mobile* (if there *was* a literal *primum mobile*), but that hardly detracts from the figurative value of the belief in order. Elizabeth was enough like the *primum mobile* for her courtiers to take the idea seriously, rebellion was enough like the wrath of God to be avoided at all costs, and peace was enough like cosmic harmony to be the desire of every honest London merchant. It matters not whether this idea of order was kept alive through political expediency or genuine and unshaken religious belief: it existed and was a potent force in the Elizabethan conduct of affairs.[17]

This is not to suggest that the so-called Elizabethan world picture is so much self-seeking hypocrisy. Human belief is an

[16] The subject is excellently studied by Karl R. Wallace, *Francis Bacon on Communication and Rhetoric* (Chapel Hill, N.C., 1943).

[17] J. W. Allen, following a widely held belief of the historians, considers the myth of order a combination of Elizabethan political propaganda and a somewhat alarming quality which he labels 'the common sense of the English people, or at least of its upper classes' (*A History of Political Thought in the Sixteenth Century* (London, 1928), pp. 131-3). Rejecting the notion that the belief springs from deep religious conviction, he declares (p. 133): 'At the end of Elizabeth's reign it was, on the whole, just the most thoroughly religious people, Catholic or Puritan, who were nearest to revolt.' But Catholic resistance to a Protestant monarchy found support in the belief that the Protestant rulers were subverting the natural order, and the Puritan mentality, strong in the conviction of man's total depravity, was naturally reluctant to submit to a system based on an optimistic view of the cosmos.

altogether more delicate affair than that. Above all, one should not underrate man's infinite capacity to adapt his beliefs to prevailing circumstances—to develop a set of beliefs often of great sophistication and to find rational explanations for such beliefs, all in order to satisfy certain underlying psychological needs dictated by the social and cultural conditions which surround him. Certainly the Elizabethan idea of order coincided with the psychological needs of the Tudor citizens.

Nonetheless, confidence in historical destiny, the sense that events move forward under the direction of God's universal will, was on the wane. Sir Walter Ralegh's magnificent opening to his *History of the World* was perhaps its last major statement by an important historian. The disappearance of this confidence had effects which easily escape the attention of the student of literary history. With its passing went one of the main elements in the quest theme, certainly as Spenser chooses to use the theme. The image of history framed by the *Faerie Queene* invests all events with significance in a gradually culminating sequence, the sequence of the quest. The faltering quest theme of Spenser's Book VI seems expressive of a certain malaise, a feeling that history itself may lack significance and momentum. The particular combination of the theme of the quest with the cyclical myth of death and rebirth embodied in pastoral reads like a collision between the Christian view of history as manifest destiny and the Greek belief in historical cycle, or perhaps an effort to shore up history by linking it with nature, and nature by linking it with historical event.

The universe of the *Faerie Queene* is in certain respects a mirror of the outside world. Faeryland itself is intrinsically good, but it is constantly under attack by the powers of evil. So we see the two views of nature in constant play. In Book I, for instance, the lion is made submissive by the sight of Una's beauty; it is naturally good. Orgoglio, on the other hand, appropriately enough a personification of pride, represents a disordered Nature. In Book VI we find a similar contrast between the Salvage Man who befriends Calepine and the Salvage Nation which attacks Serena. Orgoglio, as pride, is a product of man's sin. The Red Cross Knight comes into his clutches because he is a prisoner of his own imperfections. Instead of acting in accordance with those of his faculties most akin to the godlike aspects of his nature, he surrenders to his imagination, a lawless faculty which, unless it acts in conjunction with will and reason, leads to a reversal of the normal ascent towards God.[18] This ascent should be channelled via reason and, ultimately, intellect—the former being what we should now call discursive reason, the latter a higher faculty more akin to revelation.[19] When this breakdown takes place, when the normal ascent is interrupted, the system, like Shakespeare's 'universal wolf', turns upon itself, and nature is perverted.

This upsetting of the natural order is sin. Sin has no existence of itself; it is simply a breakdown in the lines of communication between God and his creation, some force which has stepped out of line. It follows, then, that if we can eliminate disorder we shall eliminate sin itself. Thus it is that when Arthur reclaims Redcross from the sin symbolized by Orgoglio, Orgoglio simply ceases to exist:

> But soone as breath out of his breast did pas,
> That huge great body, which the Gyaunt bore,
> Was vanisht quite, and of that monstrous mas
> Was nothing left, but like an emptie bladder was.
>
> (I. viii. 24)

But while the only solution to the problem of sin may be to remove the disordered element altogether, not every evil character in the *Faerie Queene* figures forth the sin itself. Crudor is disordered, but he is a cruel *person*, not Cruelty itself. Calidore succeeds in reintegrating him into society. Mirabella, who also became the victim of disorder, is likewise in the process of reclamation.

A society's belief in the efficacy of the natural order, the Book of God's Works, logically will lead it either to try to imitate the action of the hand of God in so far as that action is visible in the natural world, or to repudiate itself in favour of the nature upon which it is supposedly fashioned. The first results in pastoral, the

---

[18] See Spencer, *Nature of Man*, p. 24, who follows Ruth L. Anderson, *Elizabethan Psychology and Shakespeare's Plays* (Iowa City, 1927), pp. 23–4.

[19] 'Our medieval ancestors acknowledged two valid ways of knowledge. The first was through *ratio*, i.e. discursive reason; the second through *intellectus*. The word "*intellectus*" is not easy to define exactly. It carried something of the meaning of intuition or creative insight or imagination, in the sense Blake used that word. *Intellectus* they considered a higher faculty of the mind than *ratio*; one capable of bringing men to a more profound knowledge than could be gained through discursive reason.'—F. C. Happold, *Mysticism* (Harmondsworth, Middx., 1963), pp. 27–8.

second in poetry of retreat. Belief in man's ability to deal with his own problems, without reference to the occult powers of nature, leads in the other direction, towards utopianism. Utopianism involves a belief in progress—which may account for the fact that it does not appear in England before the early seventeenth century[20] —and is usually mechanistic. Pastoralism can be associated with an organic view of social processes—society is the body politic, similar to the human body; societies decay and die as men decay and die. Since society's desire to stand back from its problems and evaluate them in terms of some larger construct, or simply to stop thinking about them for a while, is a good deal more common than an attitude of self-reliance, so pastoral and its variations are legion. Indeed, literature itself is a form of pastoral (how slippery the term is!) both in what can only be described as its escapism and in its attempt to impose order on the disordered.[21] It is clear why the pastoral mode often provides a vehicle for poetic discussions of the function of literature.

3. The fall from perfection

The attraction of the life according to nature was given new impetus in the sixteenth century through a number of national economic and political changes, among them urban growth and colonial expansion. The former made men remote from the rural world and hence made it easier for them to idealize something they had not experienced at first hand—to say nothing of the fact that the anxieties of city life led them to desire retirement all the more. The latter led to the discovery of new communities in remote parts of the world—communities which to some European eyes seemed evidence of a more nearly perfect civilization because their standards were closer to the ideals of nature as conceived in turn by the Europeans.[22] This somewhat roundabout logic was

[20] I am thinking of course of the earliest genuinely prescriptive works. The thrust of More's *Utopia* is principally satiric, but the seventeenth-century's interest in the pansophical college (Bacon, Hartlib, Evelyn, etc.), in constitutional schemes (Harrington, Milton) and in language (Wilkins, Dalgarno, Urquhart) was prescriptive in its intent. See Nell Eurich, *Science in Utopia: a Mighty Design* (Cambridge, Mass., 1967); Humphrey Tonkin, 'Utopias: Notes on a Pattern of Thought', *Centennial Review*, 14 (1970), 385–95.

[21] See below, pp. 290ff.

[22] See Roy Harvey Pearce, 'Primitivistic Ideas in the *Faerie Queene*', *JEGP*, 44 (1945), 139–51, esp. 141, 143–4, 149–51; Lois Whitney, 'Spenser's Use of the Literature of Travel in the *Faerie Queene*', *MP*, 19 (1921), 143–62.

the less challenged owing to the geographical remoteness of the colonies.

It seemed to many sixteenth-century thinkers that in some way these remote Indians had escaped the ravages of the Fall or were otherwise immune to its effects. At least, they kept this fiction alive as a foil for social criticism: man's misguided belief in the virtues of the Noble Savage proves an admirable means of pointing out to him how stupid he really is. This myth of a natural perfection existing outside the confines of society has been with us as long as society itself. In its various manifestations it has been subjected to the scrutiny of anthropologists, historians of religion, literary historians.[23] It has provided peoples with a sense of their origins, mystics with a glimpse of God, writers with a setting for the description of ideal virtue. In some measure, Spenser, in his version of the myth, combines all three.

Because the tradition of primitivism has been much studied before, we need do no more than touch on it here—though its relevance to our later discussion of pastoral will be obvious. But one fact cannot escape reiteration. Sixteenth-century writers were extraordinarily fascinated by myths of the Golden Age, of sinless perfection, of gods and goddesses and all those fabulous creatures who supposedly walked the earth when the earth was yet young. In the maze of cultural history, our scholars have long since ceased to ascribe cause and effect, and so I will not hazard a guess as to whether the popularity of the myth of the Golden Age led to a preoccupation with the definition of ideal virtue, or whether attempts to define ideal virtue led to the revival of the myth. Either way, the myth of the Golden Age, by giving physical embodiment to an abstract ideal, brings the whole question of the relationship of man's individuality, on the one hand, to the standards of his social existence, on the other, into sharp and impressive focus.

Any attempt to describe ideals through the relative structure of literary narrative inevitably raises questions about the nature of imitation itself. The sixteenth-century adaptation of Petrarch, its delight in the extraction of universal moral allegory from narrative

[23] See Harry Levin, *The Myth of the Golden Age in the Renaissance* (Bloomington, Ind., 1969); Elizabeth Armstrong, *Ronsard and the Age of Gold* (Cambridge, 1968); Arthur O. Lovejoy and George Boas, *Primitivism and Related Ideas in Antiquity: Contributions to the History of Primitivism*, vol. 1 (Baltimore, Md., 1935); Mircea Eliade, *Cosmos and History: the Myth of the Eternal Return* (New York, 1959).

sequence, and similar phenomena, account for the prevalence in contemporary literary treatises of the discussion of imitation, and may go some way towards accounting for the treatises themselves. Today, we have to make an effort to understand what the Elizabethans *meant* by imitation. The combined effect of romantic poetry and representational art has led us to stress the validity of the moment, of individual experience—an idea antipathetic to the Elizabethan view of the nature of art.[24]

The idea of imitation, what Aristotle calls *mimesis*, has its origin in Greek aesthetic theory (and its later elaboration), particularly in the *Poetics* of Aristotle. Essential to Aristotle's aesthetic, as any undergraduate may tell us, is not the *possibility* of an action, but its *probability*. All art is imitation; it supposes the pre-existence of a model and the observer's acquaintance with the model or others like it. If artistic imitation involves the copying of a pre-existent model, then it follows that the most accurate imitation of a thing will show that thing at its fullest development. This is so because then the imitation will be closest to the sum of the observer's experience of the model. When we apply such a theory to the practice of the artist, it is clear that when he imitates an action he does more than imitate the particular action of a particular person. He imitates a representative person in a representative action; behind the individual stands the general. The awareness of this generalized quality inherent in the artistic moment leads to a further observation. The representation of a particular man's action is in fact the representation of a man showing the ideal characteristics of a man, in an action which is characteristic of such an ideal.[25]

It is the strength of art, then, that it mediates between the particular event and the general principle. It shows the individual the relevance of his own actions to the cosmic forces which surround him. It is, in the most literal sense, mythic. A theory of art which draws on hypotheses like these is readily adaptable to theories of allegory. Allegory, after all, only makes explicit what is implicit in the artistic process itself.

The Aristotelian doctrine of mimesis can be made to apply not

---

[24] On the general question of realism, see Johan Huizinga, 'Renaissance and Realism', in *Men and Ideas* (New York, 1959), pp. 288–309.

[25] See Geoffrey Shepherd's introduction to *An Apology for Poetry*, by Sir Philip Sidney (London, 1965), esp. pp. 47–50.

only to the imitation of actual models, but also to the imitation of literary models. The Renaissance delight in what might be called imitating literature through literature was inherited from the Middle Ages. It led, of course, to the development of literary *topoi*, prescribed in turn by medieval handbooks on writing. The existence of ready-made *topoi*, combined with a sense of tradition and what was in any case a desire to imitate the ideal, conducted writers inevitably towards the ideal landscapes we meet so often in all the literature of the Western tradition even up to the early nineteenth century (Romantic poetry, for whatever reasons, is full of them). These idealized natural descriptions go under various technical names—*hortus conclusus*, *locus amoenus*, pleasance—but they all have a number of characteristics in common.[26] What is more, the idealized landscape is linked in turn with such northern phenomena as the Fortunate Islands, descriptions of paradise like Virgil's Elysium, and perhaps even the various supposedly natural descriptions we find in pastoral poetry.

The idealized landscape is only one of many literary *topoi* dear to the hearts of medieval and Renaissance writers. But it shows rather clearly how the imitation of man's natural surroundings may lead to something which, for twentieth-century sensibilities at least, seems to have little to do with the 'real' natural world at all. The most interesting situation arises at the point where men begin to wake up to this fact. Under the influence of an alien aesthetic, they are at least led to question the validity of the images of perfection passed on to them under the benevolent seal of literary tradition. At this point there enters into the idealized landscape an element of nostalgia, largely lacking in medieval literature. Sannazaro's haunting lines come to mind. Of course, the emphasis on the disparity between real and ideal may lead in the other direction, towards the satire of Ariosto and, later, Cervantes.

If this element of nostalgia is in part the consequence of doubt about the validity of an aesthetic, it is also the result of the introduction of a further element into the idealized landscape and *topoi* like it.[27] The myth of the Golden Age implies not only a

[26] Curtius (*European Literature*, p. 195) summarizes: 'Its minimum ingredients comprise a tree (or several trees), a meadow, and a spring or brook. Birdsong and flowers may be added. The most elaborate examples also add a breeze.'

[27] On pastoral nostalgia, see Erwin Panofsky, '*Et in Arcadia Ego*: Poussin and the Elegiac Tradition', in *Meaning in the Visual Arts* (Garden City, N.Y., 1955), pp. 295–320.

distance in *space* between the model and its representation, but a
distance in *time*.[28] The perfect society made famous in the lines
from Ovid's *Metamorphoses*, echoed throughout literature from
then until now, is irrecoverable, lost at the very beginning of time
itself:[29]

> Then sprang up first the golden age, which of it selfe maintainde,
> The truth and right of every thing unforst and unconstrainde.
> There was no fear of punishment, there was no threatning lawe
> In brazen tables nayled up, to keepe the folke in awe.
> There was no man would crouch or creepe to Judge with cap in
>   hand,
> They lived safe without a Judge in every Realme and lande.
> The loftie Pynetree was not hewen from mountaines where it stood,
> In seeking straunge and forren landes to rove upon the flood.
> Men knew none other countries yet, than were themselves did keepe:
> There was no towne enclosed yet, with walles and ditches deepe.
> No horne nor trumpet was in use, no sword nor helmet worne.
> The worlde was suche, that souldiers helpe might easly be forborne.
> The fertile earth as yet was free, untoucht of spade or plough,
> And yet it yeelded of it selfe of every things inough.
> And men themselves contented well with plaine and simple foode,
> That on the earth by natures gift without their travell stoode,
> Did live by Raspis, heppes and hawes, by cornelles, plummes and
>   cherries,
> By sloes and apples, nuttes and peares, and lothsome bramble berries,
> And by the acornes dropt on ground from *Joves* brode tree in fielde.
> The Springtime lasted all the yeare, and *Zephyr* with his milde
> And gentle blast did cherish things that grew of owne accorde.
> The ground untilde, all kinde of fruits did plenteously avorde.
> No mucke nor tillage was bestowde on leane and barren land,
> To make the corne of better head and ranker for too stand.
> Then streames ran milke, then streames ran wine, and yellow honny
>   flowde
> From ech greene tree whereon the rayes of firie *Phebus* glowde.[30]

Golding's racy translation gives Ovid's lines a contemporary ring
which helps capture their relevance to the plight of the Eliza-

[28] Levin, *Golden Age*, p. 8.

[29] The main lines of the myth first appear in Hesiod's *Works and Days*, 109–201.
See also Plato, *Menexenus*, 6–7, *Politicus*, 271E–272B. Note that the translation of the
Axiochus attributed to Spenser contains what is essentially a Golden Age description.
See *Variorum*, 9: 36–7.

[30] *Shakespeare's Ovid Being Arthur Golding's Translation of the Metamorphoses*, ed.
W. H. D. Rouse (London, 1904), I. 103–28.

bethan citizen, caught among the brick and stone of overcrowded London.

The myth of the Golden Age, as set forth for us here by a sixteenth-century translator, may be dismissed by the twentieth-century reader as a delightful piece of folklore and little else. But it is in the nature of poetry to deal in fictions. 'The poet nothing affirmeth and therefore never lieth', declares Sidney. Nevertheless, there is an inescapable truth to his fiction; he displays the true and single Nature underlying its outward manifestations:

Only the poet, disdaining to be tied to any such subjection, lifted up with the vigour of his own invention, doth grow in effect into another nature, in making things either better than Nature bringeth forth, or, quite anew, forms such as never were in Nature.[31]

We shall have occasion to examine Sidney's *Apology* in a later chapter. Here, we need only notice that he is using the word 'nature' in conflicting senses, and that his argument implies that the mimetic process is not to be considered within the narrow compass of the imitation of single things and single actions, even if these things and these actions, through the process of imitation itself, are invested with wider significance. The mimetic process involves nothing short of the *creation* of a nature, the imitation of some aesthetic form developed in the poet's mind (the analogy with God is of course relevant) and given material existence in the poem.

This has the effect of turning the conventional idea of mimesis on its head, and it opens the way to an essentially Platonic view of the poetic process. The poet's world glimpses at perfection, while we, hedged about with time and historical event and abstract concept, attempt to come to terms with a universe flawed by the sin of our First Parents. In this sense, the world of poetry is more natural than nature itself.

More natural than nature itself is also Ovid's Golden Age. The operative phrase throughout is 'sua sponte'; the earth brings forth fruit *of its own accord*, men are naturally good, there is no need of law, warfare is unknown. It is hardly surprising that pastoral, offshoot of the myth of the Golden Age, should so frequently be used as a vehicle for discussions of the nature of poetry. It brings

[31] *Apology*, ed. Shepherd, p. 100.

us face to face with questions of tradition, of imitation, of the feasibility of natural perfection. At the same time, it is a poetic metaphor with a life of its own; the ordered society of the Golden Age is like the ordered movement of the poet's verse. If the perfect nature which it portrays is lost in the distance of time and space, perhaps poetry is the only means by which we may have any idea of such perfection.

4. Nature in the 'Faerie Queene'

My earlier remark that Spenser's view of nature was essentially conservative perhaps requires some modification. Spenser views the natural world not simply as a constant battleground between order and disorder, good and evil, but also as a complex and multifarious whole in which the disordered elements provide the dynamic force which makes generation and natural processes possible. The theme is slow in developing. The contrast between the lion who protects Una and Sansloy, who attacks her, is a rather obvious contrast between benevolence and malevolence, perhaps with an underlying irony that it is the *man* who is lawless, the *animal* who follows the natural law. The unreasoning satyrs are less obviously good or evil, though their happy life in the forest, while it offers little in the way of salvation, is at least carefree and apparently devoid of sin. One thing is quite clear: it is nature that supports Una during her sojourn in the countryside, just as natural law supports the English church in Hooker's apology. In later books, though, we begin to understand that the element of lawlessness in nature is not without its compensations. The boar beneath the Mount of Venus plays its role in the process of generation, just as Time with his scythe and his flaggy wings gives some point to Genius's activities. Even Acrasia is not destroyed. Guyon and the Palmer, returning from the Bower, are confronted by her victims, whom she has transformed into beasts. These beasts 'fierce at them gan fly', until Guyon restores them to human shape—all except for Grill, who chooses, 'with vile difference', to remain a beast. 'The donghill kind,' declares the Palmer, 'Delights in filth and foule incontinence: / Let Grill be Grill, and have his hoggish mind.'

It is just such individuals as Grill who keep Acrasia and similar evils alive; nevertheless, without this hoggish element in man generation would be purposeless. Cambina, in Book IV, rides in a chariot drawn by 'two grim lions, taken from the wood . . . Now made forget their former cruell mood'. Such elements are not destroyed but controlled.[32] Even in the Temple of Venus Scudamour uses violence to win Amoret; and we are told very specifically that Busyrane, the abuse of marriage, must not be killed. As with Acrasia, and later with the Blatant Beast, the enchanter is led off to captivity, controlled but not destroyed.

Our initial simple division between optimistic nature and pessimistic nature must therefore be adjusted to take into account the importance of the disordered elements in the overall picture. Spenser's conception of nature is related directly to the style and mood of his poetry of reconcilation: Britomart's aggressiveness is not so much a negation as a part of her eventual union with Artegall. But it is really not until Book v that the pessimistic and the optimistic views are presented in any kind of equality. The twin emblems of Astraea's justice and Artegall's, which stand at the beginning of the book, may be linked together through the historical fact that Artegall learned from Astraea, but they in fact represent two different ways of looking at nature, the first as something to be participated in, the second as something to be brought under control. The former may seem preferable, but the burden of Book v is that such perfection is beyond man's grasp, that the Golden Age of virtue is gone.

Nevertheless, Artegall's justice seems somehow limited and incomplete. Mercilla's court implies the existence of some higher standard. Book vi has the air of a pipe dream, a book more fictional than the other books, but its final statement is surely that the higher standard which may supplement and control Artegall's justice is not merely the feminine powers of Britomart and Mercilla (prefigured, I might add, in Cambina) but also the ordering powers of art, of poetry. The series of intrusions which run through Book vi are further emblems of the activities of the boar. Without them, nothing would be discovered, nothing known, yet with them much is destroyed as well as discovered. It is the old paradox of knowledge, the old problem of the Fortunate Fall.

With the corruption of reason by the Fall comes violence, and to counteract violence comes law. But Artegall, knight of Justice, has only a limited role, since law itself cannot operate properly

[32] Thomas P. Roche, Jr., *The Kindly Flame* (Princeton, N.J., 1964), pp. 23–4.

without the mercy and equity personified by Mercilla and Isis. The Book of Justice and the Book of Courtesy form a continuum, both dealing with similar problems of social exploitation, the one through law, the other through courtesy. Law can only deal with wrongs once they have arisen, but Courtesy can create an attitude which renders law superfluous: 'But where ye ended have,' says Calidore to Artegall at the beginning of his quest, 'now I begin.' Yet he might have turned his comment the other way round: when the Golden Age virtue of courtesy ends, Justice must begin. Book VI is an attempt to return to a lost perfection.

After his picture of the Golden Age, Ovid goes on to recount the myth of Astraea. Like Plato, he subscribes to the view that the best law is no law at all: Plato's Republic, of course, is based on government by knowledge rather than a body of laws.[33] Aristotle, with his famous dictum 'man is by nature a political animal', stressed the value of law, and his sentiments were echoed by the overwhelming majority of medieval political philosophers, particularly Aquinas. The later fifteenth and early sixteenth centuries, however, saw a revival of interest in Platonic concepts of the governor and government by knowledge. Such humanistic interests lie behind the changes in educational method which we noticed in the previous chapter, and they are discernible also in imaginative literature—for example in Douglas's translation of the *Aeneid*, which puts particularly strong emphasis on the example of Aeneas as virtuous ruler. The political evolution of the period seemed to bear out this renewed hope in the ruler, and the development of the humanists' programme gave it support. Today it seems strange that a great deal of the resistance to Greek studies at Oxford and Cambridge came from scholars fearful of turning the universities into finishing schools for government officials, but such was the case.

Just as the optimistic view of nature was opposed by a pessimistic view, so political philosophy developed along two opposed lines, the supreme example of the pessimistic view being the political realism of Machiavelli. But it is very easy to exaggerate Machiavelli's iconoclasm, as his contemporaries themselves tended to do. His conclusions were based on classical precedent, a procedure impeccably humanistic, and even his philosophy itself— Reason and Might as necessary and complementary in the process

[33] See *Politicus*, 292B–302A.

of government—is far more unconventional in its application than it is in its logical foundation.[34]

Machiavelli cast grave doubt on the idea of a universe ordered around a God-given law, and consequently he also repudiated the connection between natural law and the law of nations. It is part of Spenser's purpose in Books v and vi to reassert the concept of natural order in civil society. He approaches the problem from two opposite directions—the role of justice, of the enforcement of law, as a means to compel the balance of society; and the role of courtesy, of social harmony, as a peacefully persuasive means towards social equilibrium. That both are in some measure necessary is implied in the doctrine of opposites, which derives ultimately from Plato and Plutarch and to which I shall have occasion to refer later in this study. But the fact that Book vi is essentially an extension of the higher principle in Book v—that embodied in Mercilla and Britomart—again suggests that courtesy is in the final analysis the higher virtue. Artegall's justice is linked with natural process through Astraea and also through Britomart, who unites natural and social virtue in her person; Calidore's or Pastorella's courtesy is based upon nature itself, and in turn reflects back on Mercilla and Britomart. We might go so far as to suggest that Pastorella is another in the line of representatives of the ordering female principle which imposes Form on inchoate Matter and orders and controls the male energies. In fact she is the very embodiment of the poetry of reconciliation.

Books v and vi are therefore both opposite and consecutive. They are also complementary, since Spenser emphasizes the need for martial prowess in the defence of the precepts of courtesy, either to add authority to the teacher or to enable him to enforce his standards upon recalcitrant believers in self-interest. Most important of all, both books are 'anti-Machiavellian' restatements of the interrelation between the natural world and those patterns of conduct derived from it—on the one hand the law of nations and civil law; on the other the precepts of courtesy and 'civil conversation'.

The pattern established in Books v and vi extends into the 'Mutabilitie Cantos', which pick up where Book vi leaves off. It is

---

[34] An admirably concise treatment of the political theory of the period can be found in Myron P. Gilmore, *The World of Humanism 1453–1517* (New York, 1952), pp. 127–38.

a commonplace of artistic theory, a philosophical idea which still
retains some potency, that the poet is engaged through the creation of poetry in a search for order. If this idea is today sometimes
challenged, it was accepted more or less implicitly by most
Elizabethans. In a cultural environment which laid great stress on
order—in the state, in nature and in the individual—the artistic
metaphor of order, the Golden Age and pastoral, enjoyed a popularity unrivalled before or since. The theme of order, or of order
destroyed, echoes through Sidney's poetry, through Shakespeare's
plays, through all of Ralegh's writing.

It is not my purpose to enter into a discussion of the relation of
the 'Mutabilitie Cantos' to the published portion of the *Faerie
Queene*, though the conclusion seems inescapable that they provide a kind of coda, a kind of final statement relevant to the work
as a whole.[35] It is tempting to read them as a separate work of art
—a sort of masque, one critic has called them;[36] or an epyllion,
complete with Ovidian borrowings and mythological digression.[37] In any event, it is arresting that Spenser's most notable
statement regarding change and eternity, and perhaps his nearest
approach to a resolution, takes place outside the scope of the quest
theme. There is no mention of a quest of Constancie, or a titular
hero—if, indeed, the reference to Constancie is Spenser's at all.
Mutabilitie is both villainess and heroine, a virago who combines
the characteristics of a Radigund with perfectly legitimate control
over sublunary affairs, and who can reduce the gods themselves
to a state of rather pathetic consternation. Other critics before me
have pointed out that Faunus wins Molanna over by offering her
fruit amidst the beauties of a pre-lapsarian Arlo Hill; they have
shown that the episode depicts a kind of Fall, in which Diana
withdraws from the world, Molanna is 'whelm'd with stones', and
Faunus is hunted down like Actaeon.[38] But it is a fortunate Fall:

---

[35] They are so read by William Blissett, 'Spenser's Mutabilitie', in Millar Mac-
Lure and F. W. Watt, ed. *Essays in English Literature . . . Presented to A. S. P. Woodhouse* (Toronto, 1964), pp. 26–42.

[36] Sherman Hawkins, 'Mutabilitie and the Cycle of the Months', in William
Nelson, ed., *Form and Convention in the Poetry of Edmund Spenser* (New York, 1961),
pp. 76–102.

[37] Blissett, 'Spenser's Mutabilitie', p. 37. See also William P. Cumming, 'The Influence of Ovid's *Metamorphoses* on Spenser's Mutabilitie Cantos', *SP*, 27 (1931), 241–56.

[38] See William Nelson, *The Poetry of Edmund Spenser* (New York, 1963), p. 300;
Hawkins, 'Mutabilitie', pp. 85–6 (Hawkins, I think, misses the lightness of tone in
this episode).

Molanna wins her Fanchin, Faunus is more scared than hurt, and
the only penalty that is paid (large penalty though it may be) is
that Arlo Hill and its vicinity are no longer the haunt of Diana,
whose withdrawal has led to the advent of wolves and thieves.

This inset story mirrors the larger action. Mutabilitie, whose
tussle with Cynthia might well have caused anxieties among
Elizabethan readers all too aware of the Queen's age,[39] is ultimately worsted by her own evidence. The long line of months
and seasons which she evokes, far from indicating disorder in the
world, is merely an indication of the complexity of its order. Their
abundant variety, like the variety of Faeryland as Spenser alludes
to it in Book VI, is part of the attraction of the natural world, and
those final stanzas, instead of indicating a kind of retractation,
merely confirm that the very diversity of earthly phenomena
provides the dynamics for the gradual movement towards perfection which is part of God's purpose. Ultimately, the abundance
of the natural world (represented by Mutabilitie here on earth,
though the Goddess Nature is representative of all creation) is
gathered into the final still point where history and movement
end: 'O! that great Sabbaoth God, grant me that Sabaoths sight.'

Above all, it is the range of the 'Mutabilitie Cantos' that im-
presses. The cosmic vision which they afford reflects on the salmon
of the Shure and the hills around Kilcolman: the actual world outside Spenser's window is imbued with hope through its connection
with a vaster pattern. This sense of order in variety is, I suppose,
the most abiding impression which Spenser leaves his readers.
Order, of course, is thematically central in the seventh canto—a
fact which has led some readers to see the pageant of the months
itself as expressive of some sense of artistic order, as though we
are witnessing a series of poetic images evoked by the advocate
Mutabilitie—images which form, willy-nilly, a pattern. They provide a perhaps rather unexpected answer to the disappearance of
Diana's Golden Age haunts—another kind of beauty and purpose
which supersedes the old idea of a perfect world in the past and
which projects our minds forward, to the present and to the future.

But this kind of forward-looking is only possible, paradoxically,
when the quest is dispensed with. In Books V and VI, the paradigm
of artistic order remains the Golden Age, and it is of course a
Golden Age scene that stands at the climactic point in the Legend

---

[39] Blissett, 'Spenser's Mutabilitie', pp. 31–3.

of Courtesy. The book suggests that ideally order in nature should parallel order in society. Natural man and social man ultimately coalesce in the figure of Pastorella, who unites the two in her noble birth and rural education. Opposed to this union of nature and society, which is really what Spenser means by courtesy (or at least it is a part of his definition) is discourtesy. The spirit of discourtesy manifests itself in natural disorder (the cannibals) and social disharmony (Crudor, Turpine, Mirabella). The preservation of order in society depends on the necessary qualities of strength and reconciliation, forces roughly parallel to Justice and Courtesy. But just as Venus must include something of Mars, to represent the aggressiveness of love,[40] so courtesy needs martial prowess to maintain it.

In all the events leading up to the intrusion on Calepine and Serena, Calidore is able to mediate in terms of ideas of courtesy (supported by knightly strength) well within the range of Spenser's readers. But with the arrival of the Blatant Beast, Calidore's limitations stand revealed. Unlike Priscilla's parents, the Beast is not the kind of enemy with whom one can come to terms. Serena, gathering flowers for her garland, moves in one concept of nature, the Beast in the other. The first is the creation of a benevolent God, the second the wild forest whose horrors we meet in Dante's *Inferno* or Douglas's *Palace of Honour*. Flowery garland and wild beast stand opposed. Essential to Spenser's argument, though, is that only by experiencing the former, only by understanding the natural order, can we defeat the latter.[41]

The book's second section is dominated not by flowery garland but by wild beast. 'Optimistic' nature breaks in on the beast's domain, not the other way about. The Salvage Man saves Calepine and Serena from Turpine, Calepine rescues the babe from the bear, Matilda is saved from a hopeless situation by the discovery of this same babe, Calepine arrives in the nick of time to rescue Serena from the Salvages. Occupying the centre of the stage are Turpine, Mirabella, and the Salvage Nation, all of them representative of discourtesy and unnatural behaviour. The Salvage Nation, for example, 'serve their own necessities with others need' and

---

[40] Edgar Wind, *Pagan Mysteries in the Renaissance*, 2nd edn. (Harmondsworth, Middx., 1967), pp. 86ff.

[41] On combinations of the *locus amoenus* and *selva selvaggia*, especially through the Tempe motif, see Curtius, *European Literature*, pp. 198–202.

perpetrate 'monstrous cruelty gainst course of kynde'. Mirabella, too, offends against 'course of kynde' in her treatment of her suitors. In his discussion of her story, Berger's reference to Neoplatonic psychology, for all its needless complexity, does help to emphasize the point that Mirabella causes love to turn in upon itself—'outward and "downward" to her body'.[42] Turned aside from the creative ascent towards God, it must inevitably lead to self-destruction, just as the Salvage Nation destroys and consumes its victims. One reason for this is the fact that though she is 'deckt with wondrous gifts of Natures grace', Mirabella is 'of meane parentage and kindred base'. The discrepancy leads to pride, to the abuse of the gifts freely given her by nature: her beauty becomes sterile.

This spectacle of beauty misused, of a gorgeous exterior hiding an inner unfruitfulness, carries us forward to the elaborate artificiality of the 'Petrarchan' terms used to describe the cannibals' feelings towards Serena. Mirabella, of course, is also a kind of cannibal: her graceful appearance contrasts with the scornful reality beneath it, just as the courtly Petrarchan terminology stands in ironic contrast with their vicious behaviour. Mirabella and the cannibals make use of art to subvert nature; they put art and nature in opposition. The Salvage Nation, at least, therefore has a dual existence, as an anarchic force in the natural world and as a disrupter of harmony in the court. We can at once recognize their role as not unlike that of Lucifera and Acrasia, Malecasta and Busyrane, all of whose perversions take the form of a kind of moral involution which forces art into artificiality and which dries up, in the latter cases, the powers of generation. This separation of art from nature (which critics have long recognized as a characteristic feature of Spenser's idea of evil) and the related question of artistic creation itself, will form our next line of investigation.

[42] Harry Berger, Jr., 'A Secret Discipline: *The Faerie Queene*, Book vi', in Nelson, ed., *Form and Convention*, pp. 35–75.

VIII

Art and Grace

1. Art and nature

AMONG the more persistent topics in Renaissance literature is what may best be called the writer's justification of his own writing. Frequently such apologies are aimed at explaining the value of some particular genre or literary type, like Guarini's pastorals, round which so important and extended a controversy developed;[1] or like Giraldi Cintio's discussion of romance, which was really only a part of a controversy extending through most of sixteenth-century Italian literature and perhaps even spilling over into English in Spenser's Letter to Ralegh and Harington's preface to his 1591 translation of Ariosto.[2] A second kind of self-justification is aimed less at vindicating a method or genre and more at attacking critics. The prefaces of Elizabethan writers seem filled with vituperative contempt for backbiting detractors and unlearned philistines who would ruin a writer's reputation with their slanders, or who fail to understand the spirit or the value of what he has to say. Contrasted with such curs, a writer's patron grows in stature: he is humane, learned, and discriminating; he understands and appreciates his author.[3]

---

[1] Walter W. Greg, *Pastoral Poetry and Pastoral Drama* (London, 1906), pp. 203ff.; Bernard Weinberg, *A History of Literary Criticism in the Italian Renaissance* (Chicago 1961), 1: 27–31, 2: 679–84, 1074–1105.

[2] See Weinberg, *History, passim*, esp. 1: 433–52, 2: 954–1073; Graham Hough, *A Preface to 'The Faerie Queene'* (London, 1962), pp. 48–58; E. M. W. Tillyard, *The English Epic and its Background* (London, 1954), pp. 222–33; C. P. Brand, *Torquato Tasso* (Cambridge, 1965), pp. 119–32; W. L. Renwick, *Edmund Spenser: an Essay on Renaissance Poetry* (London, 1925), pp. 43–55; John Arthos, *On the Poetry of Spenser and the Form of Romances* (London, 1956), *passim*; Baxter Hathaway, *Marvels and Commonplaces: Renaissance Literary Criticism* (New York, 1968), pp. 133ff.; *Giraldi Cinthio on Romances*, trans. Henry L. Snuggs (Lexington, Ky., 1968); Sir John Harington, 'A Preface, or rather a Brief Apologie of Poetrie', in *Elizabethan Critical Essays*, ed. G. Gregory Smith (Oxford, 1904), 2: 194–222.

[3] H. S. Bennett, *English Books and Readers 1558 to 1603* (Cambridge, 1965), pp. 30–55; Eleanor Rosenberg, *Leicester, Patron of Letters* (New York, 1955), *passim*. Less

The terms in which such self-justification is generally couched would seem to suggest that good literature was under fierce attack. But when we come to look at the history of the period we find that there is not much evidence of these attacks outside the prefaces where they are described. Certainly, there was a good deal of corruption among London publishers, and there was not a great deal of money in writing, but even relatively mediocre writers seem to have found a market for their wares without too much difficulty. It seems most likely that the alleged attack on the writer was a kind of literary device, to impress patrons with their munificent good will, and to justify the writer's efforts. What attacks there were, came mostly from the occasional intervention of the authorities to suppress a volume they found politically unacceptable. Nevertheless, Spenser's Blatant Beast is evidently one of those 'crabsnowted beastes' which populate Elizabethan prefaces and, we are led to suppose, prey on unsuspecting men of letters. The identification is made explicit in the closing stanzas of Book VI and lies behind much of the preceding action. It is significant that after 1596 we find the Blatant Beast turning up not infrequently in just such prefaces as those I have described.

But Spenser makes the Blatant Beast much more than a mere detractor of good literature, nor does the Beast enjoy a monopoly on philistinism in Book VI. Behind the Beast's attacks is a serious attempt at a positive justification of literature. Spenser's work, in fact, is related to a third type of literary apologia, the justification not of a single genre but of literature and figurative expression in general. In this respect Spenser is at one with Sidney, whose *Apology* really amounts to a theoretical defence of art in the neo-Platonic tradition. Sidney's work is of little value as a work of formal theory: his mind is too lively to submit to such discipline, and the range of his imagination covers too disparate a collection of ideas. But it is immensely valuable as an indication of the way in which a gifted Elizabethan writer might think about matters aesthetic, and it is a creative work of great power in its own right. The balance of scholarly opinion seems now to discount the notion that Sidney's essay was written in response to Gosson's *School of Abuse*, but it is worth pointing out that in this as in many other

reliable, but with useful incidental information, is Phoebe Sheavyn, *The Literary Profession in the Elizabethan Age*, 2nd edn., rev. J. W. Saunders (Manchester, 1967), pp. 8-38.

ages the spirit of controversy has inspired many notable defences as well as some notable attacks. In Sidney's day, the intense discussion of the abuse of art, of art and nature, of disguise, of imitation, is all in some way related to the overriding concern of defining and delimiting art and literature. Speculation concerning the nature of literature is inevitably much preoccupied with the question of literary form; in fact this is perhaps the major question in an age coming to believe that literature constitutes a unique activity unlike all others. Sidney, in discussing the role of the poet, echoes the standard commonplaces of his century. If the world before the Fall represented perfect form, the product of God-as-artist, the artist's search for form can be allegorized as the re-creation of the Golden Age, an attempt to redeem nature, to impose order on it. This process implies interaction: from fallen nature derives the inkling of form (man's reason is impaired, but not hopelessly); the artist, by a process of idealization and augmentation, adds definition to it. This artistic redefinition in turn reflects back upon nature and moves men to the good.

The contrast between art and nature is therefore not a matter of mere aesthetic theorizing, but the very essence of man's teleology.[4] Ernst Cassirer on Ficino will give us some idea of the importance of its implications for the neo-Platonists. Later theorists of course adapted Ficino's ideas to their own ends, just as Ficino adapted from Cusanus and others.

According to Ficino, the whole point of religious and philosophical *knowledge* is nothing other than the eradication from the world of everything that seems deformed; and the recognition that even things that seem formless participate in form. But such knowledge cannot content itself with the mere concept; it must be transformed into action, and prove itself through action. Here begins the contribution of the artist. He can fulfil the requirement that speculation can only state. Man can only be certain that the sense world *has* form and shape if he continually *gives* it form. . . . If redemption is conceived of as a renovation of the *form* of man and of the world, i.e. as a true *reformatio*, then the focal point of intellectual life must lie in the place where the 'idea' is embodied, i.e. where the non-sensible form present in the

---

[4] On the range of its implications, see Edward William Tayler, *Nature and Art in Renaissance Literature* (New York, 1964); Madeleine Doran, *Endeavors of Art: a Study of Form in Elizabethan Drama* (Madison, Wis., 1954), esp. pp. 53–84; Millar MacLure, 'Nature and Art in *The Faerie Queene*', *ELH*, 28 (1961), 1–20; Hiram Haydn, *The Counter-Renaissance* (New York, 1950), pp. 468–97.

mind of the artist breaks forth into the world of the visible and becomes realized in it.[5]

This far-reaching and all-inclusive theory accords the artist an overwhelmingly important role in the active life of society. Art becomes the one means towards public, societal redemption: the artist acts as mediator between the Golden and Iron Worlds. Thus artistic creation becomes a sacred act, but a sacred act with direct social implications. In fact, the well-being of society depends on the artist's ability to give it form and meaning.

This enormous responsibility thrust upon the artist obliges him to distinguish and define the various aberrations which pass for art but are in fact mere travesties of the truth, and to define true art itself. While the principal yardstick employed by the Romantic artist was the validity of the individual experience, the Renaissance looked not for experience but for reason in art; while the Romantics developed an elaborate theory of imagination, the Renaissance delineated the doctrine of imitation. But imitation, as we have discovered, is actually a very flexible concept, broad enough to embrace Aristotelian *mimesis* on the one hand and, on the other, the Plotinian and neo-Platonic idea that the artist himself is a kind of god. This latter view does not conflict with the suggestion that the ground of art is reason. On the contrary, it actually reinforces it. Just as God's creation was ordered through Right Reason, so the artist must employ the same faculty in his artistic creation. Reason was impaired by the Fall. It may be the task of the artist to make good the flaw caused by Adam's sin by repairing the image of the universe, or perhaps his task is to create anew—to form a new universe of poetry. So art itself constitutes a kind of redemption—perhaps a grand term to use, but not too grand for the intensely serious purpose of a Sidney or a Spenser.[6]

The idea that the artist creates his own universe, his own 'nature', is espoused by Sidney in a passage made familiar by frequent quotation. No art, he says (using 'art' in the sense of 'discipline' or 'activity'), exists that is not based on natural phenomena. Only the poet rises above such limitations:

Nature never set forth the earth in so rich tapestry as divers poets have done; neither with pleasant rivers, fruitful trees, sweet-smelling flowers,

[5] *The Individual and the Cosmos in Renaissance Philosophy* (New York, 1963), pp. 66–7.
[6] On Right Reason, see Robert Hoopes, *Right Reason in the English Renaissance* (Cambridge, Mass., 1962).

nor whatsover else may make the too much loved earth more lovely. Her world is brazen, the poets only deliver a golden.[7]

If art is not based on reason, it fails in its primary purpose—the imitation of perfect nature. Bad art is unreasonable art, or (since reason is order) disordered art. It follows, too, that the imagination (a rather slippery term in Renaissance aesthetic theory) must remain subordinate to reason.

But let those things alone, and go to man . . . and know whether she [Nature] have brought forth so true a lover as Theagenes, so constant a friend as Pylades, so valiant a man as Orlando, so right a prince as Xenophon's Cyrus, so excellent a man every way as Virgil's Aeneas. Neither let this be jestingly conceived, because the works of the one be essential, the other in imitation or fiction; for any understanding knoweth the skill of the artificer standeth in that *Idea* or fore-conceit of the work, and not in the work itself. And that the poet hath that *Idea* is manifest, by delivering them forth in such excellency as he hath imagined them. Which delivering forth also is not wholly imaginative, as we are wont to say by them that build castles in the air; but so far substantially it worketh, not only to make a Cyrus, which had been but a particular excellency as Nature might have done, but to bestow a Cyrus upon the world to make many Cyruses, if they will learn aright why and how that maker made him.[8]

Sidney's claim for the validity of the Golden World is based on the assertion that it is more 'real' than visible nature[9] (what Sidney calls 'nature')[10] because closer to a universal, eternal reality. It is an imitation of nature, but of perfect nature (perhaps it would be better to call it perfect form, and Sidney himself avoids calling it nature), where no contrarieties or irregularities exist. This line of reasoning is in perfect accord with the doctrine of Imitation: the function of the poet is not to imitate imperfection but to

---

[7] *An Apology for Poetry*, ed. Geoffrey Shepherd (London, 1965), p. 100.

[8] *Apology*, ed. Shepherd, pp. 100–1.

[9] Cf. Mircea Eliade, *Cosmos and History: the Myth of the Eternal Return* (New York, 1959), p. 92: 'Primitive behaviour . . . is governed by belief in an absolute reality opposed to the profane world of "unrealities"; in the last analysis, the latter does not constitute a "world", properly speaking; it is the "unreal" *par excellence*, the uncreated, the non-existent: the void.' The myth of the Golden World is itself an objectification of this belief in a truth not tied to the particular event. See also Eliade's chapter 'Myths and the Rites of Renewal', in *Myth and Reality* (New York, 1963), pp. 39–53.

[10] He actually uses the term two ways—as *natura naturata* ('. . . such as never were in Nature') and as *natura naturans* ('Nature bringeth forth . . .', '. . . doth grow in effect into another nature').

figure forth the Idea present in his mind, using sense-impressions only as they assist him in this figuring forth. The theory is based, then, on the ideal conjunction of nature and art. Art controls nature (fallen nature) and imposes order upon it, even as it derives its authority in turn from nature (the ideal nature).

There were those, in this age as in preceding ages, who denied the poet's ability to penetrate beyond the sensible world to the Idea. Following the Plato of the *Republic* and the *Laws*, they concluded that art was an imitation of an imitation—an imitation of a visible nature which is in turn but an imitation of the Idea lying behind it. The argument boils down to the question of the validity of the Golden World. Is it a figment of the poet's imagination—an escape or retreat—or is it so universal as to be more 'real' than the nature we see around us, as Sidney concludes? Today we might ask the same question in other terms—does literary form provide a *retreat* from psychological pressures, or is it a means of coming to terms with them, a kind of problem-solving mechanism providing solutions which can then be reapplied in the reader's (or perhaps the writer's) everyday living? The controversy has important repercussions, since upon its resolution depends the social utility of the poet, one of the cornerstones of Sidney's argument.[11]

Sidney's essay extends far beyond the utilitarian, however. The conclusion that art is useful might provide a fitting response to a man like Gosson, but Sidney is also interested in establishing that art itself is not something immediately accessible to discursive reason, as the useful arts might be, but something altogether higher. Put in other terms, Sidney is claiming that Wisdom, the highest entity man's intellect can attain to, is not contained in a body of knowledge, *scientia*, but involves some higher, God-given virtue, *sapientia*. This distinction between utility and virtue is of crucial importance.[12] It implies that Art is a part of, a mark of, a man's humanity.

[11] Cf. Herbert's well-known discussion of the nature of poetry, 'Jordan' (1), in which the poet contrasts true plain statement against pointless artificiality and complexity, 'Catching the sense at two removes'.

[12] The 'Golden World' theory supposes an inability to explain nature in nature's own terms. Here Spenser and Sidney part company with Bacon. As Geoffrey Bush puts it (*Shakespeare and the Natural Condition* (Cambridge, Mass., 1956), p. 13), 'It cannot be said that Bacon's vision excludes the religious explanation of nature, or that Spenser's excludes the secular explanation; but Spenser's tendency is to join these explanations and Bacon's is to set them apart. What is in question is whether the temporal aspect of the world is an arrangement that would explain itself, if it

Art and Nature go hand in hand. It is Art, King Lear learns, that separates man from the animals; it is Nature, Leontes discovers, that makes sense of Art. Ideally, the two are so closely bound up in human affairs as to be indistinguishable. Declining to give Polixenes 'carnations and streaked gillyvors, / Which some call nature's bastards', Perdita is making an ironic comment on her own situation, a kind of combination of Art and Nature. She also gives Polixenes the opportunity to state the true, ideal balance between the two:

Polixenes.   Wherefore, gentle maiden,
    Do you neglect them?
Perdita.   For I have heard it said
    There is an art which in their piedness shares
    With great creating Nature.
Polixenes.   Say, there be;
    Yet nature is made better by no mean,
    But nature makes that mean: so, over that art
    Which you say adds to nature, is an art
    That nature makes . . . You see, sweet maid, we marry
    A gentler scion to the wildest stock,
    And make conceive a bark of baser kind
    By bud of nobler race. This is an art
    Which does mend nature . . . change it rather, but
    The art itself, is nature.   (*Winter's Tale*, IV. iv)

Shakespeare's play reminds us that the contrast of Art and Nature has wide implications, extending far beyond poetic creation,[13] and ultimately fusing with the question from which our discussion began in the previous chapter—the relationship of society to nature. Art distinguishes man from the beasts. The clothes he bears on his back do more than keep him warm; they are symbols of his natural superiority, of his reasonableness.

At least that is one view. But man's art is ambiguous. It may show his reasonableness, but it may also show his inability to understand and to share in the reasonableness of nature. This ambiguity provides the central conflict in *King Lear*. In Shakespeare's play, however, it is resolved not by proving the ambigu-

---

were fully understood, or whether, because it is part of a divine arrangement, it leans on a further explanation, already partly revealed.'

[13] See Tayler's chapter 'Renaissance Uses of Nature and Art', *Nature and Art*. My quotation is from *The Winter's Tale*, ed. Sir Arthur Quiller-Couch and John Dover Wilson, rev. edn. (Cambridge, 1959).

ity false but by rising above it. From the unbuttoning scene in Act III ('Off, off, you lendings'), when the artificiality of a corrupt court is finally sloughed off, to Lear's final 'Pray you undo this button', he finds the value of humanity (in this context, of Art as against Nature).[14] But the very process of discovery takes him out of the mundane: it becomes a kind of transcendence, a kind of visionary reconciliation.

The two types of Art are evident throughout the *Faerie Queene*—the Art which distorts and isolates, like Acrasia's or Busyrane's,[15] and the Art which unites, which reconciles, like Colin Clout's on Mount Acidale. As we have already observed, Mirabella and the cannibals are examples of the sterile and evil art, the art of artificiality.

2. *The role of the poet: the myth of Orpheus*

To the kind of artificiality which Spenser portrays in the cannibals, the true artist is implacably opposed.[16] The artist is a restorer of order and decency in society; some even call him god-like.[17] As the transmitter of a body of ethical standards, what

[14] Dean Frye, 'The Context of Lear's Unbuttoning', *ELH*, 32 (1965), 17–31. I use the term 'artificiality' here in its modern, pejorative, sense.

[15] The key to an understanding of this type of art as against 'good' art lies in the idea of counterfeit. When art merely *pretends* to be nature it is generally evil and insidious (the False Florimell, the False Una). Lewis's generalization, that outside the House of Alma art suggests artificiality in a bad sense (*The Allegory of Love* (Oxford, 1936), pp. 326–7) is, as the critics now agree, an oversimplification. MacLure ('Nature and Art') distinguishes between 'good' nature and 'evil' nature and between 'good' art and 'evil' art. Evil art and evil nature contribute nothing to, indeed work against, the natural movement upwards towards God. Reason and prudence reject such evil art as false (the House of Pride for instance). Mirabella's superficial beauty is an example of 'evil art'. Timias succumbs to it in trying to rescue her. On the Bower of Bliss and C. S. Lewis, see Harry Berger, Jr., *The Allegorical Temper* (New Haven, Conn., 1957), pp. 226–40; MacLure, 'Nature and Art'; N. S. Brooke, 'C. S. Lewis and Spenser: Nature, Art, and the Bower of Bliss', *Cambridge Journal* 2 (1949), 420–34; Ruth Nevo, 'Spenser's "Bower of Bliss" and a Key Metaphor from Renaissance Poetic', in *Studies in Western Literature*, ed. A. Fineman (Jerusalem, 1962), pp. 20–31. The last-mentioned comes to substantially the same conclusions as MacLure.

[16] We can perhaps see in the dance around Serena the dance of apes so frequently portrayed in Renaissance art, generally to signify artistic imitation, in the 'Platonic', derogatory sense of aping nature (cf. the Ape in *Mother Hubberds Tale*). See H. W. Janson, *Apes and Ape Lore in the Middle Ages and the Renaissance* (London, 1952), and E. Curtius, *European Literature and the Latin Middle Ages* (London, 1953), Appendix 19.

[17] For the history of this tradition, see E. N. Tigerstedt, 'The Poet as Creator: Origins of a Metaphor', *CLS*, 5 (1968), 455–88.

might be called a poetic tradition, the poet stands in a relationship to his predecessors not easily understood by a twentieth-century public bastioned about with copyright laws. Far from being an isolated individual in search of originality, the individual experience, the poet writes as a representative of his own time entrusted with a great theme and the task of expounding this theme to his contemporaries. Poetic inspiration, as far as the concept was developed at all during the Renaissance, comes from forces outside the poet, not within. When Spenser speaks of overgoing Ariosto he does not mean 'doing the same thing as Ariosto, only better', but 'taking the theme, the Idea, of Ariosto further than Ariosto did'.

The ethical standards of the poet, the tradition of poetry, serve as bulwarks against disorder. Only a god or a godlike man, says Spenser, can suppress discord; as examples he singles out the archetypal poet of the classical tradition and his Jewish counterpart—poets and minstrels both:

> Firebrand of hell first tynd in Phlegeton,
> By thousand furies, and from thence out throwen
> Into this world, to worke confusion,
> And set it all on fire by force unknowen,
> Is wicked discord, whose small sparkes once blowen
> None but a God or godlike man can slake;
> Such as was *Orpheus*, that when strife was growen
> Amongst those famous ympes of Greece, did take
> His silver Harpe in hand, and shortly friends them make.
>
> Or such as that celestiall Psalmist was,
> That when the wicked feend his Lord tormented,
> With heavenly notes, that did all other pas
> The outrage of his furious fit relented.   (IV. ii. 1–2)

The principal purpose of these stanzas is to illustrate the value of friendship against the incursion of discord, but the simile transforms them into an affirmation of the poet's role in society. Like the reference to the 'fierce Lapithes' and Ariadne's crown in Book VI (Canto x), this image portrays order transcending chaos. Shakespeare puts the same image to work in a rather similar way:

> For Orpheus' lute was strung with poets' sinews;
> Whose golden touch could soften steel and stones,

> Make tigers tame, and huge leviathans
> Forsake unsounded deeps to dance on sands.
>   (*Two Gentlemen of Verona*, III. ii)

The image of Orpheus making the trees and stones and wild beasts move in time to his music is a symbol of man's power to restore, or impose, harmony upon nature. The huge leviathans called up from unsounded deeps 'dance on sands', like the strange monsters of the artist's imagination set in order on the empty canvas of the artistic universe.

The myth itself was a particular favourite of the Renaissance neo-Platonists.[18] Some writers saw in Orpheus the archetypal poet. Others, like Bacon, explained the myth of Orpheus in terms of man's imposition of knowledge on nature, the discovery of a pattern to which all of nature danced. The broad outlines of the myth are readily discernible beneath the surface of Spenser's Book VI.[19] The Graces' dance in Canto x is the Orphic dance of the natural world, Colin piping is like Orpheus touching the strings of his lute, the dancers like the trees and rocks and wild animals which moved in order to his harmony. Eurydice disappeared beneath the earth, and was finally rescued (or almost rescued) by Orpheus after he had charmed Cerberus and all the powers of hell. In similar fashion, Calidore, made strong by his unexpected vision of perfect harmony on Mount Acidale, descends to rescue Pastorella from the hellish cave of the Brigands. Likewise Serena is victim of an attempted capture by the Blatant Beast which is distinctly reminiscent of Eurydice's rape by Pluto, and she too must be rescued, from the hellish torment of the cannibals. We might remember, too, Orpheus' worship and praise of Apollo, patron of music and light, and his antagonism to Bacchus, lawgiver but also patron of the Maenads. In Spenser's poem the Dance of the Graces is contrasted with the wild and uncontrolled dance, the bacchanalia, of the savages around Serena.

18 See the early chapters in Edgar Wind, *Pagan Mysteries in the Renaissance*, 2nd edn. (Harmondsworth, Middx., 1967). On the ramifications of the Orpheus myth in the sixteenth century and later, particularly in relation to science, see Elizabeth Sewell's fascinating study, *The Orphic Voice* (New Haven, Conn., 1960). One important point which Miss Sewell emphasizes is the logical confusion surrounding the various attempts to relate philosophy to poetry, among them Sidney's *Apology*. The classical period is covered in W. K. C. Guthrie's *Orpheus and Greek Religion*, 2nd edn. (London, 1952), which, however, is largely concerned with the Orphic mysteries and Orphic religion.

19 See Robert Graves, *The Greek Myths* (Harmondsworth, Middx., 1955), I: 111–13.

Now I am well aware that these supposed parallels are neither
very close nor very sustained. But they are also more than casual
coincidences. Orpheus, to be sure, is equated now with Colin
Clout, now with Calidore, now with Calepine; Pastorella succeeds
where Eurydice fails; there is no specific mention of Bacchus or
Orpheus in Book vi. Nevertheless, it can with justification be
asserted that the book turns on the same contrast that informs the
Orpheus story: the contrast between the powers of hell (the
Cerberus-like Blatant Beast, the brigands, the cannibals) and the
radiant powers of beauty and poetry. That Spenser associates the
Orpheus story with such contrasts is evident from similar passages
elsewhere. Scudamour's removal of Amoret from the Temple of
Venus is a case in point. Critics have seen this episode as symbolic
of Amoret's growth into womanhood.

> No lesse did *Daunger* threaten me with dread,
> When as he saw me, maugre all his powre,
> That glorious spoyle of beautie with me lead,
> Then *Cerberus*, when *Orpheus* did recoure
> His Leman from the Stygian Princes boure.   (iv. x. 58)

The journey of Orpheus with his Eurydice, avoiding the perils of
Cerberus and his confederates, is like the journey of Calidore with
his Pastorella, beset by the perils of the Blatant Beast and its
various henchmen—

> All as the shepheard, that did fetch his dame
> From *Plutoes* balefull bowre withouten leave:
> His musicks might the hellish hound did tame.
> (*Shepheardes Calender*, October, 28–30)

But if we are looking for parallels to Book vi elsewhere in
Spenser's poetry, we must look above all at the *Epithalamion*.
Surely Colin Clout's piping for the Graces on Mount Acidale is
paralleled in that strange and still unexplained passage at the end
of the first stanza of Spenser's marriage poem:

> Helpe me mine owne loves prayses to resound,
> Ne let the same of any be envide:
> So Orpheus did for his owne bride,
> So I unto my selfe alone will sing.   (*Epithalamion*, 14–17)

If there is a suggestion of a parallel between Colin Clout and
Orpheus, C. S. Lewis's suggestion that the dance of the Graces is

symbolic of fleeting poetic inspiration takes on added meaning.[20] In a sense the remark is inadequate to explain the complexity of the episode. The unreality of the scene springs not so much from its fugitive quality, though that is important, as from the fact that it is an attempt to give artistic representation to what is in essence a mystery, in the neo-Platonic sense. The dance of the Graces *is* the inner truth of poetry, the Platonic Idea from which the poem is, as it were, extrapolated. Of course, to describe the dance as symbolic of inspiration is in some ways anachronistic, though the association of Orpheus with the powers of the imagination was already well established in Spenser's day, and certainly the dance suggests a reaching beyond the discursive reason whose virtue is extolled in the early cantos of Book VI. There we learn that reason is the ground of courtesy—'What haps to day to me to morrow may to you'—but the later vision of harmony includes this reasonable courtesy within a greater all-embracing emblem. Closest to this idea of the connection between harmony and mankind, in which the poet acts as mediator, is George Puttenham's interpretation of the Orpheus myth.[21] Instead of setting poetry apart from other human pursuits, he sees it as the source of these pursuits, poets being 'the first Astronomers and Philosophists and Metaphisicks . . . and historiographers'.[22] This implicitly gives to imagination a status higher than that of discursive reason—if we can describe as imagination the quality of mind which Puttenham labels as 'the phantasticall part of man'.

So is that part, being well affected, not onely nothing disorderly or confused with any monstruous imaginations or conceits, but very

---

[20] *Allegory of Love*, p. 351.

[21] See Sewell, *Orphic Voice*, pp. 76–7.

[22] Cf. Golding's variation in his Epistle to the *Metamorphoses*, which connects the myth of Orpheus with the proper government of a commonwealth:

So Orphey in the tenth booke is reported too delight
The savage beasts, and for too hold the fleeting birds from flyght,
To move the senselesse stones, and stay swift rivers, and too make
The trees too follow after him and for his musick sake
Too yeeld him shadowe where he went. By which is signifyde
That in his doctrine such a force and sweetenesse was implyde,
That such as were most wyld, stowre, feerce, hard, witlesse, rude, and bent
Ageinst good order, were by him perswaded too relent,
And for too bee comfortable too live in reverent awe
Like neybours in a common weale by justyce under law.

(*Shakespeare's Ovid, Being Arthur Golding's Translation of the Metamorphoses*, ed. W. H. D. Rouse (London, 1904), Epistle, lines 517–26.)

formall, and in his much multiformitie *uniforme*, that is well propor-
tioned, and so passing cleare, that by it, as by a glasse or mirrour, are
represented unto the soule all maner of bewtifull visions, whereby the
inventive parte of the mynde is so much holpen, as without it no man
could devise any new or rare thing . . . and of this sorte of phantasie
are all good Poets, notable Captaines stratagematique, all cunning
artificers and enginers, all Legislators, Polititiens, and Counsellours of
estate, in whose exercises the inventive part is most employed, and is
to the sound and true judgement of man most needful.[23]

But if the dance suggests a reaching beyond reason, that is not
apparent in Colin's explanation of the dance to Calidore. He
explains only the broadest lesson which can be drawn from it.
However, there is a deeper meaning to the dance, not antagonistic
to Colin's explanation but *beyond* it. We shall be examining this
meaning in a later chapter. Colin seems to fly off at an irrational
tangent when he comes to the central figure in the dance, thereby
suggesting to us that there is more to the whole episode than the
bare bones of his explanation. But this extra dimension, which is
really what the whole poem is *about*, cannot be articulated apart
from the dance itself; the poetry, in other words, is a comment
upon itself. If rational unconflicting interpretations were all that
were needed, the *vision* of courtesy would have no point. In fact
Faeryland itself would be consigned to inutility as an elaborate and
unnecessary lie. The dance is above and beyond the particular, *and
yet* Colin Clout's beloved is part of it. This is the essential paradox:
courtesy involves the giving of oneself, but the very process of
giving brings with it greater reward; poetry, like love, is the
sacrifice of one's self, but the reward is another self, another
nature—the beloved, the poem.

Puttenham's extension of the terrain of inspiration makes the
Golden Age myth no longer the property solely of poetry: there
is a Golden Age behind all forms of human activity. As the point
from which time began, the Golden World lies in the infancy of
Nature; it is not so much a place of retirement as a place of learning, a place from which all knowledge derives.[24] The paradox of

---

[23] Sewell, *Orphic Voice*, p. 76, quoting from *The Arte of English Poesie* (1589), in
G. Gregory Smith, ed., *Elizabethan Critical Essays* (Oxford, 1904), 2: 19–20.

[24] In fact, the myth is ambiguous and is so applied. Bacon put his finger on this
ambiguous quality of time in Book 1 of the *Novum Organum* (Aphorism 84): 'The
old age of the world is to be accounted the true antiquity; and this is the attribute
of our own times, not of that earlier age of the world in which the ancients lived;

man's relation to the Golden Age is therefore similar to the relation of Art to Nature: the Golden Age contains within it the origins of man, man's infancy if you like; it also contains within it all knowledge. Man has fallen. The Golden Age is an ideal for which he seeks, and simultaneously a teacher giving him the knowledge to continue the search. It is a place of peace and a place of education: 'all things stedfastnes doe hate / And changed be . . . And turning to themselves at length againe, / Doe worke their own perfection so by fate.'

The idea of the Golden World as a place of education raises further questions related to the connection between Art and Nature. To what degree can Art supplement the deficiencies of Nature by means of education? Polixenes touches on the question in the passage from *The Winter's Tale* already quoted: 'You see, sweet maid, we marry / A gentler scion to the wildest stock / And make conceive a bark of baser kind / By bud of nobler race.' Polixenes is careful to correct himself when he first suggests that art amends nature, though the passage sets up a remarkably complex pattern of irony in the play itself and makes suggestions which seem to undermine the whole pattern of hierarchy presumably approved by Shakespeare.

3. Nature and nurture

The relation between birth and breeding, if only because it is so frequently reiterated, is clearly one of the more important questions of Book VI—either for its own sake or because it implies some larger issue. In the present study we have touched on the problem on several occasions, and it would perhaps be helpful to take stock of our findings and to relate them to the larger issue of the relation between Art and Nature.

It is not too outrageous a generalization to say that the traditional Elizabethan view of questions of heredity is that breeding will out[25]—a view illustrated rather well in the story of Tristram.

---

and which, though in respect of us it was the elder, yet in respect of the world it was the younger.' (Quoted by Sewell, p. 101.) On the importance of this reassessment of the ancients see J. B. Bury, *The Idea of Progress* (New York, 1932), pp. 50–63. Cf. Rosemond Tuve, 'Ancients, Moderns and Saxons', *ELH*, 6 (1939), 165–90, and Richard Foster Jones, *The Triumph of the English Language* (Stanford, Calif., 1953), *passim*.

[25] See Frank Kermode's discussion of nature and nurture in his edition of *The Tempest* (London, 1954), pp. xliii–xlvii.

He is of noble birth, and his handsome exterior, graceful movement, and costly clothing all make this abundantly clear—in spite
of the fact that when Calidore meets him he is engaged in what
appears to be a gross breach of the rules of chivalry. The child
given to Matilda, on the other hand, appears to give promise of
total malleability:

> If that the cause of this your languishment
> Be lacke of children, to supply your place,
> Lo how good fortune doth to you present
> This litle babe, of sweete and lovely face,
> And spotlesse spirit, in which ye may enchace
> What ever formes ye list thereto apply,
> Being now soft and fit them to embrace;
> Whether ye list him traine in chevalry,
> Or noursle up in lore of learn'd Philosophy.
>
> And certes it hath oftentimes bene seene,
> That of the like, whose linage was unknowne,
> More brave and noble knights have raysed beene,
> As their victorious deedes have often showen,
> Being with fame through many Nations blowen,
> Then those, which have bene dandled in the lap.
> Therefore some thought, that those brave imps were sowen
> Here by the Gods, and fed with heavenly sap,
> That made them grow so high t'all honorable hap.
>
> (VI. iv. 35–6)

But the issue is not as simple as it seems. The final lines throw the
actual *nature* of these children into doubt, and the rest of the
passage is not so much an affirmation of the efficacy of education
as a reminder that there is something very special about foundling
children discovered in the forest. They are sturdier, for one thing—
and a stay among the rigours of nature, in infancy or (like Tristram) in young manhood, is good for young bones.

If Spenser is here setting up any contrast at all, it is between the
two ways to knowledge—precept and experience. We are certainly
apt to think of courtesy as largely the province of the former; it is
a set of rules, presented to us for our instruction by a Guazzo or a
Castiglione. We have seen how Spenser, describing Elizabethan
gentlemen through the metaphor of knighthood, has his heroes
follow or transgress rules of *chivalry*, the metaphorical equivalent
of sixteenth-century courtesy. The effect of the transgressions is

to demonstrate that courtesy does not consist in rules and precepts entirely, but also in empirical experience. Courtesy is discoverable through the operations of nature.[26]

Artegall learned justice by practising it upon the beasts; Satyrane learned to fight in this same way; in the woods Belphoebe received her education. By contrast, Amoret, brought up in the Garden of Adonis, was protected from the rigours of experience, and in consequence found herself immediately in trouble when beyond the loving care of her foster-mother Venus. But if Amoret must learn to live with man's inhumanity, Artegall must learn mercy, and Satyrane is denied the holy precepts bestowed upon the Red Cross Knight. Belphoebe's chastity may merit our admiration, but she is hardly a picture of perfect womanhood. *That* is reserved for Britomart, who combines Belphoebe's experience with Amoret's innocence. As is so often the case with Spenser, the mean between two extremes constitutes the pattern to be followed.

If education and experience have their value, so does birth. Tristram is descended from noble stock, so we expect him to behave nobly. Matilda's child, it is hinted, is grown of seed 'sown by the gods'—grown of an uncorrupted nature.[27] Tristram's noble birth is what is normally meant by 'nature' in the nature–nurture antithesis, but the babe is *in himself* a child of nature. The apparent contrast between the babe and Tristram turns out to be less of a contrast than we might think. The very fact that children can be sown by the gods (as some think) suggests that the idea of natural hereditary superiority may have some justification. We might notice, too, that Tristram has been preserved in the forest by a benevolent nature, and that he is firmly identified with the world of natural change by the image of the flower, also an anticipation of the story of Pastorella.[28]

[26] Note, however, that learning was sometimes regarded as one branch of nobility and hence of courtesy. See, for example, my quotation from La Primaudaye, p. 167 above.

[27] Cf. Castiglione, *The Book of the Courtier* (London, n.d.), p. 32: 'Some there are borne indeed with such graces, that they seem not to have been borne, but rather fashioned with the verie hand of some God, and abound in all goodnes both of bodie and minde.' Drawing attention to this passage, MacLure ('Nature and Art') mentions a similar one in *Nennio, or A Treatise of Nobility* (1595), Book I. MacLure (p. 16) draws a parallel between this child and Tristram, but this only tends to undermine his argument in favour of the 'aristocratic' view (noble characters nobly born, base characters basely born), which seems to me too categorical and simplistic.

[28] The image of the flower bursting forth to honour, or unfolding its silken leaves, is especially appropriate. If the root of the flower of courtesy is in nature, it

Matilda's child forms the subject of a series of observations on the effects of education on the young mind. The child can be trained, says Calepine, for a life either of action or of learning.[29] His abundant confidence in the child's teachability would have struck a responsive chord among Spenser's readers, since it is very much in keeping with the optimistic views of education current among the Elizabethans. In an age characterized by social mobility, a proper education was frequently the key to success for an ambitious young man.

But social mobility does not necessarily breed egalitarianism. A man newly risen on the social ladder may prove more jealous of the privileges accruing to him than the man born into social prominence. The Elizabethans, precisely because so many of them were trying so hard to imitate the ways of social groupings to which they were new, were intensely conscious of what makes an aristocrat, how one can recognize a man of breeding from a boor. In a society so obsessed with externals—in its architecture, its decoration, the way it dressed, its manners—wiser men were newly anxious to convey the qualities of *intrinsic* nobility. If in Calidore Spenser sets up an ideal of the combination of noble breeding with education, he is only being realistic; it was just such an ideal that men of social pretensions in Elizabethan England were attempting to imitate.[30] It does not, of course, preclude

---

nevertheless blossoms forth in the court; the court is therefore the culmination, the highest point, of human civilization. Cf. Milton:

so from the root
Springs lighter the green stalk, from thence the leaves
More aerie, last the bright consummat floure
Spirits odorous breathes. (*Paradise Lost*, v. 479–82)

Here, of course, the plant climbs through, and hence unites, the four elements. On similar passages in other poets, see Marjorie Hope Nicolson, *The Breaking of the Circle* (Evanston, Ill., 1950), p. 13.

[29] 'Chevalry' might correspond to experience, 'philosophy' to precept.

[30] Kermode (*Tempest*, pp. xlv–xlvi) quotes an interesting passage by Milton's nephew, Edward Phillips, in which the relation of birth to education is spelled out and the Orpheus myth is linked with education. Phillips is speaking of the two forces which distinguish the better part of mankind: 'The first is that *Melior natura* which the Poet speaks of, with which whoever is amply indued, take that Man from his Infancy, throw him into the Desarts of *Arabia*, there let him converse some years with Tygers and Leopards, and at last bring him where civil society & conversation abides, and ye shall see how on a sudden, the scales and dross of his barbarity purging off by degrees, he will start up a Prince or Legislator, or some such illustrious Person: the other is that noble thing call'd *Education*, this is, that Harp of *Orpheus*, that lute of *Amphion*, so elegantly figur'd by the Poets to have wrought such Miracles

aberrations, either in noblemen who turn out bad or men of lesser stock who make good. What is apparently essential in *every* case is the seed of virtue, which must somehow be implanted by nature in the object of her attentions. While the usual means for so doing may be aristocratic birth, the case of Matilda's babe suggests that other miracles are possible. Priscilla's prissiness (the term might almost have been created for her) in disdaining to carry the wounded Aladine shows too great a reliance on supposedly 'natural' superiority—superiority of breeding. Thus she shows herself a snob, perhaps bearing out the reservations expressed when the other knight's lady first describes her (or is this merely Spenser's skill in female psychology?). Aladine, furthermore, is in no sense base, even if he does not measure up to Priscilla's parents' standards. Their choice is evidently the richer in wealth but the poorer in valour, and in the scale of values operative in Book VI this gives the palm to Aladine. Perhaps Calidore's white lie on Priscilla's behalf is a tacit acknowledgement of the rightness of her choice—an assumption borne out by the story of Bellamour and Claribell, whose union produced Pastorella.

   Though Spenser does not invariably support social status, nobility of birth, against all other qualities, Mirabella's lowly birth serves to emphasize the fact that she is a fraud; her superficial beauty is supported by no hidden seed of virtue. The Salvage Man, by contrast, is probably of noble birth but utterly lacks the courtly training which presumably Mirabella has received. Yet he is naturally courteous, deriving his courtesy from his ancestry rather than his habitat. 'Of court it seemes, men Courtesie doe call', but this second figure raised in the woods (Tristram being the first) implies that courtesy is no court monopoly. There is, of course, some justification for supposing that gentle behaviour will follow from a life in the woods. When we first meet Belphoebe, the poet expresses wonder at her grace, but perhaps closeness to nature is itself a reason for gracefulness. There are, after all, two

among irrational and insensible Creatures, which raiseth beauty even out of deformity, order and regularity out of Chaos and confusion, and which, if thoroughly and rightly prosecuted, would be able to civilize the most savage natures, & root out barbarism and ignorance from off the face of the Earth: those who have either of these qualifications singly may justly be term'd *Men*; those who have both united in a happy conjunction, *more* than *Men*; those who have neither of them in any competent measure . . . *less* than *Men*. . . .' (*Theatrum Poetarum*, 1675.) On other treatments of nature and nurture see Kermode's note to this passage.

aspects to nature, and they are not both inimical to order. In fact, even disordered nature may prove a good teacher of order, as was the case with Artegall. This love of order, or of gentleness, to be found among the inhabitants of the forest is a characteristic of some types of the wild men who populate medieval art and literature. Thus Walter Map, in a passage quoted in a previous chapter,[31] refers to one Edric Wilde, 'that is, the man of the woods, so called from the agility of his body and the charm of his words and works'. We hardly expect such gentleness from a denizen of the forest—until we realize that the creatures who brought help to wounded travellers, who had knowledge of herbs and forest lore, were also men of the forest as much as the wodwoes and the trolls, with this difference, that they were creatures of *benevolent* nature.

Of course, Spenser's reference to the Salvage Man's noble birth also helps to add credence to his story (and to provide hints of new stories). But the stamp of noble birth is also a stamp of humanity, and it certainly would add probability to some future story of the Salvage Man's development into a courtier, if this was intended. In fact, I would be inclined to suggest that this consideration, and not some doctrinaire conservatism, leads Spenser to mention the Salvage Man's background. There is another reason, too, why it is appropriate; the Salvage Man is thus allied with Tristram, the babe and Pastorella as a fugitive from a court overrun by the forces of discourtesy.

We could conclude, then, that there are two ways of looking at the term nature in relation to nurture, and that there are also two ways of looking at the term nurture. Both court and natural world may be sources of the superiority derived from nature, either separately or together (the noble Tristram comes from the court, Matilda's babe from the natural world). Both may also provide nurture. But the one quality consistently praised, regardless of its subjects' background, is harmony, and with it reciprocal love. Man's art, the art of education, can supplement and augment nature, but there must be some ground of goodness for education to work upon. In Mirabella, for example, such goodness is lacking.

As part of the natural order, man needs the strength which nature provides. As a social being he needs the support of nurture. But this nurture, this external overlay of good manners and breeding, may easily become a sham. The story of Pastorella is based

---

[31] See above, p. 134.

on a very careful differentiation between intrinsic goodness and external ceremonies, and it provides the best gloss on the whole question that Spenser gives us. Pastorella was born of noble stock, though that stock was not as noble as it might have been (Bellamour was not of as distinguished a family as Claribell). Living in the country, cut off from the court, she yet becomes the epitome of the *true* courtesy. Is this courtesy derived from *nature*, her gentle birth; or is it derived from *nurture*, her upbringing close to the harmony of the natural world? Of course, it is both. A series of miracles is responsible for her surviving at all, and yet it is her birth that shines through her conduct so conspicuously that Calidore halts in his quest. Though a creature of the court, she nevertheless displays the courtesy of the natural world—grace, gentleness, harmony. These qualities seem often to be lacking amid the welter of meaningless politenesses taught and displayed in the court. But, Spenser says, they constitute the fundamentals of all courtesy.

> Amongst them all growes not a fayrer flowre,
> Then is the bloosme of comely courtesie,
> Which though it on a lowly stalke doe bowre,
> Yet brancheth forth in brave nobilitie,
> And spreds it selfe through all civilitie. (vi. proem. 4)

The parents of Priscilla were in danger of forgetting this; 'But vertues seat is deepe within the mynd'—in nature, not in art.

Through all this, the issue of nature versus nurture recedes in importance. Spenser is never really interested in arguing one or the other. He is simply concerned to show the *variety* of circumstances under which natural virtue, natural courtesy, can manifest itself. However, as was emphasized in the previous chapter, Book vi is ultimately a poem *about* society. Thus Calidore, integrated into society, nobly born, nobly educated, is Spenser's ideal courtier. Book vi tells the story of how even the ideal courtier needs to understand that the roots of courtesy lie outside the court, though their blossom is within the court. Both Tristram and Pastorella burgeon like flowers as they move into the courtly world, but the seeds of the flowers, though planted perhaps by the gods, are in nature.

4. Nature and Grace: the poetry of vision

One term which I used in connection with 'natural' courtesy was the word 'grace'. It is a word often used in Book VI, from passing references to beauty of appearance (Mirabella's, for instance), to the dance of the Graces themselves. The fact that the Graces exist in a region approaching the celestial reminds us that the word is essentially a pun. How seriously are we supposed to pursue the logic of this pun?

It is difficult to establish to what degree Spenser conceives of Grace theologically in this book: to what extent, in other words, it is a quality sent from heaven rather than simply a way of behaviour. Many readers would no doubt dismiss any suggestion of a theological reading of Book VI without further thought, but the word is used too often, and it is too closely associated with the book's central virtue, to be dismissed quite so casually.[32] Some years ago, A. S. P. Woodhouse, in a study of the Orders of Nature and Grace in the *Faerie Queene*, made Spenserian scholarship more acutely aware of the rather unusual qualities of the titular virtue of the first book as against those of later books. Woodhouse reminds his readers that the Elizabethans conceived of man as situated in the framework of two separate orders of existence:

To the Christian, of course, both orders were subject to the power and providence of God, but exercised in a manner sufficiently different to maintain a clear-cut distinction between the two. In the natural order belonged not only the physical world, what is commonly called the world of nature inanimate and animate, but man himself considered simply as a denizen of that world. The rule of its order was expressed not only in the physical laws of nature, but in natural ethics . . . and even in natural as opposed to revealed religion. This order was apprehended in experience and interpreted by reason. . . . To the order of grace, on the other hand, belonged man in his character of supernatural being, with all that concerned his salvation, under the old dispensation and the new. The law of its government was the revealed will of God, received and interpreted by faith, and it included a special kind of experience called religious experience.[33]

Woodhouse points out that there are two ways of approaching the relationship between the two orders: either to recognize their

[32] Maurice Evans, 'Courtesy and the Fall of Man', *ES*, 46 (1965), 209–20, reads the book in these terms, and I think he is partly right, though I disagree with his interpretation of Calidore's supposed truancy.
[33] 'Nature and Grace in *The Faerie Queene*', *ELH*, 16 (1949), 195.

divergence or to stress their unity. Those who choose the first path do so in order to emphasize the one and depress the other (ascetics at the one extreme, naturalists at the other) or to keep them separate so as to apply methods of examination to the one not acceptable in the context of the other (Bacon). Those who choose the second path correspond to the 'optimists' who see in nature the pattern of God's order—Hooker, for instance. Spenser falls between the two categories, being more strongly aware than Hooker of a dichotomy in nature, of a defective pattern.

Woodhouse does not touch on Book VI. He spends some time speculating on how Spenser might have formed a final synthesis of Nature and Grace had he reached the end of his undertaking. He does not believe that such a synthesis is achieved in that part of the work which we now have. Here he may be right, but it is difficult to know just what kind of a synthesis he envisions. What has to be brought together? Presumably the synthesis must involve a Christian element, and in consequence it is not enough to propose a solution based on 'eterne in mutabilitie'. Nevertheless, this *is* a form of solution, since it in effect nullifies the corruption of the Fall while at the same time acknowledging that the Fall happened. Mutabilitie's struggle at the sphere of the moon represents the first sign of disorder in the cosmos, brought about by Adam's sin. In fact, her attack on Cynthia, her subverting of nature, represents her coming into existence: were there no Fall there would be no Mutability.

The theme of the 'Cantos of Mutabilitie', the reconciliation of supposed opposites by finding that in fact they are in harmony, is, as we have seen, a constant theme in the *Faerie Queene*. In reconciling the realm of matter and the realm of forms, the 'Mutabilitie Cantos' are an elaborate restatement of the description of the Gardens of Adonis in Book III.[34] Of course, we can argue that neither the 'Mutabilitie Cantos' nor the Gardens of Adonis point the way to man's salvation. The Book of God's Works is supplementary rather than alternative to the Book of God's Word. Neither is the vision on Mount Acidale a vision of salvation in a Christian sense. The one final and necessary step—the crossing of the rift between classical and Christian—is only hinted at. But the

---

[34] That it should be Diana who retires from the world at the end of the Golden Age on Arlo Hill is logical enough. Venus remains active in this world, in her role as Earthly Venus rather than Celestial.

realization that the hint is there is enough to give the dance of the Graces exceptional importance in the structure of the *Faerie Queene*. Woodhouse's article, for all its perceptiveness, had the unfortunate side-effect of tending to blind many critics to the Christian implications of the later books. Spenser's vision, mildly neo-Platonic, is certainly not at variance with Christian teaching. In Book VI, it may look suspiciously as though he is using theology to explain poetry, rather than poetry to explain theology, but even that need hardly upset us, knowing what we do of the humanist delight in synthesis.

The hint which Spenser offers us is this term 'Grace', a term which opens up a new area of experience to the reader of Book VI. The theological meaning of the term lies behind its more mundane occurrences: grace is the means by which the spirit sloughs off the clay. Though nature is corrupt and fallen, and though man's sin filters grace so that it reaches him in a pale and wintry light, God's grace still moves the hierarchy of nature in the endless dance which the sixteenth century loved to describe.

As Spenser uses the word in Book VI, Grace has, in varying degrees, the two meanings I have already mentioned—grace of body and heavenly grace. Just how this is so will become clearer when we examine the iconography of the Dance of the Graces. Of course, even grace of body implies the operation of a power external to the individual. Speaking of women, Spenser writes

> And as ye soft and tender are by kynde,
> Adornd with goodly gifts of beauties grace,
> So be ye soft and tender eeke in mynde;
> But cruelty and hardnesse from you chace.
>
> (VI. viii. 2)

The term 'beauties grace' contains elements of both meanings. The particular individual is graceful, and through being graceful she reveals grace. But though she reveals beauty through this grace, beauty is a metaphysical principle external to her. Among the neo-Platonists, especially Ficino, this principle of beauty, the principle of perfect form, becomes central to the philosopher's world view. The beauty of the universe provides the most conclusive proof of its divine origin and consequently of its spiritual value. Spenser, echoing this idea (which was widely held by other philosophers besides the members of the Florentine Academy, and consequently might have come to him from any or many of various sources), naturally uses theological terminology to explain the phenomenon. The ideal beauty, he says, operates on man through the medium of grace, just as God reaches the soul through grace.

The word 'grace' had such wide connotations to the Elizabethans that this hint of complex meaning behind a simple word might easily have escaped their attention. The word was widely used to denote the action of the beloved's beauty upon the lover, and especially the action of the beloved's mercy upon her suitor. The metaphor is so simple and obvious that it might be difficult to decide where it started, but it became a very common means of indicating the qualities of deity present in the beloved as the Middle Ages freely adapted theological language to matters of courtly love. In time, in fact, the metaphor came close to dying completely, so that an allusion to grace in an Elizabethan love-lyric may raise in the reader scarcely a flicker of recognition that the word belongs to the realm of the spirit rather than the realm of the flesh. Spenser uses the word rather frequently in his works —three or four hundred times in its various forms. Sometimes the term's ambiguity is exploited extensively—in the *Fowre Hymnes* for example—but at others it is little more than a rather perfunctory piece of Petrarchanism. When Timias is restored to Belphoebe's favour, a second metaphor must consequently be brought in even to hint at a religious connotation in the words (my italics):

> After that Timias had againe recured
> The favour of Belphebe, (as ye heard)
> And of her *grace* did stand againe assured,
> To happie *blisse* he was full high uprear'd.   (VI. v. 12)

Of course, in the *Faerie Queene* we are more on the lookout for hints of other realms of existence than we are in a poem less evidently allegorized.

The word 'grace' carries a further metaphorical connotation. Nature itself can be bestower of grace upon the individual. Thus, we read of Mirabella:

> She was a Ladie of great dignitie,
> And lifted up to honorable place,
> Famous through all the land of Faerie,
> Though of meane parentage and kindred base,
> Yet deckt with wondrous giftes of natures grace.
>
> (VI. vii. 28)

The word 'gifts' reminds us of the movement, the bestowal, which the word 'grace' connotes.[35] And 'Nature's grace' signifies two separate things: gracefulness *in* a body, and the means of communicating gracefulness *to* a body. Neither of these meanings can be described as anything more than metaphorically akin to the realm of the spirit, but it is arguable that the grace bestowed upon its creations by beneficent nature has a higher source than the immediately tangible realm of earthly nature. Even if the order of nature extends as far as moral philosophy, still grace implies a quality beyond the reach of discursive reason. The goddess Nature rules the physical universe, as we learn in the 'Mutabilitie Cantos'; but beyond her there is a still greater power—God himself. Spenser, appropriately, likens the appearance of Nature on Arlo Hill to the appearance of Christ transfigured. If the transfigured Christ is such as to cause the Three to forget their wits (VII. vii. 7) how much greater is Almighty God! Yet God's grace, God's word, was made flesh in Christ: the two orders, of Grace and of Nature, coalesced in him, and thus he became man's way to salvation.

Una, alone in the realm of Nature, pacifies the Lion and the Salvage Nation. Serena, apparently going from frying pan to fire in being rescued by a wild man from a bad one, places her hope in 'Gods sole grace, whom she did oft implore, / To send her succour'. The succour comes, in the form of the wild man himself: the grace of heaven turns out to be the grace of nature.

Spenser's compromise (common enough in his time), his stand midway between Hooker's beneficent Nature and Calvin's fatally defective Nature, means that he sees a direct contact between Grace and Nature even if there is a dangerous fault in the communications cable. Indeed, the whole question of the relationship between the two resolves itself into the need to keep the line of communication open. The key to the problem lies in the Dance of the Graces, handmaids of Venus. As we shall see in a subsequent

[35] The reference to nature in this context is also a further indication of the ambivalence of Spenser's attitude towards the question of nature and nurture. On a previous occasion, again in reference to a morally doubtful character—Blandina— Spenser posited the simple alternative, 'Whether such grace were given her by kynd, / As women wont their guilefull wits to guyde, / Or learn'd the art to please' (VI. vi. 43). Qualities either come by nature or they are learned. But coming by nature involves an alternative, as Mirabella's qualities make clear: they may be *bestowed* by nature, independently of parentage. There are thus three possibilities, not two: grace by nature, grace by parentage, grace by education.

chapter, Venus fulfils dual roles—that of spiritual generation, as *Venus Coelestis*, and that of earthly generation, as *Venus Vulgaris*. The dance is emblematic of both these functions, and so Spenser sets it in the pre-lapsarian Golden Age, when there was no division between nature and grace.

The dance itself mirrors its setting. *Natura naturata* surrounds *natura naturans* in a single emblem. Dancing in the centre of the hundred naked maidens are the Graces:

> These three on men all gracious gifts bestow,
> Which decke the body or adorne the mynde,
> To make them lovely or well favoured show,
> As comely carriage, entertainment kynde,
> Sweete semblaunt, friendly offices that bynde,
> And all the complements of curtesie:
> They teach us, how to each degree and kynde
> We should our selves demeane, to low, to hie;
> To friends, to foes, which skill men call Civility.
>
> (VI. x. 23)

The Graces are bestowers of gifts, as their iconography, the arrangement in which they are presented in the succeeding stanza, makes clear. As bestowers of gifts they are like 'nature's grace', and their effect is to produce gracefulness of bearing in those to whom they turn. As symbols of *natura naturans* they sum up the harmony of the created universe, teaching civil society the hierarchical order natural to it. In an earlier stanza we are told how the Graces relate to Venus:

> Those were the Graces, daughters of delight,
> Handmaides of *Venus*, which are wont to haunt
> Uppon this hill, and daunce there day and night:
> Those three to men all gifts of grace do graunt,
> And all, that *Venus* in her selfe doth vaunt,
> Is borrowed of them.   (VI. x. 15)

I have drawn attention before to the ambiguity in the sentence 'and all, that Venus in her selfe doth vaunt, is borrowed of them'. Either Venus borrows, or we borrow. Or both. Spenser is looking at the iconographical significance of the figures in two different ways at the same time. Venus, goddess of beauty, sends her beauty through grace, through the Graces, to mankind. In us, it makes objects and individuals beautiful—beautiful physically but, more particularly, beautiful mentally, for 'vertues seat is deepe within the mynd'.

While grace descends to us through the Graces, we are turned towards the source of grace: communication takes place in both directions. It is an exchange of gifts. A similar idea lies at the root of neo-Platonic thought; not only does man strive towards God, but God strives toward man. 'In a free act of love', summarizes Cassirer, 'God turns toward the world; in a free act of his grace, He redeems man and the world; and the same double direction of striving is essential to all intelligences.' He quotes Ficino:

It is the peculiarity of all divine spirits that, while they contemplate the higher, they do not cease to look at the lower and to care for it. It is also characteristic of our soul that it is concerned not only for its own body but for the bodies of all earthly things and for the earth itself, to cultivate them and further them.[36]

So it is that Venus gives to the Graces the grace which they pass on to mankind. Yet at the same time the natural world rises towards God. Through the Graces flows grace to the natural world, presided over by the Earthly Venus, and from the realm of matter love rises through them to the realm of the spirit, presided over by the Celestial Venus. Beyond both Venuses stands God himself. The central 'three other ladies' not only dance but also *sing*, a reminder that music is the measure of their dance. The power of music to create and symbolize harmony is a subject dear to poets and philosophers in every age. Orpheus and his lyre not only ordered the world of nature but soothed even the gods; the spheres in their revolutions give back to God their harmony through music; Orpheus, the poet, is a kind of demigod to whom all nature is subservient. Music is the link between the two realms of nature and of grace, for it imposes order upon nature and at the same time mirrors the perfect harmony, the metaphysical principle upon which the universe is constructed.[37]

In his book *Pagan Mysteries in the Renaissance*, Edgar Wind reproduces (Fig. 20) an illustration from Gafurius's *Practica Musice* (1496), showing the eight notes of the musical scale and the Nine Muses (the ninth is Thalia, muse of pastoral poetry, who is

---

[36] Cassirer, *Individual and Cosmos*, p. 133.

[37] On Orpheus and the powers of music, see John Hollander, *The Untuning of the Sky: Ideas of Music in English Poetry, 1500–1700* (Princeton, N.J., 1961), esp. pp. 162–76.

allotted the sphere of the earth). Over them presides Apollo, linked with the earth through the *signum triceps* frequently associated with him. The *signum* is joined to him by a serpent's tail.[38] Beside Apollo are, on one side, the three Graces and on the other, his lyre and a pot of flowers. The Graces signify, according to Panofsky and Wind, the realm of the spirit, the flowers the realm of matter: Grace and Nature, united through music.[39]

Wind's interpretation of Botticelli's *Primavera* is particularly instructive as a means of explaining the episode on Mount Acidale.[40] He establishes that the painting revolves round the central figure of Venus (the earthly Venus), and also that there is a movement from right to left, from the triad Zephyrus–Chloris–Flora, to Venus, to the three Graces, to Mercury—an ascending movement from matter to spirit. This being the case, the influence of the Order of Grace upon the Order of Nature in fact goes *from* the Graces *to* Venus rather than the other way round. Wind emphasizes the difference between the rapid and violent movement of the right-hand triad and the decorous dance of the Graces, the former being more typical of the earthly natural order. Spenser's dance, with its thumping of the hollow ground, moves from one to the other—to a higher and ever higher level of abstraction. But ultimately it is the same dance: the Graces are both servants of the Earthly Venus and mediators between her and heavenly grace. Wind further shows, by reference to Gafurius, that the painting can be interpreted musically, with the lowest note of the scale at Zephyrus and the highest at Mercury, with Venus as the fourth note, the central point when the transcendent eighth note is excluded.

If the Order of Grace and the Order of Nature are harmonized within the general emblem of the musical scale, music is indeed an appropriate accompaniment for Calidore's vision of the Graces. Leo Spitzer, in one of his most remarkable studies, has given us additional evidence of this association of music with the reconciliation of Nature and Grace, or even with Grace alone. Paulinus of Nola writes, 'At nobis ars una fides et musica Christus' and

---

[38] See Erwin Panofsky, *Hercules am Scheidewege* (Leipzig, 1930), pp. 1–35 and esp. pp. 18–23. Panofsky also reproduces the Gafurius frontispiece and interprets its link with Apollo. On a later printing of the woodcut, see Wind, *Mysteries*, p. 130, n. 6.

[39] See Wind's note 'Gafurius on the Harmony of the Spheres', *Mysteries*, pp. 265–9.

[40] *Mysteries*, pp. 113–27.

alludes to this parallel in a number of other rather arresting contexts.[41] In fact, Spitzer points out, the four terms 'grace–nature–
music–harmony' are frequently associated in medieval writing.
Sometimes music is absorbed into harmony, thereby creating the
triad grace–nature–harmony. He cites the famous painting by
Raphael, 'in which Cecilia, on hearing the angelic music of the
beyond, is shown as dropping, enraptured, her earthly *organetto*,
while vielle, tambourin and other earthly instruments lie on the
floor about her'. From earthly music she has risen to heavenly
music, heard in her heart:

By now vocal music, that is, the music of the human heart, is superior
to instrumental music . . . and, significantly enough, the equation
'music equals grace' is emphasized by the presence . . . not only of
Augustine (author of *De musica*), but also of Paul ('Si linguis hominum
loquar, et angelorum, charitatem autem non habeam . . . '), of John
the Evangelist (the representative of the invasion by grace) . . . and,
especially, of Mary Magdalen, a Saint who has never been shown in
any direct relationship with music, but only with that grace-which-is
music.

To Schopenhauer this painting represents the transition from poet
to saint, the point at which the poet 'lays hold on the real'. Before
he reaches, if he reaches, such sainthood, he is bound to the work,
to 'that pure, true, and deep knowledge of the inner nature of the
world', which becomes for him an end in itself.

It does not deliver him for ever from life, but only at moments, and is
therefore not for him a path out of life, but only an occasional consolation in it, till his power, increased by this contemplation and at last
tired of the play, lays hold on the real.[42]

If Colin Clout pipes for a shepherds' dance, or for his mistress, he
is no more than the simple poet piping. But his music does far
more than this; it creates and holds together a universe of poetry
in which Nature is united with Grace, the divine principle behind
and beyond Nature. For all that Schopenhauer's idea of the Will
and Spenser's Christian neo-Platonism are worlds apart, both men

---

[41] Spitzer, *Classical and Christian Ideas of World Harmony* (Baltimore, Md., 1963),
p. 48. The quotations and the following observations are largely drawn from this
work, pp. 48ff.

[42] Arthur Schopenhauer, *The World as Will and Idea*, trans. R. B. Haldane and J.
Kemp, 8th edn. (London, n.d.), 1.iii.52 (p. 346).

are here describing a rather similar movement. The poet 'doth grow in effect into another nature'.

But when Colin breaks his pipe the gesture represents not a 'laying hold on the real' but an acknowledgement of its impossibility. Music belongs with grace; it is neither appropriate nor supportable in Calidore's presence, since Calidore, for all his glimpse of another and unknown existence, is firmly rooted in the world of here-and-now, with its comfortingly rational explanations for phenomena fundamentally irrational to those who choose truly to investigate them. Small wonder, then, that Colin's explanation to Calidore is so feeble when compared with the dance itself.[43] The breaking of the pipe, too, suggests a reassertion of the division between Grace and Nature. But it is not entirely a return to the old state, since from the dance Calidore himself learns an important lesson, and, still more important, the connection between the *natural* beauty of Pastorella and the heavenly *grace* of her womanhood is by implication firmly established. In this grand emblem of earthly and heavenly beauty, Colin Clout's mistress and Venus herself are drawn together in a single figure—and, we can conclude, so is Pastorella.

It is in the nature of the triad to bring about such conflations. Platonic theology taught that the god reveals himself in this way. Venus is unfolded in the Graces, the Graces infolded in Venus. The neo-Platonist law that contraries coincide in the One makes of the triad two contraries linked together through a quality midway between them, which thus prevents the disintegration of the figure. The use of the triad to figure forth this momentary coming together of contraries is highly appropriate. Nature and grace are held together through mediating harmony; art and nature coincide in order; Colin's mistress and Venus are brought together through the medium of the poet.

The similarity of the Platonic doctrine of the triad and the Christian doctrine of the Trinity was not lost on the neo-Platonists. In fact it became a commonplace of Renaissance thought.

[43] 'And in this movement it is not simply the described figures but the vision itself which seems stanza by stanza to shift and revolve, expand and contract, unfolding as if the poet does not know what he thinks till he sees what he says. The landscape displays a mind negatively capable, an indeterminate and creative collaboration between the epic poet and his pastoral persona.' (Harry Berger, Jr., 'A Secret Discipline: *The Faerie Queene*, Book vi', in William Nelson, ed., *Form and Convention in the Poetry of Edmund Spenser* (New York, 1961), p. 68.)

With an equal inevitability, the grace of the Graces was associated with the grace bestowed on mankind by the three theological virtues. 'Faith, Hope, and Charity, are the three Divine Graces,' declares Alexander Ross, the seventeenth-century mythographer, 'pure and unspotted Virgins, Daughters of the Great God.'[44] This connection with Christian, as well as neo-Platonist, doctrine suggests yet another way of looking at the dancing damsels, as manifestations of theological grace. The idea, of course, is not made explicit in Spenser's text, and it is at most an underlying significance—but not one which we can readily ignore.

If theological grace is associated with music and with the Three Graces, we should perhaps also observe that it was anciently connected with the dance. Max Pulver has drawn attention to a curious passage in the apocryphal Acts of St. John, in which the twelve apostles dance in a circle round Christ: 'Then he bade us form a circle; we stood with folded hands, and he was in the middle. And then he said: Answer me with Amen. Then he began to intone a hymn of praise and to say: Praise be to thee, Father. And we all circled round him and responded to him: Amen.' Later, Christ provides the music for the dance: 'Grace paces the round. I will blow the pipe. Dance the round all, Amen.' Translating the chapters describing the dance, Pulver comments, 'After [the] first confessions of Christ, Charis enters the round, for it is the grace of the supreme godhead which sent the savior, and it is grace which permits the mystes to partake of initiation in this choral song . . . . Christ appears plainly as the mystery god, playing the tune for the mystical round dance.'[45]

Christ, then, plays the tune to which the disciples dance, his music bestowing upon them the heavenly grace which harmonizes their actions and makes of these actions a ceremony of praise to God. This godlike role reminds us of the role of the poet towards his creation. While I do not suggest that this strange episode in an early part-Christian, part-Gnostic work has any direct connection with Spenser's Acidale, it does suggest one way in which theological grace and human gracefulness may be expressed through the dance. The range of associations evoked by the Dance of the

---

[44] *Mystagogus Poeticus or the Muses Interpreter* (1648), p. 141.
[45] Max Pulver, 'Jesus' Round Dance and Crucifixion According to the Acts of St. John', in *The Mysteries: Papers from the Eranos Yearbooks* (New York, 1955), pp. 169–93.

Graces seems almost limitless. Spenser draws into his poetry of reconciliation neo-Platonism and Christianity, folklore and literature, political order and natural harmony. The result is a fleeting glimpse of an eternal and perfect world—and in the paradox which my observation contains lies the essence of Spenser's argument and of his success.

IX

Courtesy Redefined

1. Courtesy and the vision of order in the dance

In an earlier chapter we noticed how sixteenth-century courtesy books, though used by Spenser, are inadequate to explain the complex presentation of courtesy which the poet gives us in the sixth book. Particularly when set next to the remarkable pastoral episode late in the book, the precepts of the literature of courtesy provide little more than a beginning point for Spenser's exposition. There is, however, another definition of courtesy which we have so far not considered and which is of great importance to Spenser's theme.

This definition is associated particularly with the traditions of chivalry and courtly love. Lewis cites a typical observation from Andreas Capellanus's *De Arte Honeste Amandi*: 'It is agreed among all men that there is no good thing in the world, and no courtesy, which is not derived from love as from its fountain.'[1] Love, of course, ennobles the mind and leads to virtuous deeds: these virtuous deeds, or the virtue which lies behind them, constitute 'courtesy'. *Cortesia*, then, is the projection of love into human society—the social effects of a lover's actions. The word turns up in the following centuries with bewildering frequency and in any number of contexts. It seems to suggest not only the virtuous conduct of the lover but also the proper relationship of man and his fellows, the understanding which binds courtly society together. D. S. Brewer, in his important study of courtesy and the Gawain-poet,[2] finds that courtesy covers man's relationship to God as well as his peers, and to his inferiors and superiors as well as his equals. He quotes from *Patience*, commenting, '*Cortaysye* is a word describing a relationship between persons,

---

[1] *The Allegory of Love* (Oxford, 1936), p. 34. See Lewis's chapter on courtly love, pp. 1–43. Cf. R. F. Hill, 'Colin Clout's Courtesy', *MLR*, 57 (1962), 492–503.

[2] In John Lawlor, ed. *Patterns of Love and Courtesy* (London, 1966), pp. 54–85.

here God and mankind. The relationship is not between equals; it is from high to low. Yet it is marked by warmth which may be greater than the merit of him who receives it, even though it must be earned. . . . As applied to God in these few lines it is very much like Grace' (p. 57).[3] Courtesy embraces prudence and self-control, and it is manifested above all in gentle speech, which should flow from inner virtue. Of course, all these meanings will not be present in any given usage of the term, but the medieval tradition does supply ample precedent for the broad virtue which we find described, or depicted, in Book VI. Above all, the association of courtesy with man's relationship to God should not be forgotten. It was a commonplace of medieval thought. The poet of *Pearl* refers to Our Lady as 'Quene of cortasye' (456–7), and Chaucer's Parson speaks of 'the curteis Lord Jhesu Crist' (245).[4]

Much of this breadth in the meaning of the word disappears in common sixteenth-century usage. Guazzo's moral earnestness lacks a spiritual dimension, and for Della Casa even the moral aspects of the virtue seem relatively unimportant. But Spenser's chivalric metaphor affords him a unique opportunity to rescue from medieval literature aspects of the virtue neglected by its sixteenth-century bourgeois proponents, and, as it were, to recreate the medieval conception of social harmony for his Elizabethan readers. This chapter will attempt to show how Spenser redefines his titular virtue in these terms.

Stefano Guazzo's emphasis on honesty and moral awareness is rare among courtesy books, Castiglione's emphasis on show widespread. By choosing a pastoral setting for his climactic statement of the meaning of courtesy, Spenser does make clear where his preferences lie. Courtesy, he claims, is rooted firmly in nature— the flower of courtesy bowers on a lowly stalk. The setting among simple shepherds suggests that the ground of courtesy is not a superficial showiness, a set of tricks to impress the world, but a moral principle with its origin in nature itself. At the same time, the setting implies that the court lacks this moral grounding.

This double direction—the praise of nature and the criticism of art—is inherent in the very character of the pastoral mode. Since

---

[3] Cf. Rosemond Tuve's description of Christine de Pisan's *Épitre d'Othéa* as a 'double courtesy-book', concerning the earthly fight against evil and the pilgrimage towards heaven: *Allegorical Imagery* (Princeton, N.J., 1966), pp. 44–5.

[4] See P. C. Bayley, 'Order, Grace and Courtesy in Spenser's World', in Lawlor, *Patterns of Love and Courtesy*, pp. 178–202.

pastoral repudiates the court and its standards, it can be used as a base from which to attack the courtly world. Spenser himself uses it this way in *Colin Clouts Come Home Again*. On the other hand, pastoral also involves a return to the standards of what Huizinga, in a perceptive discussion,[5] calls natural love. The glorification of such standards may lead the poet not into satire but into a praise of perfection. If he goes further and attempts to show how this perfection may be brought back to revitalize the courtly world, he is at the opposite pole from satire, which depends above all on contrast and dichotomy. Thus romance replaces irony.

It is this second technique that is used in the climactic episode in Canto x, though Canto ix, with Meliboe's speech criticizing the court, makes effective use of the satiric variety of pastoral. The very contrast between Meliboe's speech and the Dance of the Graces strengthens the transcendent qualities of this mysterious dance, in which the critic's usual tools of analysis are strangely inadequate. In fact the critic finds himself in a methodological quandary. He may base his analysis on the literal meaning of Colin Clout's explanation. He may emulate this explanation by examining the iconography of the scene presented to him. He may look for literary antecedent—the symbolism of the dance, the fairy ring, the Golden Age, and so on. He may identify literary archetypes in the episode; they abound. All these lines of approach have partial validity, but even a combination of all of them leaves a great deal unsaid.

We have already observed that as the dance is presented to us it grows increasingly formalized, leading us gently from an immediate complete yet confused impression towards an appreciation of the perfect arrangement of all its details. Spenser's contemporaries, quick to perceive that all dancing has this quality, suggested that the dance is an admirable way of inculcating a sense of order and decorum. In fact, dancing holds a surprisingly high place in the esteem of authors of courtesy books. Castiglione stresses its value in the education of a courtier, and Sir Thomas Elyot, in a discussion made famous by his twentieth-century namesake, extols its virtues as a means of teaching by delight:[6]

---

[5] Johan Huizinga, *The Waning of the Middle Ages* (New York, 1949), chapter on 'The Idyllic Vision of Life'.

[6] On the significance of the passage, see J. M. Major, 'The Moralization of the Dance in Elyot's *Governour*', *SRen*, 5 (1958), 27–36. See also Tillyard's chapter 'The

And because that the study of virtue is tedious for the more part to them that do flourish in young years, I have devised how in the form of dancing, now late used in this realm among gentlemen, the whole description of this virtue prudence may be found out and well perceived, as well as by the dancers as by them which standing by will be diligent beholders and markers, having first mine instruction surely graven in the table of their remembrance. Wherefore all they that have their courage stirred toward very honour or perfect nobility, let them approach to this pastime, and either themselves prepare them to dance, or else at the leastway behold with watching eyes other that can dance truly, keeping just measure and time. But to the understanding of this instruction, they must mark well the sundry motions and measures which in true form of dancing is to be specially observed.[7]

Aquinas linked prudence with reason, and made it a prerequisite for the attainment of wisdom.[8] Clearly we can discern in the dance a kind of key to proper education; and behind proper education Elyot sees proper government, and peace and prosperity for the common weal.[9]

While so high an opinion of the merits of dancing was by no means universal, it is a not uncommon theme among Tudor thinkers of a humanist turn of mind. Both dancing and music are defended against occasional Puritan attacks in rather similar terms. Elyot is only one of the earlier writers to suggest that they mirror the perfect harmony of the state, in which the various hierarchies move as circles round a central point—the prince

---

Cosmic Dance' in *The Elizabethan World Picture* (London, 1943). T. S. Eliot quotes from Elyot in 'East Coker'.

[7] *The Book Named The Governor*, ed. S. E. Lehmberg (London, 1962), I. 22.

[8] Robert Hoopes, *Right Reason in the English Renaissance* (Cambridge, Mass., 1962) pp. 51–2.

[9] Elyot's theory of education provides a perfect complement to Spenser's notion of the seed of virtue. He writes early in the *Governor* (1.4): 'To the intent that I will declare how such personages may be prepared, I will use the policy of a wise and cunning gardener: who purposing to have in his garden a fine and precious herb that should be to him and all other repairing thereto excellently commodious or pleasant, he will first search throughout his garden where he can find the most mellow and fertile earth, and therein will he put the seed of the herb to grow and be nourished, and in most diligent wise attend that no weed be suffered to grow or approach nigh unto it. . . . Semblable order will I ensue in the forming the gentle wits of noblemen's children, who, from the wombs of their mother, shall be made propise [proper, fit] or apt to the governance of a public weal.' Not only are we reminded of one of the principal ideas set forth in the Garden of Adonis, but Elyot's notion of the seed of nobility requiring special attention from the tutor reads like a gloss on Book VI.

himself. *The Praise of Musicke*, published in 1586 and attributed
to John Case, gives perhaps the most extensive defence of the
study and practice of music, stressing its value as a calmer of
troubled nerves, a teacher of discipline, a conveyer of happiness
and, above all, a means to move men's hearts to God.[10] Richard
Mulcaster, Spenser's headmaster, emphasizes the value of musical
training in developing young joints and voices. In a dedicatory
poem to *Cantiones Sacrae*, by Tallis and Byrd (1575), he also
points out that the Queen herself is an accomplished musician—
a theme constantly reiterated by her subjects in prose and verse.[11]
Thomas Churchyard, a poet more typical than elegant, alludes
gently to this fact in a passage which delineates another aspect of
the metaphor of musical order, even as it hints at heavenly grace
and mysterious triads:

> An Empresse heere, three kingdoms showes us plaine
> On which three realms, our Queen may rightly raine.
> O treble Queen, the sweete and highest part
> That we like best, and shrillest voice doth sound
> The onely meane, to shew deepe musicks art
> Where all the skill; of well set song is found.
> Grant silly man, a grace that meanes to sing
> Of heavnly love, and of none other thing.[12]

Elizabeth was not only a musician; she was a skilled dancer too.
Sir John Davies, in *Orchestra*, surely the most delicately graceful
of all Elizabethan works in praise of order, seems to posit his
argument on this fact. The poem, published in 1596, assembles
the commonplaces found in Elyot and his successors, adds a
series of glancing allusions to contemporary science, and,
throwing over all a gentle veil of irony, gives rise to speculation
whether Spenser borrowed from Davies, Davies from Spenser, or
both from Case.

The dance, therefore, means more than merely harmony in the

---

[10] On Case, see Morrison Comegys Boyd, *Elizabethan Music and Musical Criticism*,
rev. edn. (Philadelphia, Pa., 1962), pp. 28–33, 292–300.

[11] The text of Mulcaster's poem is in Boyd, *Elizabethan Music*, pp. 286–9. See also
his *Elementarie* (1582), ed. E. T. Campagnac (Oxford, 1925), and *Positions* (1581),
ed. Robert H. Quick (London, 1888).

[12] *A Musicall Consort of Heavenly Harmonie . . . called Churchyards Charitie* (1595),
A*1r. On triads, see below, p. 258. For examples of rather similar musical imagery
at this time, see John Hollander, *The Untuning of the Sky* (Princeton, N.J., 1961),
pp. 124ff.

abstract. It shows Calidore the function of the perfect state, the heavens wheeling round the earth, the courtiers moving in due order around their sovereign. But there is still a dimension of the dance which escapes such rational explanation. Earlier, I proposed that hints of fairy dances imply a touch of the supernatural. But even the setting of the dance—a mysterious hilltop in a pastoral world—suggests that we are somehow beyond nature.[13] Below is the movement of the seasons with their ever-changing procession of months; above us is the realm of the divine. Here on Acidale we find unchanging nature in its first paradisal form, for this is where earth and heaven touch. It is a frequent poetic symbol, this scene, and it is common in myth and in the Bible. Northrop Frye calls it the point of epiphany—'the point at which the undisplaced apocalyptic world and the cyclical world of nature come into alignment'.

Its most common settings are the mountain-top, the island, the tower, the lighthouse, and the ladder or staircase. . . . In the Bible we have Jacob's ladder, which in *Paradise Lost* is associated with Milton's cosmological diagram of a spherical cosmos hanging from heaven with a hole in the top. There are several mountain-top epiphanies in the Bible, the Transfiguration being the most notable. . . . Purgatory in Dante is an enormous mountain with a path ascending spirally around it, on top of which, as the pilgrim gradually recovers his lost innocence and casts off his original sin, is the garden of Eden. . . . The sense of being between an apocalyptic world above and a cyclical world below is present too, as from the garden of Eden all seeds of vegetable life fall back into the world, while human life passes on.[14]

While we should not draw over-ambitious conclusions from a general poetic symbol isolated for the benefit of critics in the twentieth century, we must recognize that there is more to Calidore's vision than a lesson in how to behave when one is in company or even a lesson in the proper orderliness of human

[13] Note the connection between music and grace mentioned in my previous chapter, and also the important connection, according to many writers, between music and ecstasy—a link made the more credible by the assumption that music mirrors the harmony of the universe. In the seventeenth century the question of the divine power of music became a central issue in the controversy over the use of music in churches. See Gretchen Ludke Finney, *Musical Backgrounds for English Literature 1580-1650* (New Brunswick, N.J., n.d. [1962]), chapter on 'Music and Ecstasy: a Religious Controversy'.

[14] *Anatomy of Criticism* (Princeton, N.J., 1957), 203-4. Cf. Arnold Williams, *Flower on a Lowly Stalk* (Michigan State University, 1967), p. 57.

affairs. The joy, the beauty, the music, the graceful movement of
the dancers suggest a glimpse of cosmic harmony which responds
to that yearning for perfection, for the release from selfhood,
whose traces can be found in all human pursuits since the world
began. Mircea Eliade describes it as the Symbolism of the Centre
—the point from which all creation emanates, the first seed, or
divine spark, or 'navel of the earth'.[15] In the broadest sense, every
representation of the Garden of Eden or the Golden World makes
use of the Symbolism of the Centre, but in the case of Spenser's
vision the setting on a hilltop, and above all the dance (which is
itself a symbol of all creation's connection with a single point),
help reinforce the archetype. Spenser's vision is a variant of the
myth of human origin, here adapted to a particular purpose and a
particular situation, but almost miraculously retaining its wider
implications—cosmic and divine.

There are two earlier episodes in the *Faerie Queene* which can be
compared to Calidore's vision of the Graces. The Garden of
Adonis in Book III represents the origin of matter, the beginning-
point for the natural world, the place of generation. It is in the
most obvious sense the navel of the earth. An investigation of
the episode would show very clearly how it is an example of
Spenser's brilliant mythmaking, a focal point in his argument
whose influence stretches throughout the three succeeding books.
But in many respects more interesting at the present stage of our
study is the Red Cross Knight's Pisgah vision in Book I, first
because it comes at the same point in the narrative, Canto x,
second because it involves the book's titular hero, third because

[15] Mircea Eliade, *Cosmos and History: the Myth of the Eternal Return* (New York,
1954), pp. 12–17. Eliade connects the symbol with the Sacred Mountain, where
heaven and earth meet, situated at the centre of the world. 'The summit of the cosmic mountain is not only the highest point of the earth; it is also the earth's navel,
the point at which the Creation began. . . . Paradise was the navel of the Earth and,
according to a Syrian tradition, was established on a mountain higher than all others.
According to the Syrian *Book of the Cave of Treasures*, Adam was created at the center
of the earth, at the same spot where the Cross of Christ was later to be set up. The
same traditions have been preserved by Judaism. The Jewish apocalypse and a
midrash state that Adam was formed in Jerusalem. Adam being buried at the very
spot where he was created, i.e., at the center of the world, on Golgotha, the blood
of the Saviour . . . will redeem him too.' There is a fuller discussion of the symbolism
of the centre in an earlier study by Eliade, *Images et Symboles* (Paris, 1952). See also
Joseph Campbell, *The Hero with a Thousand Faces* (New York, 1949), esp. pp. 40–6.
Angus Fletcher, *Allegory: the Theory of a Symbolic Mode* (Ithaca, N.Y., 1964) alludes
to the reverse of the optimistic, heavenly symbolism of the centre: the cave or prison
which is a symbol of hell (pp. 210–19). See p. 312, below.

these two episodes are the only two full-scale visions to occur in the *Faerie Queene*.[16]

Redcross, coming to the House of Holiness, is shriven and instructed in good works and prayer. Finally, he is conducted to 'an hill, that was both steepe and hy',

> On top whereof a sacred chappell was,
> And eke a litle Hermitage thereby,
> Wherein an aged holy man did lye,
> That day and night said his devotion,
> Ne other worldly busines did apply;
> His name was heavenly *Contemplation*;
> Of God and goodnesse was his meditation.
>
> Great grace that old man to him given had;
> For God he often saw from heavens hight.
>
> (I. x. 46–7)

It is here that Redcross sees a vision of the New Jerusalem, from atop a hill likened to other 'points of epiphany' in the Old Testament and in the New, and likened also to the Hill of the Muses:

> Or like that sacred hill, whose head full hie,
> Adornd with fruitfull Olives all arownd,
> Is, as it were for endlesse memory
> Of that deare Lord, who oft thereon was fownd,
> For ever with a flowring girlond crownd:
> Or like that pleasaunt Mount, that is for ay
> Through famous Poets verse each where renownd,
> On which the thrise three learned Ladies play
> Their heavenly notes, and make full many a lovely lay.
>
> (I. x. 54)

The stanza betrays a poetic habit of mind typical of Spenser. The desire to create the all-inclusive symbol leads him to move freely between classical and Christian, and to pick old ideas and use them anew, in new situations which yet remind us of their predecessors. Thus Mount Acidale seems another Mount of Olives 'For ever with a flowring girlond crownd', another mount

---

[16] The only possible exceptions are Britomart's vision of Artegall and their progeny, in Book III, and the dream in Isis Church in Book V, both of which (especially the former) are of a quite different character. Although the 'Mutabilitie Cantos' do not involve a vision, they do present a point of epiphany—in fact the greatest representation of the symbol in the whole of the *Faerie Queene*. See Frye, *Anatomy*, p. 204.

of Venus like the Garden of Adonis, and a haunt of the Graces similar to the 'pleasaunt mount' of the Muses.

Redcross, gazing on the Holy City now revealed to his sight, sees the 'blessed angels to and fro descend' and the pattern of the Faerie city Cleopolis, which in turn is the most perfect city on earth. He hears that he will be made a saint, 'Saint George of mery England'—the man who, more than all others, was supposed to have united the active chivalric life with true holiness. It is little wonder that Redcross turns to his mentor in anguish:

> 'O let me not (quoth he) then turne againe
> Backe to the world, whose joyes so fruitlesse are;
> But let me here for aye in peace remaine,
> Or streight way on that last long voyage fare,
> That nothing may my present hope empare.' (1. x. 63)

Of course, it is not to be. Redcross must descend to the plain below, to fight the dragon and liberate Una's parents, Mankind, from the monster's ravages. Calidore, too, must descend. He is also an active chivalric hero, for whom a life of contemplation, like that of the Hermit perhaps, will come only after long travail and many hardships. He, too, is tempted to abandon his quest and remain forever in an ideal existence above the petty cares of the world: 'Great grace that old man to him given had; / For God he often saw from heavens hight.'[17]

The topography of Redcross's vision, the terminology, the circumstances, the shape of the narrative in which it occurs—all these point to a direct parallel between Book I and Book VI. Seen in this light, the term 'grace' in Book VI suddenly takes on theological implications, the vision itself becomes mystical.

Two modern scholars throw light on the nature of the vision. In his book *Poetry as a Means of Grace*,[18] Charles Grosvenor Osgood gives a scholarly and absorbing introduction to Spenser originally intended for students of theology. Considering his audience, he naturally turns his attention to the *Fowre Hymnes*, pointing out how, from the 'romantic, even sensual' first two hymns, Spenser moves to the hymns 'Of Heavenly Love' and 'Of Heavenly Beauty', which are deeply imbued with Christian mysticism tempered by Platonism. He identifies these two hymns with two routes of ascent to the Beatific Vision of God:

---

[17] 1.x.47. Cf. vi.x.30.   [18] Princeton, N.J., 1941.

The Theocentric route of ascent proceeds by contemplation of the works of God, ascending from the study of Nature from lower to higher forms, at length to the stars in their spheres and orders, to the empyrean, the nine orders of angels, the Attributes of God, and thus to the Divine Presence. At once you will recognize Dante's course of ascent. The Christocentric route of ascent proceeds by a contemplation of our Lord . . . until at last we see Him face to face even while in the body.[19]

F. C. Happold's volume on mysticism distinguishes two types of mystical experience, which the author calls the mysticism of love and union and the mysticism of knowledge and understanding.[20] The former involves complete obliteration of selfhood in union with God, while the latter constitutes knowledge of God based on a direct experience of him and including a new understanding of the ultimate reality of things through revelation rather than speculative reason.

The experience which Calidore undergoes on Mount Acidale is neither a theocentric vision pure and simple, nor a mystical vision of 'knowledge and understanding', but it involves elements of both of these things.[21] Calidore is vouchsafed a glimpse of the harmony of the created universe and an awareness of the spirit which moves it, the grace of God. In the coming together of the heavens and the created world, of art and nature, there come together also nature and grace, the one operating upon the other to order and control and create.[22]

[19] *Poetry as a Means of Grace*, p. 74. Osgood is following Joseph Burns Collins, *Christian Mysticism in the Elizabethan Age* (Baltimore, Md., 1940). Collins devotes detailed attention both to the House of Holiness and to the *Fowre Hymnes*. His analysis, particularly of the latter, is extremely illuminating. On the Theocentric and Christocentric routes of contemplation, see his chapter 'The Method of Christian Mysticism', pp. 36–70. Cf. Adolf Katzenellenbogen's chapter 'Man's Arduous Ascent to God' in *Allegories of the Virtues and Vices in Mediaeval Art* (London, 1939), pp. 22–6.

[20] *Mysticism: a Study and an Anthology* (Harmondsworth, Middx., 1963), pp. 40–2.

[21] Describing the nature of mystical experiences, Happold gives data showing striking similarity with Calidore's vision. Of such experiences in general he writes: 'While mystical states are akin to states of feeling, they are also states of knowledge. They have a *noetic* quality. They result in insight into depths of truth unplumbed by the discursive intellect, insights which carry with them a tremendous sense of authority. Things take on a new pattern and a new, often unsuspected, significance. Even though he may not be able to say, in the language of the intellect, what he knows, one who has undergone mystical experience is convinced with absolute certainty that he does know' (p. 45).

[22] Cf. the relationship of microcosm and macrocosm: man, who holds all the universe within him, united in a mystical union with the macrocosm, both of these

2. The iconography of the Graces: 'Discordia Concors'

Spenser's, or Colin Clout's, description of the Graces is contained in three stanzas in the middle of Canto x:

> They are the daughters of sky-ruling Jove,
> By him begot of faire *Eurynome*,
> The Oceans daughter, in this pleasant grove,
> As he this way comming from feastfull glee,
> Of *Thetis* wedding with *Æacidee*,
> In sommers shade him selfe here rested weary.
> The first of them hight mylde *Euphrosyne*,
> Next faire *Aglaia*, last *Thalia* merry:
> Sweete Goddesses all three which me in mirth do cherry.
>
> These three on men all gracious gifts bestow,
> Which decke the body or adorne the mynde,
> To make them lovely or well favoured show,
> As comely carriage, entertainement kynde,
> Sweete semblaunt, friendly offices that bynde,
> And all the complements of curtesie:
> They teach us, how to each degree and kynde
> We should our selves demeane, to low, to hie;
> To friends, to foes, which skill men call Civility.
>
> Therefore they alwaies smoothly seeme to smile,
> That we likewise should mylde and gentle be,
> And also naked are, that without guile
> Or false dissemblaunce all them plaine may see,
> Simple and true from covert malice free:
> And eeke them selves so in their daunce they bore,
> That two of them still froward seem'd to bee,
> But one still towards shew'd her selfe afore;
> That good should from us goe, then come in greater store.

(VI. X. 22–4)

The passage is of great importance, because a great deal of our understanding of the thematic content of Book VI and of the

---

universes represented in the circling movement of the dance. C. G. Jung, in 'The Interpretation of Nature and the Psyche' (*Psyche and Symbol*, ed. Violet S. de Laszlo (Garden City, N.Y., 1958), pp. 251–2), quotes Pico (*Opera Omnia*, pp. 40–1): 'Firstly there is the unity in things whereby each thing is at one with itself. Secondly, there is the unity whereby one creature is united with the others and all parts of the world constitute one world. The third and most important [unity] is that whereby the whole universe is one with its Creator as an army with its commander.'

character of Grace as Spenser describes it depends on how we interpret these stanzas. There are three important aids to interpretation, two modern and one contemporary: the researches of Edgar Wind into the iconography and symbolism of the Graces,[23] the work of the late D. T. Starnes on Renaissance dictionaries in relation to Spenser,[24] and E. K.'s note to a passage in the April eclogue of the *Shepheardes Calender*. We can usefully begin with this last. Here is the passage, followed by E. K.'s gloss:

> Lo how finely the graces can it foote
>   to the Instrument:
> They dauncen deffly, and singen soote,
>   in their meriment.
> Wants not a fourth grace, to make the daunce even?
> Let that rowme to my Lady be yeven:
>   She shalbe a grace
>   To fyll the fourth place,
> And reigne with the rest in heaven.

The Graces) be three sisters, the daughters of Jupiter, (whose names are Aglaia, Thalia, Euphrosyne, and Homer onely addeth a fourth. s. Pasithea) otherwise called Charites, that is thanks. whom the Poetes feyned to be the Goddesses of al bountie and comelines, which therefore (as sayth Theodontius) they make three, to wete, that men first ought to be gracious and bountiful to other freely, then to receive benefits at other mens hands curteously, and thirdly to requite them thankfully: which are three sundry Actions in liberalitye. And Boccace saith, that they be painted naked, (as they were indeede on the tombe of C. Julius Cæsar) the one having her backe toward us, and her face fromwarde, as proceeding from us: the other two toward us, noting double thanke to be due to us for the benefit, we have done.

While the antecedents of E. K.'s note are extremely complex, Starnes feels justified in identifying it with one principal source, which it echoes not only in substance but also verbally. This is Thomas Cooper's *Thesaurus Linguae Romanae et Britannicae*, first published in 1565.[25] Cooper, in turn, based his explanation on

---

[23] *Pagan Mysteries in the Renaissance*, 2nd edn. (Harmondsworth, Middx., 1967).

[24] DeWitt T. Starnes, 'Spenser and the Graces', *PQ*, 21 (1942), 268–82; *Classical Myth and Legend in Renaissance Dictionaries* (Chapel Hill, N.C., 1955) [with E. W. Talbert].

[25] Starnes, 'Spenser and the Graces'. See also Starnes's 'E. K.'s Classical Allusions Reconsidered', *SP*, 39 (1942), 143–59. Much of this material was later incorporated into *Classical Myth and Legend*.

Charles Stephanus, whose *Dictionarium Historicum, Geographicum, Poeticum* was published four years earlier. (This feature of Renaissance dictionaries, that they borrowed so extensively from one another, makes the pinpointing of particular sources almost impossible.)

While there are several parallels between the April eclogue and Book VI, the two passages describing the Graces are more notable for their differences than their similarities.[26] There are two principal differences. The first concerns the movements among the Graces. E. K. describes two such movements, one circular and one involving a movement back and forth. The circular movement, which derived ultimately from Chrysippus, Seneca explains as indicating the triple rhythm of generosity: giving, accepting, and returning.[27] Though it is better to give than to receive, yet the circle continues endlessly and must never be interrupted. Servius adds the dual movement, giving and receiving: 'That one of them is pictured from the back while the two others face us, is because for one benefit issuing from us two are supposed to return.'[28] In Book VI, Colin Clout limits his explanation to the Servian meaning, or at least to the movement which we find in Servius, since the line 'That good should from us goe, then come in greater store' is distinctly ambiguous. Not knowing whether 'then' has its modern meaning or the common Elizabethan meaning 'than', we shall have to reserve judgement on the meaning for the moment.

The second principal difference between the passage in the April eclogue and that in Book VI is the positioning of the Graces. E. K. explains that one Grace has her back towards us and two face us, whereas Colin Clout reverses the arrangement, having two Graces turned from us and only one facing us. If we bear in mind that the direction in which the Graces are facing is crucial to the Servian interpretation, the reverse order in Book VI may

[26] Starnes lists the following similarities: in each scene there is a company of ladies in a ring; in both, the Graces dance and sing; in both a maiden admired by the piper forms the centre; in both she is crowned and flowers are brought to her; in both she is said to be worthy of being a fourth Grace; finally, there are a number of verbal parallels.

[27] Wind, *Pagan Mysteries*, p. 28, cites Seneca, *De beneficiis*, 1.3.

[28] Servius, *In Vergilii Aeneidem*, 1.720. Among writers mentioned by Wind are Fulgentius, Mythographus 2 and Mythographus 3, Boccaccio, Niccolò Perotti and Ripa. See also the discussion of Spenser's Graces in Starnes and Talbert, *Classical Myth and Legend*, pp. 50–5, 87–96.

have a bearing on our interpretation of Colin Clout's meaning, and hence the prickly word 'then'.

There is, however, one difficulty which we need to dispose of before we proceed further, and that concerns the word 'froward', on which Colin Clout's description turns. In the first two editions of Book vi, in 1596 and 1609, this word is printed as 'forward'. Because of the word 'towards' in the following line, most later editors emend 'forward' to read 'froward'. Starnes concludes that Spenser is echoing E.K. and Cooper, both of whom use 'fromwarde' in precisely this context. We should be wise to go along with Starnes—though Wind does not. He reads 'then' in its modern sense, concluding that good is therefore being returned twofold. But his assertion that the group is exactly as it is in the April eclogue cannot go unchallenged. Since he retains the reading 'forward', he must perforce be reading 'towards' to mean 'backwards'—an interpretation which makes no sense at all. He does not explain how he interprets 'afore'.[29] Taking Wind's reading just as it stands, it is hard to avoid a mental picture of a line of chorus girls.

Wind's interpretation is obviously unsatisfactory. The group in Book vi is not a further example of the traditional grouping, but a remarkable departure—one which would have struck home to Spenser's readers particularly forcefully if they remembered the April eclogue with its pattern of giving and receiving. If 'towards' and 'afore' mean what they say, then one Grace is quite evidently facing the onlooker. This in turn leads us (and evidently led Spenser's editors) to conclude that the other two are facing in the other direction—so, froward. As Starnes and Talbert explain, this arrangement is very unusual since it reverses the normal order of the figures. The question now arises as to where the giving and receiving movement originates. If it originates with the single figure, it is untraditional because the first movement is *towards* the viewer, not away from him. If it follows the traditional *direction*, it is untraditional because it originates with

---

[29] He may be thinking of Cooper and presuming that Spenser did not explain himself sufficiently clearly. Cooper writes: 'Wherefore they paint the Graces in this manner, that the ones back should be *towarde* us, and hir face *fromwarde*, as proceeding from us, the other twoo *towarde* us: noting double thanke to bee due for the benefite we have done.' (Quoted by Starnes, 'Spenser and the Graces'.) Cooper's confusing terms, reproduced by E.K., may possibly have caused Spenser to muddle things still further.

two figures instead of one. Starnes and Talbert produce one answer. Cartari, they tell us, interprets the Graces as an object lesson in self-sacrifice: good should from us go *than* come in greater store:

> Though Cartari follows the conventional pattern in his picture of one Grace with her back turned and therefore going away, and two coming towards, he has the unconventional, though not illogical, interpretation for his picture that we should repay twofold any good or benefit received, and that doing a good with expectation of compensation is a form of usury.[30]

The claim of Starnes and Talbert, that Cartari is Spenser's only precedent for this interpretation, is not, however, entirely true.[31] There is another more likely source nearer at hand. Although Starnes considers Cooper's *Thesaurus* a probable source for the Book VI passage, along with Cartari, it seems likely that Spenser turned not to Cooper but to the well-known dictionary of Richard Huloet, in its revision of 1572 by John Higgins.[32] The description of the Graces which he found there is in many respects different from the version which he finally assembled, but there are enough similarities to suggest a likely source. Huloet and Higgins tell us that the Graces are 'fayned three, Aglaia, Thalia, Euphrosine, The daughters (as Hesiodus writeth) either of Jupiter and Eurymone [sic], or els of Bacchus and Venus . . .'

> whome antiquitie did painte naked, because friendship and good wyll among frendes ought to be naked, simple and voyde of covine & deceit: They were three in numbre, for that the one gyveth th'other receiveth, and the thyrde requiteth: they semed yonge, because the memory of a benefite, ought never to cease or waxe olde: chereful and smyling, for that a benefite should be bestowed cherefully: Two of them looked towarde the beholders, and the thirde turned her backe,

---

[30] *Classical Myth and Legend*, p. 93.

[31] Cartari's work (*Imagines Deorum*) also yields a list of the Graces in the same order as Spenser lists them. However, this is not as unusual as Starnes and Talbert claim. Caelius Rhodiginus (1516), for example, does the same: 'Nomina haec facit, Euphrosynen, Aglaiam, Thaliam' (nn3r). The 1564 French translation of Alciati's emblems lists 'Ioye Euphrosyne, Aglaie beauté vive / Et Pitho a parole persuasive' (N3r). As Starnes points out, Spenser's order may be forced on him by the metre. (Pitho, or Suada, was sometimes identified as one of the Graces. She was regarded, of course, as goddess of persuasion.)

[32] Starnes considers both passages, in the April Eclogue and in Book VI, derived from Cooper. This seems to me unlikely.

whereby is signified that a benefit ought to be requited, with greater good wyll: They were knitte together, shewing thereby the knott of frendship, should be indissoluble.[33]

The attentive reader will notice several points of similarity with Colin Clout's speech, especially stanza 24, whose first two and a half lines are close to the meaning of Huloet, and whose fifth line ('Simple and true from covert malice free') seems a direct verbal echo of Higgins's English ('Simple and voyde of covine & deceit'). More important, however, is the fact that, like Cartari, Higgins emphasizes not a double reward but a sacrifice: we should give in greater measure than we receive.[34]

If this reading seems to square well with the notion that 'good should from us go, *than* come, in greater store', we should note, however, that there are several occasions in Book VI where the opposite interpretation would seem to hold good. By deferring to Coridon, Calidore demonstrates his courtesy and wins the prize of Pastorella's love, which he had wanted all along even if he seemed to give his rival a sporting chance.[35] Is this self-sacrifice or good policy? In the Brigands' cave, Pastorella's pleasantness to the Captain, designed to placate him and keep him at bay, is justified with the words, 'A little well is lent, that gaineth more withall.' Does this contradict Calidore's vision or reinforce it? If we accept wholeheartedly the suggestion that Spenser's Graces are modelled on Huloet–Higgins,[36] these contradictions will doubtless prove bothersome. We shall return to this point shortly.

Also bothersome is the positioning of Spenser's Graces, which Starnes and Talbert consider to be without precedent.

[33] *Huloets Dictionarie, Newely Corrected, Amended, Set in Order and Enlarged . . .* (*STC*. 13941). The first edition, the *Abcedarium Anglico Latinum*, appeared in 1552.

[34] There is a passage in Perottus (Niccolò Perotti), *Cornucopiae Sive Linguae Latinae Commentarii* (Basle, 1521), which is at least ambiguous on this point and is perhaps a precursor of Higgins and Cartari. Perottus describes both Senecan and Servian movements, saying of the latter: 'Alii ideo dicunt treis gratias esse, quia acceptum beneficium cum foenore reddi debet' (col. 345). What we do not know, of course, is who is receiving, who giving.

[35] I am not convinced by the argument that such a reading 'cheapens the actions of Calidore' and is 'quite wrong'. See R. F. Hill, 'Colin Clout's Courtesy', *MLR*, 57 (1962), 492–503, esp. 497. Hill is in accord with Hallett Smith, *Elizabethan Poetry* (Cambridge, Mass., 1952), p. 12.

[36] This is, however, traditionally the more accepted interpretation. See the note in Todd's edition, *The Works of Edmund Spenser* (London, 1805), 7: 103.

There is, however, one likely precedent in Pico della Mirandola. In his commentary on Benivieni we read:

Una delle gratie e dipinta col volto verso noi, come precedente & non ritornante. Laltre due, perche apartengono al lo intelletto & alla volonta, la operatione dellequali e reflessiva, pero sono dipinte col volto in la, come di chi ritorna, imperoche la cose sono dette venire ad noi dalli Dii, & da noi alli Dii ritornare.[37]

Pico is describing not a Servian exchange of gifts but the operations of Beauty, an altogether less mundane way of reading the Graces, which was of considerable importance among the neo-Platonists.[38] It suggests, in fact, an association of the Graces with philosophical concepts and it perhaps points the way to a theological reading of the figures. I have mentioned in passing one such reading—that of Alexander Ross.[39] We should take another look at it:

Faith, Hope and Charity are the three Divine Graces . . . but their posture is somewhat different from the other Graces: For of the other, two look on us, the third hath her back to us. But in these three Divine Sisters, one only looketh to us, to wit Charity; the other two, Faith and Hope, fix their eyes from us upon God. Faith is Aglaia, the glory and honour of a Christian: Hope is Euphrosyne, that which makes him joyful, we rejoyce in Hope: And Charity that is Thalia, which would make our Christian state flourish and abound with all good things, if we would admit of her company amongst us.[40]

---

[37] *Opere di Girolamo Benivieni firentino* (Venetia, 1522), D5v. (One of the Graces is painted with her face towards us, as coming forward and not returning. The other two, because they belong to the intellect and the will, the operations of which are reflexive, are therefore painted with their faces away from us, as if returning; thus things come to us from the Gods and from us to the Gods they return.)

[38] Wind (*Mysteries*, p. 67) maintains that Pico has in mind the conventional configuration and that the orientation of the Graces is defined in this case 'by the posture of their heads rather than their bodies'. Such a reading seems to be unnecessarily grotesque, but in any case it does not really affect my argument, since it seems highly probable that if I and others misread this passage so would Spenser's contemporaries. (Kathleen Williams, *Spenser's 'Faerie Queene': the World of Glass* (London, 1966), p. 213, quotes from *A Platonick Discourse upon Love*, trans. Thomas Stanley, ed. Edmund G. Gardner (Boston, Mass., 1914), p. 35. Stanley's translation (1651) is an abridgement of the *Commento*. Miss Williams comes to the same conclusion as I do.)

[39] See p. 236, above.

[40] Alexander Ross, *Mystagogus Poeticus or the Muses Interpreter* (1648), p. 143. I do not rule out the possibility that Ross's interpretation is derived from a reading of Spenser's Book VI, which would obviously weaken my argument.

The reader will notice immediately that the three Graces are
arranged just as they are in Book VI, and that they imply a spirit
of Christian self-sacrifice, of faith and hope even in excess of the
love received from God. According to this interpretation, then,
the movement begins with the two figures facing away from us:
'Good should from us go, *than* come in greater store.'[41]

Ross's work is, of course a good deal later than the *Faerie
Queene*, but there are strong reasons for associating theological
grace with the figures we find in Spenser—not, of course, to the
exclusion of other readings, but in concert with them. Our
discussion of music and of the dance drew us towards associations
of heavenly grace, and of course the nature of courtesy, implying,
as it does, a selfless devotion to the needs of the community and a
promotion of social harmony,[42] is in accord with the nature of
heavenly grace itself, freely bestowed upon us by the 'curteis
Lord Jhesu Crist'.

If Pico does not go so far as to associate the Graces with God's
grace, there are others who do. The late fifteenth-century com-
mentator on Dante, Christophoro Landino, is a case in point.
The three ladies who descend to assist Dante in the second canto
of the *Inferno* (Mary, Lucy, and Beatrice) are, he says, none other
than three types of grace:

... Perho ci vengono da dio tre gratie. La prima illumina la ragione
... & questa e decta preveniente ... La seconda e grati illuminante ...
La terza e gratia perficiente.[43]

But then he moves directly into a discussion of the Three Graces
'of which poets write'. Anyone with any intelligence, he says,
can see that they are not very different from the grace described
by the theologians. The fact that they are daughters of Jove, he
claims, means simply that all grace proceeds from God alone—
and he quotes Paul and James to prove his point. The etymology

[41] Note, however, that the syntax of the sentence, with 'than come' contained
by the movement of going in greater store, makes it hard to decide just where
the movement actually begins. The emphasis, in fact, is on endless reciprocity.
Cf. Kathleen Williams, *World of Glass*, pp. 213–14.

[42] See also Wind's note 'Pagan Vestiges of the Trinity', *Mysteries*, pp. 241–55.

[43] *Comento ... sopra la comedia di Danthe alighieri poeta fiorentino* (Vinegia, 1484),
c 3*v* (Therefore there come from God three graces. The first enlightens the reason
... and this is called prevenient. ... The second is illuminating grace. ... The third
is perficient). Cf. Charles W. Lemmi, *The Classical Deities in Bacon* (Baltimore, Md.,
1933), pp. 19ff.

of 'Eurymone' gives him a chance to quote the Psalms, and he ends up equating the Graces with 'le tre divine gratie'.[44]

If Landino seems rather far removed from Spenser (it is not impossible that he had read him, but at least unlikely) we can find other examples of the association of the Graces with divine grace, nearer home. Stephen Bateman, for example, builds the whole structure of his work *The New Arival of the three Gracis, into Anglia*[45] round the figures of 'Aglaia, Thalia, and Euphrosine, thankfulnes, plenteousnes and lyberalite', but the material in the book hardly mentions classical mythology (except with disapproval) and it seems to be taken for granted that the three are doubling for divine grace ('By the plentifull gracis proceading from God, the children of Israell wer delyverid').[46]

But these examples do not eliminate the problem just stated, that on occasion the giving of something does yield a greater reward. Here the ambiguity of the word 'then' comes to our rescue. While the forward-froward problem is essentially typographical,[47] the word 'then' is an ambiguity pure and simple— an ambiguity, be it noted, for the ordinary reader of Spenser at the time the *Faerie Queene* was published. But it is an ambiguity inherent in the very character of grace itself, those gifts to mankind received through Christ's death—the free flow of love made possible by the supreme sacrifice of God's only-begotten Son. 'Nor height, nor depth, nor any other creature, shall be able to separate us from the love of God, which is in Christ Jesus our Lord', writes Paul in the Epistle to the Romans, undoubtedly the clearest commentary on the nature of the New Dispensation (8: 39); and again, 'For if by one man's offence death reigned by one; much more they which receive abundance of grace and of the gift of righteousness shall reign in life by one, Jesus Christ' (Rom. 5: 17). Writing of hope, Paul declares, 'For we are saved by

[44] His discussion of the relationship between the three Graces seems also to suggest an arrangement similar to Pico's, quoted above.

[45] 1580; *STC.* 1584.

[46] Bateman gives extended treatment to the Graces as classical figures in *The Golden Booke of the Leaden Goddes* (1577).

[47] This is be no means the only typographical problem in this episode. The difficulties over 'Plexippus brooke' (vi.ix.36) may, as Upton suggests (*Variorum*, 6: 243), l·e typographical, and not some obscure allusion whose significance has since been forgotten. Note also that the 1611 edition reads, at vi.x.12, 'And in the middest of those same *there* was placed . . .'—a variant which may affect our reading of this stanza.

hope: but hope that is seen is not hope: for what a man seeth, why doth he yet hope for? But if we hope for what we see not, then do we with patience wait for it' (Rom. 8: 24-5). The fleeting vision of the Graces, with its visual and verbal ambiguities, precisely exemplifies the mystery of God's relationship to man as Paul expresses it: it is supreme benefit and supreme obligation.

As I have pointed out, a theological reading of the Graces should in no way limit our comprehension *only* to theology. Just as the law of nations mirrors the law of nature, so the more lowly operations of courtesy mirror the supreme courtesy of God. The book is largely concerned with these lesser courtesies, not with heavenly grace. But Spenser's poetry of reconciliation, here as everywhere, expresses a continuity of endeavour from the lowest of God's creatures to the highest, and a parallel effort in all of man's actions for the good. This theological reading does not render the Legend of Courtesy Christian allegory so much as render the earthly virtue of Courtesy akin, even identical, to its heavenly counterpart. To argue that the basis of the allegory in Book VI is theological (as Maurice Evans seems inclined to do)[48] seems mistaken and at odds with the book's tone, but to argue that there is a link established between the courtesy of the sixth book and God's New Dispensation to mankind seems to me both necessary and inescapable.

Despite the complexities which Spenser's depiction of the Graces has already revealed, we should now note that he chooses to expound only one of the two alternative interpretations of their positioning given by E. K. Colin Clout provides an explanation of the two-directional giving and receiving, passing over the Senecan, circular interpretation. The giving and receiving movement was the more popular way of looking at the Graces among the compilers of dictionaries in the Renaissance, but the circular movement proved particularly attractive to philosophers.[49] Although Spenser does not explicitly mention the circular movement, it is implicit in the circle of the dance itself, and it is likely that we are supposed to see both these alternatives in the iconography.

The attraction of the Graces for the philosophers lay in the fact that they represent a triad: opposites are reconciled through a third, intermediate, figure. Plato told them that communion

[48] See above, p. 226. [49] See Wind, *Mysteries, passim.*

between the gods and lesser beings is achieved through the medium of love. In consequence, Venus gained a position of special importance in the neo-Platonic pantheon. Since the Graces were traditionally the handmaids of Venus, their relationship to her was interpreted as showing ('unfolding') her characteristics or as representing the effects of her action. To the neo-Platonists, the bounty bestowed by the gods upon the lower orders was an 'overflowing' (*emanatio*), whose operations produced a vivification or rapture (*vivificatio, raptio, conversio*) which in turn drew these orders back to the gods (*remeatio*). The idea is somewhat similar to Spenser's conception of the 'infinite shapes of creatures' who go forth from the Gardens of Adonis in an ever-cyclic pattern of 'eterne in mutabilitie'. This cycle of *emanatio, conversio*, and *remeatio*, the process of *natura naturata* set in action by Venus, is frequently expounded by means of the triad of the Graces, symbols of giving, receiving (or conversion), and returning.

The connection with Venus also resulted in the use of the Graces to expound various philosophies of love, a tendency (fully documented by Wind) which need not concern us here, except to indicate to us the many possible ramifications of Spenser's emblem. The triads *Pulchritudo–Amor–Voluptas* and *Castitas–Pulchritudo–Amor* are, in their way, extensions of the personality of Venus, but there is no ready means of ascertaining whether such associations were present in Spenser's mind or may legitimately be read into the poem.[50] Perhaps we should content ourselves with the most generalized of conclusions: as well as showing the actions of giving and receiving basic to the poet's idea of courtesy, Spenser's Graces are another emblem of *discordia concors*, of the cyclical continuity which forms a part of the pattern of eternity.[51] Case summarizes these generalizations in a thoroughly Elizabethan way:

Now if Musicke can find no favour by alleadging these parentes, let us search other mens registers, and see if happily shee be more gracious

[50] Among the many interpretations of the Graces, several are based on a Senecan relationship among the three powers of the soul, Memory, Understanding, and Will (e.g. Landino), and may make use of the etymology of the Graces. The alleged ancestry of the Graces also affects the way mythographers interpret them. There are many parental candidates (see Perottus, Boccaccio, Rhodiginus, etc.).

[51] On the association of order and disorder, Venus and Mars, love and force, see Donald Cheney, *Spenser's Image of Nature* (New Haven, Conn., 1966), pp. 23 5–236.

for the graces sake. Whose handes being fast claspt without severing, their faces amiable without frouning, their youth fresh & green without waining, their garmentes loose without girding, and their chastitie perpetuall without violating expresse in sense & meaning nothing else, but concorde without breach, mirth withoute sadnesse, continuance without end, liberty without constraint, and finally purenesse without taint or corruption. And can a gracelesse fruite come of so gracious a stock?[52]

3. Venus as the Dance's central figure

Venus herself also represents the harmony of the universe, for her Love is responsible for its coherence. But she exists in two quite separate regions. Indeed, Plato goes so far as to speak of two Venuses, the one Heavenly, the other Common.

We all know that Aphrodite is inseparably linked with Love. If there were a single Aphrodite there would be a single Love, but as there are two Aphrodites, it follows that there must be two Loves as well. Now what are the two Aphrodites? One is the elder and is the daughter of Uranus and had no mother; her we call Heavenly Aphrodite. The other is younger, the child of Zeus and Dione, and is called Common Aphrodite.[53]

The difference between the two Venuses, the one coming into existence in an earlier stage in the development of the cosmos than the other, was eagerly expounded by the neo-Platonists, particularly in the seminal works for the neo-Platonic philosophy of love, Ficino's Commentary on Plato's *Symposium* (the *De amore*) and Pico's *Commento sopra Benivieni*. As Panofsky[54] explains, these works were not themselves widely read, but their influence was enormous.[55] Ficino follows the pattern of Plato's exposition. Panofsky summarizes:

Venus Coelestis . . . dwells in the highest, supercelestial zone of the universe, i.e., in the zone of the Cosmic Mind, and the beauty symbolized by her is the primary and universal splendour of divinity. She

[52] John Case, *The Praise of Musicke* (1586; STC. 20184), A3r–A3v. Cf. *Apologia Musices* (1588), attr. to Case, A4r.
[53] Pausanias, in the *Symposium*, trans. W. Hamilton (Harmondsworth, Middx., 1951), p. 45 (180D).
[54] Erwin Panofsky, *Studies in Iconology* (New York, 1939), p. 145.
[55] On the later influence of neo-Platonic philosophy in England, see Ernst Cassirer, *The Platonic Renaissance in England* (Austin, Tex., 1953). Such works, Panofsky points out, spawned a huge number of dialogues on love, of which Pietro Bembo's *Asolani* (1505) and Castiglione's *Courtier* were the most influential.

can thus be compared to 'Caritas,' the mediatrix between the human mind and God. . . . The beauty symbolized by [Venus Vulgaris] is . . . a particularized image of the primary beauty, no longer divorced from, but realized in the corporeal world. While the celestial Venus is a pure *intelligentia*, the other Venus is a *vis generandi* which, like Lucretius' Venus Genetrix, gives life and shape to the things in nature and thereby makes the intelligible beauty accessible to our perception and imagination.[56]

The Venus Vulgaris is, therefore, particularized. Her domain, human love, is characterized by visible beauty. He who would rise above such 'active' love must pass from the particular beauty to contemplation of the universal, divine beauty beyond the reach of the senses. That one can lead to the other is basic to Ficino's (and Plato's) philosophy, though sometimes the aberration of 'amor ferinus', love by touch rather than by sight— 'bestial love'—may reverse the upward progress.

> Par Venus terrestre j'entendz
> L'amytié de ce monde immunde
> Par Venus celeste pretendz
> L'amytié de Dieu pur et munde.[57]

So writes a mid-sixteenth-century poet, giving his own particular twist to Ficino. But whereas Ficino's Venus Vulgaris is readily distinguishable from the Venus Coelestis and seems almost to invite this kind of distinction, Pico relegates her to the position occupied by Ficino's 'amor ferinus', creating a second Venus Coelestis, slightly lower than the first, to fill her place.[58] This weakens the distinction between the two realms and makes credible the kind of synthesis-by-progression that we find in Spenser.

> All they without were raunged in a ring,
> And daunced round; but in the midst of them
> Three other Ladies did both daunce and sing,
> The whilest the rest them round about did hemme,
> And like a girlond did in compasse stemme:
> And in the middest of those same three, was placed

---

[56] *Iconology*, p. 142.
[57] Quoted from the anonymous *Cercle d'Amour* (1544) by W. A. R. Kerr, *PMLA*, 19 (1904).
[58] This second Venus is daughter of Saturn. See Panofsky, *Iconology*, p. 145.

Another Damzell, as a precious gemme,
Amidst a ring most richly well enchaced,
That with her goodly presence all the rest much graced.

(VI. x. 12)

We have seen how the stanza moves us gradually towards the starry heavens, to the crown of Ariadne 'being now placed in the firmament'; and the ascending order of the images (girlond–gemme–Ariadne's crown) is matched by the singing of the Graces themselves, their song reminding us, with its music, of the realms of grace, harmony and order. We are reminded, too, of the similar upward progression in the 'Mutabilitie Cantos'—from the mutable world, to the moon, to the planets, to the goddess Nature (herself a variant of Venus), and finally to God himself.

As for Pico's third love, Ficino's 'amor ferinus', which causes a doubling back in the natural ascent, it is suggested in the wild and savage dance of the cannibals round Serena. By contrast, the human love in the uncorrupted universe of Acidale moves naturally towards the divine, caught in the image of the gem, symbolic of the bounty freely rendered by the earth yet closest to the heavens in its perfection, linked with them through its native influence, and possessing a permanence setting it above the ever-changing leaves and flowers of a garland. There could hardly be a more fitting symbol of the harmonious union of art and nature.

But observations about the union of art and nature still do not do justice to the scene. Edward Tayler, in his study of Book VI,[59] criticizes C. S. Lewis for his vagueness in describing the dance as 'inspiration', but the term sums up its fleeting, ambivalent nature rather well, even if, as I previously remarked, it is somewhat limiting. If Lewis oversimplifies, so does Tayler, principally because he ignores the implications of the dance's central figure. After Colin Clout has given his explanation of the Graces (an explanation surprising in its conclusions rather than its conception), he passes to the fourth maiden in the midst of the circling graces:

> Such were those Goddesses, which ye did see;
> But that fourth Mayd, which there amidst them traced,
> Who can aread, what creature mote she bee,

---

[59] Edward William Tayler, *Nature and Art in Renaissance Literature* (New York, 1964), p. 115. Cf. Lewis, *Allegory of Love*, p. 351.

> Whether a creature, or a goddesse graced
> With heavenly gifts from heven first enraced?
> But what so sure she was, she worthy was,
> To be the fourth with those three other placed:
> Yet was she certes but a countrey lasse,
> Yet she all other countrey lasses farre did passe.
>
> (VI. X. 25)

Colin is unable to assign a place to this figure—'Whether a creature, or a goddesse graced'—whether part of the natural world or the world beyond it. The point, of course, is that she is both—both country lass and more than a country lass:

> So farre as doth the daughter of the day,
> All other lesser lights in light excell,
> So farre doth she in beautyfull array,
> Above all other lasses beare the bell,
> Ne lesse in vertue that beseemes her well,
> Doth she exceede the rest of all her race,
> For which the Graces that here wont to dwell,
> Have for more honor brought her to this place,
> And graced her so much to be another Grace.
>
> Another Grace she well deserves to be,
> In whom so many Graces gathered are,
> Excelling much the meane of her degree;
> Divine resemblaunce, beauty soveraine rare,
> Firme Chastity, that spite ne blemish dare;
> All which she with such courtesie doth grace,
> That all her peres cannot with her compare,
> But quite are dimmed, when she is in place.
> She made me often pipe and now to pipe apace.
>
> (VI. X. 26–7)

While the stanzas pay an elaborate compliment to a living girl, they are also a description of an ideal: the beauty of Venus herself, perhaps even a hint of the triad *castitas–pulchritudo–amor* in the terms 'firme chastity', 'beauty soveraine rare', 'divine resem-blaunce'.[60] That they are also an oblique compliment to Queen

---

[60] The term 'daughter of the day' is difficult; I take it to mean Venus. Kermode (ed. *Selections from the Minor Poems and 'The Faerie Queene'* (London, 1965), p. 224) glosses 'Venus (evening star)', and Upton (ed. *Spenser's 'Faerie Queene'* (London, 1758), 2.653) identifies her with 'the morning star'. The evening star is commonly called Hesperus, the morning star Lucifer. Both are, of course, the planet Venus. Sometimes Lucifer is named Aurora, and this name is a favourite with Spenser (see

Elizabeth is obvious from the stanza that follows; the Queen, it is implied, is greater than all such compliments paid to one of her subjects.

By leaving the relationship of Venus to the Graces ambiguous, Spenser is able to soften the distinction between Venus and the shepherd maid; we do not know who borrows grace from whom. This confusion of absolute and particular is matched by the impossibility that Calidore, imperfect man, could enter the Golden World. But a miracle has taken place—foreshadowed in that first, static picture in the shepherds' country:

> Upon a litle hillocke she was placed
> Higher then all the rest, and round about
> Environ'd with a girland, goodly graced,
> Of lovely lasses, and them all without
> The lustie shepheard swaynes sate in a rout,
> The which did pype and sing her prayses dew,
> And oft rejoyce, and oft for wonder shout,
> As if some miracle of heavenly hew
> Were downe to them descended in that earthly vew.
>
> (VI. ix. 8)

To spell out the implications of Spenser's ambiguity would take long indeed, for they are endless. The central figure round whom the Graces move in due order can be seen as the unity above the triad of the Graces, the meeting-point of the universal order, the single representative of the harmony of creation. Shakespeare, we remember, spoke of love as 'an ever fixéd mark'. This is Spenser's version of the same vision. But it is foreshadowed in this first sight of Pastorella, in fact seems almost the mystical equivalent of that very particular scene. St. Augustine, describing the mystical experience, uses terms which apply well to Calidore's situation on Mount Acidale:

And thus with the flash of one trembling glance it arrived at THAT WHICH IS. And then I saw Thy invisible things understood by the

---

1.iv.16; 1.xi.51; III.x.1; III.iii.20; *Gnat* 9)—cf. Henry Gibbons Lotspeich, *Classical Mythology in the Poetry of Edmund Spenser* (Princeton, 1932), pp. 6–8. Kermode's identification I think leaves the wrong impression, since it implies that darkness is on its way. The overwhelming appropriateness of identification with Venus is clear, because of Venus's connection with the central figure in the Dance. Spenser's failure to be specific is in accord with his general ambivalence about this central figure. Cf. III.iv.59.

things which are made. But I could not fix my gaze thereon; and my infirmity being struck back, I was thrown again on my wonted habits, carrying along with me only a loving memory thereof, and a longing for what I had, as it were, perceived the odour of, but was not yet able to feed on.[61]

So it is, we suppose, when Calidore returns to the actual world; so it is when the poet descends from contemplation of beauty to the routine matters of existence. In the final, mystical vision of Dante's *Divine Comedy*, there come together in a blinding and inexplicable understanding the general and the particular: man in God's own image, God in man's image. Gavin Douglas, describing the same vision in the *Palace of Honour*, falls back on explanation after the fact. Dante does not make the mistake of attempting to *explain*. Spenser chooses to explain the readily explicable but to leave the central idea—the unity of general and particular, of harmony and love and the movement of the universe—unexplained. Ultimately, he seems to say, there are things beyond the reach of simple logic, things real and conceivable only in poetry, because poetry transcends logic in transcending oppositions and particulars.

4. The choice of Hercules: pleasure and active virtue

Like Augustine, Spenser's knight must finally descend to the world again, since in the world of the *Faerie Queene*, where moral problems are given physical embodiment and moral rectitude is associated with knightly prowess, the hero's principal task is to combat the effects of 'moral wretchedness' and champion virtue. If he is to do this, he needs martial prowess—of the kind demonstrated by Calidore against Crudor, but so lacking in Calepine's encounters with Turpine. Fortune, we are told, favours the brave. Whether this be true or not, misfortune certainly afflicts the weak. There is a succession of such misfortunes throughout Book VI—the squire tied to his tree, Serena wandering in the fields, Calidore intruding on Calepine and Serena. It is clear that the main cause of misfortune is a kind of social defencelessness, the product of isolation from the group. We have already noticed how medieval writers conceive Courtesy as the virtue that orders and harmonizes society. Misfortune, then, takes its toll when men

---

[61] *Confessions*, VII, in Happold, *Mysticism*, p. 200.

are beyond the reach of the power of courtesy. The champion of courtesy must possess the strength to withstand the attacks of ill fortune both on himself and on others, and he must appreciate the value of men's standing together in co-operation, and understand the virtues of courtesy and civility.

Among the first champions of Justice whom we meet in the imagery of Book v are Bacchus and Hercules:

> Such first was *Bacchus*, that with furious might
> All th'East before untam'd did overronne,
> And wrong repressed, and establisht right,
> Which lawlesse men had formerly fordonne.
> There Justice first her princely rule begonne.
> Next *Hercules* his like ensample shewed,
> Who all the West with equall conquest wonne,
> And monstrous tyrants with his club subdewed;
> The club of Justice dread, with kingly power endewed.
>
> (v. i. 2)

We have seen how the career of Hercules is built into a major correlative of Artegall's quest: two recent studies of Book v make this connection very plain.[62] Both Bacchus and Hercules are appropriate upholders of civil order, and as a subduer of tyrants and slayer of monsters Hercules was frequently evoked by Renaissance writers.[63] Mrs. Aptekar has explained to us the appropriateness of Artegall's meeting with the Blatant Beast. The Beast is clearly modelled on the Hydra, she maintains, and the Hydra is associated above all with evil-speaking and slander by Renaissance mythographers, since as fast as its heads are cut off new ones grow.[64]

The Beast also reminds us of Cerberus, the 'dreadfull dog of hell', whom Hercules also subdued. In fact, the animal's hundred tongues, combined with his descent from Cerberus (vi. i. 7), make him a kind of composite of the dog and the monster, a Cerberus–

[62] Jane Aptekar, *Icons of Justice* (New York, 1969), pp. 153–214; T. K. Dunseath, *Spenser's Allegory of Justice* (Princeton, N.J., 1968), *passim*.

[63] See Eugene M. Waith, *The Herculean Hero in Chapman, Shakespeare and Dryden* (London, 1962), esp. pp. 16–59; Marc-René Jung, *Hercule dans la littérature française du XVIe siècle* (Geneva, 1966).

[64] Aptekar, *Icons*, pp. 201–14. Cf. the seven-headed beast of the Apocalypse, and Duessa's monster in Book I. See Thomas Warton, *Observations on the Fairy Queen of Spenser* (London, 1762), I. 222.

Hydra with the characteristics of both.[65] At the height of his
fury he is

> . . . like the hell-borne *Hydra*, which they faine
> That great *Alcides* whilome overthrew,
> After that he had labourd long in vaine,
> To crop his thousand heads, the which still new
> Forth budded, and in greater number grew.
>
> (VI. xii. 32)

Later, Spenser alludes to Hercules' capture of Cerberus:

> Like as whylome that strong *Tirynthian* swaine,
> Brought forth with him the dreadfull dog of hell,
> Against his will fast bound in yron chaine,
> And roring horribly, did him compell
> To see the hatefull sunne, that he might tell
> To griesly *Pluto*, what on earth was donne,
> And to the other damned ghosts, which dwell
> For aye in darkenesse, which day light doth shonne.
> So led this Knight his captyve with like conquest wonne.
>
> (VI. xii. 35)

Scholars have generally concluded that Hercules appears here
because he was considered the type of virtue and dedication and
manly strength. Certainly his presence reminds us of the way in
which Book VI sums up and complements Book V, and it carries
us back to the conclusion of the Legend of Justice in a rather
obvious but satisfying parallel.

There are, however, other reasons for having Hercules appear
in the Legend of Courtesy. They have to do with Hercules'
connection with Fortune. Throughout Renaissance literature,
there are constant references to the power of Virtue to overcome
Fortune:[66] 'Though Fortune hath a powerfull name, / Yet Vertue
overcomes the same', writes George Wither, echoing a commonplace.[67] Specifically, the struggle against Fortune is commonly

[65] The Beast is probably modelled on such creatures as the Questing Beast, in
Malory, and the monster Privy Malice, in Hawes (the creation of Envy, Disdain,
and Strangeness; compare Spenser's Despetto, Decetto, and Defetto). See M. Y.
Hughes, 'Spenser's Blatant Beast', *MLR*, 13 (1918), 267–75, reprinted in *Variorum*,
6: 382–8; see also the notes in *Variorum*, 6: 268–9, 382.

[66] See Plate 2 in Howard R. Patch, *The Goddess Fortuna in Medieval Literature*
(Cambridge, Mass., 1927), for a typical confrontation. Patch's book is the fullest
and most helpful discussion of its subject.

[67] Quoted by Samuel C. Chew, *The Pilgrimage of Life* (New Haven, Conn., 1962),
p. 67.

associated with Hercules. Cassirer, for example, describes a pageant performed in Rome in 1501, entitled *The Battle between Fortune and Hercules*.[68] Juno sends Fortune against Hercules, but instead of conquering him, Fortune is overpowered and chained, finally gaining her release only at the further intervention of Juno, and then on condition that she do no harm to those for whom the pageant is being performed. Although there is a particular appropriateness to the inclusion of Hercules in the pageant, which was performed for the House of the Duke of Ferrara, Ercole d'Este, the conflict between Hercules and Fortune was in any case proverbial. Cassirer cites another, rather later work, Giordano Bruno's *Spaccio della bestia trionfante*, in which Fortune comes before an assembly of the gods (reminiscent of the court of Nature in the 'Mutabilitie Cantos')[69] to lay claim to the place in the heavens hitherto occupied by Hercules,

But her claim is declared invalid. Indeed, to her, the roving and inconstant one, no single place is denied; at her pleasure she may show herself anywhere in heaven or on earth. But the place of Hercules is assigned to *Valour*. For where truth, law and right judgment are to reign, Valour cannot be absent. It is the palladium of every other virtue, the shield of justice and the tower of truth. Valour is unyielding to vice, unconquerable by suffering, constant through danger, severe against cupidity, contemptuous of wealth—and the tamer of Fortune.[70]

Bruno was read relatively widely among scholars in England, visited the country, and was on good terms with the Sidney circle.[71] It is therefore possible that Spenser knew this story (the work was published in 1584). It is an appropriate story for Bruno, whose espousal of the Copernican theories put him in the

[68] *The Individual and the Cosmos in Renaissance Philosophy* (New York, 1963), pp. 73-4. See Ferdinand Gregorovius, *Lucrezia Borgia* (London, 1948), p. 142.

[69] Chew, in two perceptive asides (*Pilgrimage*, pp. 57, 67), suggests that there are marked similarities between the Titaness Mutabilitie and Fortune. The Bruno passage would seem to support such an identification, though Angelo Pellegrini, 'Bruno, Sidney, and Spenser', *SP*, 40 (1943), 128-44, finds the differences more striking than the similarities. See also Raymond Chapman, 'Fortune and Mutability in Elizabethan Literature', *Cambridge Journal*, 5 (1952), 374-82.

[70] *Spaccio*, Dial. II, terza parte, summarized by Cassirer, *Individual and Cosmos*, pp. 73-4. See *The Expulsion of the Triumphant Beast*, trans. Arthur D. Imerti (New Brunswick, N.J., 1964), pp. 178-81.

[71] Bruno dedicated both the *Spaccio* and *De Gl'Heroici Furori* to Sidney, though his connection with him was probably not especially close. See Frederick S. Boas, *Sir Philip Sidney, Representative Elizabethan* (London, 1955), p. 170. Cf. Frances Yates, *Giordano Bruno and the Hermetic Tradition* (Chicago, 1964).

forefront of those who stressed man's individuality in a universe neither so ordered nor so constricting as had been supposed in earlier centuries.[72] Hercules was a symbol of man's indomitable will, his ability to overcome and subjugate Fortune. He was a symbol of valour, of *virtú*.[73]

Niccolò Machiavelli, like so many of his contemporaries, writes at length on the antithesis of Fortune and *virtú*, sometimes (in the *Capitolo di Fortuna*, for example) emphasizing the inexorability of Fortune, sometimes stressing man's ability at least to mitigate her influence. The idea that Fortune may be brought under control by human power goes back to the classics; the *Consolation of Philosophy*, of Boethius, is only the last in a line of classical treatments of the relation between fortune and human fortitude. The central question in many discussions of the subject is whether fortune is an external agent or whether it is in some ways a product of human action.[74] The well-known twenty-fifth chapter of *Il Principe* characterizes fortune as an external power, but it is clear that a man's actions may determine the way in which fortune manifests itself: 'Fortune varying and men remaining fixed in their ways, they are successful so long as these ways conform to circumstances, but when they are opposed then they are unsuccessful.'[75]

The problem of the nature of fortune clearly underlies the conversation between Meliboe and Calidore in Canto ix of Book VI. In fact Meliboe's speeches are a texture of commonplaces on

[72] See Hiram Haydn's admirable summing-up, *The Counter-Renaissance* (New York, 1950), pp. 154–60.

[73] As such, he was sometimes considered patron of men, just as Juno was patroness of women. See Jean Bayet, *Les Origines de l'Hercule Romain* (Paris, 1926), p. 380. Hence the association with fecundity and the traditional opposition of Hercules and Juno, which Bayet discusses. Occasionally Fortune and Juno are associated: see Patch, *Fortuna*, p. 32. (Bayet's study is based on works of art, and there is therefore no certainty that all the associations he mentions actually transferred themselves to literature.)

[74] See Pierre Courcelle, *La Consolation de Philosophie dans la tradition littéraire* (Paris, 1967), pp. 103–58, and Plates 65–92. As well as discussing Boethius, the volume provides a good summary of views on fortune from antiquity to the Middle Ages.

[75] *The Prince*, trans. Luigi Ricci, rev. E. R. P. Vincent (New York, 1952), p. 134. A recent discussion of Machiavelli's views will be found in Sydney Anglo, *Machiavelli: a Dissection* (London, 1969), pp. 216–37. See also Joseph Anthony Mazzeo, *Renaissance and Revolution* (New York, 1967), pp. 72–8. Cf. Bacon, whose essay 'Of Fortune' rejects the idea that fortune is a power external to oneself (*Works*, ed. Spedding, Ellis, and Heath (Boston, Mass., 1860–64), 12: 215–16).

the subject. There appears to be no great consistency to Spenser's own use of the term in the *Faerie Queene*, though we do frequently have the impression that his characters are apt to blame their own shortcomings on misfortune. Una covers up for the Red Cross Knight in this way (I. viii. 42–3), and Calidore uses a similar excuse for his various intrusions. Serena, alone in the wilderness, blames her plight on fortune when she might better have blamed it on a misunderstanding of Cupid's punishments. Our reading of instances such as these naturally leads us to the conclusion that man is in reality a free agent, though subject perhaps to the stipulations and limitations of God's holy plan. Pico della Mirandola says as much in his famous *Oration*, again an assemblage of commonplaces powerfully expressed, and this optimistic idealism lives on in literature for a century or more to come. It is essentially Spenser's view, though in Book VI he never makes it categorically clear whether fortune is or is not external to the individual. He is really interested in the other side of the picture—how man's inherent qualities may mitigate fortune's influence. This *virtù*, the power of the knight and the strength of men's leaders, may help bring fortune under control.

But the optimistic note sounded by the metaphor of the chivalric quest stands in ironic contrast to the seeming futility of human action in the face of destiny and human imperfection. This nagging doubt about man's ability to change his fortune lies behind much chivalric romance and is of course a theme of Malory's work. We detect it, I think, in Spenser's Book VI, where, as we have seen, the quest of the knight is also equated with the quest of the poet, and the doubts about the ability of *virtù* to change the circumstances which beset us are matched by an uneasiness about the power of poetry to move men to the good. What is more, if *virtù* can indeed score its victories, then power misused (and poetry misused) by men *male fortes*, may spread *mis*fortune and social oppression. These considerations may lie at the back of Spenser's inspiration in the sixth book, but it is clear that his conception of Courtesy as the active promotion of social harmony through the powers of nature provides an answer to his own doubts. We are constantly told that strength well used may create harmony. It is logical, therefore, to meet Hercules, who epitomizes such a belief, in the book's final canto.[76]

[76] We might note that Poverty and Wisdom were also considered antidotes

The two similes in which Hercules appears are especially appropriate. Not only is there a physical resemblance between the many-tongued Beast and the many-headed Hydra, but they were both born of the union of Typhon and Echidna. They both represent scandal and slander. Most important of all, the battle against the Hydra was the least successful of Hercules' labours, and our reservations about his success against the Hydra cast an ominous shadow over Calidore's struggle against the Beast.[77]

Like the Hydra, Cerberus was also born of Typhon and Echidna.[78] The capture of the hellish creature that guarded the entrance to the underworld constitutes the last and most difficult of the labours of Hercules. The physical resemblance between the Blatant Beast and Cerberus will be immediately clear, and the manner in which Calidore subdues the Beast is also somewhat

---

against Fortune, and it was not unusual to pit Mercury against Fortuna. Francis Thynne has an emblem on the subject (note his equation of wisdom and art):

> On rolling ball doth fickle Fortune stand;
> On firm and settled square sits Mercury,
> The god of Arts, with wisdom's rod in hand;
> Which covertly to us doth signify,
> That Fortune's power, inconstant and still frail,
> Against wisdom and art cannot prevail.

(quoted by Chew, *Pilgrimage*, pp. 66–7). Cf. Pierre de la Primaudaye, *The French Academie*, Chapter 44 ('Of Fortune'). In his difficult and sometimes rather conjectural study *Spenser and the Numbers of Time* (London, 1964), Alastair Fowler, identifying Venus as the patroness of Book vi, shows how fortune has a more extensive role in this book than in the others, and demonstrates the connection between Venus and fortune. The connection of Venus and the hexad makes her a logical choice as patroness of the sixth book. Note also that the hexad is associated with harmony (Fowler, p. 49). Occasionally we find Fortune and Love specifically opposed to one another (cf. Calidore's intrusion on Calepine, or on Colin Clout). See, for example, Fulke Greville's poem 'Faction, that ever dwells': 'Fortune should ever dwell / In courts, where wits excell: / Love keep the wood.'

77 'The Lernaean Hydra puzzled the Classical mythographers. Pausanias held that it might well have been a huge and venomous watersnake. . . . According to the euhemeristic Servius (On Virgil's *Aeneid*, vi.287), the Hydra was a source of underground rivers which used to burst out and inundate the land: if one of its numerous channels were blocked, the water broke through elsewhere, therefore Heracles first used fire to dry the ground, and then closed the channels' (Graves, *Greek Myths*, 2: 109). Might there be some connection between the explanation of the Hercules myth found in Servius and the defeat of Cormoraunt, who will be destroyed by drinking and drying up 'all the water, which doth ronne / In the next brooke' (vi.iv.32)? (Bayet, *Origines*, p. 24 etc., points out Hercules' association with springs.)

78 The equivocation over the Beast's ancestry (vi.i.8; vi.vi.9–11) allows a link with both Cerberus and the Hydra.

similar to Hercules' tactics. Hercules was forbidden to use his club or arrows in the fight and achieved victory by choking his adversary. Calidore likewise makes no use of aggressive weapons, using his shield to press the Beast down 'till he be throughly queld'.[79]

Of course, it is not difficult to find parallels between Hercules and many of Spenser's heroes: so abundant were the stories of Hercules, and so popular were they among Renaissance writers, that there is something in the Hercules myth to suit the source-hunter's every occasion. Herein lies the danger of looking for definite and definitive sources. Plutarch, for instance, alludes to the fact that Hercules was naturally courteous; a number of writers point out that he was a skilled wrestler and musician. But such antecedents are too imprecise to have much bearing on Book VI. It does seem likely, though, that Spenser would be aware of the dimensions of the Hercules story among Christian writers, who identified him with Christian virtue and the Christianizing process. Sometimes this identification extended as far as parallels between the classical hero and Christ. Thus the *virtus* of Hercules became Christian virtue, the active virtue especially associated with the *miles Christi*.[80]

Hercules' possession of virtue was part of a conscious decision, figured in the well-known story of the Choice of Hercules, recounted by Xenophon and forming the subject of one of Panofsky's extended studies.[81] Readers will be familiar with the essential details of the legend, which particularly caught the imagination of the Renaissance.[82] Generally the choice lies between *virtus* and *voluptas*, between the active life of the hero and the allurements of a life of pleasure. Lydgate calls them Reason

---

[79] The victory over Cerberus was construed as a victory over death: 'En enchaînant et tirant à la lumière du jour le triple Cerbère, Héraclès avait vaincu le Serviteur de la Mort, ou la Mort elle-même: la puissance d'Hadès avait été brisée par la force.' (Bayet, *Origines*, p. 397.) This is the final victory over Fortune, whose final weapon is death itself.

[80] See Erwin Panofsky, *Hercules am Scheidewege* (Leipzig, 1930), pp. 151-5, 187-96. On the Christianizing of classical heroes, see Raymond Trousson, *Le Thème de Prométhée dans la Littérature Européenne* (Geneva, 1964), I: 59-82. See also Jean Seznec, *The Survival of the Pagan Gods* (New York, 1953), *passim*. On Hercules as a Christian hero, see Marcel Simon, *Hercules et le Christianisme* (Paris, 1955), esp. his chapter on 'Hercule chrétien'. On Hercules and Virtue, see Waith, *Herculean Hero*, pp. 43-8.

[81] *Hercules am Scheidewege*; Xenophon, *Memorabilia*, II.i.21-34.

[82] On its popularity, especially in the late Middle Ages, see Chew, *Pilgrimage*, pp. 175-181.

and Sensuality. For Christian writers the choice has an obvious appropriateness, echoing as it does the words of Christ (Matt. 7:13–14), 'Enter ye in at the strait gate: for wide is the gate, and broad is the way, that leadeth to destruction, and many there be which go in thereat: Because strait is the gate, and narrow is the way, which leadeth unto life, and few there be that find it.' The young man, setting out on his life's work, like Hercules embarked on his labours, must eschew Pleasure and cleave to Virtue. Mrs. Aptekar suggests that Artegall faces such a choice with Radigund and Britomart,[83] though ultimately, as in Jonson's *Pleasure Reconciled to Virtue*, he is able to enjoy both options when he is saved from the debasing captivity to Radigund. Calidore, too, confronts a similar choice, but Pastorella, miraculously, ultimately comes to symbolize both Pleasure and Virtue, pastoral and chivalry.

Sometimes the contrast of Action and Pleasure is explored through the old conflict of Love and Honour—a motif given further elaboration in Tasso's pastoral drama *Aminta*, where the Golden Age is praised not for its various physical qualities, but only because Honour had not been invented and Love still reigned supreme. A further variant of the same contrast is retreat literature, so marked a feature of the seventeenth and eighteenth centuries. The georgic theme tends to emphasize the virtues not of pleasure over action but of contemplation over action, and the retreat into the countryside away from the troubles of the city becomes a means of coming to terms with oneself, of understanding one's own nature.[84] The theme is given its most sophisticated treatment in Marvell's 'Garden'.

Emphasis on the knowledge of oneself, a favourite topic of the sixteenth and seventeenth centuries, is reflected in Spenser's emphasis in the Letter to Ralegh on the private rather than the public virtues:

The generall end therefore of all the booke is to fashion a gentleman or noble person in vertuous and gentle discipline: Which for that I conceived shoulde be most plausible and pleasing. . . . I chose the historye of king Arthure . . . In which I have followed all the antique Poets historicall, first Homere, who in the Persons of Agamemnon

---

[83] *Icons*, pp. 172–200.
[84] The definitive history of the theme of retreat is Maren-Sofie Røstvig, *The Happy Man* (Oslo, 1954–8).

and Ulysses hath ensampled a good governour and a vertuous man, the one in his Ilias, the other in his Odysseis: then Virgil, whose like intention was to doe in the person of Aeneas: after him Ariosto comprised them both in his Orlando: and lately Tasso disseuered them againe, and formed both parts in two persons, namely that part which they in Philosophy call Ethice, or vertues of a private man coloured in his Rinaldo: The other named Politice in his Godfredo.[85]

Arthur, we are told, will be 'perfected in the twelve private moral virtues'. Certainly the fact that Spenser begins the *Faerie Queene* with the Legend of Holiness and follows it with a book on Temperance gives obvious importance to self-knowledge and self-discipline. The stress on the self makes the conflicting pull of Contemplation and Action particularly poignant when we confront it in that institution of self-knowledge, the House of Holiness. The kind of self-discipline expressed in Book II, however, leads to a conflict not between Action and Contemplation but between Action and Pleasure. Book II's house of self-knowledge, the Castle of Alma, is under constant attack from the forces of the senses, and Phaedria and Acrasia are voluptuous temptations of the kind which assail the man of action. When the theme reappears in Book V, Artegall ultimately is not denied Pleasure: Pleasure is *contained within* the person of Britomart, whose quest of her future husband through the central books draws into reconciliation the conflicting claims of action and generation or, as it might be expressed in the Choice, Action and Pleasure. This does not happen, though, before Artegall has learned that fundamental lesson which Calidore later teaches Crudor: 'In vaine he seeketh others to suppresse, / Who hath not learnd him selfe first to subdew' (VI, i. 41). His fall to Radigund is an indication that the outward trappings of his Justice are not linked to an inward virtue.

Marvell's 'Garden', in spite of its ambiguities, seems to imply a drawing together of Pleasure and Contemplation in the paradise existence of the garden itself, the two being contrasted with the life of action. Hawes's *Pastime of Pleasure* moves the contrast in the other direction by widening Action to cover Pleasure and confronting the poem's hero with a choice between Action (with

---

[85] On parallels in Tasso's commentary on *Gerusalemme Liberata*, see Cheney, *Image of Nature*, pp. 88–92.

Pleasure) and Contemplation. His choice of the former is well in accord with Renaissance thinking.[86]

5. *Resolution: the tripartite life*

The Choice of Hercules was a simple one: the hero was successful in avoiding temptation: he chose virtue rather than vice. Indeed, to the neo-Platonic philosophers it was over-simple. The presentation of the two opposites precludes the choice of a third transcendent reconciliation of the two, such as Jonson presents in his masque *Pleasure Reconciled to Virtue* or such as is implied in the altogether more complex situation of the Judgement of Paris, where three figures reveal their attractions to the noble and courteous youth Paris on more or less equal terms. The sixteenth century saw nothing incongruous in conflating the Choice and the Judgement, associating the paths offered by the three goddesses with Socrates (Wisdom), Paris (Pleasure), and Hercules (Virtue, heroic action). These three paths correspond to the Platonic scheme of the tripartite life,[87] which Plato defined as consisting of Reason (contemplation), Passion (action), and Desire (pleasure), each clear and distinct from the other two.[88] Reconciling the three Platonic 'parts' became a frequent intellectual exercise for Renaissance thinkers. Ficino, writing to Lorenzo de' Medici, praises the prince for combining all three in his person—a mode of compliment which also lies behind the famous picture of Queen Elizabeth repulsing Juno, Pallas, and Venus, painted by Hans Eworth and now in Hampton Court.[89] Quite possibly the allusion

[86] Cf. Prospero's inability to achieve the proper balance and his consequent ouster from the dukedom of Milan. On the increasing praise of the active as against the contemplative life in the Renaissance, see Hans Baron, *The Crisis of the Early Italian Renaissance* (Princeton, N.J., 1955), and Eugene F. Rice, Jr., *The Renaissance Idea of Wisdom* (Cambridge, Mass., 1958). Rice lays particular emphasis on the reconciliation of the two.

[87] Wind, *Pagan Mysteries*, pp. 78–9.

[88] *Republic*, IV. 435–41; trans. H. D. P. Lee (Harmondsworth, Middx., 1955), pp. 185–93.

[89] John Buxton, *Elizabethan Taste* (London, 1963), p. 116. See also John D. Reeves, 'The Judgment of Paris as a Device of Tudor Flattery', *N&Q*, 199 (1954), 7–11. Cf. Peele's *Arraignment of Paris*, where Elizabeth reconciles Juno, Venus, and Pallas by combining their respective virtues in her own person. See T. S. Graves, '*The Arraignment of Paris* and Sixteenth-Century Flattery', *MLN*, 28 (1913), 48–9. Frank Kermode (ed. *The Tempest* (London, 1954), pp. xlix–l) quotes Cleland (*The Institution of a Young Noble Man*, II. i) on James I: '[He] standeth invested with that triplicitie which in great veneration was ascribed to the ancient

to Socrates and the presentation of Tantalus and Pilate in the Cave of Mammon presents the *triplex vita* in parodic form, though Guyon's essential task resembles the Choice of Hercules— simply to avoid all temptations to indulge the senses.

The presence of Hercules in Book VI is matched by another presence, that of Paris. Calidore, we remember, during his stay among the shepherds is likened to 'Phrygian Paris by Plexippus brooke, / When he the love of fayre Oenone sought, / What time the golden apple was unto him brought' (VI. ix. 36). Certainly this reminder of the tragic train of events set in motion by Paris's fateful choice of Pleasure casts an ominous shadow over the carefree pastoral world. But Spenser's audience was well aware of the ambiguities of the Troy story: the Fall of Troy brought about both the foundation of Rome and also the foundation of Britain. Spenser has already elaborated on these ambiguities in his treatment of the story of Troy and the myth of Helen in Book III.[90] Paris, himself a foundling like Pastorella, moved from the pastoral existence on Mount Ida to the turbulent world of the city of Troy because of his encounter with the three goddesses.

In the figures of Paris and Hercules, so carefully alluded to in Book VI, is presented the direct conflict of love and honour which Tasso makes central to the *Aminta*. Calidore as Paris and Calidore as Hercules therefore represent complete and seemingly irreconcilable opposites—the Pleasure and Virtue of the Choice of Hercules. If the *Faerie Queene* were purely and simply a work about the heroic virtues, if there were not so much emphasis on self-knowledge and the private virtues and on qualities other than those simply of the life of action, the dilemma would be as simple as the Choice: we would reject the pastoral truancy out of hand. The slightly sinister figure of Paris would simply represent a turning aside from the path of true virtue. But Book VI, especially, is not as simple as that. Within twenty stanzas of the Paris simile, we find ourselves on Mount Acidale, amidst the beauty of the dancing Graces.

Hermes, the power and fortune of a *King*, the knowledge and illumination of a Priest, and the Learning and universalitie of a Philosopher.'

[90] See Thomas P. Roche, Jr., *The Kindly Flame* (Princeton, N.J., 1964), *passim*. Most Renaissance treatments of the Paris story (including Spenser's allusion to it in the July eclogue) emphasize his folly. See Hallett Smith's helpful discussion, *Elizabethan Poetry* (Cambridge, Mass., 1952), pp. 3–9.

The key to this unresolved conflict lies not in the rejection of the life of Action or the life of Pleasure but in their reconciliation. 'Harmonia est discordia concors': from the union of Mars and Venus there came a daughter, Harmony. Wind quotes a long passage from Pico which may prove helpful in providing an understanding of this doctrine of opposites:

And for this reason no simple thing can be beautiful. From which it follows that there is no beauty in God because beauty includes in it a certain imperfection, that is, it must be composed in a certain manner: which in no way applies to the first cause. . . . But below it [the first cause] begins beauty because there begins contrariety, without which there would be no creation but only God. Nor do contrariety and discord between various elements suffice to constitute a creature, but by due proportion the contrariety must become united and the discord made concordant; and this may be offered as the true definition of Beauty, namely, that it is nothing else than an amicable enmity and a concordant discord. . . . According to the ancient astrologers, whose opinion Plato and Aristotle follow, and according to the writings of Albenazra the Spaniard and also of Moses, Venus was placed in the centre of heaven next to Mars, because she must tame his impulse which is by nature destructive and corrupting, just as Jupiter offsets the malice of Saturn. And if Mars were always subordinated to Venus, that is, the contrariety of the component elements to their due proportion, nothing would ever perish.[91]

Wind draws attention to Raphael's famous painting 'The Dream of Scipio', now in the National Gallery. The painting, illustrating Cicero's well-known work, which, along with Macrobius's commentary on it, was so popular at this time,[92] shows a choice between Pleasure and Virtue, but a choice which really presents three possibilities—Action (symbolized by a sword), Contemplation (symbolized by a book), and Pleasure (symbolized by a flower). Interestingly, the painting was a companion piece for a painting of the Three Graces, whose entwined arms and graceful expressions imply not so much a judgement among three possibilities as a reconciliation of the three.[93] This, as Wind's study amply attests, is a customary role for the Graces. *Castitas* and *amor* are reconciled through the agency of *pulchritudo*; *amor* draws

[91] Pico, *Commento*, 2.6, quoted in Wind, *Mysteries*, pp. 88–9.
[92] See C. S. Lewis, *The Discarded Image* (Cambridge, 1964), pp. 23–8, 60–9.
[93] Wind, *Mysteries*, Plates 60 and 61.

pulchritudo and *voluptas* together, and so on. In each case it is the third element in the triad which draws apparent opposites into harmony—rather like Concord with Love and Hate at the Temple of Venus in Book IV.[94]

Although Spenser does not offer a specific description of the figures of the three Graces, their differentiation extending no further than their names and a few apparently imprecise adjectives (VI. x. 22), the three are suggestive both of a combination of Action, Pleasure, and Contemplation and of the representation of Contemplation itself.[95] In other words, they both represent the *triplex vita* and stand for one element in it. This is not, of course, the first time that we have met the quality of Contemplation. Spenser has prepared us for this episode in Calepine's words to Matilda, concerning the education of the babe.[96] The choice between Action and Contemplation is presented again in the person of the Hermit, who has retired to 'observaunce of religious vow' (VI. v. 35) after a life 'in armes and derring doe' (VI. v. 37).

Canto x, however, presents a picture not of philosophy or religious observance but of the poet's own poetry: the third element in the triad Action–Pleasure–Contemplation is not some abstraction or some foreign referent but the very poem itself, which binds the pastoral and the heroic, the life of pleasure and the life of action, together in terms of a new and crucially effective myth. This myth of the Graces can be read as a restatement of the earlier motif of reconciliation-through-opposites: the Venus *armata*, and the harmonization of the quest and the generative cycle through the single person of Britomart. But if we read the *Faerie Queene* itself as an attempt to make sense of the old split personality of chivalric romance (love versus honour), we must recognize that the Graces represent a peculiarly effective solution

[94] Fowler, *Numbers of Time*, pp. 164–6.
[95] 'The first of them hight mylde Euphrosyne, / Next faire Aglaia, last Thalia merry.' The three were customarily associated with *laetitia*, *splendor*, and *viriditas* (Wind, *Mysteries*, p. 269; Pico-Stanley, *Platonick Discourse*, p. 35; Pico, *Benivieni*, D5r; Landino, *Commento*, c3v; Alciati, *Emblèmes*, N3r; Perottus, *Cornucopiae* . . . , col. 345 (Perottus reverses Aglaia and Euphrosyne, however, thereby confusing their meanings)). One has to stretch Spenser's adjectives to make them line up with these three aspects of Ideal Beauty. The order of the Graces (see n. 31 above) may just possibly reflect a descending sequence from the *laetitia* associated with the celestial realm, *splendor* with the sun, and *viriditas* with the earth (see Wind, *Mysteries* p. 269).
[96] Cf. Don Quixote's well-known discourse on Arms and Letters—*Don Quixote* I. xxxviii, trans. J. M. Cohen (Harmondsworth, Middx., 1950), pp. 342–5.

to the dilemma, because they reflect not merely on the problem itself but also on the work in which the problem is examined. The Graces are Spenser's means of justifying the life of the intellectual, the pursuit of poetry and, just possibly, his own life amid the green yet far-flung fields of Ireland.

We have discovered, then, yet another aspect of the meaning of the Graces, possibly the most important. They present the balance of the ideal man, who combines in a single person the powers of Action, Pleasure, and Contemplation, and they simultaneously justify the life of Contemplation because it provides the means by which the other two may be united. As well as the balance of the ideal man, this is also the balance of courtesy and the balance of civility, for the three parts of the tripartite life can also be interpreted in terms of the state, as Plato sets them forth in *The Republic*. The state as macrocosm exactly parallels the individual as microcosm: businessmen correspond to Desire, auxilaries to Passion, governors to Reason. The picture of Elizabeth's court given in the proem stands as a model of the harmonious state, and this same system of hierarchies is borne out in the Vision of the Graces, with the central dancer linked through simile to the incomparable figure of the Queen herself, *primum mobile* and centre of her harmonious realm. We are reminded of Churchyard's lines, 'Grant silly man, a grace that meanes to sing / Of heav'nly love, and of none other thing.' The Vision of the Graces not only draws human life into harmony but shows the source of that harmony in the grace of God himself.

But the mere fact that the Graces present a solution does not necessarily project that solution into the world of affairs in which Calidore customarily belongs, any more than the solution protects Meliboe's life of pleasure or Colin's life of contemplation against the depredations of brigands or of hostile philistines. This problem of the relationship between private virtue and public action is first presented to us in Book VI in the very first episode, with Calidore's words to Crudor:

> In vaine he seeketh others to suppresse,
> Who hath not learnd him selfe first to subdew:
> All flesh is frayle, and full of ficklenesse,
> Subject to fortunes chance, still chaunging new;
> What haps to day to me, to morrow may to you.
>
> (VI. i. 41)

The same question returns in the Hermit's advice to Serena, and it is presented in slightly different form in the episode of the monastery (which of course is also another treatment of the contrast between action and contemplation). The answer lies in the figure of Pastorella: she is the link between the vision of beauty on Mount Acidale and the world of here-and-now to which she is returned. She is an earthly representation of Calidore's heavenly vision, but she is also a flesh-and-blood girl, daughter of a knight and his lady, and loved by a questing hero.

The key to Spenser's conception of courtesy is to be found in the two related concepts of harmony and reconciliation. The theme of reconciliation embraces all those discordant elements in terms of which the Elizabethans viewed their world: nature and grace, art and nature, love and honour. Pico's aesthetic theory logically leads to the conclusion that art and nature come together in the harmony of beauty. In this instance, the conclusion is embodied in two different ways of looking at the vision on Mount Acidale: as a vision in a Golden World set at the point where art and nature coalesce, or as a vision of opposites brought together in the endless dance of the Graces, the symbol of ordered nature, or of artless art.

From an ordered world Paris went forth to the quarrels and embroilments of Greece and Troy, to return at the end of his life. Hercules, too, in his *alter ego* of Jesus Christ, went out into the world, was made flesh and returned to God. The ideal man must embody the ideals of the ideal world, but with them must come those oppositions which, considered in their separate elements, make him imperfect yet equip him for the trials of an imperfect world. In Book III, Spenser presented two alternatives in Belphoebe (Mars–Hercules) and Amoret (Venus–Paris) and the ideal combination in Britomart, who has the valour to protect herself and others, combined with the love to perpetuate the cycle of nature, and the high purpose to guide her and sustain her.

We have seen how the Golden World of birth and death, where opposites are reconciled and whence nature's creatures go forth into the sublunary world, is also a place of education and retirement, beginning life and ending it. It is a world of youth, where the trees are always in bud, where what we imagine is what comes to pass, and where there is love and sunlight. When Spenser asks

'Revele to me the sacred noursery / of vertue', he is alluding not only to the budding flowers of Tristram and Pastorella but to the youthfulness of the Golden World: Book VI is the book of youth. It is also the book of return: the principal recurrent symbol is the ring, or its natural equivalent, the garland—both associated with the process of giving, converting, and returning, symbolized in the Graces themselves. A sense of the cyclical character of nature and of society dominates the book. But Spenser implicitly repudiates the idea of the Golden World simply as a world of retreat: it cannot be a substitute for Calidore's quest, but only a place of education—and it is set not only in a nostalgic past but in the future too, for it is the beginning and end of time.

I have called Mount Acidale an amalgam, the core of the book, not simply because here all the threads of allegory come together, but also because in a genuine sense it *is* the centre of the universe of courtesy—the place of perfect harmony and perfect order. If the vision is in part mystical, its application is nonetheless a practical one: the ideas Calidore learns on Acidale return to their rightful place in society in the form of Pastorella. Her coming back from the pastoral world signals a rebirth, a rejuvenation through the power of love, and a bestowal of God's grace on mankind.

X

Pastoral and *Myth*

1. The uses of pastoral

OUR consideration of such topics as Nature and Courtesy has
focused primarily on subject matter, merely glancing at the modes
through which this subject matter is expressed—principally
pastoral and allegory. In this chapter we will look a little more
closely at what is meant by pastoral and how it works. My
intention is not to develop a theory of pastoral: that has been
done more effectively than I could by William Empson,[1] and in
some measure by the late Renato Poggioli.[2] Nor will I attempt a
history: W. W. Greg long ago produced what has deservedly
remained the standard history of pastoral.[3] Frank Kermode[4] and
Hallett Smith[5] have also made their contributions particularly on
Renaissance pastoral, and such related fields as the myth of the
Golden Age,[6] georgic poetry,[7] and romance[8] have all received

---

[1] *Some Versions of Pastoral* (London, 1935).

[2] 'The Oaten Flute', *Harvard Library Bulletin*, 11 (1957), 147–84; 'The Pastoral
of the Self', *Daedalus*, 88 (1959), 686–99.

[3] *Pastoral Poetry and Pastoral Drama* (London, 1906).

[4] Introduction to *English Pastoral Poetry from the Beginnings to Marvell* (London,
1952).

[5] *Elizabethan Poetry* (Cambridge, Mass., 1952), pp. 1–63. Cf. E. K. Chambers,
'The English Pastoral', in *Sir Thomas Wyatt and some Collected Studies* (London, 1933);
Edward William Tayler, *Nature and Art in Renaissance Literature* (New York, 1964);
Patrick Cullen, *Spenser, Marvell, and Renaissance Pastoral* (Cambridge, Mass, 1970).
On seventeenth-century pastoral, see Joan Grundy, *The Spenserian Poets* (London,
1969); Harold E. Toliver, *Marvell's Ironic Vision* (New Haven, Conn., 1965); Donald
M. Friedman, *Marvell's Pastoral Art* (Berkeley and Los Angeles, Calif., 1970), and,
in the minor but interesting area of pastoral *practices*, Christopher Whitfield, *Robert
Dover and the Cotswold Games* (London, 1962).

[6] Harry Levin, *The Myth of the Golden Age in the Renaissance* (Bloomington, Ind.,
1969); Elizabeth Armstrong, *Ronsard and the Age of Gold* (Cambridge, 1968); Patrick
Cullen, 'Imitation and Metamorphosis: the Golden-Age Eclogue in Spenser, Milton,
and Marvell', *PMLA*, 84 (1969), 1559–70.

[7] M. L. Lilly, *The Georgic* (Baltimore, Md., 1915); Dwight L. Durling, *The Georgic
Tradition in English Poetry* (New York, 1935).

[8] Eleanor Terry Lincoln, ed. *Pastoral and Romance: Modern Essays in Criticism*

attention from historians and theorists. Primitivism has been the
subject of a number of scholarly studies.[9]

As always with a field much explored, there is a great deal to
disagree about in the works on pastoral already available to us,
both the general studies and also those specifically concerned
with Spenser. In the general area, perhaps our principal problem
is deciding where pastoral stops. Is it legitimate to extend its
range to include Robert Frost or Dylan Thomas, and to see in
Thomas Hardy's peasants the descendants of Hobbinol and
Diggon Davy and the rest? Or should we conclude, with Yeats,
that the woods of Arcady are dead, that 'Words alone are certain
good'? And in the specific area of Spenser studies we are faced
with the difficulty of tracing patterns and coherence among
Spenser's many assays at pastoral poetry, so different in intention
and conception.[10]

There is, of course, much disagreement about what pastoral is.
Is it a modal, or generic, or stylistic phenomenon? Is it possible
to define it historically or is it part of man's psychological make-up
in every age? Is it a branch of romance or a branch of satire, a
consequence of urbanization or a vestige of religion? Although
both are often united in a single work, we have found it possible
to distinguish two separate general functions of pastoral. Its
first function is satiric: it serves as a device for criticism. It
distances the writer from his own milieu and forms a base from
which to attack its standards or lack of standards. The eclogue is
its special vehicle. Its second function is as a means of articulating
moral or spiritual aspirations. It creates a world where the conflicts
and pettinesses of ordinary life are eliminated, where all invest-
ments have returns, and where actions have desired results. Love
is untrammelled, and belief suffers no contradiction. Neither of

---

(Englewood Cliffs, N.J., 1969); Northrop Frye, *Anatomy of Criticism* (Princeton,
N.J., 1957); W. P. Ker, *Epic and Romance* (London, 1897); Dorothy Everett, *Essays
on Middle English Literature* (Oxford, 1955).

[9] Arthur O. Lovejoy and George Boas, *Primitivism and Related Ideas in Antiquity:
Contributions to the History of Primitivism*, vol. 1 (Baltimore, Md., 1935); Richard Bernheimer, *Wild Men in the Middle Ages* (Cambridge, Mass., 1952).

[10] Among the many relevant studies of Spenser, I have found the following particularly valuable: Thomas P. Harrison, Jr., 'Aspects of Primitivism in Shakespeare
and Spenser', *Texas Studies in English*, 20 (1940), 39–71; Roy Harvey Pearce, 'Primitivistic Ideas in the *Faerie Queene*', *JEGP*, 44 (1945), 139–51; Donald Cheney, *Spenser's
Image of Nature* (New Haven, Conn., 1966); William Nelson, *The Poetry of Edmund
Spenser* (New York, 1963).

these functions is peculiar to pastoral. The first shades into satire, the second into romance.[11]

The characteristic dynamic of pastoral satire is contrast—city versus country, art versus nature, duty versus pleasure. Such a medium appealed strongly to the Renaissance imagination, so accustomed to viewing the world in terms of paradox. The characteristic dynamic of pastoral romance, however, is quite different: it is retreat—withdrawal into an enclosed and perfect world. It expresses itself in terms of circles, of enclosed paradises, sacred areas cut off from the outside world.

These two devices are not mutually exclusive. Pastoral satire depends on an awareness of the virtues of the pastoral existence, while pastoral romance at least presupposes the existence elsewhere of urban and courtly corruption. Most pastoral works involve a combination of satiric and romantic ingredients, some leaning towards the former and some towards the latter.

The pastoral world which we meet in satire is generally separated from court and city spatially rather than temporally. Incursions from the outside remind its inhabitants and its transient guests of the shortcomings and failings of urban living, and of the cares and tribulations of governors and men of affairs. But this country of beautiful landscape and simple emotions often has an air of fantasy—a retreat into the imagination rather than an escape to the country. While it is constantly susceptible to attacks from outside, or to the emotional upheavals and tragedies of sexual love, it often serves as its own justification: less emphasis is put upon external evils, and more upon internal strengths. We might go so far as to say that the pastoral *world* (as opposed to pastoral *works*, which are often concerned with the disintegration of this world) is based upon the idea of sexual innocence. Here a temporal element enters in, because such a setting suggests make-believe and childhood and growing up. This temporal element, less apparent in satiric pastoral, is conveyed principally through imagery of the Golden Age. Golden Age and pastoral are not the same thing, because the one is a myth, an idea, whereas the other is principally a mode of thought and a way of writing. Nevertheless, the stronger the temporal pull and the less the emphasis on spatial removal and external dangers, the more the pastoral *world* becomes synonymous with the Golden *Age*. The Golden Age

[11] See Frye, *Anatomy*, p. 151.

looks back to an ideal past long ago, when cities were unknown and nature was kind.[12] In pastoral works, this collective historical myth often becomes a model for the past of the individual, and mankind's descent into the barbarism of the Iron Age is paralleled by the individual's growth to manhood.

Yet ambiguity lies at the very heart of the pastoral vision. Sexual innocence, strangely, is preserved by remaining loyal to natural process, to Artemis and to Pan. The pastoral satirist tells us that sexual experience does not unite us with natural process but separates us from it because it introduces the pangs of longing and the lack of completeness implied in human love. While some writers of pastoral romance deny this, others remind us that the innocence of the morning of our lives is replaced not only by the tragedy of adulthood but also by its heroism.

In the contrast of innocence and heroism we find a paradigm of the poet's career, at least as the Renaissance conceived it. To speak of Nature and Art and of worlds of the imagination is to remind ourselves that pastoral often has poetry itself as its subject. Even the tradition of the eclogue, associated above all with satire, embodies this interest from the very beginning. The seventh *Idyll* of Theocritus, while it contrasts country innocence and city dissension, pure love and imperfect love, is also an allegory of poetic inspiration and poetic creation.[13] The same is in some measure true of Virgil's *Eclogues*, and of course forms a central unifying theme in Spenser's own *Shepheardes Calender*, which chronicles the growth of a poet's mind even as it satirizes the shortcomings of his own era.[14]

The *Shepheardes Calender*, organized according to the circle of the year as well as the progress of the poet, combines contrast and circularity in a subtle unity. A work like Longus's prose romance *Daphnis and Chloe*, ancestor of Renaissance pastoral, goes further than Spenser or Theocritus in emphasizing circularity. While the *Idylls* depend in some measure on the contrast of

[12] The archaic element in pastoral is most notable in its language. See, for example, Veré L. Rubel, *Poetic Diction in the English Renaissance* (New York, 1941). Cf. Emma Field Pope, 'Renaissance Criticism and the Diction of *The Faerie Queene*', *PMLA*, 41 (1926), 575-620; Veselin Kostić, 'Spenser and the Bembian Linguistic Theory', *English Miscellany*, 10 (1959), 43-60.

[13] See Gilbert Lawall, *Theocritus' Coan Pastorals* (Washington, D.C., 1967), especially pp. 74-117.

[14] See, for example, Isabel G. MacCaffrey, 'Allegory and Pastoral in "The Shepheardes Calender"', *ELH*, 36 (1969), 88-109.

two geographical locations, the setting of Longus's romance is single. The pirates are not a *part* of the universe of Daphnis and Chloe any more than the Brigands are a part of the ideal world in which Pastorella moves. At the centre of this universe, an inner circle set within it, is a sacred spot. The perceptive scholar Walter Davis, who sees Longus's work as the precursor of Renaissance pastoral romance, explains its topography in this way:

The scene of *Daphnis and Chloe* . . . contains . . . a supernatural center and two surrounding areas. At the center stands the Cave of the Nymphs which is to play such a large part in the story of Daphnis and Chloe, from their discovery as infants there to their final marriage and consummation there. The region around this cave, which is the scene of most of the action, is the pastoral land. . . . Beyond these fields lies the great world of Lesbos and the sea. . . . As the geographical rhythm of the individual incidents, each driving toward the supernatural center of the land, implies, the over-all action of *Daphnis and Chloe* records a coming into harmony with the forces of nature—specifically, the accordance of two children with the force of Eros, Lord of the earth, the animals, and men . . . and all that implies about maturity and truth to one's self and nature. Therefore the plot records the growth of the two children toward sexual maturity and true identity, and envelops it in the rhythm of two seasonal cycles separated by a long winter.[15]

Here is pastoral in its romantic aspect, in which the powers of nature are finally vindicated and the transition from innocence to sexuality successfully achieved. There are similar devices at work in Renaissance pastoral romance—Sannazaro's *Arcadia* (1502) for instance, and Sidney's work of the same name. In fact one of the most remarkable features of Renaissance literary history is the emergence of a kind of universal pastoral plot, and, along with this plot, a set of standard pastoral themes and preoccupations. They remain more or less constant throughout the Renaissance.[16]

---

[15] Walter R. Davis and Richard A. Lanham, *Sidney's Arcadia* (New Haven, Conn., 1965), pp. 32–34.

[16] See n. 27 below. With equal justification one might make lists of the themes and devices used by pastoral satirists in the Renaissance, and find that they too are constantly repeated from one work to the next. Here it would be helpful to distinguish between georgic and bucolic poetry, the first being poetry of retreat pure and simple, and the second being pastoral proper—concerned with sheep and shepherds, perhaps with fishing, and all for the purpose of comparing court and country by creating a fictional world of imaginary characters. Georgic poetry claims truth for itself: bucolic poetry does not. It will be clear that there is an element of allegory

Theocritus's seventh *Idyll*, with its journey to the harvest feast at Phrasidamus's farm, preserves the satiric and romantic side by side. The festival involves a penetration from the city to the heart of the country (our own idiom preserves the sense perfectly) even as it contrasts city ways and country ways. The fact that Theocritus uses pastoral to talk about poetry is of the utmost importance, because it suggests a rather different way of viewing the pastoral tradition, not only in the classical period but in the Renaissance too—as a means for articulating a metaphor of poetic experience (and one thinks, among other more modern authors, of Wordsworth's landscape in 'Tintern Abbey', or Hopkins's 'inscape', or the poetry of Robert Frost).[17]

Though pastoral was traditionally considered the least of the kinds,[18] its allegorical tendencies widened the area open to its practitioner. Virgil's Fourth, 'Messianic', Eclogue, for example, employs an elevated tone quite different from anything in Theocritus, and later poets were to make it a precedent for similarly elevated passages in their own pastorals. Spenser's November eclogue, after Marot, is such an example. Not only was an elevated style thus justified, but descriptions of the Golden Age might take on Christian connotations. Renato Poggioli argues, with some justification, that the pastoral pursuit of pleasure and the Christian pursuit of active virtue are in direct opposition to one another.[19] Nevertheless pastoral imagery is abundantly employed in the teachings and ceremonies of the Church. Christ as the Lamb of God, as the Good Shepherd, the humble shepherds who are the first to hear of Christ's birth; pastors, the bishop's crosier—all these are founded upon, or give significance to, this same metaphor. What is more, the history of pastoral is studded with attempts to bring the classical and Christian traditions into alignment; Milton's *Nativity Ode* is one example of this persistent theme. Of course, the bucolic strain in Christianity is only one aspect of a highly complex and often paradoxical set of religious metaphors: the shepherds' news of the Messiah must be balanced

in the latter. Upland and lowland shepherds stand for types of churchmen, oaks and briars for age and youth or for conservatism and change, and so on. This element is not present in georgic poetry, or at least not in so pronounced a form.

[17] See John B. Van Sickle's perceptive remarks, 'Is Theocritus a Version of Pastoral?' *MLN*, 84 (1969), 942–6.

[18] See Kermode, *English Pastoral Poetry*, pp. 29ff.

[19] In 'The Oaten Flute'.

against the passivity of the flock before its pastor—recognition
of the peasant's humanity is counterbalanced by preaching his
obligation to strict and uncomplaining obedience.[20] But the
Christian use of pastoral motifs is no tunlike Spenser's pastoral in
Book VI: it forms a metaphorical bridge between the passive and
the active, between security and challenge, between obedience
and leadership. It is easy to see how pastoral may reflect and
characterize social movements, and how a history of pastoral
would have to take into consideration social as well as literary
history.[21]

This Christian element in pastoral explains why Spagnuoli,
Shakespeare's 'old Mantuan', chose the eclogue as a vehicle to
attack church abuses, and why this theme is so dominant in the
Shepheardes Calender. But Spenser's most elaborate use of satiric
pastoral is in *Colin Clouts Come Home Again*. The poem's wide-
eyed rustics are so naïve that the narrator must expatiate at
length upon the glories and shortcomings of the court. The
glories centre round Cynthia herself: 'But if I her like ought on
earth might read, / I would her lyken to a crowne of lillies, / Upon
a virgin brydes adorned head' (336–8). Beside this picture of an
ideal perfection, of which the imagery, be it noted, is drawn from
natural phenomena, is set the highly artificial courtier bathing in
love, so-called, up to his ears:

> For either they be puffed up with pride,
> Or fraught with envie that their galls do swell,
> Or they their dayes to ydlenesse divide,
> Or drownded lie in pleasures wastefull well,
> In which like Moldwarps nousling still they lurke,
> Unmyndfull of chiefe parts of manlinesse,
> And do themselves for want of other worke,
> Vaine votaries of laesie love professe,
> Whose service high so basely they ensew,

[20] In this religious context pastoralism is also associated with an ideal past. The
next major event after the Fall is the death of the shepherd Abel at the hands of
Cain. Symbolically, the pastoral life goes the way of Paradise itself, destroyed by
man's pride and aggression. See Hallett Smith, *Elizabethan Poetry*, pp. 3–4.

[21] William Empson touches on such matters in passing, in *Some Versions of
Pastoral*. Cf. Maren-Sofie Røstvig, *The Happy Man* (Oslo, 1954–8); Renato Poggioli,
'Naboth's Vineyard, or the Pastoral View of the Social Order', *JHI*, 24 (1963),
3–24; A. J. Sambrook, 'The English Lord and the Happy Husbandman' ,*SVEC*, 57
(1967), 1357–75, etc.

That *Cupid* selfe of them ashamed is,
And mustring all his men in *Venus* vew,
Denies them quite for servitors of his.   (759-70)

This passage is particularly interesting, since it gives some clue
about Spenser's intention regarding Cupid in Book VI: he later
goes on to an elaborate defence of Cupid as the servant and son of
Venus. The vain courtiers are the counterparts of the cannibals
and their love is in reality no love at all. But more immediately
pertinent is the fact that in this poem, as in the proem to Book VI,
there are once again three points of reference: the Queen, her vain
courtiers (not all her courtiers are vain) and the shepherds. The
shepherds, representatives of Nature, form one side of the pair of
opposites necessary to the function of satire, the opposite extreme
being occupied by the vain courtiers. But the poet's panegyric of
love rises far above this satiric distinction, and the shepherds
become honest through uncomprehending servants of a natural
power clearly operating in the court as well—among the loyal
followers of Cynthia. Fused with the satiric is the romantic.

We can trace a similar process on a smaller scale in *Prothalamion*,
where an initial antithesis of court and nature is reconciled
through the symbol of the Thames, flowing from flowery
meadows through the centre of London on its way to the sea,
and carrying the two swans, who are both swans and brides, to
their courtier husbands. The one discordant element, the poet's
own misfortune at the court, is swept aside by this stately hymn
of joy, but serves as a reminder of the satiric potential of Spenser's
lines. In Spenser's finest pastoral, the two aims of the mode—
satire and romance—both receive their attention, and sometimes
the first is subsumed beneath the second.

Prothalamion is concerned principally with effecting a resolution,
not with pointing up antagonisms. It shares this purpose with the
pastoral elegy, a genre whose beginnings lie with Theocritus but
which especially caught the imagination of the Renaissance.[22]
The pastoral elegy begins with antagonism but ends with resolution, begins by emphasizing the poet's isolation not only from his
fellow men, but also from the natural world (note, here also, the

[22] See Thomas P. Harrison, Jr., ed. *The Pastoral Elegy* (Austin, Tex., 1939);
C. A. Patrides, ed. *Milton's 'Lycidas': the Tradition and the Poem* (New York, 1961);
Erwin Panofsky, '*Et in Arcadia Ego*: Poussin and the Elegiac Tradition', in *Meaning
in the Visual Arts* (Garden City, N.Y., 1955).

essentially triangular organization), and ends by drawing all three together in harmony. Crucial to the elegy is, of course, nostalgia: it is a paradigm of the loss of innocence.

I mention the elegy because it provides a suitable point of entry to Spenser's Book VI, which also uses devices both to emphasize antagonism between court and country and to under-line their reconciliation. In an earlier chapter I suggested that the movement of the poem up to the end of Canto viii is principally linear, and I pointed out how the antagonism of court and country is continually before our eyes. Characters retreat into the country-side to escape the evils of court life, or the artificial conventions of degree, or they retire after a life of heroic endeavour. Others preserve in their persons standards of courteous behaviour scarcely known even in the court—like the Salvage Man. In Book VI, as in the *Prothalamion* and elsewhere, we found a triangular set of forces: true court, false court, nature.

But I went on to explain that in Canto ix the linear movement is replaced with a circular movement, epitomized in the garland associated with Pastorella. Pastorella is surrounded by swains, the Graces dance in the midst of the hundred maidens, Mount Acidale is in the midst of the shepherds' world. A motif already given incidental expression in earlier episodes here becomes dominant: this is the motif of the intrusion. Calidore intrudes on the shepherds; he intrudes on the dancers. But in this final intrusion, this pushing through to the Centre, he is given new strength and courage by being made witness to the mystery of courtesy itself. Clearly in these cantos the topography and the poetic principles are those described by Davis: concentric circles, and a 'supernatural centre'.

To talk of circles replacing lines is to talk in very general terms. In fact, Canto ix begins with the machinery of satire. Meliboe's speech on the court brings home to us the contrast of court and country very clearly. But the contrast is swept away by the vision on Mount Acidale. In the same fashion, motifs familiar to pastoral romance (incursions by tigers for example) are not confined to the ninth and tenth cantos. Nevertheless, this broad distinction holds good. Spenser moves from contrast to resolution and, in the final two cantos, seeks to apply his resolution to the world of here-and-now.

2. Pastoral positive: revitalization

Spenser perceived the function of pastoral very clearly, articulating this function in the opening of the proem. Although his words there are directly inspired by his idea of Faeryland, they apply equally to all imaginary realms of romance where standards are simplified, issues made clear and oppositions eliminated. What makes no sense in the complicated realm of day-to-day living suddenly fits together when acted out against a moral background where right is right, and recognizably so. As the great flaw in the everyday world, the great universal problem, is the problem of evil, so in pastoral it is possible to present a universe at least partly purged of evil and hence of contradictions. Where evil exists, it is externalized, as bears or tigers or bandits.

William Empson, in his study of pastoral, makes this general observation his starting-point, though he interprets it in a somewhat special way. Empson's versions of pastoral include not only pastoral romance but a number of other types of literature and literary devices involving an ambivalence, or movement between two planes of action which in some magical way reinforce one another. In pastoral the rich come into contact with the poor in a kind of reciprocal relationship. The rich bestow a certain power upon the poor, and the poor reinforce the social superiority of the rich by purifying their actions. To glorify the virtues of the simple life gives the patrician a licence to continue living exactly as he was before. The magic lies in the fact that the qualities most associated with the court turn up in the pastoral world apparently the characteristics of life according to nature—only to be transferred to the court through a magical discovery. Pastorella, courtesy personified, seems to belong to nature, but in fact she belongs to the court all the time; she has been temporarily transplanted into the shepherds' world. Her aloofness to Coridon's advances is therefore not misplaced pride (which should be struck down as a violation of the natural order), but a kind of subconscious awareness that despite her circumstances and upbringing she *really is* socially superior. Thus, what might seem a vice is actually a virtue. Here, there is a clear contrast with Mirabella, who rebuffs her suitors even though she is on an equal (or even inferior) social footing with them. Mirabella's behaviour shows an inability to perceive the need for social cohesion, and she is violently punished for it. Pastorella, on the other hand, may *appear* to defy social distinctions in her attraction to Calidore, but she is actually supporting them. In fact, since she loves Calidore and Calidore loves her in spite of themselves, and despite Calidore's truancy from his quest, the effect of their love, once her social status becomes known, is to reaffirm the natural foundation of social distinctions, and to bring passion and social order into harmony.

Pastoral, here as everywhere, reinforces a social structure which must have looked a little rickety in places by Spenser's day. The Elizabethan interest in pastoral can be partially explained in precisely these terms. As we have observed, the old social distinctions of the period before 1485, based above all on a man's ability to defend himself, were supplanted in the sixteenth century by less tangible indicators—wealth, administrative ability, native intelligence. The whole style of living changed as the century progressed. Students of domestic architecture will point out to us that the larger houses of the sixteenth century place less emphasis on the hall, where master and servant shared their meals and in earlier years most of their domestic life. The master and his family begin to move to upstairs apartments, sitting rooms and the like, while the servants move back towards the kitchens. These spatial distinctions replace the old distinctions based on strength; for the first time in English history, the country enters on a period of prolonged peace; battlements and towers are demolished, and replaced with long windows giving on to the Elizabethan countryside.[23] At the same time men look to the arts for the sense of assurance, the confirmation, of their social status. Pastoral reflects this need. Its workings suggest that the natural world itself approves and reinforces the social hierarchy: for all that it may look otherwise, the social system *is* rooted in natural laws. The anxieties and doubts of its readers are mirrored in the structure of romance, but then dispelled. Disguises, sexual confusions, a distinct air of revolution in the hobnobbing of aristocrat and peasant—these resolve themselves as if by miracle into a conclusion which restates the social order. Such devices are never far away in the *Faerie Queene*. They become the central principle in Book VI.

[23] See John Buxton, *Elizabethan Taste* (London, 1963); Muriel St. Clare Byrne, *Elizabethan Life in Town and Country*, rev. edn. (London, 1954).

It is reasonable to argue that the quest theme, the heroic mode, is the main ordering principle in Spenser's poem. As such, it is a metaphor for the ordering principle of virtue which Spenser discerns in his own society. Where the quest is threatened, the principle of virtue is threatened. Calidore's decision to remain among the shepherds, his apparent agreement with Meliboe's rhetoric, therefore seems to strike at the very heart of the virtuous order of Book vi. Only with Calidore's resumption of his heroic role does the quest resume. The truth is, of course, that Calidore is never really convinced of the rightness of the shepherds' way of life: he is far more interested in Pastorella. But while the action is going on we can never be totally *sure* of this. In fact the one conviction we are likely to have about Calidore by this stage is that despite appearances he is a rather limited kind of hero, likely to make mistakes. Ultimately, though, we come to understand unequivocally that Meliboe inhabits a dream world—his dreams as well as ours. Spenser gives the lie to the pastoral world in the final cruel and unforgettable emblem of the cowardly Coridon driving his sheep out into the desolated countryside where the shepherds once dwelt.

Doesn't all this add up to an indictment of the life according to nature? Not entirely. One essential element from the pastoral world—Pastorella—is preserved. Preserved, too, is the transcendent vision, set in the centre of this episode, in which court and country, all of nature and all of art, come together. Though peasants ultimately prove merely peasants, they unwittingly pass on to society a truth, a talisman—the Dance and the noble shepherdess Pastorella. It may well be that Calidore's truancy *seems* to undermine the very fabric of the Legend of Courtesy (here lies our anxiety), but the dance of the Graces, orderly, controlled, and symbolic, shores it up (here lies the miracle). The change from the image of the garland to the image of the precious stones and a crown of stars is significant: the first implies pastoral equality, but the image that replaces it implies sovereignty and hierarchy. The delicate movement from one to the other is, as it were, poetic proof that hierarchy is derived from nature, sovereignty from natural order. Calidore's problem, of course, is to bring this vision back to the world. The dance is distanced from ourselves, on the other side of Faeryland, beyond the shepherds' world. It is also halfway to heaven—the topmost point in the realm of matter, where matter resolves itself into spirit. To bring the standards set forth in this Golden World back to the lowly corrupted world of 1596, Spenser must not only employ the process of discovery normal in pastorals, but also make the heroine's captivity infernal and her rescuer a combination of Hercules and Paris. Calidore throws off his disguise and emerges as the most skilled knight of them all, as the narrator declared he was in the first place; Pastorella passes through a symbolic period of suffering for the shortcomings of the court, and her rescue reaffirms the strength of social distinctions and the need for suffering in a heroic world.

Yet behind this reassertion of the heroic there lies a vision which has, on the face of it, little to do with chivalric endeavour. Mount Acidale presents a world of perfect order, visible only to the poet and the seer. The Golden World gives us a vision of order which transcends both court and country—and which unites them, as it were, in a single supreme emblem. The emblem of Mount Acidale is really the concretization of an idea lurking in the back of Spenser's mind throughout the *Faerie Queene*—poetry as order, the true poet as the orderer and shaper of a universe. This explains Spenser's constant interest in poetic *topoi*, and in the function of metaphor and image. When Redcross and Una wander into the wood of Error, the catalogue of trees does more than remind *us* that this is a poem; it *should* remind Redcross that the beauty of his surroundings may be a treacherous fiction. When Belphoebe bursts in on Braggadocchio and Trompart, in Book II, it is, we discovered, as though she has burst the confines of the Book III to which she belongs. As for her twin sister, her troubles with Busyrane spring from an inability to understand metaphor— a failing which is satirized also in the proem to Book II. Malbecco changes levels of reality when he changes from a jealous *man* into Jealousy itself.

Such preoccupations come to the fore in Book VI, announced in the proem. Faeryland, we are told, is a creation of the poet. Earlier pastoralists had sometimes set themselves in their own works—as Philisides, or Sincero.[24] Spenser merely carries this a

---

[24] See Edwin Greenlaw, *Variorum*, 6: 371–6; T. P. Harrison, Jr., *Variorum*, 6: 379–81. There are instances of the author appearing as a minor character also in medieval French romance: see Jessie L. Weston, *From Ritual to Romance* (Cambridge, 1920), p. 189.

stage further by affirming what these other writers had hinted at: the world of perfect forms is the creation (or discovery) of the poet. It is *poetry* which strengthens and revives and purifies society. Colin's position in the *pastoral* world is a respected one, but in the *Golden* World he sustains the very universe.

But the tragedy of Book VI is that in some measure Calidore's quest fails. Scandal lives on and the poet is powerless to stop it. It is the great tragedy of poetry, the tragedy inherent in the myth of Orpheus; at the moment when his superhuman efforts seem at last close to success, when Eurydice is almost within reach of the rays of sunlight shining across the entrance to the underworld, the Poet looks back and she recedes into the darkness. In the parallel myth of Proserpine Spenser provides an optimistic alternative to the Orpheus story, but it offers but temporary respite.

Although the conclusion to his story is in part pessimistic, Spenser does provide a vision of social and natural order in the Dance of the Graces. The imagery of the book, with its garlands and flowers, receives its ultimate logical embodiment in the dance, based on the circular and hierarchical character of the natural world. It implies that nature *has* a pattern, which in turn implies that society has a pattern. Spenser's extensive examination of nature spills over into the early cantos as well as occurring in the shepherds' country—thereby implying that the pastoral proper is only one part of a much more broadly based investigation of the nature of nature. This possibility is reinforced by the fact that the machinery of the pastoral romance—the incidents which are a traditional part of the genre—is likewise scattered throughout the book, not confined to the shepherds' episode. These departures from the norm, coupled with the mythological ambiguity lying behind the work, raise questions about the generic character of Book VI. Can it be regarded as a heroic romance pure and simple, or has Spenser somehow changed his terms, making the Legend of Courtesy different from the books which precede it?

3. Calidore's truancy

The question of the character of Book VI has been an indirect concern of much of the present study. But we need now to confront directly the significance of Calidore's stay among the shepherds, surely the episode which will most determine any generic classification of the work as a whole. Should it be regarded as a pastoral episode quite separate from the main business of the book—in fact as a dereliction of knightly duty—or should we react to Calidore's abandonment of his quest in some other less disapproving manner?

Spenser's attitude to primitivism throughout the *Faerie Queene* can hardly be regarded as straightforward. The work depends upon a certain dissatisfaction with the world of here-and-now and a reaching back into a past known for heroic endeavour, noble sentiments, and a sense of destiny. The sixteenth-century social order is brought into critical contrast with the imagined order of bygone ages, through the metaphor of chivalry which forms the basis of the work and through a kind of linguistic primitivism,[25] coupled with a curious quality of space and time, which makes the poem read like a heroic romance not merely of the past but of all time.

The contrast between the present order and the past, between the corrupt morals of Elizabethan England and the romantic precision with which moral dilemmas are presented in the antique models of castles and gardens and temples, does not in itself call the idea of social order into question: it is perfectly reconcilable with the basic premiss of chivalric romance, that the values of human society are discoverable within the social order itself. But beginning with Book III, a rather different range of associations is brought into play. The emphasis on the cycle of generation, made explicit in the chivalric narrative through its female hero, does suggest an attempt to define the relationship between society and nature, and between human time (or history) and natural time (or generation). Book V, though it works out the story of Britomart, returns somewhat to the earlier pattern, its main emblems of justice being buildings, Isis Church and the Court of Mercilla, not locations outside the range of human history (as the Garden of Adonis was). The Court of Mercilla, a fictional representation of Elizabeth's own court, moves the antique model very close to the contemporaneity of sixteenth-century England. Spenser takes such contrasting parallels a stage further in Book VI, proposing two courts in the book's proem,

[25] The term is Rosemond Tuve's, 'Ancients, Moderns and Saxons', *ELH*, 6 (1939), 165–90.

one perfect and the other imperfect, though it is hard to tell
whether this perfect court still exists or not.

But Book VI also adds a third frame of reference, the natural
world. Earlier books defined such qualities as Holiness in an evil
world, Justice in a world no longer just, Temperance in moral
surroundings posing a constant threat. Book VI, however, by
examining Courtesy examines the foundations of society itself,
not some element within society. Hardly surprisingly, the book
finds its point of contrast *outside* society. As we have already
discovered, this implies a rather different relationship with the
natural world from that customary in heroic romance. The
beautiful paradises of Boiardo, Ariosto, or Tasso, like those of
the great classical epics, are sinister fictions created to deflect the
hero from his quest or his responsibilities. But side by side with
these epic narratives we do find a commingling of heroic and
pastoral in several Renaissance romances, like Montemayor's
Diana and Sidney's *Arcadia*, and here the relative values of the
two attitudes are much harder to assess. Undoubtedly Book VI
is heavily indebted to Sidney—just how indebted still remains to
be established.[26] But Spenser goes beyond Sidney in emphasizing
the positive aspects of the courtly world, and he seems more
interested than his predecessor in spelling out the qualities which
he finds in pastoral. Unlike Sidney and (especially) unlike Shakespeare in the romances, he is describing a specific virtue much
of which can be, and had been, perfectly clearly defined in a
simple unmagical prose.

The attitude towards Calidore's stay among the shepherds is
not that of a Boiardo or an Ariosto. Calidore's abandonment of
his quest is carefully prepared for in a series of semi-pastoral
episodes earlier in the book. In fact, the motifs of pastoral
romance begin in the very first cantos, with the introduction of
Tristram.[27] Tristram belongs to heroic romance, but he is

---

[26] The only extensive study of the subject is H. C. Chang, *Allegory and Courtesy
in Spenser* (Edinburgh, 1955), pp. 114–51. See also Greenlaw, *Variorum*, 6: 371–6.

[27] On the background and sources of these motifs, see Greenlaw, *Variorum*, 6:
371–6; Merritt Y. Hughes, *Variorum*, 6: 376–9; Harrison, *Variorum*, 6: 379–81;
Gilbert Highet, *The Classical Tradition* (London, 1949), pp. 162–77; Dorothy
Atkinson, 'The Pastorella Episode in *The Faerie Queene*', *PMLA*, 59 (1944), 361–72;
Walter F. Staton, Jr., 'Italian Pastorals and the Conclusion of the Serena Story',
SEL, 6 (1966), 35–42. One element typical of such works which Spenser avoids is
the complicated love situation, so notable a feature of Tasso's *Aminta*, Montemayor's
Diana, Sidney's *Arcadia*, and such later versions of the same basic plot as Fletcher's

insulated from the chivalric world until the completion of his (pastoral) education. Calidore's defence of Aladine and Priscilla symbolizes his limited espousal of pastoral values: as Poggioli points out, 'Love was born free but family and society hold that winged creature in a gilded cage. Often pastoral poetry is but a voice of protest against society's power to replace the fruitions with the frustrations of love.'[28] The story of Pastorella's parents of course constitutes Calidore's vindication and demonstrates triumphantly the poet's observation that 'a little well is given that gaineth more withal'.

We are introduced to another child in, if not of, the natural world—Matilda's babe. He, too, may grow up to be a great hero, but he may also grow up to be a philosopher—our first reminder that there is more than the simple Choice of Hercules, for there exists also the Way of Contemplation, an essential part of pastoral. In the episode of Matilda we find a riddling prophecy, and we have already met a wild man. Soon we shall meet a Hermit, who also emphasizes the value of the contemplative life, demonstrating its application to the active life in his disinterested advice to Timias and Serena. Such figures are pastoral figures, but they possess qualities which may revive and strengthen society. And, while on the subject of pastoral motifs, is it mere coincidence that Matilda's namesake was she who showed Dante the Earthly Paradise?

The 'forest figures' occupy the central episodes of Spenser's book, when Calidore is absent. Clearly, the earlier episodes set up the virtue of courtesy in society's terms—more or less within the frame of reference of heroic romance. The central episodes, however, define courtesy from first principles, by presenting, on the one hand, forest figures to whom courtesy comes not as a set of chivalric rules but naturally, and, on the other hand, aberrations like Turpine, Mirabella, and the cannibals. Although Calepine ultimately asserts his knighthood, these episodes present what is essentially the pastoral view—the assumption that

---

Faithful Shepherdess. On its implications see Margaret Schlauch, *Antecedents of the English Novel 1400–1600* (Warsaw and Oxford, 1963), pp. 176–81. Cf. Poggioli, 'The Pastoral of the Self'. See also Bruce W. Wardropper, 'The *Diana* of Montemayor: Revaluation and Interpretation', *SP*, 48 (1951), 126–44. This fascinating and important article raises a number of questions relevant to Book vi.
[28] 'The Oaten Flute', p. 158.

virtue lies not in society but in the natural world. Only when we are thoroughly acquainted with these 'pastoral' standards does Spenser place heroic and pastoral values in direct confrontation by bringing Calidore, representative of the quest for the Blatant Beast (challenger of the standards already extant, though assailed, in the court), back into his story and into a world of pastoral romance.

The fact that five cantos or more prior to Canto ix have been taken up with the definition of a possible alternative set of values to those of heroic romance, and the obvious approbation with which Spenser treats the various forest folk, make it quite clear that Calidore's truancy is no simple and automatically culpable neglect of a quest, in favour of a life of love and pleasure. This is not a representation of the clearcut issues of the Choice of Hercules. Such a view ignores the evidence, is based on a mis-understanding of the function of pastoral in Book vi and smacks of the 'mellifluous' school of Spenserian criticism which sees Spenser's high seriousness as constantly threatened by the sheer beauty of his own poetry.[29] Calidore's retreat into a pastoral world is not a simple retreat into a world of the senses—as was Guyon's enticement by Mirth or Rinaldo's by Armida—but a movement through a further circle and into the central circle of contemplation. Above all, a voluntary return then takes place, an unusual feature of truancy, especially when the return involves dragging along the supposed enchantress herself.

Even Calidore needs to be instructed in courtesy. The problem of how to behave in society cannot be resolved without stepping outside it. Yet discourtesy (the Beast) can be fought only *within* society. Although Calidore abandons his quest, although at first sight this abandonment points to a culpable truancy, we have to face the fact that the Dance of the Graces teaches Calidore what courtesy really is. If Mount Acidale is the key to Spenser's con-ception of courtesy, the Knight of Courtesy is hardly truant in lingering there. Nevertheless, his stay *does* involve an abandon-ment of the quest. Though the beauties of Pastorella may exceed those of a corrupt and unrewarding court, and though the natural

---

[29] For a rather extreme statement of this view ('The conflict between the *dulce* and the *utile* went deep into Spenser's heart') see J. W. Saunders, 'The Façade of Morality', in William R. Mueller and Don Cameron Allen, ed., *That Soueraine Light* (Baltimore, Md., 1952), pp. 1–34, esp. pp. 23–4.

world may have more to offer than the courtly, there remains the fact that the Blatant Beast is free to wreak havoc where he will, and Calidore's responsibility to the Faerie Queene stays neglected.

> Who now does follow the foule *Blatant Beast*,
> Whilest *Calidore* does follow that faire Mayd,
> Unmyndfull of his vow and high beheast,
> Which by the Faery Queene was on him layd?
>
> (VI. x. 1)

In this limited context the conclusion seems obvious. It is essentially the conclusion to which J. C. Maxwell comes in his short but important essay on the subject:[30] the pastoral world and the heroic world are irreconcilable. Paris is directly opposed to Hercules: the Way of Pleasure is opposed to the Active Life. If we do not take into consideration the Golden World of Mount Acidale, Calidore's stay with the shepherds is a truancy pure and simple.

But of course we *must* take this episode (which follows immediately) into consideration. On Mount Acidale Calidore witnesses a vision which takes him beyond the Choice of Hercules, to a reconciliation of the opposition between Action and Pleasure which both equips him for the struggle against the Blatant Beast and demonstrates in a definitive manner that Book VI is not an ordinary heroic romance. And to prove it, there is of course Pastorella herself, whose magic is brought back to society by a revitalized Calidore.

To be sure, Calidore is a bungler. His intrusion on Calepine and Serena, for example, destroys the harmony between them and forms a minor emblem of the Fall. When he abandons his quest, that too constitutes a kind of Fall. So does his breaking in on the Dance of the Graces.[31] But just as Adam's sin itself may be regarded as a *felix culpa*, so Calidore's bumbling into situations which ostensibly do not concern him ultimately leads to a knowledge of true courtesy.[32]

---

[30] 'The Truancy of Calidore', in Mueller and Allen, ed., *That Soueraine Light*.

[31] See Maurice Evans, 'Courtesy and the Fall of Man', *ES*, 46 (1965), 209–20. In a rather obvious way, Pastorella falls too. There are obvious analogies of sexual experience and the loss of innocence in her capture and imprisonment underground by the Brigands.

[32] See A. C. Hamilton, *The Structure of Allegory in 'The Faerie Queene'* (Oxford, 1961), pp. 203–4.

The episode on Mount Acidale forms the climax of Calidore's education and is therefore an integral part of the preparation for the defeat of the Beast. The fact that it takes place *outside* the quest itself really only tells us something about the nature of heroic romance, not about Calidore's sense of responsibility. Heroic romance is rooted in the active life: it leaves no scope for introspection (witness the failures of Malory's introverted knights). As Calidore tells Crudor, courtesy involves harmony with oneself. And that kind of self-knowledge is not attainable through the quest, for it involves not merely the Active Life but the *triplex vita*, that which the dance itself figures forth. In a sense, Calidore is a better servant of Gloriana for his new-found knowledge; and the vision of the dance unites not only the three ways of the *triplex vita* but all those other dichotomies—Nature and Grace, Art and Nature, Imagination and Politics, Microcosm and Macrocosm—which bewildered and inspired Elizabeth's subjects.[33]

4. *Contemplation into action: withdrawal and return*

The Red Cross Knight, given a vision of the New Jerusalem from the Mount of Contemplation, may not remain forever on the Mount but must return to his task on the plain below and defeat the dragon. Although contemplation may point the way to heaven, matters more earthly must have our attention. So it is with the pastoral world. To withdraw into the world of shepherd swains and fleecy flocks in order to escape one's responsibilities in the outside world is an offence against society. But to withdraw into the pastoral world to gain new strength to deal with the *problems* of the external world is a different matter. Davis has explained this latter process—what he calls the standard pastoral action—in these terms:

Disintegration: the sojourner-hero usually enters the pastoral land from the heroic world under the pressure of some grief or love that has left his mind a set of conflicting emotions he cannot resolve.

[33] On interpretations of the tripartite scheme in relation to the state and to the individual, see Walter Davis's chapter 'Sage Counseling' in Davis and Lanham, *Sidney's 'Arcadia'*. Pastoral romance frequently has overtones of political theory. See Ernest William Talbert's chapter on Sidney in *The Problem of Order* (Chapel Hill, N.C., 1962), and the not wholly fanciful interpretation by Witold Ostrowski, 'A Forgotten Meaning of *The Tempest*', in Stanisław Helsztyński, ed., *Poland's Homage to Shakespeare* (Warsaw, 1965).

Education: once there, he learns certain basic truths that show him how to reconcile his conflicts. He usually does this by a process of *analysis* —by seeing his situation reflected in those of other people around him, and then coming face to face with his own divided mind. . . . *Reintegration*: at the center under the aegis of a god or a magician, he adjusts his conflicts, composes his mind, and leaves for the outer world again. (pp. 38-9)

This, with certain variations, is what happens in Book VI. Calidore's entry into the pastoral world may at first sight seem to be caused not by confusion but by an overpowering certainty— that he loves Pastorella. However, the fact of his love demonstrates his own confusion regarding the purpose and means of his quest and perhaps the nature of the virtue he is supposed to be defending. In the pastoral world he gains the knowledge requisite for the completion of his quest, and, along with it, the power of love to support him and motivate his heroic endeavour.

The 'standard pastoral action' thus describes the transformation into action of the energy latent in nature. The inner workings of nature are the basis, the starting-point, of contemplation. Contemplation supports action, initiates it, and makes it possible. So Plato described it, his philosopher-ruler corresponding to contemplation and his ministers to action. The proper relation of hierarchy to hierarchy in the macrocosm, of king and subject in the social macrocosm, these depend upon the proper translation of contemplation into action, just as it is crucially necessary that the individual be equipped to put his faith into practice, to live his principles, to achieve and communicate. Man is moved to knowledge through pleasure—through the contemplation of beauty and the appreciation of harmony. Pleasure can be said to lead action to contemplation and thus to generate further action. The movement, like the movement of the dance, is circular.

In *A Study of History* Arnold Toynbee describes what he calls the movement of Withdrawal-and-Return, using as his starting-point Plato's famous simile of the Cave (*Republic*, 514A-521C), with its lessons about the difficulty of explaining perfection to those who have never known it, and the pain of abandoning the vision in order to do so:

When Plato has painted the ordeal of the return in these unattractive colours, it is almost startling to find him imposing this ordeal remorselessly on his elect philosophers. If it is essential to the Platonic system that the elect should acquire philosophy, it is equally essential that they should not remain philosophers only. The purpose and meaning of their philosophic enlightenment is that they should ultimately become philosopher-kings. . . . The path which Plato . . . lays down for (them) is unmistakably identical with the path that has been trodden by the Christian mystics. . . . The life of contemplation is placed by Pythagoras above the life of action, as well as above the life of pleasure; and this doctrine runs through the whole Hellenic philosophical tradition. . . . Plato affects to believe that his enlightened philosophers will duly obey and duly consent to take a hand in the work of the world.[34]

The Return is vital: upon its success depends the well-being of society. We might add that in Spenser's case Calidore's return will also determine the well-being of poetry, for the vision which he has beheld is also a vision of the powers of poetry. On Colin's success in enlightening and instructing Calidore depends in large measure his success in the public function of the poet: Calidore is in a sense Colin's public, his imperfect understanding representing the imperfections of every poet's public in every age. Let us not forget that all Elizabethan critics were agreed that poetry was a didactic art.

Mount Acidale may also signal a conflict in Spenser's own mind. C. S. Lewis mentions the possibility of a truancy by *Spenser* only in order to dismiss it,[35] and certainly we should not look on this episode as in any sense a loss of control on the poet's part.[36] But

---

[34] *A Study of History* (London, 1935), 3: 251ff. Cf. St. Mark's description of the Transfiguration, Chapter 9, and see also Spenser's July eclogue.

[35] 'The greatest mistake that can be made about this book is to suppose that Calidore's long delay among the shepherds is a pastoral truancy of Spenser's from his moral intention. . . . The shepherd's country and Mount Acidale in the midst of it are the core of the book, and the key to Spenser's whole conception of courtesy.' (*The Allegory of Love* (Oxford, 1936), p. 350.)

[36] William Nelson's suggestion (*The Poetry of Edmund Spenser* (New York, 1963), pp. 293–4) that Book VI is a 'failure of duty' by Spenser since he gives so little praise to the Queen and chooses to devote his attention to a country lass does not do justice to the complexity of issues here, and may well be a case of allowing our knowledge of his biography to dictate our reading of the poem. Certainly the implication that Spenser, seeing a conflict between London and Ireland, simply threw care to the winds in sensuous abandonment—a view not unusual amongst the 'mellifluous' school of Spenser criticism—is based on a substantial misunderstanding. Harrison (*Variorum*, 6: 242–3) typifies this view: 'Both poets [Sidney and Spenser] held in high contempt the shallowness and indolence of court life and voice frequently the Renaissance ideal of honor. In this regard, perhaps there is a definite parallel in Book VI . . . when Calidore doffs his armor and forgets the quest commanded by Gloriana. He, like Musidorus, assumes the garb and adopts the life of the shepherd with disastrous delay in the accomplishment of his quest. Spenser

Colin's praise of the Queen serves as a reminder that his attentions are mostly elsewhere. In the same way, Spenser himself, in exile self-imposed or made necessary by circumstances (or perhaps even desired—biographers never seem to consider this third possibility), may have felt in his own mind a conflict between his love for Ireland, for the countryside, for retreat, and his loyalty to the Queen.[37] There seems to be a conflict, too, between Spenser-the-poet and Spenser-the-civil-servant, in which the former feels the need to justify the demise of the latter and at the same time to assert the role of the poet not as mere entertainer of monarchs but as image—the voice of his time for all times, and prophet as well as historian. No man made larger claims for poetry in his era.

In one sense the Return is built into the structure of pastoral.

---

obviously censures Sir Calidore's pastoral aberration; yet he, like Sidney, is inclined to paint the rural picture sympathetically. The digression in Spenser's heroic poem affords him opportunity to describe the delightful life and scenes of this fairy Arcadia and again to introduce himself in the role of the shepherd suitor. . . . In the attitude towards such digressions as are pictured in their heroic poems Spenser and Sidney were agreed, as each succumbs for the moment to the charm of pastoral life.' Book vi is not a digression but a redefinition. There is no indication that Calidore's delay is disastrous, nor that Spenser is escaping from the central issue of the book. It is true that there are many points of similarity between Spenser and Sidney, but in Harrison's terms it is actually the differences that are striking. Basilius's retreat is essentially selfish and irresponsible—a truancy pure and simple. But Calidore's is not, for reasons which my argument makes clear. As for the writer's 'succumbing' to the pleasures of the pastoral life, that conclusion is based on the old fallacy that, when a writer writes about something pleasant, his own creation in some way takes control. A particularly erroneous expression of this view occurs in Mark Van Doren's chapter on Spenser in *Mark Van Doren on Great Poems of Western Literature* (New York, 1962). On its history, see William R. Mueller's introduction to *Spenser's Critics: Changing Currents in Literary Taste* (Syracuse, N.Y., 1959).

[37] Of *Colin Clouts Come Home Again*, Nelson (*Poetry of Spenser*, p. 62) writes: 'The sensitive and intelligent man of the Renaissance must always have been ambivalent about the pursuit of a career at court. On the one hand the "disordered thrust" (as Daniel puts it) of ambitious striving was incompatible with contemplative study; on the other, the principal justification of contemplative study was the service it could render to the state.' There remains also the fact that in Book vi Colin Clout is ostensibly praising his mistress as well as the Queen. In fact the two are in a sense one and the same. Nevertheless Frank Kermode (*Selections from the Minor Poems and 'The Faerie Queene'* (London, 1965), p. 223) feels constrained to remark: 'So, Spenser seems to say, his labours on his huge poem were interrupted by the events described in the *Amoretti* and the *Epithalamion*; he himself has been guilty of a pastoral truancy.' To accept this interpretation is to ignore the complexity of the allegory. Yet another variant in this range of opinions is that of Leicester Bradner (*Edmund Spenser and the 'Faerie Queene'* (Chicago, 1948), p. 150): 'The pastoral interlude is not merely a pretty Arcadian idyll, a dereliction from duty put in because Spenser enjoyed it. On the contrary, I think it represents Spenser's final rejection of political ambition and his defense of his retired life as an Irish planter.'

Although, or perhaps because, associated with a nostalgia for the past, for a lost innocence, pastoral frequently has to do with the process of growing up, and the breaking out of the world of childhood. Shakespeare, perhaps taking his cue from Spenser, makes a skilful combination of the two themes of growing up and withdrawal both in the *Winter's Tale* and in the *Tempest*. Pastorella in coming out of the pastoral world is like Amoret leaving the Temple of Venus: the maiden is attaining womanhood, with all the trials and dangers and misgivings which that entails. The descent from innocence to experience may be viewed with regret, yet it is a regret tempered by necessity, and by the feeling of fulfilment, of self-justification, which is the driving force in social action and in the perpetuation of society. Once again, the return to the world of nature is as important as the ascent to the realm of grace: the lines of communication go in both directions.

One cannot emphasize too strongly the importance of action, the active pursuit of virtue, in Book VI; though action too must not be an end in itself.[38] The Graces, with their giving, conversion and return, symbolize the constant exchange between man and his creator, the human end of which process is rooted in action. The whole of Canto xi, the story of Pastorella's return to society, chronicles the difficulties not only of the girl growing to womanhood but also of the process by which the harmony of the universe is applied to man's state. Man's Fall means that this process is not automatic; it is a constant struggle against the evil brought into the world through Adam's sin.

Toynbee points out that the movement of Withdrawal-and-Return is not confined merely to the relationship of human beings to their fellows. The flux and change of nature follows the same pattern: spring, summer, and autumn give way to winter, and then

---

[38] Davis (*Sidney's 'Arcadia'*, pp. 172–3) comes to much the same conclusion about Sidney—that he takes a stand midway between action and contemplation, each requiring the other to make it effective: 'The first problem to arise in Arcadia concerns the adjustment of the claims of the active and the contemplative lives. Should a man choose Pallas Athene or Juno? Does the pursuit of contemplative wisdom necessitate complete abandonment of the world? . . . Must there, in fact, be a choice, or is there possible a harmony of soul which can embrace both? . . . Sidney's position, though it stresses the need for active virtue, indicates a modus vivendi between the two ways of life rather than a rejection of one for the other. His answer is in fact the classical answer: Plato's answer (that the philosopher-king must attain a vision of the Good in order to mold his kingdom actively toward perfection), Macrobius' answer (that he is double blessed who, like Scipio, combines the political virtues with the cleansing virtues), Aristotle's answer, and Lupset's answer.'

spring returns again, in an endless cycle. Indeed, the movement of Withdrawal-and-Return is part and parcel of all activities of the fallen world. It becomes, as do all the major processes connected with human life and environment, mythologized. So the myth of Proserpine expresses the change of the seasons; the many myths of dismemberment and resurrection express this same process in somewhat more abstracted terms. Toynbee reminds us that even the plot material of pastoral is related to this same movement:

One mythical variant of the *motif* is the story of the foundling. A babe born to a royal heritage is cast away in infancy—sometimes (as in the stories of Oedipus and Perseus) by his own father or grandfather who is warned by a dream or an oracle that the child is destined to supplant him; sometimes (as in the story of Romulus) by a usurper, who has killed the babe's father or driven him out and fears lest the babe should grow up to avenge him; and sometimes (as in the stories of Jason and Orestes and Zeus and Horus and Moses and Cyrus) by friendly hands that are concerned to save the babe's life from the villain's murderous design. The next chapter in the story is that the infant castaway is miraculously saved alive. . . . In the third and last chapter the child of destiny—now grown to manhood and wrought to a heroic temper by the hardship through which he has passed—returns in power and glory to enter into his kingdom.[39]

The same motif is expressed through the story of Jesus, through the myth of the Eternal Return, the Second Coming, and the Lost Paradise. In the case of Book VI, the Return, which occupies the closing cantos, is rich in mythological allusion. Some of these myths we have already taken into account—that of Hercules and that of Paris, for instance, but there are others to which we shall shortly turn our attention.

The implications of pastoral are many—as this chapter and previous chapters have shown. Previous discussion revealed that pastoral resolves the opposition between Art and Nature, providing a medium through which this resolution may come about. In this chapter we have seen how it also resolves—through the central Golden World—the opposition of Nature and Grace, the Golden World being the point where the two come together. The idea of Art carries with it connotations of social living, of urban society and civic responsibility, of maturity within society. This is related to the notion of the pastoral world as a place of education,

[39] *A Study of History*, 3: 260.

of perfect patterns of living, and of the lost world of innocent childhood whose memory sustains us in the tribulations of adulthood. Art also means poetry, and Mount Acidale is the world of poetry, of strange and wondrous visions, which revives and strengthens the poet and his public in the workaday world.

The association of pastoral with education reminds us that pastoral is therefore a very suitable mode of expression for a poem whose main purpose is educational. Book vi is, however, a new and important departure from its predecessors, since it implies, more forcefully than any of the previous books, that the simple antagonisms and virtues and battles of heroic romance are inadequate to deal with the complexities of life in society. The values which sustain society, Spenser suggests, are not discoverable within its framework, nor are they the result of some miraculous divine intervention having no bearing on man's environment. In this imperfect world, we must understand and apply the principles underlying nature in our pursuit of grace. Unlike heroic romance, which implies antagonism, pastoral implies reconciliation—and the virtue of courtesy is founded upon reconciliation. Action requires contemplation to direct it, contemplation requires action to apply its standards to society. The process is an unending giving and receiving. The need to step outside society to define social values perhaps points to a complicating influence on Spenser's conception of his work which would have made it difficult for him to proceed further.[40] No longer is man's choice the simple choice of a simple virtue; Book vi deals with the ideal balance between the three Platonic ways of life, and its explanation of the relationship between the Active Life and the other ways for the first time defines the framework of the poem itself—at the same time as it moves beyond, or adds to, that framework.

[40] Hamilton (*Structure of Allegory*, pp. 203–4) sees the episode on Mount Acidale as what he calls the redemption of nature. Whereas the heroes of previous books had fallen, had been fatally drawn aside from their quests, Calidore 'triumphs over his vision'. Hamilton's terms are a little confusing: in point of fact the framework of the episode is different from those in earlier books. But he rightly points out that the Dance of the Graces goes beyond all previous statements of the kind in the other books, and he makes the important observation that Book vi, by including nature in the general framework of the poem, prepares the way for the appearance of the goddess Nature in Book vii. Cf. Richard Neuse, 'Book vi as Conclusion to *The Faerie Queene*', *ELH*, 35 (1968), 329–53.

5. Courtesy regenerate: the myth of Proserpine

The active life is associated with the world of achievement, with an environment in which time and change are dominant factors. Its natural means of expression is the quest theme, or the heroic romance in which nature is cruel and inimical. The contemplative life is associated with changelessness, with an environment in which everything remains the same, whose dominant symbol is the perfect geometrical figure, the circle.[41] It is naturally associated with pastoral, with an unchanging, beneficent nature. This collision of two literary modes, pastoral romance and heroic romance, is, as we have seen, one of the major dynamic forces in Book VI. It is symbolized in the intrusion of the linear active life (Calidore) upon the circular contemplative life of Mount Acidale—a pattern similar to that in the 'Mutabilitie Cantos',[42] where Spenser resolves this collision of forces through the final magnificent speech of the goddess Nature (VII. vii. 58–9), his finest statement on the subject. Symbolic of the resolution of mutability and eternity, of the change of the seasons, are two associated myths, that of the ritual killing as appeasement to the gods, set forth in the myths of Actaeon and Orpheus, and that of death and rebirth, also associated with the Orpheus myth and more particularly with the myth of Proserpine. These myths lie behind the action of Book VI, especially in its final episodes.

We have already seen how the Orpheus myth relates to the situation of Colin Clout in Book VI.[43] The pathos of this myth— the success against overwhelming odds, yet the ultimate failure; the unending power of the song, but the violent death of the poet —this pathos forms a backdrop of contrasts against which the latter part of the book takes place. The dance of the cannibals contrasts with the dance of the Graces, Mount Acidale contrasts with the Brigands' Cave, the restoration of Pastorella with the escape of the Beast. The dance around Serena is an ironic parody of the dance of the Graces, and a reminder, too, of that other

[41] On the symbolism of the circle, see Marjorie Hope Nicolson, *The Breaking of the Circle*, rev. edn. (New York, 1960), pp. 47–80; Alastair Fowler, *Numbers of Time*, pp. 225–6, 265–9; Vincent Foster Hopper, *Medieval Number Symbolism* (New York, 1938), *passim*.

[42] Cf. Frye's suggestive if vague observation (*Anatomy*, p. 140): 'If we "stand back" from Spenser's *Mutabilitie Cantoes*, we see a background of ordered circular light and a sinister black mass thrusting up into the lower foreground.'

[43] See above, pp. 213ff.

aspect of the Orpheus myth, '*Sparagmos*, or the sense that heroism
and effective action are absent, disorganized or foredoomed to
defeat, and that confusion and anarchy reign over the world'.
This, says Northrop Frye, is the archetypal theme of irony and
satire:

The turning of literal act into play is a fundamental form of the
liberalizing of life which appears in more intellectual levels as liberal
education, the release of fact into imagination. It is consistent with this
that the Eucharist symbolism of the apocalyptic world, the metaphorical identification of vegetable, animal, human, and divine bodies,
should have the imagery of cannibalism for its demonic parody.
Dante's last vision of human hell is of Ugolino gnawing his tormentor's
skull; Spenser's last major allegorical vision is of Serena stripped and
prepared for a cannibal feast. The imagery of cannibalism usually
includes, not only images of torture and mutilation, but of what is
technically known as *sparagmos* or the tearing apart of the sacrificial
body, an image found in the myths of Osiris, Orpheus and Pentheus.[44]

Whatever we may feel about Frye's theory of myths in general,
and his habitual confusion about the sequence of events in the
Faerie Queene,[45] his comments here seem helpful. The 'confusion
and anarchy' which he discerns in the cannibals' dance is the polar
opposite of the Dance of the Graces and the return of Pastorella
to society. In these later incidents we surely recognize the archetypal theme of comedy—'recognition of a newborn society rising
in triumph around a still somewhat mysterious hero and his
bride'.[46] The fate of poetry and the poet vacillates between these
two extremes—between dismemberment and victory, between
chaos and glorious order.

But related to, and counterpointing, the myth of Orpheus is the
myth of Actaeon, a myth which finds its first extended treatment
on Mount Acidale in Book VI, and which serves as an important
unifying element when it is used again in the 'Mutabilitie Cantos'.
The story of Faunus is there emblematic of the larger upheaval
in the universe caused by Mutabilitie, but whereas the logic of the
Cantos might call for the destruction of Mutabilitie and the myth
of Actaeon calls for the destruction of its protagonist, Spenser

---

[44] *Anatomy*, p. 148.
[45] See Rudolf B. Gottfried, 'Our New Poet: Archetypal Criticism and *The Faerie
Queene*', PMLA, 83 (1968), 1362–77.
[46] *Anatomy*, p. 192.

chooses another path. Arlo Hill is made desolate and forlorn through Faunus's crime in spying on Diana, and the episode is a kind of Fall:

> No way he found to compasse his desire,
> But to corrupt *Molanna*, this her maid,
> Her to discover for some secret hire:
> So, her with flattering words he first assaid;
> And after, pleasing gifts for her purvaid,
> Queene-apples, and red Cherries from the tree,
> With which he her allured and betraid. (VII. vi. 43)

But the outcome of Faunus's action is comic. Unlike Actaeon, Faunus runs faster than Diana's hounds and escapes, and Molanna, albeit whelmed with stones, marries 'her beloved Fanchin' as a result of the intercessions of Faunus on her behalf. The one total and complete loss is the beauty of Arlo, but the wedding of Molanna and the Fanchin, with its guarantee that life will in consequence go on, mitigates even this loss. Nature will continue, indeed begin, its eternal cycle after the Fall.[47]

The 'Mutabilitie Cantos' form a more satisfying unit than the final cantos of Book VI primarily because the story of Faunus is subservient to the larger overall design of the cantos. But the parallels between Mount Acidale and Arlo Hill are arresting. As we have already noticed, both are paradisal in character. Both involve intrusion from outside upon a supernatural scene. We may feel that Calidore's intrusion has nothing to do with Actaeon, being simply another manifestation of the old and well-worn device of the figure hidden in the forest and spying upon a forbidden or wonderful event—a device widely used in court of love poetry and often representative of human contact with the divine.[48]

[47] On connections between the myths of Orpheus and Actaeon, see Robert Graves, *The Greek Myths* (Harmondsworth, Middx., 1955), 1: 85, 114; 2: 181. Actaeon was associated with myths of vegetation and seasonal change. He was also, like Orpheus, occasionally identified with Jesus Christ (see, for instance, Jean Seznec, *The Survival of the Pagan Gods* (New York, 1953), p. 93).

[48] The motif quite possibly originates in folk tales. It was widely employed by writers in the courtly love tradition, with the result that Calidore's spying on the scene on Mount Acidale carries with it associations of this kind; he is the outside observer spying on the mysteries of love. Compare this with the situation in *La Belle Dame Sans Merci*, of which Arthur Piaget writes: 'As for the poet "in ambush" in an arbour, catching every word of the dialogue of two lovers, this is a situation among the most common, in which the "courteous" people of the Middle Ages saw no indiscretion. I need cite only the *Jugement du roi de Bohême*, of Guillaume de

On the other hand, the Actaeon myth itself was a mainstay of the sonneteers, symbolizing the speaker's loss of equilibrium after beholding the divine beauty of his beloved—'My thoughts like houndes, pursue me to my death.'[49] What is more, the Actaeon myth was considered an emblem of the Fall. The likelihood is that Spenser's readers would make the association.

As Spenser uses the Actaeon myth in the 'Mutabilitie Cantos', it symbolizes not the incompatibility of time and eternity, human and divine, but their reconciliation. In Book VI the same kind of reconciliation is achieved largely through the myth of Proserpine, one of the most important of the mythic structures which serve as correlatives for the action of the book. The motif of getting and spending, winter sacrifice and summer harvest,[50] unifies the book's final cantos and connects them with the earlier narrative. Our first hint of the Proserpine myth actually comes in the story of Serena, who in so many respects anticipates Pastorella.[51] Serena's name itself expresses unblemished changelessness and innocence.[52] Calidore's intrusion on her anticipates his later intrusion on Colin Clout and is, as we have seen, suggestive of the Fall. Naturally enough, it is of heroic exploits that Calidore and Calepine converse, but Serena belongs to another order. 'Allur'd with myldness of the gentle wether' and with the flowers and the fields, she wanders 'To make a garland to adorne her hed' (VI. viii. 23). Of course, the garland, the circle of flowers, remains unmade. We are reminded of the parallel myth of Orpheus and Eurydice.[53] In *Sir Orfeo* we read:

> This ilke quene, Dame Heurodis,
> Took two maydens of pris

Machaut' ('*La Belle Dame Sans Merci et ses imitations*', *Romania*, 30 (1910), 26 (my translation)). For other examples, see William A. Neilson, *The Origins and Sources of the 'Court of Love'* (Cambridge, Mass., 1899), pp. 76–7, 163.

[49] Samuel Daniel, *Delia* (1592), v. Cf. Bartholomew Griffin, *Fidessa* (1596), VIII; William Smith, *Chloris* (1596), IX. See Douglas Bush, *Mythology and the Renaissance Tradition in English Poetry*, 2nd edn. (New York, 1963), p. 72.

[50] On ritual sacrifice and rebirth, compare the seasonal movement of *Sir Gawain and the Green Knight*, John Speirs's essay on the subject (*Scrutiny*, 16 (1949), 274–300) and Sir James George Frazer, *The Golden Bough*, abridged edition (London, 1922), pp. 492–518 (chapter on 'Lityerses').

[51] On the myth of Proserpine, see Frye, *Anatomy*, pp. 138–9.

[52] Arnold Williams sees the name as ironic, *Flower on a Lowly Stalk* (Michigan State University, 1967), pp. 69–70.

[53] Williams mentions an illustration of the story in a manuscript of the *Ovide Moralisé* which is reminiscent of Spenser's presentation (*Flower*, p. 123).

And went in an undred-tide
To pleye by an orcherd-side,
To see the floures sprede and sprynge,
And to here the foweles synge.   (63–8)[54]

It was from such a world that Ovid's Proserpine was snatched away:

Neare *Enna* walles there standes a Lake *Pergusa* is the name.
Cayster heareth not mo songs of Swannes than doth the same.
A wood environs everie side the water round about,
And with his leaves as with a veyle doth keepe the Sunne heate out.
The boughes do yeelde a coole fresh Ayre: the moystnesse of the
    grounde
Yeeldes sundrie flowres: continuall spring is all the yeare there
    founde.
While in this garden *Proserpine* was taking hir pastime,
In gathering eyther Violets blew, or Lillies white as Lime . . .
. . . *Dis* spide hir: lovde hir: caught hir up: and all at once well
    neere:
So hastie, hote, and swift a thing is Love, as may appeare.[55]

Proserpine is snatched from a paradisal world ('ver erat aeternum') and this breaking of the perfect circle, symbolized by the ring of trees, begins the cycle of the seasons.

The 'faire Serena', as she is repeatedly called, now undergoes a series of tribulations resulting from this incursion of evil and climaxed by her captivity by the cannibals, whose unnatural behaviour divides her totally from the strength imparted by the natural world to those who are in tune with it. Serena is associated with light and brightness; her captivity and near sacrifice by the cannibals plunge her into darkness—for it is at night that the cannibals carry out their savage parody of religion.

If we make the possibly poetically justifiable equation of the figure in the centre of the Dance of the Graces with Pastorella, we find a series of events reminiscent of the incomplete series of

[54] *Five Middle English Narratives*, ed. Robert D. Stevick (Indianapolis, Ind., 1967), p. 5.
[55] *Shakespeare's Ovid, Being Arthur Golding's Translation of the Metamorphoses*, ed. W. H. D. Rouse (London, 1904), v. 485–96. For Celtic versions of the Proserpine myth see Roger Sherman Loomis, *Celtic Myth and Arthurian Romance* (New York, 1927), pp. 302–8. Note once again the fairly strong 'Celtic' element in this book (cf. the ending of the ballad *Childe Roland*, in relation to Calidore's rescue of Pastorella).

Serena's story. This central figure is also associated with lightness
and brightness—the sunlight of Mount Acidale itself, the crown
of Ariadne, the fact that she 'dimmed' her peers. Pastorella dims
those who surround her (VI. ix. 9), and in the Brigands' hellish
cave, the merchants see her as a rich jewel shining in the cave's
darkness:

> The sight of whom, though now decayd and mard,
> And eke but hardly seene by candle-light,
> Yet like a Diamond of rich regard,
> In doubtfull shadow of the darkesome night,
> With starrie beames about her shining bright,
> These marchants fixed eyes did so amaze.   (VI. xi. 13)

Meanwhile, on the earth all is desolation. The cottages of the
shepherds lie broken and empty, through the world outside the
Blatant Beast rages insatiable and unpursued. The situation mirrors the ravages of winter, when the light of summer is buried
deep beneath the earth and there seems no hope that the hard and
frozen earth will ever bear fruit again.[56]

From this desperate pass, Pastorella (and hence the world of
nature) is rescued by a knight no longer disguised as the shepherd
Paris, but soon to reveal himself as Hercules, victor over Fortune,
and type of the active, temporal life. Time moves forward,
destroying the brigands as the brigands have destroyed the
shepherds. As Pastorella returns to the light, brought forth by
that same Hercules-figure whose victory over the Blatant Beast
will be likened to Hercules' dragging of a reluctant hell-born
Cerberus 'to see the hatefull sunne', all nature seems to burst into
joy:[57]

> Then backe returning to his dearest deare,
> He her gan to recomfort, all he might,
> With gladfull speaches, and with lovely cheare . . .

---

[56] Cf. Fletcher's important observation, applicable to Pastorella's captivity: 'A
positive value cannot always be ascribed to the symbol of the center. Literature and,
unfortunately, history have presented the opposite kind of sacred place, and we
commonly call it "hell". Prisons are such places, in fact or in imaginative "prison
literature". Prometheus' rock was such a place. The bottomless pit of Christian
mythology is such a place. . . . Spenser, for example, is fascinated by caves, and they
are usually prisons . . . where the hero or heroine is reduced to a state of the most
acute ambivalence.' (*Allegory*, pp. 213–14.) See above, p. 244.

[57] Cf. the myth of Zephyrus and Flora, as presented for instance in the *Roman de
la Rose*, lines 8398–8412, where Jean de Meung's picture of the Golden Age is in
fact a picture of the return of spring.

(Thus far went the story of Calepine and Serena, but no further. Now, in this later, more elaborate story, central to the book, the narrative moves on, picking up as it goes not only the background to Pastorella's story but also the story of Serena.)

> ... And forth her bringing to the joyous light,
> Whereof she long had lackt the wishfull sight,
> Deviz'd all goodly meanes, from her to drive
> The sad remembrance of her wretched plight.
> So her uneath at last he did revive,
> That long had lyen dead, and made againe alive.
>
> (VI. xi. 50)

Now it only remains to bring Pastorella back to society, where the magical episode of her recognition takes place. Her parents abandoned her when their fortunes forced them to do so: they also were imprisoned beneath the earth (in a dungeon). Spenser's insertion of their story at the opening of Canto xii makes the recognition doubly forceful, for it implies not only Pastorella's return from the darkness, not only her return from exile, but also the return of her parents to happiness and joy.[58] Sir Bellamour welcomes Calidore 'sith they twaine / Long since had fought in field'—both are exponents of the Active Life which takes tribulation in its stride. As for Pastorella, she is welcomed back to this same world:

> The matrone stayd no lenger to enquire,
> But forth in hast ran to the straunger Mayd;
> Whom catching greedily for great desire,
> Rent up her brest, and bosome open layd,
> In which that rose she plainely saw displayd.
> Then her embracing twixt her armes twaine,
> She long so held, and softly weeping sayd;
> And livest thou my daughter now againe?
> And art thou yet alive, whom dead I long did faine?
>
> (VI. xii. 19)

The story parallels the story of Proserpine:

> But meane betweene his brother and his heavie sister goth
> God *Jove*, and parteth equally the yeare betweene them both;

---

[58] Cf. the extensive use of light-imagery in Shakespeare's *Winter's Tale*, whose general theme closely mirrors that of Book VI. See Honor Matthews's thought-provoking chapter on 'The New Imagery and the Final Synthesis' in *Character and Symbol in Shakespeare's Plays* (Cambridge, 1962). On Proserpine in Shakespeare, see also Frye, *Anatomy*, p. 138.

And now the Goddesse *Proserpine* indifferently doth reigne
Above and underneath the Earth: and so doth she remaine
One halfe yeare with hir mother and the resdue with hir Feere.
Immediately she altred is as well in outwarde cheere
As inwarde minde, for where hir looke might late before appeere
Sad even to *Dis*, hir countnance now is full of mirth and grace,
Even like as *Phebus* having put the watrie cloudes to chace,
Doth shew himselfe a Conqueror with bright and shining face.[59]

Inherent in the story is the foreboding at the very moment of joy, and optimism at the time of sorrow. Symbolic of this unending change is the rose on Pastorella's breast, for Pastorella herself is likened to a flower, now decayed and with only a spark of life within it, now blossoming forth in the world of society, of the active life. Tristram, too, was to blossom forth as he entered society, and the garlands and flowers decorating the brow of Pastorella emphasize her connection with the renewal and destruction of vegetation as season gives way to season. Tristram's story tells us that the seed of courtesy is in nature, its blossom in society. Hence, the prevalence of courtesy in the court depends on the court's acceptance of the powers of the natural world—an event set forth in her parents' acceptance of Pastorella.

The story of Orpheus and Eurydice is also associated with darkness and light, the darkness of the underworld against the light of the world above.[60] In its alternative form, it is an optimistic story, but the network of associations is such that to Spenser's readers this remembrance of the Orpheus myth must be tinged with the colour of tragedy.

The final outcome of Book VI is perhaps tragic, perhaps merely a reminder that man's triumphs are shortlived. The Blatant Beast is conquered, bound, and led cringing through Fairyland—yet finally he escapes again and evades capture. Perhaps Spenser's pessimistic conclusion regarding the fate of his poetry must be read in the context of the myth which underlies Book VI: even though evil mouths will slander his achievement now, there will come a time when the Blatant Beast will be captured again. Triumph and despair, says Spenser, in this book of ill-fated intrusions and fortunate encounters, are relative.

[59] *Golding's Metamorphoses*, v. 699–708.
[60] Accounts of the myths which mention sunlight will be found listed in Graves, *Greek Myths*, I: 113, subsection 3. On Orpheus, see above, pp. 213–19.

Calidore sets forth to fight the Blatant Beast before the full implications of his deed are known to him: he leaves Pastorella's parents before her parentage is discovered. This perhaps mitigates the incompleteness of his victory, reminding us that there is a hidden power ready to sustain us when we fail in the battles of this life. If this power did not exist, if nature was not divine but merely an endless repetition of endlessly identical cycles, we might well ask what the point of it all would be. Camus described Sisyphus as the absurd hero: for him the repetition is senseless since there is no possibility of achievement—the gods are scornful of his efforts and offer no reward.[61]

Spenser, not equipped with the clear-sighted futility of our own century, builds into Book VI one answer to the apparent pessimism of its ending. The path around the Mountain of Purgatory is a spiral, not a circle: it mounts upwards towards Paradise. The cycle of nature is also not a perfect circle, for the perfect circle is to be found above and beyond nature. All things, says the goddess Nature, 'worke their owne perfection', spiral upwards towards 'that same time when no more Change shall be'. Action leads ultimately to Contemplation, but (*pace* Meliboe) there is no short cut. The motive power which makes this upward progress meaningful and possible is grace, and it is grace which descends to our world in the person of Pastorella. Christ came down to earth bringing redemption, 'a full, perfect, and sufficient sacrifice, oblation and satisfaction for the sins of the whole world', he suffered in Hell and he rose again from death. Pastorella is no Christ figure, but her story follows the same pattern and holds out similar hope.

6. Book VI: myth and allegory

Any reading of Book VI which fails to take into account the presence of these major mythic forces at work in the poem will not only be defective but will miss the point of the book. Any interpretation based on a 'story' plus allegorical labels would do violence to Book I, but it would not totally bury that book's important features. Book VI, however, requires a more sophisticated reading if it is to make any sense at all. In Book I, where questions of salvation and redemption are naturally under discussion

---

[61] Albert Camus, *The Myth of Sisyphus and Other Essays* (New York, 1955), pp. 88–91.

and where the book's rational foundation is strengthened by the existence of a large body of theological material existing outside the work, even a strictly mechanistic interpretation of the allegory is likely to yield some result. But Book VI offers no adequate rational explanation to the allegory in the final cantos.

This is not to suggest that Book VI is without these larger patterns extending beyond the work itself. In Books I and VI, as everywhere in allegorical works, what cannot be understood as it stands takes on authority by allusion to an order external to the work. In Book I this order is theological dogma; in Book VI it is, above all, myth. The more complex the order and the more significant in itself, the more scope the poet has for the creation of a vast network of associations like that in Book VI, in which contradictions remain suspended or resolved by a kind of dialectic action which creates of them a new and superior unity. Mere allusion to a body of information does not create a complex pattern. The House of Holiness, for example, is an infinitely simpler episode than Mount Acidale: its broad lineaments can be reduced to a row of unequivocating footnotes. The Castle of Alma has this same simplicity. But Mount Acidale hides its allusions behind a veil of myth. Complexity, in this sense, arises when imprecise movements are reconciled through their very imprecision—a process which makes the reconciliation not less convincing but only more wonderful.[62]

The difference between allegory and myth evaporates if it is recognized that the magical quality of allegory—the quality which supplants the motivation necessary in non-allegorical works—is not confined to the story but extends to the story's significance in terms of extraneous forms, beliefs, and movements. Allegory at its most powerful is not confined by its denotation but leads to an infinite widening of the province of the literary work which contains it. It is this quality in myth that Spenser recognizes and exploits: myth deepens and universalizes human experience and endows our disparate actions with timeless significance. The vast dichotomy between private virtue and public action, between general principle and its individual manifestation, is telescoped in the *Faerie Queene* not simply because Spenser alludes to myth or to Christian story at various points in his narrative, but because the work *becomes* myth. 'So much more profitable and gratious is

62 Cf. Hamilton's perceptive remarks, *Structure*, p. 204.

doctrine by ensample, then by rule', writes Spenser in the Letter to Ralegh, and his *Faerie Queene* sets forth the 'doctrine by en-sample' which we, his readers, are asked to follow. The work is not a rule book but a model, and our response to it is properly like our response to myth: we imitate its actions, we use it as a pattern for our own experience.

It may well be objected that I am here confusing myth and litera-ture, that I am attempting to turn literature into a set of archetypes. But this is not so. My intention is not to show that Spenser repro-duces mythic patterns. On the contrary, I wish to emphasize that Spenser creates his own mythic patterns, that his literary sensibil-ity produces a work uniquely his own, which nevertheless offers itself to us as a total system for living, a pattern to be followed. The full scope of Spenser's myth-making has perhaps not been fully mapped out by his critics. It is an essential element in his vast work and it raises the *Faerie Queene* above the set of precepts which its more Blatant detractors, the enemies of allegory, sup-pose it to be.

Spenser is fully aware of these aspects of his work. In fact he is intensely interested in the way his poetry functions. His powerful use of the poetry of reconciliation to draw opposing elements into harmony bespeaks a fascination with the multiplicity of things, with how things fit together, with correspondences and contrasts. This fascination with the power that unites and contrasts causes him in the sixth book to examine that power and to call it Courtesy. In the process, he sets himself and his poem in the work: the *Faerie Queene* ends by examining itself.

How might it have continued? There is little to be said: we can only rest content with what we have. Perhaps Spenser was aware of the impossibility of the terms set up by his poem: nothing short of an apocalypse could have ended it. It may be that, like Milton fifty years later, having perceived the limitations of the Arthurian theme, which tied him to the dynamics of chivalric romance and the glorification of an aging queen, he saw that the vision of English history was too restricting a frame. The 'Mutabilitie Cantos' hint at something wider, though they dispense in some measure with the personal dimension—that quality which makes Spenser so intensely believable. Here, perhaps, we have a more important clue. Spenser's attempt to justify the ways of God to Elizabethan England, unlike Milton's epic, does not shrink from the here-and-now of its own time or from the personal concerns of the private men who live in that time. Milton, writing half a century later, has a sense of classical decorum not to be found among the writers and artists of Elizabeth's reign, but this sense of decorum shields him from an awareness of the pathetic shortcomings of his own species. Our appreciation of Book VI is symptomatic of these uneasy times. Tennyson seems a greater poet because of the discomfort so painfully evident to all but his sovereign in *In Memoriam*. Book VI is the longing and impassioned cry of the idealist faced with the personal problems of day-to-day living in a vicious and none too rewarding world. The autobiographical element naturally appeals to Spenser's readers. So, too, does his examination of the poet's role in the world, of the corruption of those standards which might never have existed, but which sometimes seem humanly possible. So many publishers' blurbs tell us that the reign of Elizabeth was a time of glory and squalor that we are resolutely determined to forget the fact. But it was so, and Spenser felt it to be so. Therefore, beside the varied course of his fortunes depicted in the conquest and escape of the Blatant Beast, he set the vision of the Graces and the beauty of Pastorella. He loved the world, and he felt its tribulations and acknowledged their truth even as he wrote. Yet here on earth the imperfection bears the imprint of Pastorella's rose, the promise of greater Love to come.

> The joyes of love, if they should ever last,
> Without affliction or disquietnesse,
> That worldly chaunces doe amongst them cast,
> Would be on earth too great a blessednesse,
> Liker to heaven, then mortall wretchednesse.
> Therefore the winged God, to let men weet,
> That here on earth is no sure happinesse,
> A thousand sowres hath tempred with one sweet,
> To make it seeme more deare and dainty, as is meet.
>
> (VI. xi. 1)

INDEX

Abessa, 151 n.

Achilles, 80

Acidale, Mount, and Dance of the Graces, 126–42, 275; and courtesy, 28, 75, 85; as climactic episode, 53–4, 156, 280; contrasted with other episodes, 102–3, 144, 152, 261, 307, 309, 316; and harmony, 123, 215, 261, 293; and Art, 213; and *Epithalamion*, 216; as vision, 227, 247, 263, 279, 289; and Venus, 233; and dancing, 236; and Nature, 243; and Symbolism of the Centre, 245; and truancy, 298–300; and poetry, 302, 306; and Actaeon myth, 308; and Pastorella, 312

Acrasia, 18, 20, 32, 142, 198–9, 205, 213, 273

Actaeon, 202, 307–10

Active Life, 22, 29, 51, 77, 141, 246, 300–7, 315; and Hercules, 264–74, 312–13; and *triplex vita*, 274–8; and pastoral, 286–7, 294–300

Acts of St. John, 236

Adams, Joseph Quincy, 60 n.

Adonis, Garden of, 6, 9–10, 53, 73, 198, 221, 227, 241 n., 244, 246, 258, 295

Aemylia, 73

Aesop, 24

Aladine, 45–9, 55, 68, 121, 148, 160, 173–4, 180, 223, 297

Alciati, on the Graces, 252 n. 277 n.

Aldus, father of Aladine, 46, 77–8, 120, 148; name, 66

Aldus Manutius, 66

Alexander the Great, 71

Alice in Wonderland, 101

Allegory, 4 n., 26, 43, 193–4, 257, 285–286 n., 315–18

Allen, Don Cameron, 186 n., 298–9 nn.

Allen, J. W., 189 n.

Allen, John, 185 n.

Alma, 72, 122, 156, 213 n., 273, 316

Alpers, Paul J., 3 n., 4 n., 100 n., 131 n., 142 n.

Amadis of Gaul, 107

Amavia, 2 n., 31

Amazons, 60 n.

Amoret, 6, 104, 106, 141, 199, 216, 221, 279, 293, 304; and Serena, 50, 98–100; and Timias, 91; and Mirabella, 100; and Masque of Cupid, 107–8

Amoretti, 131 n., 303 n.

Amorous Contention of Phillis and Flora, The, 87 n.

Amyas, 73

Ancona, Alessandro d', 69 n.

Anderson, Ruth L., 191 n.

Andreas Capellanus, 87 n., 238

Anglo, Sydney, 268 n.

Apes, and wild men, 61 n.; and art, 157–158, 162

Apollo, 215, 233

Aptekar, Jane, 33 n., 73 n., 153 n., 265, 272

Aquinas, *see* Thomas Aquinas

Archimago, 26, 154

Architecture, 4, 14, 222, 291

Arganté, 97

Ariadne, 129–31, 214, 261, 312

Ariosto, *Orlando Furioso* and characters, 3–4, 18, 56 n., 59, 63, 70, 87 n., 195, 206, 214, 296

Aristotle, 7–8, 55, 182, 200; and Letter to Ralegh, 70–1, 75; and Imitation, 194–5, 209

Armstrong, Elizabeth, 193 n., 281 n.

Art (*see also* Nature and Art), 23, 29, 194–5, 202, 213–19.

Artegall, 10–12, 14, 19, 31–4, 37 n., 38, 40, 44 n., 62, 73, 74 n., 179–80, 199–201, 221, 245 n., 265, 272–3

Arthos, John, 3 n., 12 n., 206 n.

Arthur, role in the *Faerie Queene*, 2, 5–6, 16, 30, 53, 69–75, 273; in earlier books, 12, 37 n., 48 n., 104, 125, 191; in Book VI, 62, 76, 80–6, 91–5, 105, 146 n., 161, 173, 176, 177 n., 181

Arthur of Little Britain, 107 n.

Articles of Religion, Anglican, 185–6

Ashley, Leonard R. N., 163 n.

Astraea, 12, 199–201

Astrophel, 162 n.

Até, 32, 83, 98–9

Atin, 32

Atkinson, Dorothy F., 296 n.

Augustine, Saint, 186, 263–4

Aurora, 262 n.

Babb, Lawrence, 170 n.

Bacchus, 129, 215–16, 252, 265

Bacon, Francis, 188–9, 192 n., 215, 218–219 n., 227, 268 n.